9/22

"College students will find Brennan Hill's *Explo*
thoroughly modern, unusually clear, and right on
use of student questions. Brennan Hill is a maste
the student mind very well. He lucidly shares his
of the central themes of Catholic theology with students. This is a book that professors will use with pleasure over and over in their theology classes. Excellent college theology texts are rare, but Brennan Hill has produced an exemplar text worthy of imitation."

Keith J. Egan
Chair and Professor, Religious Studies,
Saint Mary's College
Professor, Theology, University of Notre Dame

"Although Catholic systematics is a well covered field, no college text compares to Brennan Hill's *Exploring Catholic Theology.* Its juxtaposition of the voices of college students and theologians makes the book clear yet deep, relevant and scholarly, contemporary and rooted in tradition. Discussion questions and suggested readings, moreover, invite students and professors to continue the process by examining and conversing about key areas of Catholic belief."

Sally A. Kenel, Ph.D.
Associate Professor of Theology
St. John's University

"Written out of Hill's experience as an undergraduate teacher, *Exploring Catholic Theology* manifests his love for students and his concern about their search for religious meaning and value in a complex world. Readable chapters, carefully crafted in response to concrete questions on the minds of many people today, survey the history of Catholic doctrines on God, Jesus Christ, the church, and the sacraments, and explore critically the issues the Catholic community faces as it approaches the 21st century. The breadth of the research on the topics addressed, the thoughtful discussion questions at the end of each chapter, and the recommendations for further reading make this book a fine choice for college courses on Catholic theology, and for parish and adult study groups searching for ways to make the Catholic tradition more meaningful in their lives."

Anne M. Clifford, Ph.D.
Duquesne University

"*Exploring Catholic Theology* strikes me as well suited for use in undergraduate classrooms and with adult discussion groups. It is written in straightforward prose with remarkably little academic jargon, even in the discussion of finer points of doctrine. The endnotes make clear the breadth of Hill's scholarship but the text itself adopts a more interpersonal approach to the doctrine under discussion. Furthermore, Hill's technique of 'framing the question' for each chapter with a 'real-life' case focuses the attention of the reader immediately on the implications of dogma for day-to-day Christian life. Likewise, the anecdotal remarks of students interspersed through the chapters have a way of drawing the attention of the reader back to the 'real world.'

"The perspective adopted is evidently that of an open-minded, liberally oriented Roman Catholic who is willing to learn about the essentials of Roman Catholic belief from a variety of sources, both religious and secular. At the same time, the basic adherence of the author to membership in the institutional church is never in question. As such, the book could be seen as a counterpart to the recently published universal Catechism, which offers a much more traditional and conservative viewpoint. I hope *Exploring Catholic Theology* will enjoy a broad readership."

Joseph A. Bracken, S.J.
Rector, Jesuit Community
Xavier University, Cincinnati

"With characteristic lucidity and comprehensiveness, Dr. Hill introduces undergraduates to the four central beliefs of Christianity: God, Christ, church, and sacraments. Students will find here that good Catholic theology is not remote from their daily lives and concerns; rather it provides them with resources to answer their deepest questions and fears which frame the theological discussions in the book.

"With uncommon pedagogical skills Hill blends solid biblical criticism, historical scholarship, and contemporary theologies to produce a theological synthesis that is engaging, inclusive, and well informed. I highly recommend this volume not only for undergraduate courses, but also to anyone who wants to learn more about central Catholic beliefs."

Peter C. Phan
Professor of Systematic Theology
The Catholic University of America

EXPLORING CATHOLIC THEOLOGY

God, Jesus, Church, and Sacraments

BRENNAN R. HILL

XXIII
TWENTY-THIRD PUBLICATIONS
Mystic, Connecticut 06355

Acknowledgments

I want to extend my gratitude to Neil and Pat Kluepfel and many others at Twenty-Third Publications for all their encouragement and support over the years; to Tom Artz, Dan Connors, and John van Bemmel for their expert editorial assistance; to Max Keck and many others at Xavier University, who have given me time and space to write; to my colleague Bill Madges for his helpful advice; Darlene Frickman for her assistance; and to my family, Marie, Ami, and B.J., for their love and cheers while I wrote this book.

Twenty-Third Publications
185 Willow Street
P.O. Box 180
Mystic, CT 06355
(203) 536-2611
800-321-0411

© Copyright 1995 Brennan R. Hill. All rights reserved. No part of this publication may be reproduced in any manner without prior written permission of the publisher. Write to Permissions Editor.

ISBN 0-89622-661-1
Library of Congress Catalog Card Number 95-60731
Printed in the U.S.A.

Dedication

In memory of Sr. Joan Leonard, O.P.,
to all my friends and colleagues
in the College Theology Society,
and to all my students.

Contents

Introduction

This is a book written for students of Catholic theology. It is designed to help students understand with more clarity and depth the four fundamental areas of Catholic belief: God, Jesus Christ, the Church, and the Sacraments. This text will attempt to address many of the searching questions of students; thus throughout the book you will find students "framing the question," and commenting on the issues being discussed.

Religion, Faith, and Theology

Theology is a distinct area of study, and though related to both religion and faith, it should be distinguished from them. Essentially, religion describes the human inclination toward ultimacy, a drive that is apparently universal among all cultures and peoples. "Religions" are organized movements and communities dedicated to singular traditions of beliefs, rituals, and laws.

Faith is distinct from religion and has a number of connotations. On one level faith seems to be a divine gift, an invitation to a relationship with God; on another level, faith is the trusting acceptance of this gift. Faith is also a set of beliefs derived from divine revelation. Finally, faith is a course of action, a way of life that flows from a covenant with God and the beliefs connected with such a commitment.

Theology is both the human capacity to understand and interpret religious beliefs, as well as the recorded product of such an effort.

Theology is "faith seeking understanding," that is, theology is the effort to better comprehend faith in its relational, contextual, and lived out dimensions. At the same time, theology is "understanding seeking faith," since for the person of faith all our thinking and living are somehow linked with ultimacy. As Karl Rahner so often taught, we are questioners and searchers, and only God is our ultimate answer, our ultimate goal.

To sum up, as a religious person one might identify with the Catholic religion, accept the gift of Catholic faith, believe in the doctrines of its tradition, and live a faith-filled life. The same person can also benefit from exploring Catholic theology in order to better understand the content of faith.

Theology Has a History

Theology is a complex discipline that has a long history in the church.

We might say that Christian theology began in the scriptures of the New Testament, as each Christian community expressed its unique understanding of Jesus and his teachings. The body of these reflections expanded in the early centuries of the church, with the development of catechetical schools in places like Rome, Antioch, and Alexandria. Theology developed even more with the contributions of many of the early apologists, the writings of the "Fathers of the Church," and teachings of popes and bishops and saints. This early period seems to have peaked with the writings of Augustine (d. 430), a theologian whose thought still holds great sway over the church today.

The medieval period saw another explosion of theological work with the expansion of the religious orders and the rise of the universities. Theological giants like Anselm, Aquinas, Scotus, and Bonaventure developed theological works that would have profound effects on how the Catholic faith would be understood throughout subsequent centuries. This period of theology was characterized by much questioning, disputation, and argumentation. It would culminate in the Reformation, with the Protestant reformers rejecting much of this medieval theology and proposing their own methods for understanding the Christian tradition. The Catholic church would ultimately respond to this Protestant challenge with a theological stance that was both defensive and authoritative. Catholics would not again gain flexibility and openness in their theological approaches until the Second Vatican Council.

Pre-Vatican II Theology

Following the Second World War, a number of European theologians began to set new directions for Catholic theology, returning to the sources of scripture and patristics with current and progressive methods. Scholars like Karl Rahner, Yves Congar, M.D. Chenu, and Henri de Lubac were quietly developing more contemporary approaches to theology, but their efforts often did not gain official approval. For the most part a neo-scholastic approach to theology prevailed in Catholic seminaries and universities.

The neo-scholastic approach to theology that held sway previous to the Second Vatican Council was largely focused on explaining the official teachings of the church councils. The classic resources for such theology were "manuals," which stated a teaching of the church in the form of a thesis, explained the thesis in a series of notes, and then demonstrated how the teaching was supported in the statements of church councils, passages of scripture, and in teachings of the Fathers and Aquinas. In this era, the task of the theologian was largely to deliver the official teachings of the church and make sure that students clearly understood the meaning of these teachings. Any critical thinking was aimed at the proper comprehension of the teachings of the church. Little critique was focused on the scriptural, patristic, and conciliar resources themselves, and the boundaries of interpretation of the doctrines were well-defined.

The Second Vatican Council

The Second Vatican Council was undoubtedly the most significant religious event for Catholics, if not for the world, in this century. Although the first session began with a rather traditional theological agenda, the subsequent sessions introduced much of the liberal European theology that had been struggling to gain recognition since the end of World War II. Progressive theologians now joined the cardinals and bishops, some of whom were great thinkers in their own right, and many new currents of theological thinking suddenly entered into the debates. Yves Congar brought a new vision of the role of the laity in the church, while Henri de Lubac helped with a new integration of the natural and the supernatural. Karl Rahner, Bernard Häring, and others introduced a new vision of church; and the American Jesuit John Courtney Murray made significant contributions in the area of religious freedom. In addition, the visionary perspectives of past scholars like John Henry Newman and Pierre Teilhard de Chardin found their way into the conciliar considerations. By the end, the council proposed a renewed church of people committed to serving the modern world. Theology would henceforth be a much more varied and pluralistic discipline, with a critical eye turned toward the history of the church and its doctrines, as well as toward the context and meaning of the scriptures. Its philosophical tools would now go beyond Thomism to include modern existentialism, phenomenology, and other perspectives.

The Development of Contemporary Theology

Major shifts took place in Catholic theology following the Second Vatican Council, as theologians developed new methods for doing theology and continually opened fresh perspectives. A veritable explosion of theological effort ensued that would be in dialogue with secular sciences like psychology, social studies, and others, as well as with the teachings of different churches and religions. Theologies would emerge that would be concerned about the world and its political and social issues; theologies that were open to new and varied interpretations of Christian beliefs and moral values would also be developed. In the following I will list some of the new methods and perspectives, and point out how these will come to light throughout the chapters of this text.

The Historical Method

Traditional Catholic theology had often been ahistorical, often going on the assumption that the church, along with its teachings and rituals, had remained relatively in the same forms from the very beginning. For many Catholics there was little awareness of how doctrines developed, how sacraments evolved, or the manner in which laws changed throughout the history of the church. The tools of historical research gradually put to rest such assumptions.

Studies of political, social, and religious history have provided students with invaluable insights into the background of the Hebrew and Christian scriptures. Such research has enabled Catholics to better understand the historical Jesus, how the early churches first began, and the vast and complicated development of the church. Research on the various councils of the church in their historical context has brought to light new ways of interpreting the pronouncements of these councils. We are now aware that every belief has its own history of development and application, and that there are exciting possibilities for giving these beliefs new relevance in our own times.

A careful and accurate history of the church itself has helped the church celebrate its accomplishments, as well as regret its failures and resolve not to repeat them. A precise history of the rituals and sacraments of the church has been invaluable in helping the church reclaim and renew the best of its liturgical tradition. Accurate knowledge of the evolution of the ministries in the church has been invaluable in providing much-needed advances in the leadership and pastoral service in the church. Contemporary cultural and social analysis has also provided today's church with directions on how it might best serve the needs of the oppressed of the world.

In the course of this text, the value of historical and cultural studies will be made evident as we explore such areas as the appearance of modern "atheism," the varying images of God throughout history, and the modern conflicts between science and religion in the first three chapters. We shall see in the chapters on Jesus Christ how studies of the places and people of Jesus' times have helped in the search for the historical Jesus; and how the central doctrines on Jesus' humanity and divinity developed against a backdrop of religious, philosophical, and political strife. In chapters seven, eight, and nine historical studies will bring to light how the church first began, as well as its constant need to reform and renew its mission and its ministry. The chapters on the sacraments will reveal how each sacrament has a history of its own and how each sacrament has uniquely developed throughout the history of the church.

Biblical Criticism

The critical study of scripture in terms of its literary forms, cultural context, sources, editing, and multiple possibilities of interpretation is somewhat new in Catholic theology. This historical-critical approach began as early as the seventeenth century, gained prominence among Protestant scholars in the last century, but did not gain approval in the Catholic church until 1943 under Pope Pius XII. At first, Catholic biblical scholars entered the field as fledglings, but within several decades had established themselves as leaders in biblical scholarship. Today the scholarly analysis of both the Hebrew and Christian scriptures is foundational in much of the work done in Catholic theology. It has offered more accurate interpretations of scripture, and has thus provided enormous possibilities for reinterpreting Catholic beliefs. Ironically, this approach to scripture has not been widely promulgated among the Catholic membership as a whole.

The value of biblical criticism will become evident as we explore such areas as the images of God, the creation stories, and the relevance of scripture to ecology in chapters two and three. In chapters three, four, and five, modern biblical studies provide a major resource for learning more about the historical Jesus, the mysteries of Jesus' life, death, and resurrection, and about the development of Jesus' titles as savior and liberator.

Methods for Interpretation

The science of interpretation, or "hermeneutics," has made a profound impact on theology. Studies in linguistics, symbolism, metaphor, myth, and the context wherein teachings develop have provided scholars with innovative ways of interpreting the Christian traditions. Interpretative methods have made it possible to recover more accurately the original meanings of Christian beliefs, have assisted in the discovery of multiple layers of meanings of doctrines, and have also made it possible to reinterpret Christian teachings in light of the pressing questions of today. We saw earlier how, in the "manual" approach to theology, critical thinking in past theology was often limited to merely explaining the meaning of church definitions. Now theology is engaged also in serious critique of the very resources from which these definitions were derived. As a result, levels of meaning that have been long forgotten have been reclaimed, and new possibilities for innovative interpretations have been opened.

Focus on the Subject Interpreting

Interpretation of any text has both objective and subjective dimensions. Contemporary theology has often shifted the focus from the objective text to the subject who interprets the text. Contributions by theologians like Karl Rahner and Bernard Lonergan have helped theologians better understand the cognitive makeup of the believer. Rahner explored the believer as a searcher and a questioner, open to the horizons of reality, indeed capable of openness to the transcendent itself. Influenced by Heidegger's dynamic notion of being in time, Rahner was able to portray the believer as one caught up in the dynamic search to understand and become. Both believer and belief would now be seen in a much more dynamic light, and as part of a church and tradition that have been constantly moving forward. Lonergan studied the psychology of believing, as well as the levels of consciousness involved in the study of theology. He was able to relate belief to other kinds of "knowing," and to demonstrate how "doing theology" can be more than a mere intellectual exercise, and should be more properly related to religious conversion of the whole person.

This focus on the interpreter opened the way to seeing human experience as being connected with revelation and its interpretation. Revelation could come not only through texts and formulations, but also through life experiences. Human experience, whether it be the experience of nature, secular life, or personal relationships, could be the source of revelation and a starting place for learning to understand and interpret the beliefs of one's tradition. Indeed, many theologians began to suggest that revelation itself, whether biblical or doctrinal, was rooted in human experience. If this be so, then a "revelation from below" becomes possible, and profoundly new possibilities arise for understanding and interpreting revelation. As we shall see later, these insights have been crucial in the development of the liberation, feminist, and ecological perspectives.

Correlative Approaches

Many theologians see interpretations of the Christian message as a product of the interaction between culture and religion. Paul Tillich spoke of a correlation between culture, which asks ultimate questions, and religion, which proffers answers to these questions. Here religious tradition becomes reinterpreted in light of the questions arising from any given culture. David Tracy, a prominent Catholic theologian, moved beyond this and suggested a "revisionist" approach whereby both culture and religion challenge each other with a mutual exchange, with both questions and answers coming from each side. From this perspective, culture and religion reshape each other, reinterpret each other. The challenge, of course, in these correlative approaches is to maintain the continuity and truth of the Christian tradition, and at the same time allow culture the autonomy that is its right. How can tradition sustain its universal truths, and yet adapt to the constantly changing times? How can the absolute and relative be sustained in a religious tradition? These are questions that are at the very heart of the theological enterprise today. Here the theologian often finds herself or himself in a position of mediator between religion and culture, faith and life, at times even between the church and the modern world.

Throughout the text we shall see some of the results of contemporary theological interpretation. In chapters one and two we see how the emphasis on the person interpreting has given human experience a prominent position in the discussion of both the existence and identity of God. Metaphorical approaches to theology have opened up many new possibilities for imaging the Mystery we call God. In chapter three we see how an understanding of myths and models helps us better recognize the mysteries that are involved in both religion and science, and how these two areas struggle to be co-related.

The same chapter examines the pressing need to reinterpret the Christian tradition in a way it might be co-relative with the many environmental crises that we face today. In chapters five and six the multiple possibilities for interpreting the identity and the mission of Jesus

Christ are explored. In the chapters on the church we will disclose how the modern church changed its self-understanding, radically revised its mission toward the world, and resolved to be more closely related with the poor and the oppressed. The final chapters on sacraments will demonstrate how new insights into symbolism and ritual have helped Catholics gain fresh interpretations of the liturgy and sacraments.

New Perspectives

We have seen how contemporary theology has often moved to be more connected and relevant to the modern world and its issues. There has, as we have seen, been a shift to the subjective, the personal, the experiential.

Theology has often moved from the discussion of essences to dealing with existential situations. It has often shifted from the abstract to the practical. Theology now sees its own context as political, global, technological, as well as religious. Once the Catholic church decided to plant its feet solidly in the world and be a living symbol of Jesus' solidarity with the oppressed, new forces were unleashed in theology. Once people discovered that they too were church, that the Spirit was with them, and that the "sense of the faithful" was a truly operative means of locating and sustaining the Christian tradition, new ways of "doing theology" appeared. A "theology from below" began to emerge from the people of the Third World. Voices from the margins of society began to speak of a Jesus who was in solidarity with their pain and who wanted to free them—and not from the world, but *in* the world. The disenfranchised suddenly heard the gospel calling them from fear and apathy to courageous action for freedom. They also heard the gospel calling for the conversion of the greedy and violent people who oppressed them. The poor called the church to be one with them in their struggle for peace and justice.

Other oppressed peoples were awakened to the inequality and injustice to which they had almost become accustomed. Minorities pointed out that racial injustice was in opposition to the gospel way of life. The disabled began to listen to the dignity taught to them by Jesus, and they demanded respect, access, and integration into our society. Gays and lesbians were awakened to their right to human dignity and began their struggle for freedom and justice. Gradually theologies of liberation spread throughout the globe, crying out for freedom for the children of God.

Many feminist theologies have also been born out of this struggle for freedom and equality. These theologies pointed out the subjugation and oppression that is so often attached to patriarchy. They pointed to the violence, injustice, and poverty to which many women are so often subject. Women throughout the world now call for liberation, justice, and equality in both the world and the church.

Feminist theology is perhaps one of the most significant movements in the church today. Women scholars are helping us reread the scriptures and the tradition from the feminine point of view. Women theologians are offering challenging new facts about the history of the church and discovering revealing insights about the authority and ministerial structures of the church. Many women are calling for the dignity and equality that is rightfully theirs in the Catholic church.

We will see evidence of these new liberation and feminist perspectives in many areas of our text. In chapter six we will examine the role of Jesus as liberator. In chapters eight and nine we will see how the church began in solidarity with the poor and how, in its perennial efforts to reform and renew its mission, the church is called to imitate Jesus' love and care for outcasts. Chapter two deals with the suppression of the feminine in religion and discusses efforts to reclaim feminine imagery with regard to God. Chapter four discusses how unique Jesus' treatment of women was for his time, and how he selected women disciples and gave them a central role in his movement. Chapter nine discusses the rights of women to equality in the church's ministry. Chapters ten, eleven, and twelve describe the sacramental experience where Christians are inclusively called to celebrate encounters with Jesus Christ, and where in the loving covenant of marriage women have the right to equality and partnership.

"Post" Theologies

Theology today is often spoken of in a "post" position. Some claim that theology is in a period post-modern, post-critical, or post-liberal. Theologians who use these terms often indicate that we are at the end of one era and beginning another. Precisely what is ending and what is beginning largely depends on the point of view of the theologian.

I am inclined to agree that Catholic theology is in a posture of transition; theology has been continually moving forward, and one senses that with the proper atmosphere of freedom and encouragement, extraordinary breakthroughs will continue to be made in the church of the future.

If we are in a "post" position, what is being left behind, and where are we headed? It seems clear that much of Catholic theology has moved beyond looking at the Catholic tradition as static and now perceives it as a living, organic tradition that has always somehow preserved the heart of Jesus' message, but has also been able to produce new insights and structures and put archaic teachings aside. There was a time in the church when the theology of the Trinity was new, when priesthood was first thought of, when papacy was first developed. There was a period when the original catechumenate was a novelty, and when person to person confession was an innovation. There was a time when the concept of collecting a new testament was just being formulated. There was a time when marriage was first declared to be a sacrament. There was even a period in the not too distant past when the possibility of salvation for those outside the church was considered dubious at best, and when unbaptized babies were believed not to be with God. Catholic theology, the understanding of the faith, has changed and will continue to change. New realities will continue to appear in the church. Obsolete teachings and practices will be left behind. Catholic theology is also moving "post" closedness and exclusivity. It attempts to be in dialogue with other churches, other religions, and with people of all genders, races, and ethnic background. Authentic Catholic theology will welcome the voices of the poor and disenfranchised. Catholic theology must be inclusive of women in the church, as they critique abuses, and as they reinterpret the scriptures and tradition from their unique points of view.

Catholic theology is "post" responding to revelation with only the mind. Feelings, intuition, imagination, moral conscience, and action can all play a role in the holistic theology of the future. Catholic theology has moved beyond traditional "piety" to a deeper spirituality that is both contemplative and active. It is a theology concerned with a deeper participation in prayer and worship; it is a theology that empowers people to stand up for others less fortunate.

Catholic theology is challenged to maintain stability in the midst of transformation; continuity along with transition; confrontation joined with nonviolence. It is a theology that must neither jettison nor absolutize the past; and at the same time needs to connect past beliefs with present issues. Contemporary Catholic theology is world-embracing rather than world-denying. It defends the autonomy of the individual, but values the intimacy of community. It struggles for unity, but is tolerant of plurality. Today's Catholic theology respects authority, but can differ respectfully and constructively.

This book, then, offers an overview of contemporary Catholic systematic theology. It is not exhaustive by any means; no one book or person could hope to synthesize such a vast field as Catholic theology. But this text is offered as a synthesis of a theology that is dynamic, inclusive, holistic, and balanced. It is, as it were, a snapshot of Catholic theology at this moment in time.

Suggested Readings

Avery Dulles, *The Craft of Theology*. New York: Crossroad, 1992.

Sheila Greeve Davaney (ed.), *Theology at the End of Modernity*. Philadelphia: Trinity Press International, 1991.

Roger Haight, S.J., *Dynamics of Theology*. New York: Paulist Press, 1990.

Aidan Nichols, O.P., *The Shape of Catholic Theology*. Collegeville, MN: The Liturgical Press, 1991.

Leo J. O'Donovan and T. Howland Sanks (eds.), *Faithful Witness: Foundations of Theology for Today's Church*. New York: Crossroad, 1989.

Ted Peters, *God—The World's Future: Systematic Theology for a Postmodern Era*. Minneapolis, MN: Fortress Press, 1992.

Francis Schüssler Fiorenza and John P. Galvin (eds.), *Systematic Theology*. Minneapolis, MN: Fortress Press, 1991. vol. I, pp. 1-89.

Frans Jozef Van Beeck, S.J., *God Encountered: A Contemporary Systematic Theology*. San Francisco: Harper & Row, 1989. vol. I.

1.

Does God Exist?

Framing the Question

My name is Yin, and I was born and raised in Beijing, China. I had never given serious thought to this strange notion of "God" until I enrolled in my first religious studies class in college. In my country it is not permitted to speak about religion or God in school. My mother is a Communist and believes that religion is a way of controlling people. My father was a Buddhist when he was young, and he thinks that there is no way that we can think or talk about a reality such as God.

Now that I have been studying about God, I have many questions. First of all, it is hard for me to think or talk about a reality as large as divinity. It is simply beyond my grasp. Why is it that so many of my fellow students seem to be able to have so many questions about something that seems so vague and confusing? Second, how am I to answer all of the many atheists, people who simply do not believe in the existence of God? Many of them are intelligent and good people. Can they all be so wrong about this matter? And finally, can someone prove to me that such a divine being actually exists? And if such a God does exist, how does one go about the search to find such a reality?

Yin raises some difficult questions regarding the reality which many call "God." In this chapter we are going to deal with some of these questions. We will begin with some general observations about the so-called God-question. Then we will discuss atheism, considering how it began and developed, as well as how atheism is expressed today. In the final section of this chapter we will describe various paths to God: through the mind, the feelings, the will, and then more holistically through human experience.

The Question of the Existence of God

What many theologians refer to as the "God-question" is fundamental in religion. Such a question is a difficult one, and many wonder if humans even have the capacity to grapple with such a mystery. Yet humans have perennially asked about divinity, and their answers have had broad implications in other areas of belief.

A Difficult Question for Humans

Dealing with this question of God's existence presents enormous difficulties. We have finite minds, and we are attempting to grasp the infinite. We are mortal beings, and we are trying to understand immortality. As John Macquarrie, the highly regarded Protestant theologian, has pointed out: "In spite of all the countless teachings about God throughout history, God still 'surpasses all human understanding.'"[1]

Since the reality of God is so mysterious and inscrutable, one might wonder why we humans can even attempt to think about God. Perhaps the Buddha was right in teaching that we cannot think about the unthinkable or speak about the unspeakable.

For the most part Christians have disagreed with the Buddha. They have taken the position that since we have been created as questioners, we should be able to search for answers to the ultimate questions. Since we have the ability to transcend or go beyond concrete reality and investigate the unseen, we should be able to explore the transcendent God. Our human ability to listen, interpret, and understand enables us to be open to the revelation of God. Our capacity and even hunger to experience the spiritual empowers us to experience God and reflect on the significance and relevance of such experience.

A Perennial Question

We humans seem to have had the God-question on our minds since the very dawn of intelligence. It was on the mind of ancient peoples who discovered powerful deities in the crash of thunder and lightning, in the roar of the ocean, and in the awesome flight of the eagle. The Egyptian pharaohs struggled with the question of divinity as they prepared elaborate tombs for their burial. It was a question that was on Abraham's mind as he tried to fathom why he was called to be the father of a new people of God; and no doubt a concern for Moses as he wrestled with his call to lead the people to freedom. It was of such deep concern to Socrates (d. 400 B.C.E.) that he was willing to forfeit his own life in order to challenge the conventional wisdom regarding the gods. Aristotle (d. 322 B.C.E.) wrestled with this ultimate question as he attempted to reason to the need for a first cause and an unmoved mover of the world. Serious questions about God's apparent absence at a time of need came to Job in his desolation and to Jesus of Nazareth as he suffered on the cross.

In medieval times the ingenious theologian Anselm of Canterbury (d. 1109) decided that God was the greatest thought that one could think. Later the brilliant Thomas Aquinas (d. 1274) set out to offer reasonable "proofs" that God existed. Yet when Aquinas had completed his masterful summary of the Christian tradition, he looked upon it all as so much straw compared to a unique personal experience that he had of God.

In more recent times, Albert Einstein (d. 1955) wrestled with the problem of God as he attempted to measure the universe, concluding that such a complex and magnificent world could not have come about through "a roll of the dice." A contemporary astrophysicist, Stephen Hawking, still struggles to understand the mind that seems to be involved in the design of this vast universe.

Worldview and the God-Question

The worldview of each culture affects how people approach the question of the existence of God. In primitive times when people's lives were closely linked to nature, belief in God's existence was generally expressed in animal symbols and other representations from nature. When ancient cosmology viewed the earth as a level place with the sky as an overhead dome, God was seen to exist in the heavens above.

During the time of the Enlightenment when civilization experienced the birth of science, God was placed into gaps that were without scientific explanation. As science developed, these gaps became less in number. With the onset of secularization, many people began to push God to the periphery. This attitude was not so much a denial of God's existence as it was a matter of relevance. A student reflected this attitude when he said: "Even if God does exist, what does it matter?"

During the 1960s and early 1970s some who subscribed to the secularism of those years startled the world with the observation that "God is dead." This view represented, in part, a revival of the thought of Friedrich Nietzsche (d. 1900), a nineteenth-century atheist. Some theologians were describing a rebirth of atheism, while others were only attempting to show that certain outmoded concepts of God had died.

Death of God theology, however, remained in the public attention for only a very short time. One theologian remarked that he took a sabbatical to study the death of God movement only to discover that the discussion itself had passed away before he could get his research underway. Some paraphrased a classic remark of Mark Twain, declaring that the rumors of God's demise were greatly exaggerated.

The Question Today

A number of factors seem to affect the current discussion about God's existence. For some, the marked experience of God's absence or silence in the world has led them to challenge the traditional arguments regarding God's presence. For others, the many physical and moral horrors in the world seem to mount daily and raise serious questions about the existence of a God of power and wisdom. Even among some of those engaged in the struggle against oppression, there seems to be doubt about whether God can be of help in their struggle. Others have embraced secularism and materialism to the point where God seems irrelevant. An important element in the God-question today, then, is whether or not belief in God can help us better understand contemporary experience and whether such belief can assist us in addressing the many complex issues of today's world.

Recent developments in Eastern Europe and Russia have added even more factors to the equation. The collapse of Communism and the Soviet Union, which has resulted in religious freedom for millions of people throughout these countries, has provided many new insights about how people come to believe in God. The failure of nearly a century of repression and violence to force the false ultimates of State and Party upon people, has made it clear how nearly impossible it is to eradicate God from culture and the human psyche. People had grown hungry for genuine meaning in their lives and were tired of ideological slogans.[2] In the midst of their suffering and deprivation they sought a God who could relate to them humanely and suffer along with them. It is exciting to anticipate what new religious questions, insights, and actions might emerge from the revival of religion in Eastern Europe. Perhaps we will begin to see what was born in the suffering in the Gulags, in the underground religious discussions and prayers, and in the hearts of those who had to suffer so much for their faith.

The Implications of Our Answers

The way in which we answer the question about the existence of God has profound consequences for the way we view reality and live our lives. For the Christian the question of God's existence has unique significance. What a person believes about God influences what he or she understands about Jesus, the scriptures, the church, sacraments, and morality. For instance, if one concludes that God is a remote being who exists somewhere outside the world keeping track of evil deeds, it is easy to become focused on external behavior and perhaps be legalistic and even guilt-ridden. On the other hand, a person who believes that God exists as a personal and creative power within life might see the Christian life as dynamic, and might be more willing to take risks in exploring new challenges. Listen to Bill, a junior botany major, and also a recovering alcoholic:

For a long time, God was just a word I used for swearing. I heard God's name a lot in the bars and when I went on a binge with my friends. It was only after I got into Alcoholics Anonymous that I came to realize the God was a higher power who was with me and who would help me deal with this sickness of alcoholism and get my life back on track.

Atheism

Atheism, as we understand it today, often includes the denial of God's existence, the gradual exclusion of God from all aspects of culture, and the establishment of a materialistic lifestyle. Ironically, since atheism is the reverse side of belief in God, much can be learned about the question of God's existence by studying the writings of those who have denied it. In many ways, atheism feeds off belief in the existence of God, and derives its energy from struggling against religion and attempting to disprove it. In this sense, atheism has no real ideology or specific worldview of its own. Without religious belief to struggle against, atheism generally sinks into a kind of despairing nihilism.

The Beginnings of Atheism

The atheism with which we are familiar today is of recent vintage, finding its roots in the Enlightenment and fully blossoming in the nineteenth century. Explicit denial of God's existence was common neither in antiquity nor in the medieval period.[3]

In ancient times atheism seems to refer more to heretical views about God than to the denial of God's existence. The atheist was the one who disagreed with the conventional wisdom about the divinity. Such a position was often seen as worthy of condemnation and was even punishable by death.

A very early example of atheism and its effects was seen in the life of the Egyptian Pharaoh Akhenaten (d. 1399 B.C.E.) Akhenaten was condemned after his death for replacing the traditional Egyptian gods with Aten the Sun-God. It was believed that the pharaoh's false beliefs actually caused the gods to turn their backs on Egypt. For such atheism Akhenaten's name was obliterated, and nearly everything that he built was destroyed.[4]

There are other examples of atheism in ancient times. Xenophanes (d. 470 B.C.E.) was called an atheist for attacking anthropomorphic images of God, and for his oft-quoted ironic remark that if animals could draw, they would draw God with horns. Anaxagoras (d. 422 B.C.E.) was criticized for denying that the gods had a hand in storms and natural disasters, and for seeking natural causes for such physical evils. Diagoras chopped up a statue of Heracles in order to boil his turnips and ridiculed the Eleusinian mysteries. There was also the famous case of the denouncing and forced suicide of Socrates for teaching the youth of his time not to believe in the gods of the city. In the Roman era Cicero (d. 43 B.C.E.) was criticized for his disillusionment with the gods and for relying too much on philosophy as his guide to life. Pliny the Elder (d. 79 C.E.) was accused of atheism because of his pantheistic tendency of identifying the gods with reality.[5]

Atheism in the Scriptures

Atheism was rare in biblical times. The Psalmist proclaims: "The fool says to himself: 'There is no God'"(Ps 14:1). Yet this statement seems to ridicule someone who does not experience the power of God in history, rather than one who denies the very existence of God in the metaphysical sense. Jeremiah speaks of people "who do not know God" and castigates those who practice idolatry or the worship of false gods (Jer 10:25).

In the New Testament Paul speaks of those who do not know God and who will not listen to Jesus Christ (2 Thes 1:8). Luke refers to those who sit in the darkness and in the shadow of death (Lk 1:79). These remarks seems to refer to a kind of godlessness, but not an outright denial of the existence of God.[6] It is also interesting to note that the early Christians themselves were called atheists by the Romans for their refusal to accept the divinity of the emperor and to worship the gods of the empire at the state temples.

The Development of Modern Atheism

Modern atheism seems to be rooted in attempts to explain the world and its workings without reference to a deity. The ancient world had seen natural and historical events as somehow the result of some higher divine will. For the Hebrews all creation came from Yahweh—a God of punishing floods and military victories; a God of history, actively involved in liberating the people from captivity and slavery. At the same time, other ancient cultures held that all that was human also had its source in the deity. For example, the Greeks believed that love came from Aphrodite and wisdom from Athene.

It was Aristotle who supplied the crucial distinction between the world and God, viewing the world as an object to be studied in its own right. Aquinas adopted this distinction and introduced it into Christian thinking. Before Aquinas the perspective of Augustine of Hippo (d. 430) had prevailed, wherein the universe was seen as "something of God," an arena in which humans carried out their search for God. In contrast, Aquinas held that the universe was an order of being that was subsistent, autonomous, and radically distinct from God. The universe could be explored rationally as an order in itself. While the universe could reveal God, it was distinct from God. Thus God and the world could now be examined rationally. This distinction represented a significant change in how the universe was viewed. Most important, the way was now clear for the development of modern science. At the same time, dichotomies developed between the secular and the sacred, the natural and the supernatural. These distinctions deeply affected future notions of God.

The Enlightenment, with its extreme focus on the powers of reason along with the Cartesian emphasis on methodical doubt, also played a role in the development of atheism. Whereas nature and scripture previously had been the central resources for discussion of God, now the human intellect—the power of human reasoning—was acceptable as an exclusive resource. Reason cut off from faith, however, used logic and rational analysis on the question of the existence of God as the only sources of truth. It was now possible to question the very existence of God. Reason cut off from the authority of scripture and the church drew its own conclusions about the nature of God.

Nineteenth-Century Atheism

Atheism as we know it today, that is, as the outright denial of God's existence and the establishment of human nature as the only ultimate reality, seems to be largely a nineteenth-century phenomenon. During this century secularism had come to full bloom. Science was still in its infancy, and was often naively thought to have the power to solve all the mysteries of the universe. Many held that nature could now be explained by the physical sciences, the psyche could be explained through psychology, and the bible could be mastered through scientific study. The human person, many held, was positioned to achieve a rightful autonomy and assume the role of master of the universe.

One of the classic statements of this era was that of Nietzsche, who wrote of a madman running through the streets declaring that God was dead, and that the churches were indeed the tombs and monuments of God. Nietzsche, a brilliant but unstable eccentric who hoped that his writings would replace the bible, placed no trust in the Christian vision and was quite skeptical of nineteenth-century progress. He accepted the newly discovered theory of evolution and maintained that its goal was the Superman's dominion over the world. Nietzsche was a nihilist who hoped to undermine previous foundations of human knowledge and replace them with his own. For him, the God of the Hebrews and Christians was a denial of life, an illusion created by power-hungry priests and promoted by fables. Such a notion can only hold humanity back from its true goals; the will to power, the drive toward dominance, and the achievement of the Superman.[7] The death of the God, who prevents human fulfillment in a manner similar to a crippling chemical dependency, is to be celebrated. The human can now step into the place of God.

While one college class was discussing these views of Nietzsche, Andrea, an African-American majoring in history, made this comment:

Now I see where Hitler, Stalin, Pol Pot, and Idi Amin were coming from. These dictators somehow came to the conclusion that they were deities, with ultimate power over life and death. Their ideologies actually took the place of legitimate religion. The thought of Nietzsche served as a foundation for the ideology of many modern dictators.

God as a Projection of Ourselves

Another profoundly influential atheist during this period was Ludwig Feuerbach (d. 1872). Feuerbach, who moved from being a Christian theologian to become an atheistic philosopher, disagreed with Nietzsche's contention that God was a priestly fraud or a mere illusion. For Feuerbach, God was rather a human projection of what humans want to be and indeed can be.

The projection theory had been suggested by others, usually as a protest against our anthropomorphic tendencies to make God into our own image and likeness. Voltaire (d. 1778) had remarked that we tend to create God to be like ourselves. In the same vein Mark Twain once quipped: "God created man in his own image; and man, being a gentleman, returned the compliment."[8]

Feuerbach, however, was far more militant than these thinkers. He was explicitly atheistic. He maintained that only nature and humans exist, and that our images of higher beings are nothing more than images of ourselves. We have a desire to be infinite, immortal, and perfect. We project these desires outside ourselves and thereby create God. In so saying, Feuerbach takes the traditional notion of God as the fullness of intelligence and love and turns it on its head. He believes that these human powers are indeed what is divine. The religion that has God as its center is replaced by a religion that focuses on humanity.

Maryann, a junior marketing major from Connecticut, seems to agree with Feuerbach. She points out:

You know, there is a lot of truth in what Feuerbach has to say. Images of God often do seem to be projections of our ideal selves. When we studied the Hebrew scriptures we saw how a patriarchal society like Israel usually used male images of God. And today many women are advocating that more feminine images be used. Either way the images reflect ourselves. Right?

Maryann is right that our images of God are just that—images, and that they are taken from our human experience. But the fact that we use images to understand God does not logically lead to the conclusion that the ultimate reality that we are attempting to describe with the image does not exist. Nor does such image-making necessarily demean us as humans or take away our possibilities for expansion and growth. Christian faith holds that our powers come from God and are supported and strengthened by the same God.

God as a Drug

Karl Marx (d. 1883), who developed the ideology for atheistic Communism, adopted the "projection" view but developed his own interpretation of it. Marx was little interested in the abstractions found in Feuerbach's arguments. Marx was a practical man, profoundly taken up with the concrete world of economics, politics, and social conditions. He was not concerned about the ideal human, but with the oppressed and alienated labor class, whom he wished to see liberated. It was Marx's conviction that belief in God and religion was indeed a product of human suffering. Religion, for Marx, was the cry of the oppressed, as well as the drug (opium) that diverted their attention from the injustices they suffer. He believed that once the proletariat was given freedom and happiness, religion would be abolished, for it would no longer be needed. Illusions of heaven would not be needed because revolution would bring about the classless society; real happiness would eliminate the need for illusionary happiness. Atheism itself would disappear because there would no longer be a need to deny God.[9]

It was Vladimir Lenin (d. 1924) who used the Marxist ideology to begin a revolution that would profoundly affect the world for nearly a century. Lenin went beyond Marx and said that religion did not arise from the suffering of the people, but served as the "drug" for the suffering people. Belief in God was imposed on them by the church and to the ruling class in order to keep the poor blind to their sorry lot and render them incapable of revolting against their oppressors. From Lenin's point of view, religion and its leaders had to be obliterated. Persecution, exile to the Gulags, and death were the fate of anyone who attempted to take a religious stand against the revolution. Now the Party, not God, would be the ultimate reality, and the Party would be the guardian of the people and the designer of the "providence" that guided their future.

In the 1980s the entire world was astounded to see Russian Communism and the Soviet Union disintegrate. Suddenly and unexpectedly a new religious freedom emerged throughout Eastern Europe and even in Russia itself. Years of repression and violent persecution were apparently ineffective in obliterating belief in God and religion. It might well be that a new religious and theological revolution will emerge from that area, much as it has from the oppression in Central and Latin America.

God as an Infantile Illusion

Sigmund Freud (d. 1939), one of the pioneers of modern psychotherapy, spent a great deal of effort attempting to discover the psychological and historical basis for religion. He tried to make some causal connection between the neuroses that he encountered in his clinical work and the practice of religion by his patients. Once he felt that he had made that connection he proceeded to trace the connection back through religious history.[10]

A number of factors brought Freud to his conclusion that religion was a mere illusion. No doubt he was significantly influenced by Feuerbach's projection theory. In addition, Freud was a materialist and received his medical training from the mechanistic school of medicine, which allowed religion no place in science or medicine. In dealing with patients Freud seemed to view the psyche as a sort of appliance hooked up to the body-machine. He gave little credence to the spiritual aspects of human beings.

Freud, who was raised in the Jewish religion, became alienated at an early age from Christianity by the intense Catholic piety of his nanny. He became more hostile toward the Christian religion because of the anti-Semitic treatment he received at school. Freud's attraction to his youthful mother, as well as an aversion for his father, also contributed to his later work on the Oedipal aspect of religion. These and many other factors led to Freud's conclusion that religion is nothing more than illusion or wish fulfillment, and that ritual is similar to neurotic, obsessive actions. Freud held that religion had a long and complicated history, and yet could be ultimately traced back to some primal patricide.

Freud explained that the psychological basis for religion is found in the fears and helplessness that we experience in infancy. We need the truth and the protection of a father, yet we are caught in an instinctual struggle with our father as competitors for the love and attention of our mother. This need for a father-protector as well as this tense struggle to eliminate our father is part of the dynamic projections that are ascribed to God and religion. Ultimately Freud taught that belief in God is not reasonable because it finds its source in infantile projections that cannot be scientifically demonstrated.

Freud attempted to give historical foundation to these theories by researching the origins and evolution of religion. He did this, however, from the perspective of his underlying assumption that ancient people were primitive and infantile and that their religious writings were untrustworthy and full of contradictions. He believed that these primitive peoples, standing helplessly before the powers of nature and fate, projected God-figures who would protect them, reveal to them answers to their questions about life and the world, and reconcile them with such mysteries as suffering, fate, and death.

To support his conclusions Freud pointed to one pivotal historical incident. Assembling a collection of questionable cultural studies, Freud told a tale of a primal horde wherein the sons are jealous of the father for keeping the women to himself. The sons proceed to kill their father and devour him. Then filled with guilt and remorse they set up a totem to represent the father and offer sacrifices for expiation. Freud viewed this as the Oedipal link to the origin of religion. Unfortunately for Freud, however, this incident has no historical foundation. As one author puts it: "This ramshackle machine, assembled from odd parts which Freud found lying around his library, was quite incapable of flying. It bore no relation to the equivalent of aerodynamic facts, namely anthropological evidence as a whole."[11] Other scholars, such as the renowned Mircea Eliade, agree that there is no historical foundation for such a theory on the origin of religion.[12] As a matter of fact, in spite of numerous theories, religious historians have not been able to discover the origin of religion.

In spite of the weaknesses of Freud's theories, his perspective has had a profound influence on society and on the field of psychotherapy. Hans Küng, the Swiss Catholic theologian, suggests that the high incidence of atheism in the psychiatric profession might well be traced back to Freud's theories on religion.[13]

Contemporary Atheism

Atheism today appears in many forms. There is the "atheism of the academy," common among secular intellectuals who accept only those realities that can be brought before the bar of reason for critical judgment. Included here are some scientists who maintain that all reality can be understood and explained without making any reference to God.

There is also a "materialistic atheism," common among those whose ultimate values are found in consumer goods, investments, and pleasure. Similar to this is the "atheism of the marketplace," which appears among those in industry and corporate life, who absolutize profit and success. Then there is the "atheism of indifference," which does not see the relevance of God to any events, realities, or the carrying on of everyday life.[14]

The contemporary atheist does not tend to be a philosopher concerned with disproving God, as in the nineteenth century. Atheists today tend to be people who focus their life on education, science, corporate life, art, or industry and who think that any notion of God or religion simply gets in the way of what they want to accomplish in life. For them God is not part of the universe, or history, or personal life. This is not so much the post-World War II atheism that grew out of anguish and a sense of the absurd. This is an "atheism of indifference," which seems to develop out of a drive for personal autonomy and individualism.[15]

The atheism of indifference that is prevalent today is not necessarily linked to an ideology that embraces an evil lifestyle. Often this kind of atheism is quite humanistic, concerned about the well-being of all people but convinced that belief in God and religion can only diminish humankind and inhibit people's freedom. Bertrand Russell (d. 1970) described this kind of atheism when he wrote:

> The freedom that the freethinker seeks is not the absolute freedom of anarchy: it is freedom within the intellectual law. He will not bow to the authority of others, and he will not bow to his own desires, but he will submit to evidence.[16]

For the contemporary atheist, the center often lies in what is visible and measurable.

The Search for God

So far we have been discussing the difficulties and challenges that surround the question of the existence of God. We have also looked at atheism—the most radical challenge to belief in God. Now we will consider some of the approaches that have been judged useful and appropriate in the endless search for God. This discussion will continue in the next two chapters, which consider the way Christians have come to know and understand God (chapter 2) and the relationship between God and science (chapter 3).

Seeking God Through Intelligence

Reason distinguishes human beings from other creatures. As Thomas More (d. 1535) says in the classic drama, *A Man for All Seasons*, we are all driven to figure things out "in the tangle of our minds." The human person is the only creature on this planet who searches, questions, listens, and who can grow in knowledge and understanding through reflection. Thus it is no surprise that many of our great thinkers have viewed reason as an effective avenue to God. This section will consider some of the major "players" in this rational approach to God.

Ancient "Theology"

Plato (d. 347 B.C.E.), one of the most brilliant and influential thinkers of all time, maintained that the realm of ideal forms was the only permanent reality. He also concluded that there must be a creator who acts as a craftsman to impose order out of chaos and form on formlessness. Aristotle, another genius of antiquity, whose thought along with Plato's still underlies much of Christian thinking, disagreed with idealism. From his perspective, forms existed within reality. Change came about through cause and effect, and from this he reasoned that there must be an uncaused cause, an ultimate intellect that brought about the highest form of reality, the human intelligence.

It was Philo (d. 50), a contemporary of Jesus, who attempted to integrate this Greek thinking about God with the notions of the Hebrew scriptures. Since he believed in a God of history, Philo portrayed God as being intimately involved in the universe and all its creatures through an intermediary Logos. As a Jew, he could not accept God as the mere source of ideal or form, but believed that God was an active parent, very much involved in history and life. Philo was able to put the "God of the philosophers" in dialogue with the "God of the bible," a dialogue that still goes on, albeit at times with great difficulty.

Medieval God-Talk

Medieval talk of God seems to have been profoundly influenced by Anselm of Canterbury, a brilliant monk and bishop. Anselm formulated his classic ontological argument regarding God, which represents a benchmark in the theology on the existence of God. In effect Anselm said that God is "that than which a greater cannot be thought."[17] This does not seem to mean that God is the highest possible thought, or that God exists because we can have such a magnificent thought. Rather, Anselm seems to be saying that "God" is a concept which refers to that which nothing greater can be thought. God is a reality beyond all thoughts; a reality that gives us the ability to reflect on the Source of all creation. Others have suggested that Anselm was pointing out that God is to be thought of as the greatest possible being, the being with maximal perfection. Karl Rahner (d. 1984), the preeminent Catholic theologian of the twentieth century, offers another possible interpretation. He sees Anselm's ontological argument meaning that behind all perennial debates about the existence of God there must be an Existence that would provoke such debate.[18]

Later in the medieval period, interest in ancient Greek thought became more prominent in Europe. This was a result of increasing contact with the Islamic philosophers who had preserved and commented on it. It was Thomas Aquinas who accomplished the masterful integration of Aristotle's thought and the Christian tradition. Although Aquinas's heart rested comfortably in the biblical and mystical approach to God, he attempted to devise a "natural theology," whereby reason could get in touch with God in the created world and establish God's existence. Using logic, the power of observation, and reason, Aquinas presented five arguments—now viewed as classic statements—to establish clearly the existence of God. He proposed: (1) the argument from motion (there must be a prime mover), (2) the argument from causality (every effect must have a cause), (3) the argument from necessity (all beings are possible, but one must be necessary if there are to be any beings at all), (4) the argument from design (the complex and harmonious operation of the universe demands an intelligent and purposeful designer), and (5) the argument from perfection (all of creation is judged against the summit of perfection).[19]

What Aquinas called "arguments" or "ways" came, over time, to be known as "proofs." It is unlikely, however, that these or any other rational "proofs" would convince someone of the existence of God. But for someone with faith in God, the ideas of Anselm and Aquinas can make that faith seem reasonable and worthy of deeper understanding. Aquinas's "proofs" represent a rational reflection on faith in God rather than scientific proof that God exists. Faith comes from the experience of God and the acceptance of God's revelation, and not from logical arguments.

The so-called natural theology that is integral to the Catholic understanding of the existence of God, and which was enunciated at the First Vatican Council (1869-70), merely demonstrates that it is possible to gain knowledge of God from creation and that there is no contradiction between faith and reason. Both faith and reason are complementary paths to the one Truth. In practice, however, many people begin with faith and then seek to understand it more fully, and not the other way around.

Unfortunately, Aquinas's approach to God through both faith and reason eventually resulted in a dichotomy between the two. Over centuries a deep fissure developed between the supernatural and the natural, and the sacred and the secular. Such dualisms would deeply affect Christian thinking and living.

The Autonomy of Reason

The dichotomy between faith and reason began in great measure with the work of René Descartes (d. 1650), who maintained that he had a personal enlightenment to develop a new scientific perspective based on mathematical certainty. His goal was to arrive at clear and distinct ideas through a process of "methodical doubt." During the period of the Enlightenment the human mind became the ultimate authority and source of all knowledge and truth. It bent to no outside authority, whether sacred or secular. Certainty was no longer rooted in God or ecclesiastical authority, but in the self. For many, empirical evidence was the only way to truth.

What then of gaining knowledge of God? For Descartes, the notion of God comes directly from God, who implants it in us as a perfect idea. One can be certain of that by the very fact that reason is infallible. This understanding of reason's preeminence signals an important shift in outlook. Where the authority of God or the church was previously the basis for religious certainty, now it was human intelligence that was the measure of ultimate truth. This was the beginning of reason's break with faith. It eventually developed, as we have seen in the section on atheism, that reason could achieve complete autonomy. On the one hand, a philosophy of God developed that dealt with the question of the existence of God notionally and metaphysically. Here one could establish God as an "Idea." A philosophy of God emerged that dealt with God in a very abstract and clinical manner. As a result the image of God lost its personal and relational dimensions. In ecclesiastical circles, on the other hand, a theology of God was developed from biblical and ecclesiastical beliefs that was not subjected to intellectual critique. A great divide arose that separated the "God of the philosophers" from the "God of the bible." Theology often became highly speculative and quite removed from the concerns of ordinary people.

A young woman, Mary, a physics major from San Diego, recalls her experience of being turned off by classes in religion that were too abstract and theoretical. She recalls:

Some of the books we had to read for those courses were so philosophical and intellectual. They talked about God in very clinical, technical ways. Having grown up believing in a God who loved me and who was most present in Jesus, I just couldn't relate to the intellectual approaches to God. How can someone be friendly with a God who is the "Ultimate Cause" or the "Ground of Being"?

Many students share Mary's opinion, and perhaps that is why they often shy away from reading intellectual theology books.

The Path of Feeling

While many people approach the mystery of God's existence through reason or intelligence, others follow the path of feelings. Emphasis on this approach to God has often come at times of great crisis and suffering. During the Black Death—a plague that ravaged Europe during the fourteenth century and laid waste to many of the ordered medieval structures in both the temporal and spiritual spheres—the tidy proofs of God's existence and the logical ordering of Christian doctrine began to crumble in the face of daily destruction and death. The carts of bodies moving through the streets were a constant reminder of the fragility of mortal life. The relentlessness of death had no respect for throne or office. In their pain and suffering, people did not want a God who appealed to their intellect. Their minds were distracted by pain and suffering. They wanted a God who healed their hurts, comforted their sorrows, and grieved with them over their lost loved ones.

Replacing the God of reason with the God of feeling can have its pitfalls. Negative feelings such as despair and distrust can lead a distressed people to replace their reasonable God with a God who was reached through superstition. Lacking a reasonable explanation of why a good and just God would allow such terrible plagues, and fearing the dangers of suffering eternal damnation from an unreasonable, wrathful God, simple people can turn to relics, talismans, indulgences, and other practices that were grounded neither in faith nor in reason. Some church leaders, either through ignorance or callousness, capitalized on the people's fears and promoted such actions. It was Luther who most strongly voiced objections to such misguided mediations to God and who asserted that we must submit to direct trust and confidence in God's forgiveness and saving grace.[20]

For many, the avenue to God became one of fear and despair of the self. In the seventeenth century this current entered Catholicism in the form of Jansenism. Despairing of human nature, this movement reached for God through a spirituality that was marked by scrupulosity, legalism, and an accountant's view of grace. For many Christians, especially Catholics, this harsh view of Christianity affected both their personal piety and their understanding of the existence of God. It continued well into the twentieth century and only recently has it begun to diminish, thanks in great measure to the renewed emphasis on the love of God that was proclaimed in the teachings of the Second Vatican Council (1962-65).

Reasons of the Heart

In discussing the rational approach to God, we spoke of Descartes's tendency to reduce the human spirit to the ability to think. It was Pascal (d. 1662) who reacted against this and suggested that there is a spiritual center in each person that not only thinks, but also understands and appreciates. There is a "logic of the heart" through which one can approach God. His classic statement is: "The heart has its reasons of which reason knows nothing."[21]

Pascal writes of human misery and vulnerability, and stands helpless and insecure in the face of a vast universe. Yet he also is aware of human glory and courage, our ability to take a risk and gamble on the existence of a Creator. He writes of his own personal experience of an enlightenment wherein a feeling of confidence in his heart helped him overcome his fears and doubt.

Pascal placed his faith in the God of Christianity, not the God of the philosophers. The feelings of peace and joy, rather than mathematical certainty, were Pascal's signs that he had made the right wager. Pascal's views seem to have a good balance between reason and faith. He held that the two excesses in the questions of the existence of God are: (1) the exclusion of reason; and (2) allowing only the use of reason. For him faith comes first and then a person can use reason to attempt to understand more clearly what one believes. Proofs are only useful to those who already believe. Where Descartes moved from the certainty of self to the certainty of God, Pascal began with the certainty of God and then is enabled to have a confidence in self.

The Feeling of Absolute Dependence

Friedrich Schleiermacher (d. 1834) has been called the "Father of modern Protestant theology." For him the human link to God was not through Immanuel Kant's (d. 1804) moral imperative or G.W.F. Hegel's (d. 1831) notion of Absolute Spirit, but through the human feeling of absolute dependence. An idealist, Schleiermacher held that the human person comes into existence through God's thinking and speaking. The human feeling of dependence comes from God, and once it has been experienced, it permeates people's lives.[22] This led much of Protestant thinking into a significantly more personal and subjective approach to the God-question throughout the nineteenth century and well into the twentieth century.

The Highway of Despair

Where some followed a road of intellectual skepticism in their search for God, others moved along on a "highway of despair." The phrase was coined by Hegel, but was moved into theological discussion and dealt with in great depth and feeling by Søren Kierkegaard (d. 1855). He believed that it was in the face of despair toward oneself that one comes to accept the existence of God. Following in the footsteps of Luther, Kierkegaard maintained that only in facing the despair of oneself and the dread regarding one's own salvation can people come to faith in God.[23] These words on dread and despair became the seeds from which grew twentieth-century existentialism. This existentialism gave a framework of meaning to the anxiety that seems to have been drawn from the horrors and absurdity attached to two World Wars.

In many ways this same feeling of despair seems to attach itself to all wars. Listen to Bill, a Vietnam veteran and now an MBA student, as he comments on how his tour of duty affected his religious faith:

When I came home from Vietnam I felt like an empty shell. I had seen so much suffering and killing on both sides that I was not sure that I had the desire to start over and make a life for myself. As for religion, I could not see how any kind of a good God could be in charge of all this mess. Then I met my wife Louise. It was her faith and courage that brought my spirit back to life. Without her I don't think I would have been able to find any meaning in life or come back to believing in God.

Fascination and Awe

Following the first World War, a German Protestant theologian, Rudolph Otto (d. 1937), published a book that was to become a classic in the discussion of the God-question. In *The Idea of the Holy,* Otto, who had studied many world religions, describes the human encounter with the "Holy," the "Awesome Mystery" that we call God. Otto speaks of a whole range of feelings that attach themselves to such an experience. He writes of the feeling of fascination, of being drawn to the Holy; of feelings of awe and fear in the presence of the divine. He tells of feeling overpowered at one time, and of being filled with a unique energy at another. He speaks of the hushed and speechless feeling of the creature before the Creator; of the ecstatic feeling of being in communion with the divine; of the shuddering, quaking feeling that can come when standing before the infinite and timeless.[24]

The Feeling of Trust

Some theologians today propose that the feeling of trust is the link with God's existence. Hans Küng maintains that fundamental trust—a basic option that life and being, as well as the source of life and being, are trustworthy—is the foundational indication that God exists.[25] Such trust cannot be based on demonstration or proof. It is risky (Pascal would say a gamble), and yet if freely given, it offers ample returns of value and meaning. This trust grows from the repeated exchange of love and fidelity. It provides a base of security from which one can confront injustice and oppression. Trust is relational, part of a sacred covenant; so when God is the central reality underlying all else, ultimate trust is placed in God. As Paul Tillich (d. 1965), the German Protestant theologian, would say, such trust gives us the "courage to be." It gives us the power to overcome the anxiety so common to all of us, and to reach out in trust to being. Ultimately we are led to trust in the very "Ground of Being," which is Tillich's description of God.[26]

The Reaching Out of the Will

While some have tried to bridge the gap between our finite and limited existence and Existence itself through thinking and feeling with mind and heart, others have tried to reach out to God with their will. Augustine wrote of an innate restlessness that is deep within us, moving us to reach out to God for fulfillment: "Thou has made us for thyself, O God, and our hearts cannot rest content until they rest in thee." A notion that runs through Augustine to Aquinas to Rahner and others seems to indicate that we are created with a drive to choose good, and ultimately the absolute Good. Just as our mind reaches out for the fullness of truth, our will desires the fullness of goodness.

In philosophy Immanuel Kant maintains that pure reason cannot reach out to God. It is practical reason, the dimension of reason that is manifested in human action, that enables us to speak of God. Kant argues to the existence of God from the moral and responsible dimension of human life. God becomes the presupposition for our capacity to strive for happiness through moral actions. For Kant, God is a "regulative idea," that helps us make sense of our feelings of moral obligation. He writes: "Do what will make you worthy of happiness."[27] Any other notion of communion with God, such as the mystical, is not acceptable to Kant.

Today the Kantian perspective becomes popularized in the argument that our values, our sense of justice, and our horror over evil all demonstrate the existence of a God. It is argued that such values cannot be purely subjective, but must come from a higher power. Closely aligned with this are the questions: Why is it that people experience feelings of guilt? And why is it that some guilt is so deep that it seems only a God can heal it? Philosophers reason that without God, without an ultimate source of meaning and value, we would have no source of value, nor any ultimate goal for life. As Dostoevsky wrote in *The Brothers Karamazov*, "If there is no God, everything is permitted."

The God of Freedom

For some the existence of God is best discussed in terms of our seemingly innate personal and communal drive for autonomy and freedom. It seems at times that this drive has even been projected onto God, making God into an autonomous and distant divine figure. This is the portrait of God given to us by James Joyce (d. 1941), the Irish novelist, who speaks of God as a being in the sky dispassionately watching life on earth as he files his fingernails.

At the other extreme, however, God is deprived of all autonomy by identifying God with reality in a pantheistic notion of creation. In this worldview, God is everywhere and in everything. It is always a balancing act to maintain the notion of God's independent transcendence, and yet not lose the notion that God is immanent and related to all reality. Tillich speaks of a "God above God," God as a reality that goes beyond the metaphors, images, myths, and notions that are used to craft an image of God to fit within human limitations.[28] As Alexander McKelway points out in *The Freedom of God and Human Liberation,* God is never exhausted or encircled by human thought, and therefore the "freedom of God" must be maintained as a constant corrective to any theology of God.[29] God is indeed a free Spirit, "blowing where God wills, creatively and surprisingly—within nature, within all people, and both inside and outside of organized religion. This is a God who transcends our well-ordered and often safe religious positions." From this perspective, God is free and is therefore the very source of human freedom.

Human beings are made in God's image and likeness, and thus enjoy the "freedom of the children of God." The *Pastoral Constitution on the Church in the Modern World* of the Second Vatican Council put it this way: "Authentic freedom is an exceptional sign of the divine image within [the human person]."[30] In our own limited way, we participate in and reflect a God who is free. Through grace we can create, nurture, and extend freedom to others. The ultimate free choice, of course, is the choice of faith—to choose God, the very source of freedom. Deep in the Christian tradition is the awareness of being liberated by Jesus Christ, and of continuing this mission of liberation among the oppressed. Dietrich Bonhoeffer (d. 1945), the German pastor who died in a Nazi concentration camp while awaiting execution for his struggle in the cause of freedom, wrote: "Freedom, how long we have sought thee in discipline, action and suffering; dying, we now behold thee revealed in the Lord."[31]

We encounter God within ourselves when we freely choose to discover the authentic self within. Freely choosing to put aside the masks and the false selves, we reach deeply within our consciousness and there discover God imaged in ourselves. Thomas Merton (d. 1968), the Trappist monk and renowned spiritual writer, who spent most of his life searching to know God better has written:

> If we enter into ourselves, finding our true self, and then passing "beyond" the inner "I," we sail forth into the immense darkness in which we confront the "I am" of the Almighty.... Our inmost "I" exists in God and God dwells in it.[32]

We can also encounter God when we engage in liberating action for others. We see this phenomenon demonstrated in a person like Harriet Tubman (d. 1913), a shy slave girl who became a great role model of freedom in the emancipation movement. She freed herself of a poor self-image, of fears, of suffering and death, by making many trips to the South in order to bring over three hundred slaves to freedom.

Today one reads of other testimonies of people in Central and South America who have personally become liberated through the struggle for freedom of the oppressed. One thinks of Archbishop Oscar Romero who was able to move beyond being a shy and cautious church administrator to the point where he could fearlessly stand against violence and injustice. He once wrote to Pope John Paul II about how he had found God in the poor and their struggle for justice:

> From the beginning of my ministry in the Archdiocese, I believed in conscience that God has asked of me, and gave me, a pastoral strength that contrasted with my conservative inclinations and temperament. I believe it is my duty to take a stand in defense of my Church, and from the Church, at the side of my oppressed and abused people.[33]

The God-Question After Vatican II

Prior to the Second Vatican Council in the early 1960s Catholic theology addressed the question of the existence of God in an intellectual manner in most instances. Academic theology was largely cognitive, but not so much in an investigative or critical mode. Before Vatican II the task of academic theology was largely to hand on the officially sanctioned teachings of the pope, the bishops, the church hierarchy, and the councils (also known as "the magisterium"), and to help in the understanding of these teachings.

The faithful often approached God on an emotional and devotional level, especially in the context of the sacraments, rituals, and devotions. Cognitive instruction about God in the pre-Vatican II church commonly involved the memorization of doctrines found in question-and-answer books like *The Baltimore Catechism*, and in a literal reading of scriptural stories. There was little room in this approach for questioning or critique. "Take it on faith" was the standard injunction that often quieted the inquiring mind.

Theology regarding the existence of God as well as the other major elements of the Christian theological tradition was often studied in a timeless, unchanging context that was cut off from the contemporary world and its scientific, political, and social issues. For the most part, Catholic theology used philosophy (generally nineteenth-century neo-scholasticism) only for the purpose of generating supportive proofs, alongside biblical proofs, to reenforce official magisterial teachings.

The proofs for the existence of God initially developed by Thomas Aquinas gradually were recognized by many Catholics to be inadequate. They had been developed in a pre-scientific era, were based on a classical Greek cosmology, and thus were cut off from the contemporary experience of life. Such proofs were no longer convincing to post-World War II Catholics who were studying astrophysics and evolution in progressive universities. There was obviously a growing need for new views on all sides of the equation: new insights on God, fresh views on both the human person and the world, and new ways to make connections between human beings and God.

New Foundations

For Catholics there seemed to be an immediate need to move away from the dualisms that were prevalent in Catholic thought for so many years. The splits were manifold: natural theology vs. dogmatics, the secular vs. the sacred, nature vs. grace, human vs. divine.[34] There was now a desire to bridge gaps and develop a fresh outlook on the relationship between God, humans, and the world in which they lived.

In what is generally accepted to be the standard approach to God taken by many Catholic teachers and pastors prior to the Second Vatican Council, God was perceived mainly as an "outside God," a being above and beyond the world. The practical and theological implications were manifold: lack of appreciation for nature and the environment; withdrawal from political and social issues; disdain for the material and the physical; a threatened, if not hostile attitude toward science; exclusion of the laity, except for religious Sisters and Brothers, from the active ministry of the church; lack of appreciation for the humanity of Jesus; and the development of a legalistic morality that perceived God as a judge.

Henri de Lubac (d. 1991), a French theologian, challenged this dualistic thinking. He was one of the first to propose that reality is not bileveled. Reality for de Lubac was unified, and yet was perceived as being two-dimensional, with the natural and supernatural both integral to the whole. He suggested that dualistic thinking be abandoned, believing instead that God created humans with a natural aspiration for the infinite and a natural desire for eternal happiness. A distinction between reason and faith would remain, but reality would be perceived as whole and undivided. God could now be perceived as an "inside God," still transcendent yet known and experienced as immanent in all of reality. Karl Barth (d. 1968), a renowned Protestant theologian, called this God the "Beyond Within."

The Experience of Mystery

Karl Rahner also did his share of bridge-building as he redefined the understanding of the relationship between the human and God. Using a dynamic notion of Being developed by philosophers Martin Heidegger (d. 1976) and Joseph Maréchal (d. 1944) as a framework, Rahner proposed that all human beings have been created with a "supernatural existential," a kind of supernatural imprint that orients all humans toward God. He believed that deep within our conscious self-awareness there is a potential that moves us, sometimes grasps us, to be open to God and God's revelation. This experience of God as Mystery is integral to human nature as gift. We are created as questioners, and God is our ultimate answer. We are by nature hearers, and God is our ultimate Word. Everyone is called to touch this Mystery in nature, in revelation, in the individual self, and in communal experiences. Rahner succinctly put it this way: "We are oriented toward God."[35]

Karl Rahner believed that all proofs and theories about the nature and existence of God must be seen against the background of this fundamental realization of Mystery experienced as being within the human person. God was accessible through the gifts with which humans were endowed. God could be experienced, and then that experience could be reflected on and interpreted theologically.

Rahner encouraged people to seek to know God through a holistic process incorporating the intellectual, emotional, volitional, and indeed, all the elements of human nature. The search for God, as Rahner described it, was experiential, involving the whole person opening oneself to God's revelation in nature, scripture, and everyday living.

Different Levels of Consciousness

Bernard Lonergan (d. 1984), renowned Catholic philosopher and theologian, also attempted to build bridges between the human and the divine. In part he did this by suggesting ways of linking the philosophical efforts to know God with similar discussions in systematic theology, thereby spanning a separation that he thought was unnecessary. He connected reason and faith in human experience through his theory of differentiated consciousness. By this Lonergan meant that within human history as well as within each individual there is a development of levels of awareness. At the first level humans learn to go beyond their senses and move toward an awareness of the factual, the temporal, and the abstract. People have reached the second level when their language moves from the practical to the creative. This is demonstrated in literature with the progression from functional writing to highly artistic writing. The third level is characterized by systematic, metaphysical, and scientific thinking in which individuals define and explore meanings and their inter-connection. At this level, a move is made from physics to "meta"physics, and then on to mathematics; from what might be so to what can be verified factually. Lonergan proposed a fourth level of consciousness that is religious. This he attributed to a graced gift from God, a flow of God's power and love which is "a dynamic state that fulfills the basic thrust of the human spirit to self-transcendence."[36] As Pascal had said long before, no one would be seeking God unless somehow God had already found that person.

Lonergan maintained that our philosophical search for God takes various forms and is not limited to the cognitive. While it is true that we question the existence of God with our intelligence, we also reflect on what we have learned of God, and deliberate on a course of action that is a worthy response to such a highly moral being as God. Finally, we reflect on our religious experiences of awe and love, asking from whence these experiences come and where they are going.[37] Tillich said we are grasped by ultimate concern. Ignatius Loyola (d. 1556), the founder of the Jesuits, wrote of a "consolation that has no cause."

Similar to Rahner, Lonergan maintains that the question of God's existence is found within the human horizon. At the very root of our consciousness there has always been a tendency to get in touch with the divine, a questioning and searching that is only satisfied with answers and fulfillment from the Ultimate Being itself. Lonergan maintains that our consciousness is so structured that once we have experienced something we are driven to try to understand, judge, and make choices based on that experience. The fact that humans can question the existence of God indicates that the Creator has suited us to deal with that question.[38] God not only gives us this dynamism toward the infinite, but also provides everyday experiences, persons, and events that tug and grasp at us to respond. It is our experience of frailty and wickedness that first raises for us the question of salvation, and then the question of God.

Some theologians think that today we are making new breakthroughs in the understanding of personal presence and the sacramental dimension of reality. This enables us to appreciate the consciousness of "God among us," which was characteristic of early Christianity's understanding of salvation in Jesus as the Christ.[39]

For the Christian, the revelation of God through Jesus Christ is normative for encountering God. But this realization comes in and through human experience. As Tillich once said in his criticism of Barth: "Revelation does not drop from the sky like a rock. The experience of God is an interplay among the revelation of God, the faith of the individual, and human experience."[40]

It was prevalent throughout the first half of the twentieth century for Catholic theologians to shy away from discussing the existence of God in terms of personal and cultural experience. But as Catholicism began to find its place in the modern world, it discovered correlations between life and beliefs.

Protestantism also moved in this direction. Paul Tillich led the way with his "co-relative method" wherein the culture raises the ultimate questions and the Christian tradition attempts to answer the queries. Then David Tracy, a Catholic theologian at the University of Chicago, developed a revisionist model of theology, wherein human experience and the tradition challenge each other, and where both human experience and tradition become the sources for theology.[41]

One theologian underlines the necessity of using human experience as the starting place for experiencing God: "The world of human experience is the only access to the saving reality of revelation and faith....How can we listen to a revelation from God, how could it be a revelation...if it falls outside our experience?"[42] It is in our hunger for recognition, security, and meaning that we find God. It is in our experience of suffering, sickness, and abandonment that we can discover the divine.

Alfred North Whitehead (d. 1947), a mathematician turned philosopher, once observed that this God is not the First Cause, or the Divine Watchmaker, or the Great Architect of the universe. This God is the Fellow-Sufferer who exists within the process of life.[43] This is a God who is rediscovered in history as a force that energizes the poor and the oppressed. In the past this God has been revealed as a loving and faithful companion in life. Present experience should confirm this; and the future is the perspective toward which God draws people. This is a God of possibilities and creativity, a God of promise and newness. For those who suffer affliction, lack of work, hunger, sickness, and death, this is a Source of life and strength. For those who grieve for loved ones who have been tortured and massacred, this is a God who truly cares. This is the Mystery that gives the power of love, forgiveness, courage, and hope to those who seem to be in desperate situations.[44]

Maria, an exchange student from El Salvador, wanted to share with her class how this way of approaching God has been made real by the events in her life. She spoke for many whose sufferings and oppression have produced a deep hunger for God and a dedication to justice when she quietly told us:

One night the authorities came and took my father because he had been part of a labor meeting where the government was criticized. He was tortured so badly that night that his mind snapped and he has had to be institutionalized ever since. I was a "daddy's girl," as you say in this country, and I was crushed by the loss of my father. But I grew up fast after this and lost all my fears, even my fear of death. My faith in God was strengthened, and this faith helped me realize that my father was still with me. When I return to my country I will never give up the struggle for freedom, no matter what they do to me. This loss and suffering have actually made me closer to my father and to my God.

A Connected Experience

Today many people seek God not only within human experience that is personal and private, but also in human experience that is social and political. As a missionary visiting a theology class once put it: "God is not in heaven watching this; God is a fellow-sufferer who is with us, giving us the power and the courage to help build the kingdom." People are beginning to make connections between their experience of God's existence and the critical issues in their world. There is a connection to be made between one's perception of God and one's concern for serious issues such as environmental destruction, world hunger, the spread of AIDS, racism, and violence.

Conclusion

We have seen that the question about the existence of God has apparently risen within the human psyche from the beginning of recorded history. All people have the capacity both to ask this question and to search for its answer. They have done this in many different ways within manifold cultures and religions.

In this chapter we have also examined atheism, a phenomenon that has developed in the context of the human search for an ultimate being. Atheism began as a critique of certain perspectives on the God-question and ended in the outright denial of the very reality around which this question revolves.

This chapter also considered how humans have searched and grappled with the question of God's existence through the use of their minds, hearts, and wills, and in the daily experiences of their lives.

None of what we have said proves that God exists. The cumulative effect of everything that has been discussed, however, might make faith in God seem reasonable and more understandable. For the person of faith who believes in the existence of God, it is quite difficult to accept the possibility that all the thinking, feeling, choosing, and acting that have gone on for so long by so many have been concerned with nothing more than a projection or an illusion. Ultimately, however, the answer to the question about the existence of God lies in trust and faith. For the Christian, the answer lies in trust in Jesus Christ and faith in his message that God exists as a loving and forgiving parent.

Discussion Questions

1. How does ancient "atheism" differ from the forms of atheism in modern times?

2. How would you answer some of the classical atheistic positions of Feuerbach, Marx, and Freud?

3. Which of the various approaches to God (mind, heart, will, etc.) most appeals to you? Explain why one or the other approach is more appealing to you.

4. It is said that many young people today prefer to approach God through experience rather than through reflection. Do you think this is true? Please explain your position on this.

5. Write a reflection on some significant experience you may have had of the presence of God in your life.

Suggested Readings

Denis Carroll, *A Pilgrim God for a Pilgrim People.* Wilmington, DE: Michael Glazier, 1989.

Bernard Cooke, *The Distancing of God.* Minneapolis: Augsburg Fortress Press, 1990.

John Farrelly, *Belief in God in Our Times.* Collegeville, MN: Liturgical Press, 1992.

Barbara Fiand, *Embraced by Compassion: On Human Longing and Divine Response.* New York: Crossroad, 1993.

Gustavo Gutiérrez, *The God of Life.* Maryknoll, NY: Orbis Books, 1991.

John Haught, *What Is God?* New York: Paulist Press, 1986.

William Hill, *Search for the Absent God.* New York: Crossroad, 1992.

Harold Kushner, *Who Needs God?* New York: Summit Books, 1989.

John Macquarrie, *In Search of Deity.* New York: Crossroad, 1985.

2.

Who Is God?

Framing the Question

My name is Carole. I come from a large family of eight children and I grew up on the north side of Chicago. I run track and am an art major. I have been a Catholic all my life and have a strong faith in God, but since I have been in college my beliefs about who God really is have become somewhat vague and a bit confused. When I was small I believed that God was like a grandfather, a kind person who watched over me. I remember getting confused about God when I first heard the bible stories that they told in school. The God in those stories seemed to be angry and even mean. It scared me to think that God would punish Adam and Eve so much for just eating some fruit. And I was even more shocked when I read about God killing off all those people in the flood, and allowing all the first-born sons of the Egyptians to be killed. But in spite of all that, I kept experiencing God as a kind of loving grandfather.

My mother describes herself as a feminist. She used to bother me with all her talk about praying to God as her mother or her sister. Now that I am in college I am more aware of how our society and our church are so male-dominated. I am beginning to see why my mother was bothered by all the male images of God. My mother has been reading a lot of feminist theologians, and we have been having some interesting conversations about goddesses and about priestesses. It is hard for me to know where I stand on all these issues, but one thing is for sure: My ideas about God are going through a lot of change.

No Easy Answers

Carole is beginning to see how difficult it is to speak about or image God. It seems that as Carole matures God becomes a more complex reality for her. She is coming to an awareness that there are many ways to understand and image God, and that as we mature there can be a high degree of confusion about who God is.

The Mystery of God

Christians use the word "God" in their attempt to name the mysterious reality that is the foundation for all of their tradition. This reality, called "God," is the ultimate reality, the source, and the sustaining power of all that exists. This reality is called "Mystery" because it is beyond all comprehension, all expression, and yet, at the same time, is the most profoundly evident reality. This mystery is a nameless and faceless reality that seems to be ever-present and yet ever-absent; absolutely beyond yet profoundly within reality.[1] This inevitable ambiguity was evident even to the extraordinary genius, Thomas Aquinas. After years of working diligently on questions surrounding God, he wrote: "One thing about God remains completely unknown in this life, namely, what God is."[2]

In this chapter we will discuss some of the efforts throughout history to understand God. We will begin with a brief consideration of metaphor and myth and then move on to consider some the images of God in both the Hebrew and Christian scriptures. Then we will turn our attention to the perspectives on God arising today from the feminist movement and other contemporary approaches to theology.

Names, Images, Myths, and Notions

Throughout history humans have attempted to name this reality. Zeus, Baal, Isis, Yahweh, Asherah, The Great Spirit, Demeter, Allah, Brahman, and many other names have been given to the Supreme Being. Each of these names has expressed a different understanding of and relationship with this mysterious reality. Along with the names, many metaphors and images have been used in attempts to express an individual's or, more often, a community's understanding of this mystery.

Ongoing efforts have been made to use images from the created world to fathom the uncreated; to use the physical to construe the spiritual. The human images of father, mother, shepherd, and king as well as the inanimate images of rock, shield, and fortress were used in efforts to comprehend the incomprehensible. Human experiences of love, love-making, war, floods, disease, wisdom, justice, and manifold others were used in religious traditions to explain the inexplicable. Stories of liberation, mountaintop mystical revelation, and dying and rising were told to describe this reality. Others have used philosophical concepts such as "being" or "existence" to explain the deity. Some have gone about this religious search for understanding mystically, some imaginatively, and others logically and systematically.

Inevitably the names, the images, the myths, and the philosophical concepts fall short of capturing the reality of God. Yet we continue to go on in our efforts, probably because even though this means looking "through the glass darkly," it is better than having no look at all. We know that life is mortal and limited and so we are modest in our expectation of grasping the reality of God.

We continue on with this search because we are convinced that there is some connection to be found between the reality around us and the Reality that is its source. The Judeo-Christian religion believes that somehow all creation comes from God and that human life reflects the image of God. Integral to this traditional belief is the conviction that God is immanently present in all reality, especially in human historical experience. If this is true, then there is good and valid reason to see a connection between creation and the Creator, and to use reality and human experience to come to a deeper understanding of God. For example, since fatherhood comes from God, "father" can be an authentic image to use in our search to understand God. But motherhood also comes from God, and therefore can be an equally valuable image for learning about other dimensions of this mystery we call God. By the same token our experience of a friend or a lover can help us see unique dimensions of God's existence. And, of course, since nature itself finds its source in God, it is reasonable to use natural images such as the eagle, the rock, the buffalo, or even the earth itself as an image for God.

James is a Native American who has helped his classmates to develop new images for God. James grew up in Arizona where his grandfather was a member of the Hopi tribe. James learned as a child that the Great Spirit, which is what his grandfather called God, could be experienced in many ways: in the soaring flight of the eagle; in the majestic red-rock mountains, and in the mighty rivers. James once told us in class:

For me God has many names. God is the sun, the stars on a clear summer night, a young deer in the forest. God has come to me in many things and in many people.

The Problem with Literalism

Carole pointed out at the beginning of this chapter that her mother is quite comfortable with feminine images of God. This is a marked contrast to her grandmother who understands the bible in a literal manner. Some would say that her grandmother is a fundamentalist, someone who takes the bible literally, and believes that in it we have God's own words as dictated to the inspired writers.

Literalism is one of the hazards that arises from using image, metaphor, or myth to describe God. Finding similarities and insights about God from these devices is one thing, but actually identifying or equating God with a particular metaphor can result in simplistic or distorted notions about God.[3] To say that God is a father attributes to God the image of the male parent who cares, protects, and loves his children while possessing a certain authority and strength. This is not to say that God is actually a male or a father, nor is it correct to use this image to imply that the patriarchal social system is divinely ordained. Conversely, to say that God is a mother is to indicate that God uniquely gives and nurtures life in a maternal fashion, but does not imply that God is literally a female or a mother.

In the use of all these comparisons it is important to note that the mysterious reality we call God pre-exists and transcends creation, sexuality, and familial roles. When we use images from human experience we are drawing from a created reality that is only several hundreds of thousands of years old to describe a God that "always was and always will be." We are using finite and mortal images to describe a Reality that is both infinite and immortal.

We know that projection is often present in our efforts to image or construct myths about God. Distorted projections can result in strange images of God. The "warrior God" of the Book of Exodus from the Hebrew scriptures (Old Testament) can bring out God's protection and strength during oppressive times. At the same time, however, our dark desires for revenge and destruction can be projected onto this image of God in such a way that it seems that God is ordering and presiding over the massacre of innocent people. Myths are meant to narrate the sacred action of God within reality.[4] They are not intended to convey distorted or savage notions about God.

The God of the Hebrews

The Hebrew notions of God are at the base of the Christian tradition. Jesus of Nazareth was a Jew attempting to reform Judaism, and his teachings about God were in the context of the Hebrew tradition.

Moreover, many of Jesus' early followers were Jews, and their beliefs profoundly affected their shaping of the Christian tradition. For example, Paul of Tarsus, whose theology significantly influenced the foundations of Christian thinking, was a Pharisee (a Jewish religious party criticized by Jesus for its merely external observance of the law) before he became a Christian, and brought a rich background in Judaism to his reflections on the revelation of Jesus Christ.

The theological understanding of God that we find in the Hebrew scriptures is not abstract, philosophical, or logically constructed. Rather it is a complex tapestry of images, metaphors, and myths. Reflecting on this approach to God, a Jewish student observed:

We don't use the God-talk of Western Christian theology. The Orthodox Judaism I was brought up with never bothered itself with such abstractions. Instead Judaism was focused on doing what we call "mitzvahs," good deeds which we were told would make us better Jews.[5]

The God Yahweh

The Hebrew understanding of God arises largely from the religious influences of other cultures as well as from the interpretation of historical events. The Hebrew search for God seems to be largely an effort to rise constantly from lapses into idolatry and infidelity, and to once again walk faithfully with their own personal God, Yahweh.

We know that the Hebrew people were originally a semi-nomadic people who migrated from one place to another. Along the way the Hebrews were eclectic in their understanding of God. The Semites from the Mesopotamian area hailed El Shaddai, a mountain deity, as their chief god. When we read of the God of Sinai we see the influences of this mountain god. One might even hears echoes of the mountain god in the story of Jesus' transfiguration on the mountain (Matthew 17). We know that the Semites ultimately migrated to Canaan and were deeply influenced by the Canaanite culture and religion. In fact, early Israelite culture cannot be easily separated from the Canaanite culture, for both cultures overlap in language, social customs, and religious beliefs. When the Hebrews migrated into Canaan they were influenced by the Canaanite belief in Baal (Lord), who was a god of nature and storms, a deity who owned the land and made it fertile.[6] We can see the influences of this god in the Yahwist creation story (Genesis 2) and in the story of the great flood (Genesis 6–9). One might also hear the memory of the storm god in the miracle of Jesus' calming of the storm (Mark 4) or in the prayer of a farmer asking for rain.

Although the Hebrew people's notion of God was influenced by beliefs they incorporated from Canaan and other cultures, ultimately they developed a unique religious tradition. The Mosaic recognition of God as Yahweh represents a marked departure from the so-called pagan notions of god. First and foremost, Yahweh is recognized as the only God, before whom no other gods are to be worshiped. At first this was not so much a denial of the existence of other gods as it was a conviction that no other god is to have their allegiance.[7] The Exodus experience was most significant in moving the Hebrews to realize that they could only put their ultimate trust in Yahweh. Eventually they rejected all other gods.

Unlike the gods worshiped by the Canaanites and other peoples around them, Yahweh was not viewed as a sexual being. In the Canaanite religion, sex was elevated to the divine level. The forces of nature were manipulated through the sexual relations of the chief gods and their consorts. Worship included sexual rites that imitated the actions of the gods and persuaded them to make the land fertile and the crops bountiful through their divine love-making. All of this was rejected by the Yahwist tradition. Yahweh was thought to be autonomous and completely free. Yahweh could not be manipulated. Orgies, magic, and other pagan notions about divine influence over nature fell by the wayside.

An unfortunate result of the rejection of the sexual characteristics of God was the fact that the sacredness of human sexuality was also deemphasized in the Hebrew tradition. In a related development, the feminine characterizations of God gave way to an almost exclusive emphasis on the male image of God in the Hebrew tradition. The God of mountains, nature, and fertility gave way to the God of history, often portrayed as the warrior God, the Judge, the King. Yahweh becomes the all-powerful Creator and the Savior.

Ernest is an African-American student in ROTC. He generally sits up straight in his desk when he hears someone putting down the "warrior image" of God. Ernie's brother fought in Operation Desert Storm in the Persian Gulf and was told by his commanding officer that God was on their side in this war. Ernie remembers reading that in a letter from his brother and he is convinced that this is true. Ernie was not too happy when one of his classmates, Heather, said: "Well, what about Allah? The Iranians were praying to Allah. Whose side was he on?"

I Am Who Am

For the ancient Hebrews the name of a person had great significance because the name stood for the person's identity and innermost self. In the story of Moses' conversation with God in Exodus 3:13–14, Moses asked God his name in an obvious attempt to discover the identity of this God who was giving him a mission of liberation. In the story, God simply used the verb "to be" (YHWH), telling Moses to inform the people that "I am who am" has sent him.

"Yahweh" implies the lack of a name more that is does knowing the identity of God. It is not so much a name for God as it is a description of God's activity of being with the people and somehow causing to be all that happens. God is unnameable and cannot be known directly. God can be known only indirectly through creation and living. The name Yahweh implies that God is the very source of existence and will be with the people. God is a savior and protector; a God active in history. The name Yahweh eventually was considered too sacred to use, and it was gradually replaced by Adonai or Lord.

The Hebrew scriptures do not give us a treatise on the understanding of Yahweh. Rather they attempt to acknowledge Yahweh's revelations and actions in history and call for an acknowledgment of God's glory through a response characterized by obedience and service. Throughout the Hebrew scriptures a number of images of God emerge.

Creator

In the Book of Genesis we find two stories that portray God as the creator of the world and the first humans. In the older of the two versions of the creation story (Genesis 2) the Yahwist author (one of four major authors of the Pentateuch, the first five books of the Bible) portrays a resourceful and sharing God who brings growth from the dry land, forms the first human person, generously creates a marvelous garden for him, and with trust and confidence gives him the responsibility of caring for the garden. This is a kind and compassionate God who perceives the loneliness of his creature and creates companions for him. First he makes animals and birds for him and when they are not enough, God creates woman from the man's own flesh and blood, someone he can join with in the unity of bonded love. This Yahwist God is also portrayed as a lawgiver and a firm punisher of those who break the law. And yet this is a God who promises to overcome evil and forgive people's offenses.

The other creation story, apparently written later than the first, by the so-called priestly author (another of the four major writers of the Pentateuch), portrays a powerful and distant God who creates the universe in seven days with a mere word, declares it all good, and shares the power of creativity with living things. This is a God who is eager to share the gift of life with others and who creates both male and female to reflect the divine image. It is a God who blesses creatures and who entrusts this creation to them.

One God

The nomadic Hebrews had lived in a variety of areas and had come to know and revere many gods associated with the forces of nature and the many mysteries connected with human living. In most regions this was not so much a case of believing in many gods as it was acknowledging a supreme God or an inclusive divine reality that manifested itself in the image of many gods.[8] The Hebrews knew the frustration of trying to manipulate these gods through elaborate rituals. Often these gods seemed whimsical and little different from the creatures over whom they were supposed to rule.[9] Gradually Israel seems to have moved from having a number of deities in its early period to an eventual commitment to one God.

In the belief system of the Hebrews the image of Yahweh eventually assimilated the imagery of the other primary deities. Centuries of experiences and reflection had moved the Hebrews to the conviction that only one God was their Creator, Father, and King. They were called to love this one Lord and God with all their heart, spirit, and power. Only Yahweh was worthy of their worship, and this worship was intended as praise or repentance. It was not, as it was in the other religions they had experienced, a means of manipulating the gods.

Yahweh is described as a jealous God who will not tolerate worship of another deity. It was the experience of the Hebrew people that there was but one God who saved them, and only this God would continue to save them. The movement toward monotheism began gradually with the patriarchs (leaders of the Chosen People prior to the establishment of the monarchy under Saul), who generally seemed to accept polytheism, and culminated with the triumph of monotheism during the Mosaic period. In the incident of the Golden Calf (Exodus 32) Moses makes it clear to the people that no image may represent Yahweh. Nor could any other idols such as greed, power, wealth, or pleasure be given ultimacy. This belief was galvanized in the Exodus experience and prevailed from the time of Moses onward, in spite of periodic lapses into polytheism.

A God of History

Yahweh was worshiped as a God who was actively involved in history as the ruler of the world. For the Hebrews history was the place to discover the self-revelation of God. In contrast to the fatalistic Eastern notions of time as an endless cycle of events, the Hebrews viewed time as moving ahead in linear fashion, drawn forward by a God of the future. Yahweh was, above all, their Liberator and Savior. Their God was one in whom a trusting hope could be placed, no matter how dire the circumstances, no matter how horrible the oppression.

As a God of justice, Yahweh would restore justice to those who are oppressed and execute justice against oppressors. As opposed to other gods, who were capricious and unpredictable, Yahweh was absolute and trustworthy in the ways of justice. Yahweh protected his own with tenderness, mercy, and love. Israel had not been elected exclusively to enjoy this protection, but to witness to its accessibility to all nations.[10]

Contemporary liberation theologians (Jon Sobrino, Gustavo Gutiérrez, and others from Central America and Third World countries) have called our attention to the fact that Yahweh's justice is extended uniquely to the poor. Those who were liberated in the Exodus were poor slaves, and they symbolize the kind of people who are especially blessed with God's care. For this reason the widows, orphans, and strangers are uniquely protected in the Jewish tradition and remain a special concern of Christians today.[11]

The prophetic tradition of Israel is a tradition of protesting unjust offenses against God's law of justice. The prophets cried out against the oppression of the poor and downtrodden by the rich and powerful. The prophets pointed out the incongruity and hypocrisy of considering oneself to be one of God's chosen and at the same time imposing injustice and oppression upon God's people. An authentic sign of being created in God's image was to imitate Yahweh in feeding the hungry, giving shelter to the homeless, and clothing the naked (Isaiah 58:6–7).

Pedro, who recently came to the United States from El Salvador, can always be counted on for stories about the power of God as a liberator. He has often experienced the freeing power of God in his own life. Pedro tells the story of the time when his father took him to the funeral Mass of several people who had been killed by the death squads. He says:

I was scared going into church because the soldiers had surrounded the church with armored vehicles. I remember feeling sad that my favorite priest from the parish, Father José, was not at the funeral. They said that Father was hiding in the mountains because the army wanted to kill him because he was always helping the poor. During Mass, a funny-looking peasant with long hair and a beard came to the altar, sat down, and sang a song for those who had been killed. When the man finished the song, he left by a back door. After Mass, I asked my father who the funny-looking man was. He whispered: "That was your friend Father José. He sneaked into the church and sang a song he had written for his people who were murdered." After that I was never again afraid of anything. I really believe that through the courage of Father José, God freed me of all my fears, even the fear of death.

Scripture's Unique Notion of History

When describing Yahweh as a God of history we must be cautious not to use the concept of history that began to develop in the Enlightenment and reached decisive form in the nineteenth century. Biblical history is not always a factual or accurate description of what really happened at a given time and place. It is properly described as "salvation history," as opposed to secular history. In the Hebrew scriptures we have a unique notion of history, whereby events are viewed and interpreted as interactions between people and God. The actual presentation tells us much more about this interaction and about the beliefs flowing forth from it than it tells us about what happened. Historical events are viewed primarily as encounters with the saving God. The story that is told about the event is intended to convey the meaning of the encounter rather than present a picture of exactly what happened. The mythical nature of the stories conveys levels of reality that go much deeper than those in mere surface actions.

The Holy One

The Hebrews saw Yahweh as a Spirit who was absolutely distinct in holiness. This radical holiness separated God from all creation, and rendered God transcendent and beyond the limited experience and understanding of humans. Rudolph Otto in his classic study of God's holiness observed that such holiness rendered God both fascinating and terrifying.[12] This holiness exploded into creation in Genesis, was experienced in the destruction of enemies in Exodus, and thundered out against injustice and oppression in the prophetic tradition. The miracle stories throughout scripture, including those of the New Testament concerning the life and times of Jesus, proclaimed this holy power.

The need of an Ark of the Covenant (Exodus 25) and a Holy of Holies in the Temple (1 Kings 6) testify to how this Holy God is to be set off from the profane. Likewise the Sabbath, setting off sacred time and sacred space, indicates the value of stepping aside from mundane occupations in order to contemplate the holiness of God for one day each week. Traditions and rituals regarding particular times, objects, and places being set aside and consecrated all flow from this notion of the holiness of God and the need to attend to worship and service of God. For this reason the Hebrews viewed the entire people as "a kingdom of priests and a holy nation" (Exodus 19:6).

Spirit

Although the Israelites often used human imagery to portray God, they believed that God was a transcendent Spirit beyond perception and beyond sensible experience and comprehension. They allowed oral and written images, but never material images of God in the temple or synagogues. This explained Moses' horror when he beheld the golden calf constructed by the people in his absence, as well as the fury shown by the Jews of Jesus' time when the Romans installed the Roman Eagle over the temple gate.

As a Spirit, Yahweh was perceived as invisible to the eye, but always in reach of the hearts of the people. God was compared with life, the wind, and love; a Spirit with inexhaustible energy and power. God was not subject to suffering or death, but was the very source as well as the goal of life. Yahweh stood in contrast to the flesh or to earthly life, which was mortal, transitory, and weak.

When God is described as being a Spirit, this is not to be taken in some abstract sense as being opposed to the material and the human. The Spirit of God moves freely within creation and is openly manifest within all things. No magic can manipulate this Spirit to come and go; yet because of God's own freely made promise the divine power acts in the world and among all people.

A Personal God

To the Hebrews Yahweh is a personal God who calls people to form a relationship with the divine being. This is not to say that God is a person, but rather that God is personal, one who intimately shares in the personal and historical lives of all humans. For the Israelites the "God of places" is not so important as the "God of persons" who walks among the people. This is evident in the expression "God of our fathers," which seems to indicate that each of the patriarchs had his own personal god to accompany him and protect him and his extended family. This is a God who was always nearby and intimately involved in the families and the tribes.

The personal God of the Hebrews is different from the metaphysical gods of the Greeks. This Hebrew God is not to be identified materially with natural forces and things. This God transcends all and yet is close to all. This is a God who can be experienced in the sandstorm as well as in the breeze, in the heartache as well as in the joys and pleasures of life. Yahweh is accessible, constantly revealing God's self. This intimacy is expressed in the biblical images of human mercy, compassion, tenderness, fidelity, and love that seem to come from God and which give an image and a glimpse of their source. Here there is a personal God who invites people to share happiness and life. This is a God who especially loves and blesses the poor and the outcast. It is One who awaits a response of friendship, loyalty, obedience, prayer, and action for justice from all who believe.[13] Yahweh is One who takes initiative toward people, and uses a myriad of means both to reveal and to conceal the divine presence. Yahweh is an awesome and gracious personal presence who expects an equally personal response.[14]

A Free God

The God of the Israelites is neither a manipulative puppeteer nor a master of fate, as was the case with some to the pagan gods. Yahweh chooses freely out of a creative love to share existence, power, and life with others. Although sovereign, Yahweh extends an invitation to form a relationship and then awaits a free answer from the people. As Peter C. Hodgson, a major contributor to the contemporary theology of freedom, puts it: "Freedom is the essence of divinity; to be sure, it is also the image of God in humanity."[15] From this perspective, God is a free Spirit, blowing where God wills through all of creation. God is free and cannot be limited by our projected images or our theological explanations. This God of the Israelites could not be made into a household god, domesticated by human images, myths, and beliefs.

God of the Covenant

For the Hebrews, the experience of the personal God culminates in their election to be God's covenanted people. As Lawrence Boadt points out: "They clung stubbornly to a conviction that God had indeed entered into a special relationship of covenant with them—a covenant that established bonds of loyalty and responsibility between God and humanity in the person of Israel."[16] The story of Abraham is written around the memory of the beginning of this covenant (Genesis 12–25). The Hebrew scriptures carry forth the theme that in spite of Israel's repeated infidelity to this covenant, they are steadfastly forgiven and reconciled with their God.

This covenant was a bond between God and the chosen people as well as among the people themselves. Although it often was misread as a sign that they were an exclusive community, the Chosen People were to proclaim in word and deed that God had called all people to the covenant.

This covenant is not a bilateral contract between two equal parties. Rather it is an agreement where the initiative is graciously taken by a higher power toward one who is lower in status. The higher power can, by right, impose duties and obligations on the less powerful party to the agreement. In exchange for fulfilling the obligations of adoring only one God and following that God's laws, Yahweh agreed through the provisions of the covenant to protect and assist the people. The laws proclaimed by Yahweh show how the covenanted relationship is to be lived out by the people. They lay out the way of life with love of self, God, and neighbor as the standard.

This covenant continues to give direction and meaning to Jewish life today. For the Jews, the covenant is their occasion for celebration, their source of strength in the midst of oppression, and their standard of hope for the future. It is an ancient bond that finds its way into the stories of creation, Noah's survival of the Flood, the migrations of Abraham, the Exodus of Moses, and many other stories throughout the Hebrew scriptures.

God the Father

The image of God as Father is not original either to the Christians or even to the Hebrews. It is a primordial image found in many religions including those of the Assyrians, Babylonians, and Greeks. A key belief for the Greeks was that Zeus was the father of the gods as well as of all people.[17] This notion may have arisen from the understanding in those societies that the father was the source of life, the provider and protector of all people. This paternal image seemed appropriate for referring to God, the ultimate source, sustainer, and unifier of all that exists.

The question arises, of course, whether or not this primal image is to be taken literally. The answer hinges on how one locates the source of the metaphor. Are metaphors part of God's revelation in that they come from God and therefore are not negotiable? Or do metaphors come from human efforts to understand the revelation of God found in experiences that are deeper than spoken language? If the latter be the case, then metaphors are more negotiable and we need not be so locked into the ones of the past that have lost much of their currency.

The Hebrews saw God as the source of their life and the wellspring of meaning. Since they came to know God through the experiences of their lives and their history they felt justified in using their human experiences as metaphors in their ongoing search to understand their God. As in most cultures, the role of the father was significant. Living in a culture where patriarchal structures prevailed, the Hebrews used the image of father to describe God's authority and caring protection. Unfortunately, there were often aspects of domination and even enslavement that developed with patriarchy. At times these were not only projected onto God, they were also used as divinely decreed justification for violent conquest and oppression.[18]

Michael, a student from South Africa, can tell you how these patriarchal beliefs are still operative. He reports:

There were many people in my country who truly believed that they were created by God to dominate the indigenous people of my country and that God gave them this country as their promised land. They had to learn that God is a father to all people. We are beginning to wake up to that in my country, but much blood has been shed in the process.

Among the Hebrews the notion of father in biblical language seemed to begin with the notion of the "Father of the Gods" and moved toward The "God of the Fathers,"and then to Yahweh, the God of Moses. Abraham probably saw his God, El, as the head of all the other gods. Hundreds of years later, during the Mosaic period, the Yahwist (one of the four major authors of the Pentateuch) left no doubt about the oneness of the deity. Yahweh was proclaimed to be the God of the Fathers and the only God to be worshiped. He was viewed as the God who called Abraham, Isaac, and Jacob (the patriarchs) and their descendants to be his people.[19] They were elected to be the children of God.

In the Hebrew covenantal relationship, in contrast to much of pagan mythology, there was no sexual begetting. Rather than a physical begetting there was a calling or electing of Israel to be the children of God and to testify to all nations that this calling extended to them also. (The covenant of Noah had been given to the whole earth and all living creatures.) The Father-God would be protective and merciful, but also demanding. Thus the prophet Malachi proclaims: "Have we not all the one Father? Has not the one God created us?" (Mal 2:10). Isaiah prays: "O Lord, hold not back, for you are our father. You, Lord, are our father, our redeemer you are named forever"(Is 63:16). And several hundred years before the time of Jesus of Nazareth, another sage named

Jesus, who authored the Book of Sirach, prayed to God as "Lord, Father and Master of my life" (Sir 23:1).

The ideal of fatherhood as exhibited by God had become for the Chosen People the standard against which all human fatherhood was measured. "Father" helped define God, and then "God" helped define the role of father. The latter dynamic is perhaps most relevant today at a time when the role and influence of the father is often in decline. It can receive new clarification and importance from religious tradition. The fatherhood of God certainly stands in prophetic challenge against the neglect, abuse, violence, and abandonment that is evidenced by many fathers today.

An Uncommon Hebrew Image

Even though the Hebrews generally used male pronouns to describe God, the use of the father image for God occurs less than a dozen times in the Hebrew scriptures. The image is much more common in the New Testament where Jesus used the image of God as a loving Father to describe his unique relationship with God.

The Hebrew understanding of God began with their seeing God as the father of all, and then gradually seeing themselves in a unique covenant with this fatherly God. This image may well have been a prophetic device "for summing up the good that God had done and continued to do for his people, in order to provide a foil for their ingratitude or a basis for their plea for pardon."[20] Their sins became the sins against their father and took on all the seriousness of infidelity within the patriarchal framework. It would be a device to show why they deserved punishment as well as a sign of the availability of mercy and pardon.

God in the New Testament

The Christian understanding of God has its source in the life and teachings of Jesus Christ. As David Tracy states: "For the Christian, God is the one who revealed Godself in the ministry and message, the cross and resurrection of Jesus Christ."[21] The fullness of the Christian understanding of God begins with the image of God as revealed in Jesus Christ and then enriched by the living tradition that has developed from this teaching.

It is important to note that Jesus of Nazareth was a Jew whose life and teachings were touched by a lively and highly debated Hebrew tradition. For Jesus, God was Yahweh, the One true God, the Creator and Master of History. God was also the Holy One, the intensely spiritual

God who freely offered a covenanted relationship to all people, the Father who loved and cared for his people.

While he was steeped in the Hebrew tradition, Jesus' revelation gives a new fullness and an authenticity to the teaching about God. He accepted certain understandings of God drawn from his tradition, such as the loving, caring, forgiving nature of God; the sense of God offering fatherly protection and sacrifice; and the intimacy possible with God. Then he wove these strands into a new garment, a unique and fresh perspective about God which still today is heralded as the Good News. He proclaimed this Good News by his teaching and by his very presence.

Jesus incarnated this teaching and led a godly life of self-sacrifice, tenderness, and care for the downtrodden. He lived a life that was both simple and yet complex, a life that was contemplative and yet quite active, a life that was noteworthy for its dedication to justice and its fervent commitment to doing the will of his Father. Jesus' unique perspective was true to the God of the Hebrews, and further revealed and incarnated God with a depth and clarity that remains unparalleled in religious history.

My Father and Your Father

Although the image of God as a Father was an an important image for the Hebrews, it was rarely used in the Hebrew scriptures. In the New Testament, however, it became the central image as it was used by Jesus in the gospels about 170 times. The tradition of referring to God as Father, although elaborated on and developed by the later Christian communities, originated with the preaching and ministry of Jesus.[22]

Jesus perceived his mission as coming from the Father and he proclaimed that the way to this godly Father is through Jesus himself. In Matthew, Jesus praises his Father for revealing the presence and person of God to the childlike people and then proclaims: "All things have been handed over to me by my Father. No one knows the Son except the Father, and no one know the Father except the Son and anyone to whom the Son wishes to reveal him"(Mt 11:27).

In Matthew's Gospel, Jesus finds approval from his Father at his baptism in the Jordan when Jesus comes up from the water and a voice is heard from the heavens saying: "This is my beloved Son, with whom I am well pleased" (Mt 3:17). Similar words are heard at the Transfiguration to affirm Jesus' unique relationship with God (Mt 17:5).

Jesus teaches that this Father who is pleased with him also loves all people: "For he makes his sun shine on the bad and the good, and causes the rain to fall on the just and the unjust" (Mt 5:45). This is the loving Father who knows our needs before we ask and to whom we can confidently pray the "Our Father." This is the Father who cares for the birds of the air, the lilies of the field, and all his children, especially the little ones, the lost sheep, and the outcasts. This Father, who seems to be Jesus' constant companion, offers healing and forgiveness for their transgressions to all his children.

Jesus' distinctive confidence and authority arose from a unique intimacy that he experienced with God. This is evident in his use of "Abba" when referring to God the Father. This word means "Daddy" or "my own dear father," a term of familiarity that was used for human fathers but not generally used in public discourse or prayer to refer to God. Even though scholars are more cautious today about affirming Jesus' complete uniqueness in using "Abba" to refer to God, there is still a strong consensus that the term as we know it in the New Testament originated with Jesus. It comes from his original experience of intimacy with God, and what is even more unusual is that he invites his disciples to the same familiarity with God as Abba.

Jesus' followers join with him in a common sisterhood and brotherhood under the same Father. The Father seeks them out if they should go astray, and blesses them when they are hungry for justice. At the Last Supper and in the Agony in the Garden, Jesus turns to his Father as he agonizes over the crucifixion. In the passion stories Jesus cries out to his Father in near desperation, asks forgiveness for his persecutors, and commends himself into his Father's hands. It is this Father that raises Jesus from the dead and in the name of whom, along with the Son and Spirit, his disciples are commissioned to baptize. It is in this Father's house that Jesus prepares many mansions for the faithful. Jesus perceives himself to be one with this Father and, in virtue of this unity, to draw all things to God. Matthew's gospel reflects the early communities centering their prayer, way of life, and missionary outreach around this image of God as a Father. The Gospel of John emphasizes the oneness of Jesus with the Father to the extent that Jesus becomes the embodiment of the "I am."

The Reign of God

Jesus generally integrated the image of God as a Father with his central message of the kingdom or reign of God. This notion, which began in Judaism, speaks of God's Lordship manifested in history. God's loving and saving presence draws the world to its fulfillment in God. Jesus taught that this reign of God is in our midst as a pure gift. Nothing we ourselves can do will bring this reign about, yet we are called to pray that "thy kingdom come," and to do all that we can to help it to fruition.

Many of Jesus' parables describe the dynamic power and presence of the reign of God's kingdom. These parables teach that the reign is not remote or abstract, but a prevailing presence that can be felt now and in the future. God is both within history as well as ahead of history, drawing creation to its fulfillment.[23]

The reign of God is intended neither as a political nor as a social structure. Rather it is the dominance of God's constant love, which saves all people. The kingdom of God is not intended to result in a nation or a state, but in a movement of liberation from oppression and poverty. This notion has gained new prominence and meaning in liberation theology. In the Third World, where governments are often oppressive, the poor have gained new courage and vigor knowing that God is not remote and does not want them to suffer quietly, but is actively by their side in the struggle for freedom and justice.

Danielle, a social studies major and feminist from Detroit, takes in all these explanations about the kingdom of God, but is not impressed. She says:

There are some powerful ideas in the New Testament about love and compassion, but all this terminology about kingdom has to be changed. It is too medieval and too prone to promote male domination. The idea of a kingdom of God might have worked in Jesus' day, but it doesn't say anything positive to a lot of people today. In fact, it has many negative connotations.

Paul's Testimony

The early writings of Paul are especially valuable in witnessing to Jesus' teachings about God as Father. His Letter to the Romans and the First Letter to the Thessalonians predate the gospels and are thus quite close to the historical Jesus and the early communities. Paul firmly connected God with the image of a Father and constantly spoke of God as the Father of both Jesus Christ and the disciples. He viewed the Father as the origin as well as the goal of all Christ's redemptive work. The Father is our liberator and for this we should offer praise and thanksgiving.

Early Christian theology also echoed the image of God as Father. Irenaeus (d. 140), Justin (d. 165), and Tertullian (d. 225), three leading theologians and church leaders, referred to God as the "Father." Early creeds are directed to "God, the Father almighty," and many prayers commonly used by early Christians also are addressed to God as Father.

The Triune God

The Christian tradition speaks of God as a Trinity, as a God revealed in three manifestations. Efforts to trace this understanding of God to the Hebrew scriptures are generally judged to be futile, but there are justifiable arguments for tracing the roots of this teaching to the New Testament. In the gospels Jesus is proclaimed to be the Son of God and is portrayed as having a uniquely intimate relationship with God as Father. Jesus also promises his disciples that he will send the Spirit. While the New Testament seems to present three manifestations of God, precious little is said about the inner relationship among Father, Son, and Spirit.

The Christian doctrine of the Trinity developed during the debates in the patristic period (the era that began with the death of the last apostle and continued in Europe until the fall of Rome in 410 C.E., and for several centuries longer in the Christian Middle East). A clearer understanding of the nature of God and the relationship of Father, Son, and Spirit arose during the discussions concerning the identity of Jesus Christ, especially with regard to whether he was substantially identical with God.

Theological opinions that the Son was subordinate to the Father, or was of "like substance," or was merely a creature were rejected. The Council of Nicea (325) solemnly defined that the Father and the Son were coequally divine. The council delegates formulated a creed (Nicene Creed) that proclaims that the Son was "begotten of the Father" and was "of one substance with the Father."

During this time of patristic writings and conciliar debate, conclusions were reached about the proper way to explain both the inner and outer working of God, and how the Trinity related to each other as "persons." Throughout the discussions marked differences existed between theologians and church leaders from the cities of Alexandria and Antioch, and between Eastern and Western Christianity. Much debate focused on whether the Spirit proceeded from the Father through the Son (East) or from the Father and the Son (West).

Augustine used a psychological model to show how the Father's self-reflection expresses itself as Word in the Son. Both Father and Son, in loving each other, breathe forth the Spirit. Augustine's formulation held the field in the early centuries, was given new credence by the great Thomas Aquinas, and still stands as a traditional theological understanding of the Trinity.

Belief in a triune God has been defined and given great prominence in the Christian tradition. Precisely how the Trinity operates and how it is best explained continues to be a matter of theological speculation. Some would place the teaching regarding the triune God at the very center of the Christian tradition. Others such as Karl Rahner, one of the most profoundly influential theologians of this century, have observed that the church has never clearly defined the "why" and the "how" of the Trinity, nor has it explained how it might apply to everyday human living.[24]

Many average Christians have difficulty understanding the doctrine of the Trinity. There is a popular misconception among some well-meaning Christians that there are three gods: a Father in heaven, a Son who came down to earth to be our redeemer, and a Spirit who comes to us through the church. The notion of three "persons" in one God can easily reinforce this misconception. So can sacred art that depicts the Trinity as an old man in a flowing robe, an adult male nailed to cross, and a white bird hovering above the two human figures.

In the early centuries the word "person" did not mean, as it does today, a center of consciousness. Our contemporary psychological understanding of person could well lead people to the conclusion that there are three distinct Gods. That is not the intent of the teaching. Rather the church's traditional explanation of the Trinity is intended to protect the divinity of the Son and the power of the Spirit, and to teach that there are three distinct ways in which God's presence can be manifested and experienced.

The Feminine Dimension of God

In recent decades feminist theologians have expressed concern that the traditional understanding of God and the Trinity is exclusively male and thus intensifies the patriarchal structures that are so oppressive throughout history. Tammy, a young single parent who is studying to be a nurse, reflects these concerns. She writes:

It has been hard for me to relate to a male God. My experiences of men have not been very positive. The teaching about the Trinity makes it that much more difficult for me since it seems to say that God is really three male figures.

Recently there has been a heated debate on the use of male language for the Trinity.[25] Some feminist scholars feel that the doctrine is irrelevant and that it should be put aside. Others want to neutralize the language and use such terms as Creator, Redeemer, and Comforter. Against traditionalists who insist that God actually is a Father, there are those that maintain that Father is merely a metaphor and that feminine or neutral metaphors are equally appropriate for God. Finally, there are those who point to ancient Syriac and Eastern traditions where the Spirit is addressed in feminine terms, and offer that for a solution. To some, however, this seems to be a reversion to literalism and can overlook the appropriateness of using feminine metaphors for God.

Since bonding and relating often hold such a strong value with women, perhaps the communal aspects of Trinitarian theology need to be given more emphasis. From this perspective, the life within God is seen in terms of equality, partnership, and interaction. Perhaps less emphasis should be placed on individualism in trinitarian theology and more attention given to complementary interaction.[26] These new approaches offer women many more possibilities for exploring the mystery of God than do the more traditional patriarchal notions. This section will consider several avenues by which all Christians can expand their knowledge of God by including both feminine and masculine images and language.

Archetypes, Gender, and God

One of the creation stories presented in Genesis tells us that both genders, female and male, are images of God. Many ancient religions portrayed this literally and described their gods with human genitalia and as undertaking acts of sex. The Judeo-Christian tradition has viewed God with both female and male images, but has not taken this to the literal extremes of other traditions. In the Judeo-Christian tradition, moreover, there has been a notable predominance of male imagery. The future will no doubt see more and more protests of this male dominance and more calls for inclusion of the feminine dimension in the Christian understanding of God.

Jungian psychology has played an important role in raising the awareness that the feminine (anima) as well as masculine (animus) do not exist separately, but are blended in each individual. The masculine and feminine are complementary of each other, and each dimension of sexuality carries its own distinct contribution. From the religious point of view, both come from God and both are needed if we are authentically to understand the ultimate Mystery.

Archetypes and the collective unconscious are two other Jungian notions that are useful in this discussion of feminine images of God. Carl Jung (d. 1961) maintained that the human mind is shaped by heredity as well as by tradition. Each person is born with a mind that already has been influenced by millennia of imagining. Each person thus carries within herself or himself an already highly influenced capacity to formulate archetypal images—primordial symbols of humankind's most profound experiences and deepest longings. In other words, the human race seems to share collectively in its unconscious with its capacity to bring forth primordial images about life and death.[27]

Archetypes enable us to explore other dimensions of reality, even the ultimate reality we call God. The person of faith might approach these archetypes as having their source in God, and use them to explore the very mystery that is the source of all reality. We might say that our myths and mythical figures are the embodiments of these archetypes and have always been used in the human search for answers to ultimate questions.

Jane, a psychology major and a fine musician from Oklahoma City, can relate to this part of our discussion. She points out:

For me, different archetypes for God have been important at different stages of my life. After the death of my sister in a riding accident, I spoke to God as a sister for a long time. Now that I am older, I see God as my friend, and gender is really not important. I now feel free to pray to God in many different ways.

Feminine Images of God

For the entire 4000 years of the Judeo-Christian era, male images of God have prevailed. We have already discussed how the image of God as Father began in Judaism and then was given prominence in the Christian era. It comes as a surprise to many Christians to learn that feminine images of God prevailed in earlier times. Unfortunately, much of this rich imagery was lost when Judaism rejected the religions and the cultures that developed and fostered feminine images of the divine. When Christianity suppressed the Greek and Roman religions, and when the Old World explorers crushed the indigenous religions of the New World, much that was rich and authentic in the human search to understand ultimate questions was written off as pagan or heathen and cast aside. Feminine images were among the casualties of these cultural conquests. It is only recently that we are beginning to rediscover some of the teachings of these ancient religions. Movements such as those of liberation theology, feminism, and environmentalism have taught us that many of these ancient images and truths need to be revitalized in order to point us in new directions as we deal with oppression and destruction.

The Goddesses of Old Europe

Evidence of the use of feminine images for God has been found in excavations of civilizations dating back 30,000 years in France, Siberia, and the Ukraine.[28] The advent of an agricultural system brought with it an emphasis on the fertility of the earth that was commonly symbolized by female images. The earth was seen as a mother, from which came forth life and vegetation.

Marija Gimbutas has assembled, classified, and interpreted some two thousand symbolic artifacts from the earliest Neolithic village sites of what she calls "Old Europe." With these items from 7000–3500 B.C.E., she has given us the main lines and themes of a female-centered religion. In this context the universe is viewed as the living body of the goddess-Mother Creator who gives meaning to the mysteries of the birth, life, and death of all that exists. All living things participate in her divinity.

The mythologies of these religions stand in marked contrast to the male-dominated pantheons of the Indo-European tribes that overran these territories in the fourth millennium B.C.E. In the goddess-centered art there is a striking absence of images depicting male domination and warfare. This art also reflects a balanced social order where woman were free to play important roles.

This period was not just a short aberration in history. Gimbutas' study reveals that "the goddess-centered religion existed for a very long time, much longer than the Indo-European and the Christian (which represent a relatively short period in human history), leaving an indelible imprint on the Western psyche."[29] These feminine-centered cults seemed to prevail until the cultures with patriarchal religions and warrior deities began to conquer and dominate the known world. These factors as well as the shift from rural life to city culture ultimately supplanted the feminine influence in religion. Gallic and Celtic remnants of the feminine images of God seem to have lasted well into the fourth century of the Christian period. Homage to the earth mother seems to have been replaced gradually in Christendom with devotion to the Blessed Mother and to female saints.[30]

Hellenic Culture

The Hellenic culture has had a profound influence on Judaism as well as on Christianity and the shaping of Western civilization. This culture is foundational to Western language, literature, art, government, philosophy, and religion. Its religion was eclectic, gathering and blending various traditions from conquests in Egypt, Persia, Syria, Phrygia, and Israel.

The mystery religions that were so much a part of the Hellenic culture honored women and enthusiastically used feminine images for God.

Demeter is "one of the oldest representations of the feminine archetype in religion."[31] She was an earth-mother figure who helped the Greeks see the hand of God in the seasons and the harvest. She was a mother who lamented the abduction of her daughter. With Demeter as an image, women could use their experience of motherhood as well as the unique mother-daughter relationship to explore the mysteries of God. In addition to Demeter, Isis was a significant feminine archetype for God. Her origins are found in Egypt, but her influence on the relationship of the gods to the sacred earth was felt through the Western world.

It is important to note, however, that despite the importance of the Greek goddesses, the society still remained patriarchal. The same dichotomy continues to apply in the Hindu culture where goddesses are common and yet do not serve to change a rigid patriarchal system. Feminine goddesses do not necessarily mean a just and fair society. Precisely how their recognition affected various cultures is hard to ascertain given what little we know of these ancient cultures.

Jonathan, a classics major who grew up in Greece but came to the United States with his family when his father's company transferred him here, offers several useful insights on these Hellenic images of God. Jonathan writes in an essay:

Even though I lived in Greece, I always looked at the old gods and goddesses as ridiculous inventions of the pagans. Once I started studying the classics, however, I began to realize that the people who developed the stories of the gods and goddesses were just like us, struggling to find meaning in life and searching for God. Sure, some of their stories were pretty bizarre, and yet we make a big mistake if we simply disregard all these ancient religions. They have a great deal to teach us. And you know, some of our stories and images would probably have sounded very strange to them.

The Near East

The image of the goddess was also significant in the ancient Near Eastern culture of Sumeria where both gods and goddesses controlled and supervised the natural elements and all aspects of human life. Each city, indeed each family, had its own god or goddess. In some cases the gender of the god was not really important since the functions of the deity were often interchangeable. At other times the role that the goddess played in defining family, culture, cosmos, and city was "quintessentially female."[32]

The goddesses of Sumeria serve as an interesting case study to demonstrate the value of goddesses. Apparently the goddesses were projections of what that society thought a woman should be. Once projected as goddesses the examples of femininity then became role models for the society. It was a valuable way of sacralizing values. There were goddesses to show one how to be a mother, a queen, a wife, a daughter, or a sister. Both men and women could go to the female deity to learn compassion, love, lamenting, power, and many other virtues uniquely expressed in the feminine. The mother-goddess, from whom comes life and to whom all go in death, could teach treasured lessons about life's mysteries. As in the case of so many other cultures, however, the goddesses of the Sumerian culture eventually fell victim to social, political, and religious change and were eventually marginalized.

The Emergence of Patriarchy

A number of factors seem to have led to the marginalization of the goddess, including a shift from rural to city living, the dominance of warrior tribes, and the spread of Christianity. Another key factor was the emergence of the patriarchal social structure, which served as the predominant model for interpreting God as a male Lord and Father.

Patriarchy is a cultural structure where the fathers are viewed as the founders and heads of the clan and its family. The father is the supreme authority and the women and children are dependent upon him and subject to him.[33] It is a social system that is thousands of years old and which even in the modern day holds sway in many of the cultures throughout the world. In recent times many have linked it with colonialism, racism, capitalism, and sexism. Many feminists view patriarchy as the cultural *bête noire* that is the basis for social and religious oppression. They call for its demise. Others recognize that patriarchy is the social structure that helped bring about the cultural and economic achievements of our world and that its abuses should be recognized without condemning present-day males as being the culprits responsible for past abuses.[34] Men as well as women have been oppressed by the abuses of patriarchy. Many want to move beyond the recriminations and build new social structures that are egalitarian.

It is not easy to determine when or how patriarchy was born. Some maintain that it began about 6000 years ago with the notion of ownership and private property, with the males becoming the chief owners. Land, flocks, even wives and children became mere property.[35] Heritage became important and strict control was maintained over the wives to keep the blood lines pure. To protect and acquire possessions, military might was developed and exercised by the male who was more competitive and stronger than the female. The competitive male spirit might also become enveloped in a power struggle with the women whose powers of reproduction and nurturing had given them so much influence in the past.[36]

Patriarchy and the Hebrew Religion

The Hebrew scriptures were shaped and written over a period of 1000 years. This library of religious literature reflects the gradual development of ancient Israel out of the cultures of the Near East, especially Canaan, Egypt, and Mesopotamia. This religion developed amid patriarchal structures that greatly influenced both its image of God and the role that women played in religion. By the time of Moses, the only God to be worshiped in this religion was Yahweh, a God portrayed throughout the scriptures as a king and father. All of the powers and functions that had been distributed to many gods by the other religions were absorbed by Yahweh. He would now be the Sky God, the Storm God, the Warrior God, the Creator, Law-giver, Punisher, and Redeemer. Yahweh replaced the female goddesses and subsumed their powers over fertility, sickness and health, and all of nature. In spite of many lapses, Yahweh's people developed a monotheistic religion that would hear of no other gods.

The Hebrew religion reflected the influence of the patriarchal structures. All the God-images were predominantly male. The priesthood and the religious leadership of education and administration were in the hands of males. Yahweh was the God of the Fathers and the Father-God.

Only minor remnants of the feminine image of the deity remain in the Hebrew scriptures. God is imaged as a mother in Isaiah: "As a mother comforts her son, so I will comfort you" (Is 66:13); "Can a mother forget her infant, be without tenderness for the child of her womb" (Is 49:15). The same prophet images God as a woman in labor: "I have looked away, and kept silence, I have said nothing, holding myself in; But now, I cry out as a woman in labor" (Is 42:14). In Deuteronomy, God is compared to a mother eagle caring for her brood and teaching them how to fly by bearing them upon her wings when they falter (Dt 32:11).

The Hebrews also personified Wisdom as a woman and raised Wisdom to the level of the divine.[37] "Sophia" was thought to have existed from all eternity and is the word and power of God. The feminine notion of Wisdom prevailed in the Gnostic Christian communities. In Eastern Christianity there are also some portrayals of the Holy Spirit as a feminine figure. Such feminine images of God, however, have had little impact on Western Christianity.[38]

Reflecting the patriarchal structures of Judaism, Israel is spoken of as the spouse of God. In the writings of Hosea and Jeremiah she is repudiated for her promiscuity and infidelity. If anything, this image only intensifies the image of the female as weak and seductive. Similarly, Eve, the first woman, was portrayed as weak and the one who led Adam into sin.

Jesus and Women

Scholars today are rediscovering and reconstructing the crucial role that women had in the origins of the Christian tradition.[39] Many observe that Jesus' treatment of women was markedly different from the patriarchal practices of his time. He treated women with the same dignity that he showed toward men, stood firm against the abuse of outcast women and widows, and used feminine images to describe his mission and God's love. He used the image of a mother hen to describe his care and love for his people (Mt 23:37), and he imaged God as a woman looking for a coin to show God's intense love for the lost (Lk 15:8–10).

Perhaps Jesus' most radical step toward restoring women to a key role in religion was his choice of women to be his disciples. No other rabbi did that! The gospel images of his mother Mary, Mary Magdala, the Samaritan woman, Martha and Mary, and Joanna are convincing symbols of how Jesus gave women equal status in bringing God to the world.

For the early Christians, Jesus was the primary image of God, the full revelation of the love, compassion, forgiveness, justice, and self-sacrifice of God. Though Jesus himself was male, he was the incarnation of God as a human person. Jesus commissioned both women and men to carry his message to all the world. For these early believers, "There is neither Jew nor Greek, there is neither slave nor free person, there is not male and female; for you are all one in Christ Jesus"(Gal 3:27–28). Since both women and men have been created as images of God, both can represent God's presence and power.

Other Contemporary Images

There are many contemporary efforts to extend the imaging of God in a manner that finds acceptance in today's world among a broad spectrum of people. Karl Rahner has called for the use of the word "Mystery" when referring to God, to remind us of how unfathomable God is for the human. Paul Tillich has suggested a more metaphysical image that goes beyond sexual roles, and referred to God as the

"Ground of Being." Liberation theologians have portrayed God as the risen Lord suffering among the poor and courageously struggling with them for justice. As liberation theology spreads throughout the world, the image of God takes on the new colors of black, yellow, and red. God is no longer simply a middle-class, European or American male.

Theologians who concentrate their study on the Mother of God hope to restore the image of Mary as "the maternal face of God," an image that perhaps can help restore the dignity and role of women in the church.[40] Process theologians have described God in dynamic and changing categories and view God as a fellow sufferer in the world. Other theologians have suggested that in this age of personalism and relationship we use the images of friend or lover to describe God. Whatever our choices, it would seem that in the future Christianity will be open to go beyond the limited patriarchal images of the past and search for God in metaphors that are inclusive and liberating both for God and for people.

Conclusion

We have surveyed some of the major efforts to discover the identity of God through image and metaphor. We have seen that the Christian image of God builds on that of the Hebrews. With the person and teaching of Jesus, human understanding of God comes to a new fullness in meaning. The patriarchal social structure has provided both for Judaism and Christianity a father image that has predominated in the official teachings of many Christian churches.

In the immediate future we can hope that there will be more openness to images that are feminine as well as images of God that are dynamic, prophetic, and cognizant of minorities and people of color. The God of the global village will no doubt be a God of many faces and many shapes.

Discussion Questions

1. What do theologians mean when they speak of God in terms of "Mystery"? In what sense is God a Mystery to you?

2. Compare and contrast some of the key images of God in the Hebrew scriptures with some in the New Testament.

3. Sketch and then discuss an image of God that you had as a child. How has your image of God changed since then?

4. Are you comfortable with feminine images of God? You might want to discuss your answers to this question in small groups.

5. In what ways has patriarchy affected Christian understandings of God as well as Christian liturgical celebrations?

Suggested Readings

Bernhard Anderson, *Understanding the Old Testament*. Englewood, NJ: Prentice Hall, 1986.

Karen Armstrong, *A History of God*. New York: Random House, 1993.

Elizabeth A. Johnson, *She Who Is*. New York: Crossroad, 1992.

Walter Kasper, *The God of Jesus Christ*. New York: Crossroad, 1988.

Gerda Lerner, *The Creation of Patriarchy*. New York: Oxford University Press, 1986.

Thomas Marsh, *The Triune God*. Mystic, CT: Twenty-Third Publications, 1994.

Sallie McFague, *Models of God*. Philadelphia: Fortress Press, 1988.

Carlos Mesters, *God, Where Are You?* Maryknoll, NY: Orbis Books, 1977.

Elizabeth Moltmann-Wendel and Jürgen Moltmann, *God—His and Hers*. New York: Crossroad, 1991.

James Schall, *What Is God Like?* Collegeville, MN: Liturgical Press, 1992.

Mark S. Smith, *The Early History of God*. San Francisco: Harper & Row, 1987.

Terrence Tilley, *Talking of God*. New York: Paulist Press, 1978.

3.

God, Science, and Creation

Framing the Question

My name is Bruce. I am a college sophomore from Sandusky, Ohio. My major is environmental science, and I am hoping to get a job in some area of environmental management. My brother works for New York State as a deputy environmentalist in the Adirondack Region. I have camped with him in those mountains and really want to do something to help protect areas like that.

I have always been interested in science, and study in this area has always come easy for me. As for religion, I have been a Presbyterian all my life, and I take my faith pretty seriously. One area that has always given me trouble is connecting my knowledge of science with my religious beliefs. My minister seems to take the bible stories about creation literally, and that just doesn't fit with my understanding of evolution and astrophysics. When I am in church, I have to put on my religious head and forget all that I've learned in school. And when I'm in the lab at school, my religious tradition seems to be out of touch.

One thing I'm glad to see, is that my church has made some important connections between religion and ecology. The General Assembly of Presbyterians has put together some really good papers on how our church must seriously engage in restoring the environment. It's about time that religions connected their beliefs with some practical issues. I am still wondering if my own religious beliefs will be at all relevant to the environmental work that I want to do in the future.

Bruce has put his finger on two issues that concern many young people today: how to integrate science and religion, and how to use religious values to make a difference in the environmental movement. These will be two of the main issues we will discuss in this chapter as we look at Catholic beliefs about God, science, and creation. We will begin by looking at the relationship of science and religion, and then move on to see how religious beliefs might effectively address environmental concerns.

The Relationship of Science and Religion

The relationship between science and religion has had an interesting and varied history. In this chapter we will see how religion helped in the emergence of science, and discuss some of the tensions as well as accords that have existed between the two disciplines over the years. We will then look at the shifts that have gone on in both science and theology, and observe how we have now entered into a time filled with new possibilities for interdependence and cooperation in dealing with questions surrounding nature and creation.

Religion and the Origins of Science

Some scholars believe that religion was actually instrumental in getting modern science started. A.R. Peacocke, the English scientist-theologian, maintains that Western Christendom provided the intellectual climate for empirical natural science to emerge. Its biblical approach to creation viewed nature as good, but also de-sacralized nature so that it could be studied on its own apart from the Creator. Christianity did not view nature as being filled with capricious gods as did other religions. Rather, nature was viewed as separate from God. Even though God could be revealed through either nature or the scriptures, nature could be studied separately.

Use of Aristotle's scientific perspective helped Christianity de-sacralize nature and contributed further to the development of science as an independent intellectual discipline. Science began well-disposed toward religion, but eventually the rationalism of the Enlightenment and the materialism of the nineteenth century cut science away from religion. Since then many scientists have believed that the two disciplines should be "separate and mutually exclusive realms of thought."[1]

Science's Hostility Toward Religion

Some scientists have clearly been hostile toward religion. The Enlightenment philosopher August Comte (d. 1857), for example, maintained that human thought had gone through three stages of growth. The first and most primitive stage was theological, wherein natural phenomena were viewed as products of supernatural forces. The second stage was metaphysical, in which the supernatural forces were replaced by abstract forces. Finally, human thought progressed to the present (third) stage and gave up the search for hidden causes in favor of a pure description of observable phenomena.[2] Comte concluded that in the final stage human thought had simply outgrown the need for religion.

The Roman Catholic church, in particular, was the object of attacks from eighteenth-century deists and materialists who held that science exposed the absurd beliefs of the church. Voltaire (d. 1778), a devout popularizer of Sir Isaac Newton's scientific theories, seldom missed an opportunity to show his disdain for the church. The rationalists of this period extolled the powers of reason over revelation. They believed that human problems could be solved by human effort and that there was no longer need for the teachings or powers of the church. Diderot (d. 1784), who was perhaps the first modern atheist, held that matter was the cause of all things and that questions about God's existence or creative powers were of little consequence.[3]

During the nineteenth century an American chemist named J. W. Draper (d. 1882) explored the history of the conflict between science and religion. He maintained that the struggle was, in fact, between the expansive power of reason and the restrictive power of faith. Draper's views had a profound effect on the debates about science and religion for the next hundred years.

In 1860 there was a legendary encounter between Thomas Huxley (d. 1895) and Bishop Samuel Wilberforce of Oxford (d. 1873) over Darwin's theory of evolution. Huxley is said to have bested the bishop in the debate. The fatal blow was a remark where Huxley all but said that he would prefer to have descended from an ape than from a bishop. Huxley, a colorful crusader for evolution and a formidable opponent against reactionary theologians, maintained that "extinguished theologians lie about the cradle of every science as the strangled snakes beside that of Hercules."[4] Other nineteenth-century scientists went so far as to maintain that science had replaced religion, with scientists acting as the new priests.

Sigmund Freud, who maintained that religion was a mere illusion, argued that the narcissistic myths of religion had been dispelled by science. He pointed out that Copernicus humbled humans by revealing that the earth was not the center of the universe. Darwin showed humans that they were no different from the animals. Freud himself brought humans down a peg or two by showing them that "the ego is not the master of its own house."[5] This further convinced Freud that God and religion were mere illusions, imaginary products of primitive times, and no longer relevant in this modern scientific era. In his later years, he came to believe that while religion would remain valuable as a resistant to the on-coming horrors of war, it remained a mere illusion.

Some contemporary scientists show somewhat the same disdain for any religious interpretation of creation. Jacques Monod, a celebrated scientist, has concluded that "chance alone is at the source of every innovation, of all creation in the biosphere." G.G. Simpson points out that "man was certainly not the goal of evolution, which evidently had no goal. He was not planned, in an operation wholly planless." The well-known American evolutionist, Stephen Gould, has written that "we are the accidental result of an unplanned process."[6] Carl Sagan, a popularizer of modern cosmology, also shows little regard for religious traditions regarding the origins of the universe. It is obvious that for some scientists religion is irrelevant.

Science's Acceptance of Religion

The first modern scientists were well disposed toward the religious perspective on creation. Galileo (d. 1642) was loyal to the church and its teachings. His condemnation seemed to arise more out of ecclesiastical politics than it did out of a question of orthodoxy.[7] Sir Isaac Newton (d. 1727) was a devout believer and had an intimate sense of God's presence as he explored the immensity of space. Robert Boyle (d. 1691), the renowned anatomist, viewed scientific inquiry as a form of worship. Nature for him was God's temple and the scientist was, in a sense, a priest. Even the hard-nosed Descartes (d. 1650) believed that as a mathematician he was discovering the "laws that God has put into nature." And the great astronomer Johannes Kepler (d. 1630) believed that in exposing the geometry of creation one was thinking God's thoughts after him. Today these views sound rather quaint and even a bit naive. Both science and religion have come to a clearer awareness regarding their disciplines and no longer see the connections so explicitly.

Some contemporary scientists, while not being as devout or explicit as earlier scientists, still appreciate the religious dimension of reality. Albert Einstein (d. 1955), the scientific giant of the modern era, once pointed out that "science without religion is lame; religion without science is blind."[8] Einstein spoke not of formal religion but of a cosmic religiosity that arises out of the experience of the mysteriousness of the cosmos. He writes:

> A knowledge of the existence of something we cannot penetrate, of the manifestations of the profoundest reason and the most radiant beauty, which are only accessible to our reason in their most elementary forms....It is this knowledge and this emotion that constitute the truly religious attitude; in this sense and in this alone, I am a deeply religious man.[9]

It was Einstein's conviction that every serious scientist must be inspired by a kind of religious feeling. He could not imagine that the extremely subtle relationships uncovered by scientists were being uncovered for the first time. Someone or something had been there before and the scientist was "like a child trying to understand the superior actions of grown-ups."[10] Neither could he accept the possibility that the atomic world was ruled by chance. "God does not play dice!" is his oft-quoted observation.

Stephen Hawking, the astrophysicist who is extraordinary not only for his intelligence but also for his amazing courage in overcoming physical handicaps, also recognizes the religious dimension of reality. In attempting to bridge the puzzling gap between the theory of relativity and the quantum theory, he hopes to discover "the mind of God."[11] Whether this reflects a naivete or is said with tongue in cheek, there does seem to be a concern in Hawking's work for discerning ultimacy.

Many brilliant thinkers are working to relate the various sciences with religion and theology. A. R. Peacocke, who is both a scientist and a theologian, is a pioneer in this area of integration. He has written widely on the relation of religion and science, especially on what the new biology might tell us about the immanence of God.[12] The great mysteries that are emerging in modern physics have moved scholars to compare contemporary physics with parallels in the Christian theology of the kingdom.[13] Fritjof Capra has made amazing connections between the new physics and Taoism.[14] New developments in cosmology have moved scientists like Brian Swimme to retell the creation story in terms of scientific insights.[15] Finally, the work of Michael Polanyi (d. 1976) has had a profound effect on the link between science and religion. He has pointed out how the contemporary scientific method has a built-in openness to religious thinking. He believes that science calls for the personal and responsible participation of the scientist, and that such personal knowing can open and expand to include acceptance of the supernatural.

Betsy, a junior from Dubuque, Iowa, and a chemistry major, maintains that she can relate to what philosopher Michael Polanyi has said.

She writes:

> *Often when I am in the lab at night working with the microscope, I am overwhelmed by a feeling of awe. The items that I am looking at in the microscope are all so complex and often really beautiful. It is as though I am in the presence of something much bigger than myself. Sometimes I find myself actually saying a little prayer when I am moved like that.*

Religion Challenged by Science

Christianity's beliefs have been perennially challenged by scientific advancement. Early Greek cosmology threatened Christian beliefs during the fifth century. As a result, Augustine was moved to view some of the scriptural accounts of the cosmos as metaphorical, observing that the scriptures tell us how to go to heaven, but not how the heavens go. During the Renaissance a Polish astronomer named Copernicus (d. 1543) proposed that the earth and all planets revolve around the sun. This theory was later verified through telescopic observance by the Italian astronomer Galileo. Because this finding posed a threat to statements in the bible and to many of the teachings of Aristotle which the church had accepted, Galileo became the center of a controversy that was both political and religious. He was subsequently condemned for his views, required to recant, and forced to spend the rest of his days under house arrest.[16] Only in the latter stages of the twentieth century has Galileo been exonerated by Rome, and only then with careful reservations.

Perhaps the most serious clash between science and religion came with the publication of Charles Darwin's *Origin of the Species* and its presentation on evolution. The renowned historian of Christian doctrine Jaroslav Pelikan writes:

> Seldom in the history of the Christian church have theologians reacted as violently to a non-theological book as they did to Charles Darwin's *Origin of the Species*. Neither the *True Word* of Celsus, nor *The Revolution of the Heavenly Bodies* of Copernicus, nor even perhaps *The Communist Manifesto*, damaging though they all were to the cherished beliefs of many Christians, evoked so many wounded reactions in their own time from so many theologians, bishops, clergymen, and Christian laymen.[17]

Later breakthroughs such as Hubble's big bang theory and Einstein's theory of relativity seemed to pose little threat to the Christian tradition compared to that presented by the theory of evolution. Even today there are strong reactionary movements among conservative religionists who defend "scientific creationism," and insist that the bible be viewed as the main scientific resource for discovering how the world came into existence.

Today the controversies over the earth orbiting the sun, natural selection, and the expansion of the universe have subsided. They are being replaced on the science versus religion field of debate with such issues as genetic manipulating, test tube babies, fetal transplants, the use of life-sustaining technology, and medically assisted suicide. Is science "playing God," or "assisting God," or simply carrying out its work in areas where religion has no relevance? The answers are not always clear. Science and religion remain in tension, often seeking mutual understanding, a better awareness of their interdependence, and some common ground for dialogue.

Religious Antagonism Toward Science

Although Western theology seems to have been at least partially responsible for the development of modern science, it has not always been open to science's discoveries. We have already mentioned the threat that the findings of Copernicus and Galileo posed for many Christian theologians and church leaders. The Roman Catholic church also kept its distance from evolution and forbade its presentation in its schools and universities well into the 1950s.

The most celebrated instance of Catholic resistance to the theory of evolution arose in the response of the magisterium (the official teaching office of the Catholic church) to the writings of the Jesuit scientist-theologian, Pierre Teilhard de Chardin (d. 1955). Teilhard was a geologist and paleontologist who supported the evolutionary theory and made brilliant attempts to integrate modern cosmology with the Christian tradition. Early on he was removed from his university position in Paris, sent into virtual exile as a missionary in China, and forbidden from publishing any of his revolutionary theological ideas. His writings appeared posthumously and he was partially vindicated by the Vatican in 1981, but his rather tragic life stands as a witness to the fact that the church has had a history of being uneasy with the theological implications of scientific findings. There is still a fundamentalism and absolutism among some officials (and non-officials) in the church, who resist change and are threatened by the notion of newness and discovery.

A New Openness Toward Science

Pope John Paul II wrote a papal letter in 1988 that inaugurated a period of greater openness on the part of the church toward science. In this letter the pope called for greater dialogue between religion and science. He pointed out that both disciplines must respect the other's competencies and limitations, and that each must maintain its own foundations, procedures, interpretations, and conclusions. The church can accept scientific theories that are well-supported, and should not take it on itself to decide the truth of the findings of science. Both can benefit from the other. Science can help theology rid itself of superstition and pseudo-science, while religion can help science avoid becoming absolutist or thinking of itself as a religion in its own right. This papal letter contains much that can be used for successful bridge-building between the two areas of scholarship.[18]

Science began in a period where it was controlled and dominated by the church. At present the reverse is often true. Science has the power to ignore the church and reject the church's teachings as irrelevant to the "real world." It may be, however, that contemporary scientists are again willing to dialogue with theologians. Many outstanding modern scientists have moved away from the crass rationalism of the last century, and speak from a position that is often much more modest. This is evident in the physicist V. Weisskopf's reminder to his fellow scientists: "Our knowledge is an island in the infinite ocean of the unknown."[19] A perspective like this opens the possibility of productive dialogue with the church. Conversely, many Christian theologians have moved away from the extreme dogmatism of the past and have come to realize that much of their thinking will have to be done in the framework of modern science rather than in that of Aristotle or Aquinas. Nevertheless, theologians want to hold science to value systems and ideals that will turn science away from technology that is destructive to human life and the environment.

Common Bonds Between Science and Religion

A bridge of understanding and cooperation can be built between science and religion if both disciplines realize how much they have in common. Both are striving to understand the same reality, albeit different dimensions of that reality. The past dualisms of matter and spirit, natural and supernatural are no longer appropriate. For the person of faith there is but one reality, yet this one reality is multi-dimensional and encompasses what used to be separated into human and divine or natural and supernatural. Science has its own particular methods and tools to unlock reality's secrets that are observable and measurable. Religion, on the other hand, has its own methods and tools to explore the ultimate dimensions of reality. Theology attempts to interpret the divine revelation that comes through experiences of reality. For the person of faith there is an Ultimate Reality and Ultimate Mystery that is the source, ground, and sustaining force of all reality.

Both Science and Religion Require Faith

Both science and religion require faith, albeit different kinds of faith, in order to carry out their unique mission. Science needs to have faith in the varied structures of reality: that they hold together, that they can be systematically searched and understood. The scientist has to believe that there are patterns and systems in both the microcosm and the macrocosm, and that truth and meaning can be attained by probing the inner and outer mysteries of the cosmos.

Religion also has to have faith, a faith grounded in the existence of an Ultimate Reality that both transcends and yet is grounded in the cosmos. Religion reaches for something beyond the observable and the measurable, something eternal, something divine. The Judeo-Christian tradition believes in a God who has somehow created the universe, and who continues to sustain life and purpose. This same tradition believes in the goodness of all aspects of this creation and operates on the assumption that God has a covenant with the earth and all its creatures. This tradition also has faith in the ultimate fulfillment of all reality in some "end time," a time of resurrection and transformation of all that has existed.

Many students find a positive, hopeful interpretation of the end of the world more appealing than the apocalypse-now theories that predict the imminent end of the world due to a major cataclysm. Listen to Marsha, whose mother is Seventh-Day Adventist:

I've been worried about the end of the world since I was small. It seems like every time some impending disaster was reported in the paper, my mother would say: "This is it!" I remember going door-to-door with her, giving out magazines and warning people that the end was near. But, you know, it is hard for me to believe that God created all this beauty, just so he could destroy it. I'd rather believe and hope that this world is going somewhere positive, and stop being afraid. I saw a cartoon the other day that made me laugh. On it there was a man with a long beard holding up a sign that said: "The end of the world has been cancelled for lack of interest." I wish some of my family would lighten up on this whole topic!

Both Science and Religion Encounter Mystery

Science and religion are both familiar with mystery. Gone are the optimistic days of science's infancy when it looked forward to unlocking all the secrets of the world. Today many scientists have more questions than answers. The deeper they delve into their research, the more mysteries they seem to encounter. There seems to be unlimited complexity as science moves into the outer reaches of the cosmos and into the inner depths of the atomic world. Scientific models reach their limits and have to be discarded for new ones. Theories have to be constantly reinterpreted and reapplied.

Religion, of course, deals with the central mystery of reality, the Mystery that is the source, sustenance, and goal of all creation. Where science deals with the what, the when, and the how, religion deals with the who and the why. Christian theology, in particular, ponders the revelation of the Divine Mystery throughout history, a revelation that climaxed in the birth, life, death, and resurrection of Jesus, the Christ. As with science, the answers are elusive, tentative, limited, and often lead to more questions. The models and myths support the faith of people as they attempt to understand a Divine Reality that is far beyond their comprehension and yet at the same time close to their hearts.

Both Science and Religion Value Tradition

Science and religion both value tradition. The scientist knows that she or he must understand and build on the work of those that went before. This tradition, though valuable and an indispensable foundation for what is to be understood in the present, must be reinterpreted, improved upon, and carried on beyond where it has been. Likewise, religion values tradition, not as some static or frozen body of knowledge, but as a living and developing story that needs to be rediscovered, reinterpreted, and told anew in each age.

Both science and religion are looking at creation, and yet each discipline must have its own autonomy and methodology, and have the freedom to reach its own findings. The scientific description of nature can be given with precision and without any reference to God's creative power or action. The theological description of creation can be taught without reference to the facts and figures of science. The believer comes to a clear and holistic picture of reality, however, only through an integration of both the scientific and theological understandings of reality. The two become integrated in the believer who stands, as Karl Rahner put it, as a "spirit in the world," a person open to the truths of both science and religion.

Paradigm Shifts in Science

As science and religion enter into a contemporary dialogue about creation, both must be aware of the methodological shifts that have taken place in the two disciplines. The pre-twentieth-century scientist operated out of a Newtonian model of the universe, a model that was mechanical. The universe, the earth, and the human person were viewed as mechanisms—finished products that were parts of a complex, interrelated system. This model, although scientific, was based on the belief that God created everything once and for all in the beginning, and that science's task was to study and eventually to understand and master first the parts and then the whole. It was believed that reality had fundamental structures and that models could be constructed to approximate these structures. This older approach to natural science was objective, calculated, and independent of the human observer or that observer's process of knowledge. Gaining scientific knowledge was a building process that grew with exactitude and absolute certainty, one law and one principle at a time.

With the appearance of the so-called new cosmology based on the discoveries of such greats as Einstein, Planck, Heisenberg, and Bohr, science has entered a new era. With theories such as relativity and quantum mechanics, with astounding breakthroughs in the fields of astrophysics, microbiology, the new physics, and biology, it has become evident that old frameworks no longer apply. The universe is no longer viewed as a mechanism, but as a dynamic and expanding system. The entire system is not a series of parts to be studied, but an integral whole with all the elements interconnected in a web of inseparable relationships. Scientists, moreover, are not investigating this dynamic web of relationships objectively as if it were outside of themselves, but as persons related to and contributing to the process. Scientists are no longer building with blocks of knowledge; they now describe networks of related phenomena. The older models no longer apply and neither do their claims of absolute and final certainty. The findings of science are viewed as being much more tentative and limited. Rather than stating absolute truths about nature, scientists deal with limited and approximate descriptions of reality.

Paradigm Shifts in Theology

There have also been many shifts in theological methodology, especially in the last half of the twentieth century. The traditional approach to theology, that prevailed in most seminaries until the early 1960s, was a "manual theology" which largely consisted in explaining the definitions of the various church councils, and then "proof-texting" these with quotations from scripture and from the scholastic theology of Saint Thomas Aquinas. When theology was explained in this way, the system of beliefs was understood to be final and closed. All that was needed was a careful explanation of each tract in the system. There was little relationship among the various doctrines, and each branch of theology—scripture studies, moral, doctrinal, liturgical, and mystical theology, and related disciplines—was studied in isolation.

While science was busy studying nature and its laws and principles, theology gave little heed either to nature or to science. Traditional theology viewed creation as part of a study of the activities of God, and made few connections with either the scientific views of the day or the pertinent biblical texts. Church councils had said very little about creation, other than to declare that God was the Creator and that humankind was responsible for the disastrous Fall of creation.

By the mid-1900s, those scholars who had access to contemporary biblical criticism understood that the stories of creation found in the Book of Genesis were mythic, not literal accounts. Other theologians rejected the new findings of biblical scholars and still accepted the stories as being literally accurate. Both groups were generally so isolated from the ongoing research in cosmology and evolution that they were not aware of the conflicts and controversies between religion and science.

If the findings of science were brought into discussions on creation, the usual theological approach was what is now called the "God of the gaps." Originally this meant that when early astronomers found any deviation in the patterns in the cosmos that they were plotting mathematically, they accepted the variance as a result of the direct intervention of God. Despite mounting evidence to the contrary, Copernicus struggled to explain that orbits were perfect circles, thinking that this is the way God designed orbits. When Kepler discovered that orbits were elliptical, it was decided that God preferred ellipses to circles. If a comet appeared unexpectedly, many felt that this was also a direct intervention of God. It was assumed by the early scientists that they were discovering the plan set forth by God, and if there were any deviations it was simply God directly intervening in the plan.

As science grew apart from religion during the Enlightenment, religious thinkers often accepted the findings of science and used these in their apologetics to prove doctrinal positions about creation. It was also common for theologians to fill in the gaps left by science with the divine action of God. When Darwin proposed his theory of evolution, for instance, many religious thinkers accepted this theory as long as God could be inserted as the Creator who infused an immortal soul in the gap between the evolution of animals to humans. Later theologians accepted the Big Bang theory as long as God could be seen as the one who caused it all. And the gradual evolution of life could be accepted by theologians as long as God could be seen as the one who began life.

Laurene, a communication major and a fine musician from Phoenix, says that she has difficulty with the "God of the gaps" approach. She writes:

I remember one theology professor telling us that he had no problem with the Big Bang Theory, as long as we never forgot that it was God that started it all. I could just picture God as some kind of cosmic bomber with his hand on the detonator, ready to set off the Big Bang. God's place in creation is just not that simple.

The apologetic use of science and the use of the "God of the gaps" methodology has always presented a perilous road for theologians seeking to understand and integrate science into their theological system. Scientific theories change, and the theologians wedded to them for apologetic reasons often find themselves widowed—figuratively speaking. For instance, science gradually explained why planets traveled in ellipses and why comets shot through the sky; the gap left for God's action was no longer available. God was removed from other gaps as natural selection, genetics, and environmental factors explained the gradual and uneven development of human life. The Big Bang was explained in terms of gases being under enormous pressure and producing an immeasurable explosion. The discovery of DNA explained the origin of life. Human life could now be started in a test tube, genes could be manipulated to change forms of life, and life could be prolonged artificially through modern technology. As technology and scientific knowledge grew there were fewer and fewer gaps for God to fill. Many theologians have thus moved away from the "gap" approach to God, and developed new ways to show how belief in God as Creator can be compatible with the ongoing discoveries of science.

New Paradigms in Theology

Catholic theology has continued to undergo major shifts, especially since the conclusion of the Second Vatican Council in 1965. Many new theological currents had already been in vogue for decades in parts of Europe, but these had been often ignored in North America, and even suppressed by traditionalists around the world. As the council progressed, however, these new currents of theology were allowed to flow into the mainstream of Catholic thinking, and major changes began to take place in the Catholic consciousness. Catholic theology opened itself to philosophical perspectives other than scholasticism, to the exciting and challenging findings of the biblical movement, to the insights of other churches and religions, to the issues of the modern world, and to the findings of modern science. Tradition was now viewed as a living and developing process, interacting with historical events, cultural changes, and scientific discoveries. It was recognized that the church was in the modern world, and that it had to read the "signs of the times," including the discoveries of modern science, as a way of discerning how God was calling the church and its members to live. The Catholic framework of beliefs had to be reinterpreted and restructured to address the social, political, and scientific issues of the times. A universal and global church had to be intensely concerned about issues affecting the universe and the globe. To carry out this mission effectively, the church could no longer afford to distance itself from or be threatened by science.

A Re-Examination of Creation

The creation stories of Genesis are foundational to three major religions: Judaism, Christianity, and Islam. All three speak of God as a Creator, a being who is responsible for and covenanted with the cosmos.[20] Contemporary biblical studies tell us that these creation stories are mythological stories adapted from earlier Babylonian myths. The stories that appear in the bible developed over centuries through continuous oral retelling, with the written versions found in the bible dating back to the sixth-century B.C.E. They are less attempts at accurately describing creation than they are a celebration of God's presence in history, of God's covenant with the earth and its creatures, and of a liberating God who, by the time these stories were written, had liberated them from both Egyptian and Babylonian exile. The story of creation "is not principally an account of origins, but of dependence. It is not intended to say primarily how things began, but how they are in relation to God."[21]

The creation of the world is one of the central beliefs of the Christian faith. Almost from the start of the Christian era particular attention has been given to the historical and theological understanding of this doctrine. The controversy concerning this belief began when Christianity confronted the Hellenistic Roman world. The Apostle Paul and many Church Fathers such as Justin Martyr, Theophilus of Antioch (the first to speak of "creation from nothing"), and Tertullian (d. 225) defended the church's doctrine of creation against such pagan notions as the pre-existence of matter or the evil of the material world. Aquinas, whose *Summa Theologiae* has been the basis of much Catholic thought since the thirteenth century, did not follow the rational approach to creation that was later espoused by secular thinkers. He simply declared creation by God to be a doctrine known by revelation. (This position would later make it difficult for the church to deal with the reasoned observations of science about creation.) On the other hand, Aquinas's notion of the doctrine of creation included God's actions both in the origin as well as the continuation of creation. His recognition of the dynamic aspects of creation proved useful when Catholic thinkers recognized the validity of some theories of evolution.

The classic Protestant explanation of the mystery of creation emphasized God's governance of creation rather than God's continuing creativity. Protestant theologians also emphasized that creation was "once and for all," just as were the crucifixion and redemption. This resulted in a finished and static notion of creation, one that was resistant to the expansive and evolutionary views of science. Karl Barth, for instance, fixed such a gulf between revelation and reason that he and his followers gave little consideration to the way their belief in creation related to scientific theories of evolution. It has only been with the work of late twentieth-century theologians Wolfhart Pannenberg and Jürgen Moltmann that German Protestant thought has attempted to link creation with modern scientific thought. Contemporary Catholic systematic theologians, for the most part, have accepted more readily the findings of modern science and routinely work within that context.

New Approaches to Cosmology and Theology

Theologians realize today that they must move beyond the ancient Near Eastern cosmology of the Genesis myths and rethink the notion of direct creation by God. Scholars now work within the framework of a new cosmology in which they generally accept the contemporary advances in scientific theories related to the creation of matter and all living beings.

Contemporary theology is also carried out within a new anthropology that accepts evolution and natural selection through genetics, adaptation, and other scientific factors. Human beings are no longer viewed as the nucleus of reality living on a central planet. Rather, humans are viewed as dwellers on a fragile blue planet in a billion-starred galaxy amidst millions of galaxies. Theologians accept the fact that the universe is twenty billion years old and continues to expand into infinity; that the planet is five billion years old and depends on a sun that will one day burn out and possibly bring life on earth to a frozen end.

In seeking to understand the nature of God and the relationship between God and all creation, theologians generally view humans as one small part of a life-process that emerged hundreds of millions of years ago, and where the human species has been in its present form for only about 100,000 years. If the entire history of the universe were written in ten 500-page volumes, each page would record a million years of development. Primitive life forms would appear in volume eight and human beings would be written about only on the last page of the tenth and final volume.[22] We are newcomers, and yet we are unique. Although we are made of the same "stuff" as the universe, we are the self-conscious ones, the creatures who reflect on meaning, the weavers of symbol and myths.

Tony is a zoology major who has been interested in animals all his life. He always has some interesting things to say on the relationship between humans and animals. He once commented in class:

It is a big mistake to think that we are superior to animals and therefore that we can do what we want to them. Many animals can do things that are far beyond the human capability. They might have a sense of smell, or sight, or instinct that really astounds humans. We have to start seeing ourselves as closely related to all living creatures and not simply as superior beings who can do anything we want with other creatures.

God's Role in Creation

In struggling with the question of where and how God fits into this complex picture, the Christian believer stands at a crossroad with many choices of direction. One road is that of secularism where there is no room for God in the natural process of creation. Another is that of scientific creationism, which accepts the scriptural account of creation as scientifically accurate and discounts the findings of modern science. Still another path is followed by those who continue to place God in the gaps left by science, viewing the laws of nature as God's ways of doing things and using scientific findings to prove the magnificent power of God. Others prefer to view God as a passive observer who got all this started and now watches with concern or even with amusement. The most common perspectives among Christian thinkers today, however, seem to view God either as somehow within the process, or conversely, that the process is actually within God. As Paul is quoted as saying in the Acts of the Apostles, "In God we move and live and have our very being" (Acts 17:28).

For many Christian thinkers, God is the "beyond within," the personal power of creativity and love. God is beyond the measures of time and space within which science works. God is perceived only in faith, yet can somehow be experienced and perceived within the work of scientists. This is a God who is "in, with, and under the background 'noise' out of which all creativity comes, masked by this noise, but detectable in what results from it. God is in, with, and under the superimposed quantum states out of which potential all that is actual comes."[23]

Linking God with Reality

Those influenced by either Teilhard de Chardin or by the later process theologians recognize that there is a "within-ness" in all matter, a mentality or a potential for consciousness that ultimately emerges in the self-consciousness of human persons. Some suggest that this drive toward intelligence and awareness might serve as a link with God. Through the process of reflection one can understand God, who is metaphorically described as "cosmic intelligence," the creative power that has somehow from the beginning been the designer of the universe. Could this perhaps be what the myths of the world's religions are trying to develop with their images of Tao, Logos (Word), and Nous (Mind)?[24]

Others have found a link between nature and creation in the anthropic principle. This principle, which was enunciated in the mid-1970s, maintains that in the first moments of the universe there had to be an extraordinary degree of fine-tuning in order for the universe to emerge and for life to be possible. Stephen Hawking, one of the leading astrophysicists in the world, points out that if the rate of expansion had been smaller by the smallest fraction of a millisecond, the universe would have recollapsed before it reached its present size. One has to be on guard against seeing a gap and making God into the fine-tuner, and yet the anthropic principle does argue for a grand designer. In Hawking's opinion, "there are religious implications" in such considerations.[25]

Others are influenced by the writings of Alfred North Whitehead (d. 1947) and the process theology that grew out of his philosophy. In process theology God is understood in a dynamic and changing fashion. God is not only a sustainer and preserver of the universe, God is actually a fellow sufferer. In this perspective, the universe and its processes are in God, the creative force who communicates self through an on-going process of creation. In this approach to the understanding of God, feminine imagery is more appropriate than male as we think of the universe and all life being born from God.[26] The metaphor of God as the Creative Mother is valuable for seeing the world as a means of God's self-manifestation. The world becomes God's body.[27]

Both science and theology have turned to the aesthetic sense to see the beautiful side of nature and creation. It is said, for instance, that it was Einstein's striving to explain the consistency and beauty of the universe that led to his discovery of the theory of relativity. Among many scientists today, there is a new sense of awe in the face of the wonders amid the reality which they study each day. Theologians are also turning to an artistic model as a way of understanding creation. This model sets aside the tendency toward human domination of all other creatures that was so prevalent in the mechanical model of creation and seeks rather to be linked to the magnificent creative forces that are at work.[28]

Science and religion often seem to be merging in the quest to understand the mystery of nature and creation. Science increasingly discovers new mysteries in the reality that it scrutinizes. Religion develops new models and metaphors in its endless struggle to understand the Ultimate Mystery. To the person of faith, science and religion can merge if the Divine Mystery and the mysteries of nature can be perceived as intimately connected.

Religion and Ecology

So far we have been discussing how both the beginnings of science and the emergence of the "new science" have caused Christian thinkers to reinterpret their theology of creation. Today another phenomenon, the environmental crisis, is also moving Christian theologians to re-examine the theology of creation and to develop an environmentally friendly theology of creation. In this section we will observe how the environmental crisis developed, and then look at some efforts growing out of biblical studies and theology that attempt to integrate the Christian tradition with ecological issues.

The Crisis in Ecology

The litany of damage done to our environment is alarming, for some even apocalyptic. The waterways are being severely polluted. The land is being stripped of its resources, its forests, and the topsoil so necessary for growth. The air is also being fouled to the extent that the greenhouse effect could drastically alter the world's climate. The ozone layer, so necessary to protect the earth from ultraviolet rays, is being dangerously depleted, putting living things in jeopardy from overexposure to the sun's harmful rays. Never before in history has the very life of the earth been so threatened. Many believe that if drastic steps are not taken within the next 10-15 years, it will be too late to save many of our valuable eco-systems.

Ellen is a senior from Minneapolis. When the topic of the environment comes up, she has fire in her eyes. She writes:

I was in the eighth grade before I finally woke up to the fact that our planet is being systematically destroyed. Many people are simply in a state of denial about all the things that are tearing the earth down. Or else they feel so helpless that they just give up and go about their business. We all have to come to our senses and realize that time is running out if we are going to turn around all this deterioration. Concern for ecology is not a fad: It is the most urgent crisis that we have.

The deterioration of the earth dates back to the marauding armies of conquering empires. The Babylonians, Persians, Greeks, Romans, and later the Barbarian hordes stripped the resources from huge tracts of land in their conquests. Although most Native American tribes held their land sacred, some tribes devastated the areas in which they lived. The Spanish Conquistadores did untold damage to the environment in Latin America, robbing the continent of resources and replacing the natural crops with ones that often were not compatible with the land. Europeans who came to America often relentlessly cleared the land for grazing, overworked the land for cash crops, and began a process of environmental devastation that has reached frightening proportions today. The colonial movement in Africa and Asia also did untold damage to the ecology of those continents.

The global deterioration of the environment reached enormous proportions with the onset of the industrial revolution, particularly with the modern era of chemical manufacturing, the widespread use of fossil fuels, and the development of nuclear weapons and nuclear energy. With the collapse of the Soviet Union, we have discovered the horrible devastation to the environment that has taken place throughout Eastern Europe. In addition, the Third World is now poised for an industrial revolution that will likely allow environmental concerns to give way to the pressure of competition. A Fourth World of destitution has now developed throughout the world, and the sheer numbers and desperate needs of these people will put additional and dangerous stress on resources and the environment.

Mechanistic Notions of the Earth

Most of the scholars who are credited with the beginning of science were well-disposed toward religion, and yet their theories often provided the Western mind with perspectives that would ultimately lead to a lack of regard for the environment. Thinkers like Francis Bacon, Isaac Newton, and René Descartes "contributed significantly to the development of the modern scientific and technological paradigm which regards the world as complex and intricate, but ultimately a lifeless machine."[29]

Bacon (d. 1626) is seen as the father of the scientific method. He developed his inductive method of investigation as a way of subjugating and ruling over nature, a means of regaining the domination over creation that was lost at the Fall in Paradise.[30] Descartes (d. 1650) put the thinking mind at the center of existence and put mind over matter, viewing nature as mindless and soulless. For Descartes, all nature, including the human body, was a machine. The true element of transcendence was thought, contained in God and the human mind. The rest was matter, working in clock-like fashion. This led to Paley's notion of God as the clock maker and to a deistic notion of a God far removed from the workings of nature. Newton (d. 1727) continued with the clock and clock maker model and devised the mathematical principles that explained how nature operated through the laws of force and gravity. Newtonian physics, which prevailed until the breakthroughs of Einstein, provided the mechanical model of the world.

Using the insights of Bacon, Newton, and Descartes, moderns proceeded to make the earth their slave and began the process of its manipulation and domination. Nature's spiritual elements were eliminated, and nature was no longer linked to the divine creator or to the human spirit. Nature was not viewed as a "fellow being," and humans replaced God as the "clock maker." We both knew and ruled nature from the outside. Soon, in the secular society that developed, "the presupposition of God could itself be discarded, leaving the scientist, together with the rulers of state and industry, in charge of passive matter which could be infinitely reconstructed to serve their interest."[31] This replaced the medieval view of nature as a fixed and finished creation, a hierarchically ordered environment, which humans were to master and use as a means to get to heaven.

The secular view of the world rejected the notion of the sacredness of nature and the human connection with nature that had been held by Saint Francis and other medieval mystics. Also rejected were the ascetic and world-denying tendencies of medieval spirituality. In their place a materialistic view of the world was substituted, one that would ultimately culminate in modern secularism. Nature, which had been a "thou," now was seen as an "it." Eventually God was viewed by many as being in the way of human progress, and was either denied altogether or made so remote in the heavens of the deists as to have little relevance.[32]

The Christian theology of creation eventually was cut off from the study of nature. As Catarina Halkes put it: "The natural scientists keep themselves busy with nature and the theologians with creation in the context of salvation history. The price of this division is the separation between creation and nature."[33] The church, often caught in its own world-denying and spiritualistic position, had little to say about what happened in the environment. The traditions of closeness to nature that had been expressed in Celtic Christianity, Eastern Christianity, and the Franciscan tradition did not prevail in Western theological thinking. Only in our own times are they being reclaimed.

The world-denying aspects of Christianity influenced many to withdraw from the world and abandon their responsibility to care for it. There were many factors that helped bring about this withdrawal from the world. Gnosticism, Jansenism, and elements of monasticism had taken positions against the material world and had advocated withdrawing from it rather than caring for it. The aftermath of the Black Plague, which killed off one-third of the population of Europe, instilled in many a fear of a material world that could produce such sickness and moved many to emphasize the life of the Spirit and the afterlife rather than life here on earth.[34] Protestants often put so much import on personal salvation that global and material issues were given little emphasis. Christians who emphasized the apocalyptic end of the world were also not inclined to be concerned about long-term preservation of the environment.

Even Catholics, who preserved a strong sacramental tradition that was rooted in experiencing God through natural things, did not generally connect this sacramental tradition with a love of nature or ecological awareness. Surprisingly, the Second Vatican Council, which revolutionized the Catholic church and situated it firmly in the modern world, did not put environmental issues on its agenda. For many Christians, heaven, not the world, was their real home, so there was little concern about taking care of this passing and fallen world. Redemption and salvation seemed to pertain to souls and thus somehow got cut off from the theology of creation. As Matthew Fox, the ardent promoter of creation spirituality, has emphasized, Christianity accented original sin rather than original blessing, and neglected its rich tradition linked to the theology of creation.[35]

The Rise of Eco-Theology

For many Christian thinkers, an important wake-up call on environmental issues came in 1967 when Lynn White wrote a challenging essay on this topic. White pointed out that not only is Christianity unaware of environmental problems, but it is largely responsible for the crisis. He observed that Christianity has been a human-centered rather than an earth-centered religion. Christians have overemphasized human superiority, and have used this belief to justify domination over nature. These beliefs, according to White, have provided a religious justification for widespread abuse of the earth and its resources.[36]

Soon after this article appeared, a lively discussion began concerning the relation of the Christian tradition to ecology. John Cobb, a process theologian, wrote one of the early books on the topic, and soon after, other theologians in Germany and Holland addressed this issue.[37] The World Council of Churches in its General Assembly of 1975 focused on the sustainability of society and the deterioration of the natural environment. Since that time there has been a growing interest in integrating the Christian tradition with ecological concerns. The scriptures have been reexamined with this focus in mind, and theologians have made some important contributions to the discussion of ecology and the preservation of the earth's resources. Some churches have also published significant documents on the topic of religion and ecology.

Re-Visiting the Creation Stories

There can be no doubt that modern theories on evolution and cosmology have moved theologians to reexamine seriously their understanding of creation. The environmental movement has stirred up renewed interest in creation theology, raising some seminal questions. Scholars ask: What is the true meaning of dominion in relation to the creation of humans? What do the scriptures mean when they say that humans are created in "the image and likeness of God"? How can Christian beliefs about creation move Christians to be more active in saving the earth?

Should Humans Dominate the Earth?

Biblical scholars have pointed out that the account of creation in chapter one of the Book of Genesis, where the domination motif occurs, is the work of the so-called priestly writer who contributed his insights to the Pentateuch (the first five books of the Bible) in the fourth century before Christ. This account of creation does not carry the weight of the earlier creation story that appears in Genesis chapter two, which arose from the tradition of the Yahwist (another of the four major authors of the Pentateuch) in the tenth century before Christ. In the earlier tradition, humans are not told to dominate the earth, but to cultivate and take care of nature.[38]

It must also be noted that the dominion given in the first creation story is bestowed on women and men made in the image and likeness of God. Like an "image of God" they are to act as a symbol of God and carry out their stewardship creatively and responsibly. Human beings are to represent a God who cares and shares, not a God who is greedy and destructive. Creation belongs to the Creator. Humans have been given the sacred trust to preserve it and care for it.

In the stories of the Fall and the Flood it is clear that disruption and chaos can be brought to creation through the sins of humans who are unfaithful to their responsibilities. The Creator in whose image they are made, however, is portrayed as a redeeming Creator. God vows to overcome chaos and restore harmony and hope to creation through faithful servants.

If this interpretation of the creation stories is correct, then the biblical narratives have been distorted and wrongly used to justify environmental destruction. It should be remembered, however, that much of the environmental devastation has been done, not by people who have used the creation stories to their benefit, but by materialists and secularists who have seen no relationship between the scriptures and ecology.

Creatures who have been made in the image and likeness of God do not exercise the privilege of lording it over creation as superior beings. They come to creation, rather, as servants of a loving and creative God, stewards acting in this God's place. The notion of being a steward of God's creation can be visualized as a people standing before God in a posture of worship, "joyfully accepting responsibility for managing human affairs and promoting the well-being of creation."[39]

Humans are not the center of creation, as those who have emphasized the anthropocentric notion of reality have proposed. The creation stories in Genesis use the cosmos as a background for the earth, which is the true center of creation. This earth brings forth all kinds of living creatures. Adam, the first human, is made from the earth and is closely related to it. The first humans are given the command to procreate, which is part of having dominion.[40] It implies co-creativity, responsible stewardship, and fidelity to a creative and sharing God. Humans are to share the earth with other land-creatures. When all is brought to destruction in the Flood epic, the new creation is a rebirth for all living creatures as well as for humans. God's covenant with Noah is actually declared to be with the earth and with all living things, all of which are good because they come from the creative power of God.

Brandie, a photography major who has won awards with her photographs of nature, comments:

I had never before heard that God's covenant is with all living creatures. I was always taught that the covenant was with the Jews and then the Christians took their place as the chosen people. I find this inclusive notion more believable. God is the creator of all things, and has a covenant with all creatures. This will really help me in my photography. When I am taking pictures of nature I often feel close to God as well as to the things I am photographing. We all seem somehow to be related so closely.

God's Covenant and Ecology

God's covenant with the earth and all living things is certainly useful for developing a sensitivity toward the environment. It is a cosmic covenant that began with Noah and that has been reiterated throughout Jewish history. This covenant is not limited to the events of creation but has much to say about redemption and liberation as well. The stories of creation and covenant developed after the Hebrews had been brought out of exile many times. They are a testimony to the fidelity of Yahweh toward the chosen people who had brought chaos upon themselves again and again.

The stories of creation and covenant have special meaning today when all the world's citizens need to be liberated from the chaos in the environment. The possibility of a covenant with God gives hope for such liberation and guides people to put their faith in a God who will bring it about. As scripture scholar Bernhard Anderson says:

> The dimension of chaos has not been erased from God's creation; indeed, human beings in their freedom can act to unleash the powers of chaos. Human responsibility, however, is grounded in God's covenant which is universal and ecological. Its sign is the rainbow after a storm.[41]

The Book of Genesis presents us with a rather sophisticated Hebrew perspective on creation. It explains that all creation finds its source in God, is therefore good, and is protected by virtue of a covenant with God. The care for creation has been entrusted to human beings, who act as images or representatives of God and who have the responsibility of carrying out a loving and creative stewardship.

Other Hebrew Perspectives on Creation

Beyond the Book of Genesis, the Hebrew scriptures contain other traditions that are useful in developing a religious perspective on the environment. For example, the Book of Deuteronomy points out that "the heavens, even the highest heavens, belong to the Lord, your God, as well as the earth and everything in it" (Dt 10:14). The Book of Leviticus explains that the land of Israel belongs to God and that humans are only sojourners on the land. Creation may be in our care, but it is still the creation of God held in trust by humans (Lv 25). Psalm 19 celebrates how all creation declares the glory of God. Psalms 96, 97, and 104 are magnificent proclamations of God's power and tender care of all creation. It is difficult to pray these psalms and still see the environment as an object to be mastered and used.

The Hebrew notion of Sabbath means that a day is set aside as a sacred time and sacred space to celebrate creation and the gifts of God. The sabbatical year is set aside in an agrarian society to provide the land, fruit trees, and animals with rest and a time to recover. The prophet Joel observes that earth will strike back with barrenness if is too greedily used (Jl 1:16–18). Isaiah warns the greedy who live lavishly off the land and deprive others of the earth's bounty that they will bring desolation upon themselves. He proclaims that Yahweh desires fruitfulness and harmony in his creation (Is 5:8–10; 11:6–9). The Book of Job, especially in Yahweh's speeches to Job, clearly reflects the Hebrew notion that God and not humans is the center of creation and that the master of creation should be served without question.[42]

The New Testament on Creation

It is only recently that Christians have begun to reclaim elements in the New Testament that might provide a foundation for a theology of the environment. Caution is needed, of course, so that the biblical texts are not twisted to fit our present needs. Neither should we imply that Jesus spoke as a kind of early environmentalist. At the same time, it is legitimate to apply gospel values to this present-day crisis. The scriptures are a living word and have for millennia been applied to deal with other cultural and social crises. The gospels have a timeless quality about them and can be invoked to deal with newly arising issues. The Christian tradition is an old story, but it is also new to each believer, and it can bring renewed hope when problems seem overwhelming.

As for Jesus of Nazareth, he was raised in a Judaism that revered creation as coming from God. His unique teaching of Abba's love for creation was extended to the birds of the air and the lilies of the field. His notion of the kingdom of God was that it signified the saving power of God, a power made manifest through all of history and throughout the earth. The new covenant brought about by Jesus' death and resurrection is actually a renewal of the original covenant which, as we have seen, was made with the earth and all living things. This extraordinary kingdom of God was at hand, and can be found wherever there is the power of love, harmony, creativity, and restoration.[43]

The memories of Jesus' life and teaching that underlie the gospels recall a man who held all things to be sacred, indeed sacramental. The rain, loaves and fishes, a mud pack for blind eyes, the mountains, rivers, even the cross—the Roman instrument of execution—could reveal the saving presence of God. All kinds of people, rich or poor, highly educated or illiterate, esteemed figures or outcasts, saints or sinners, were children of God and truly blessed.

Jodi, a junior from Miami, seems to be quite sensitive to the plight of fish and sea mammals and wants to be a marine biologist. She once told the class an astounding story of how she experienced the power of God in nature. She said:

There is a cove up the coast from where I live. Dolphins swim around there and they interact with the people who go there. One physical therapist noticed that the dolphins really had a way with many disabled people that went into the water. The therapist had been working with a little boy named Eric, who had multiple heart surgeries and could hardly move. One day I was there when Eric was put in the water near one of the dolphins. The dolphin slowly and gently came up to Eric, and then began to nudge his bottom and his legs. Eric was so thrilled that he began to move a bit. His legs got stronger by trying to get to the water each day to see his new friend. He began to get strength in his hands from trying to feed the dolphin. Eventually Eric made great progress and can now do many things for himself.

Jodi said that the whole experience was a deeply religious experience for her.

Jesus' many parables with natural images of fruit, mustard seeds, salt, harvests, the sun, lightning, sheep, and many other natural images show the loving and dynamic presence of God in the world.[44] His miracles of feeding, healing, calming a storm, or walking on water are stories of God's power over creation. They give witness to God's determination creatively to bring harmony out of chaos.

At the same time, the teachings of Jesus emphasize detachment from material things. His disciples are reminded to share what they have, especially with the poor (Mt 25:31–46). In the gospel stories, Jesus often warns of the dangers of greed and wealth. Recall how saddened Jesus was over the rich young man who was so attached to his wealth that he could not give it away and accept Jesus' invitation to be one of the disciples (Mt 19:16–23).

Creation and the Jesus Events

The theology of the incarnation (God becoming human in the person of Jesus Christ) has ecological ramifications. In the incarnation, God enters the material world and becomes part of it. Creation will never be the same now that God has been revealed as part of our world. Jesus reveals for all time a God who is friend and companion, a God who has entered into the stuff of life, the very bloodstream of creation, in order to accompany humans in their struggles. The belief that through the incarnation God in Jesus touches creation is a useful element in the developing theology of the environment.

The theological understanding of salvation also has relevance here. Salvation need not be restricted to human souls, but can be extended to all creation, to the entire earth, and all its people. Indeed the saving power of God applies to people, but also is applicable to the saving of the earth and its resources. By the same token, the resurrection applies to all creation for it represents a transformation of all material things.

Leo, a Baptist from Montgomery, Alabama, and a business major, doesn't buy into all this talk about environmental crises. He points out:

I was taught that there are many signs that the end of the world is coming soon. If this is true, then why are we so concerned about environmental issues? It's all going to erupt into a raging fire anyway. Besides, I think that all this talk of environmental problems is made up. Things are not as nearly as bad as people say.

Many of Leo's classmates do not accept his views on the end of the world. Christine, a French major and a formidable debater, challenges his views. She wonders aloud:

Why would God create such a beautiful and wonderful world just to destroy it in the end? In my opinion, if the world is going to come to an end, it will be through our stupidity. It will be because of pollution or nuclear bombs, not through God's actions.

Many theologians agree with Christine. They offer the theory that the world is headed for transformation and fulfillment rather than collapse. The Apostle Paul maintains that Jesus Christ has ushered in a "new creation," one where God's power indicates that he is leading his followers to a new creation. Paul writes to the Romans that "creation awaits with eager expectation the revelation of the children of God" (Rom 8:19). The Second Letter of Peter states: "According to his promise we await new heavens and new earth in which righteousness dwells"(2 Pt 3:13). For Teilhard de Chardin and many other theologians, it is in the Cosmic Christ that everything is to be fulfilled. Jesus Christ is the "first-born of creation" (Col 1:15–16), and in Christ, God "has made known to us the mystery of his will in accord with his favor that he set forth in him as a plan for the fullness of time, to sum up all things in Christ in heaven and earth" (Eph 1:9–11).

New Perspectives on Theology and Ecology

Environmental study is an exploding area of research, an area that has now incorporated the sciences, mathematics, history, technology, ethics, and many other disciplines. Religious thinking on questions about the environment is attempting to keep pace, and in last few years there have been a number of interesting developments that are worthy of note.

The Voice of the Churches

The churches were slow to respond to the environmental crisis. The Roman Catholic church had made passing remarks about the dangers to the environment in some of its official documents, but it was only in 1990 that the first papal document devoted exclusively to environmental concerns was published. Pope John Paul II points out in this document that today we are witnessing the widespread destruction of the environment. He reiterates Christian values regarding the sacredness of creation, and points out the moral dimensions of ecological problems. He is critical of greed and selfishness, and calls for a new sense of ecological responsibility and more simple lifestyles.

In 1992 the United States Catholic bishops prepared a document that was similar in content to the pope's 1990 statement. Around the world several other national Catholic bishops' conferences have published significant documents. Most notable of these is a statement entitled, *What is Happening to Our Beautiful Land?* written by the Catholic bishops of the Philippines.[45] The Protestant churches have been leaders in this movement connecting the Christian tradition with contemporary ecological concerns. The World Council of Churches, the Conference of European Churches, and the Council of European Episcopal Conferences have given significant attention to environmental issues. In 1990 in the United States, the General Assembly of the Presbyterian Church published an outstanding document entitled, *Call to Restore Creation.* The National Religious Partnership for the Environment, and the North American Coalition on Religion and Ecology are two powerful interfaith groups that are working to sustain the earth and its resources.

Thomas Berry

A Catholic priest, Thomas Berry is widely recognized as a significant voice today in the discussion of religious traditions and the environment. Berry describes himself as a "geologian," one who is dedicated to studying the dynamics of the earth and the role humans should play with regard to the earth. He is a student of Teilhard de Chardin as well as of Eastern religions, and he brings to his work a wealth of knowledge on modern cosmology. Berry writes and speaks with great fervor and insight about how human technologies are destroying the earth's eco-systems. He is critical of the West's false notion of progress, and its almost religious reliance on science for the solutions to all its problems. He agrees with those who put part of the blame for the environmental crisis on the Christian tradition and its reluctance to worship the divine in nature, its over-emphasis on redemption, its neglect of creation, and it focus on the spiritual over the physical.[46]

Berry maintains that it is time for a new religious orientation, a new revelation that will come from listening to the universe and to the earth, both of which he views as primary "religious realities." He also advocates that Christians begin listening more intently to the teaching of the non-Christian world, especially the Eastern and Native American religions. He believes that they contain values and insights that are sorely needed in this critical time. "Diversity is enrichment" seems to be one of his central themes. For Berry the main human task of the immediate future is "to assist in activating the inter-communion of all the living and non-living components of the earth community in what can be considered the emerging ecological period of earth development."[47]

Feminism

Eco-feminism links the environmental movement and the women's movement. It arises out of an awareness that the domination of the patriarchal and hierarchical structures have been responsible for the oppression of both women and the earth. It is also founded on the recognition that the poverty that is connected with the destruction of the earth and its resources most seriously affects women and children.[48] Catarina Halkes, a Dutch theologian, points out that women are often associated with nature, while men are more likely to be understood as the makers of culture and the leaders of industry. As a result, when people lose their appreciation for nature and abuse nature, there can be a resulting loss of appreciation for and abuse of women. The enslavement of nature can include the enslavement of women. The use of nature as a machine to be manipulated can also have an effect on the way men see women. They treat women as objects to be used without concern for their feelings or their intrinsic worth. Halkes calls for an end to domination and exploitation, and calls for a return to the values of connection, integration, and interdependence.[49]

Women are becoming more aware that as male domination became more prevalent, society and religion lost much of the treasured feminine dimension of nature and religion. There is a new call today to appreciate the value of the feminine and a conviction that such an appreciation is desperately needed if we are to have a sensitive and caring attitude toward the earth. Rosemary Radford Ruether, who has been a pioneer in this movement, points out that we must regain a consciousness of the connection of female and male, of human and non-human. She writes:

> Compassion for all living things fills our spirits, breaking down the illusion of otherness. At this moment we can encounter the matrix of energy of the universe that sustains the dissolution and recomposition of matter as also a heart that knows us even as we are known....Surely, if we are kin to all things and offspring of the universe, then what has flowered in us as consciousness must also be reflected in that universe as well, in the ongoing creative Matrix of the whole.[50]

Eco-Spirituality

New ecological spiritualities are emerging that hold the possibility of helping Christians to engage actively in sustaining the earth and its resources. For some this means reclaiming some of the values of medieval monasticism and mysticism, which stressed the immanence of

God in nature. Others find their strength in reinterpretations of the Hebrew and Christian scriptures. Some go beyond the Judeo-Christian religion to Buddhism, Hinduism, Islam, Tao, or the Native American religions to rediscover reverence for the oneness in all reality. There are also those who have come to see the earth itself as Gaia, a living organism in its own right, which must be cared for and sustained as a gift from God.[51]

Concern for justice and for the poor, the ones who are always the most oppressed by the abuse of resources and the environment, is at the heart of many of these spiritualities. Some have also focused on the ethical dimensions of the environmental crisis and accented a restoration of the moral values of connectedness and human dignity. They also stress the value of all life and the need to show solidarity with the poor through a simple lifestyle. Nurturing these spiritualities is a contemplative spirit that values silence, prayer, and reflection on the beauty and goodness of the world and all its creatures.[52]

Conclusion

In biblical times creation and nature were one, and God was held to be the ultimate source of the world. With the advent of science, creation and nature came to be viewed as separate, even mutually exclusive realities. Christian theology often moved in an older context, isolated from modern science. By the same token, science often carried on its work looking on God and religion as irrelevant. The mechanistic view of the Newtonian world rendered God as a remote and disinterested clock maker, who at best intervened occasionally to adjust the mechanisms of the universe.

Today many scientists and theologians want to put such dualisms behind them. They prefer the perspective that recognizes one reality with multiple dimensions. While science and religion deal with different dimensions of reality and need to undertake their own distinctive tasks, they have much in common. God is the Creator, Sustainer, and ultimate goal of all. Religion can challenge science to be conscientious and attentive to revealed values, and science can warn religion about the consequences of taking its myths too literally, and being so world-denying as to become an obstacle for science. Both can view God as the creative and unifying force within the world, and both can operate within the new cosmology that tends to humble both science and religion.

The environmental crisis has brought additional challenges to both religion and science. Science has come to realize that its relentless dedication to progress has brought society and the world to the brink of ecological disaster. The Christian religion, at the same time, now realizes that it has not only been unaware of the problem, it has even been part of the problem through its human-centeredness and its acceptance of human dominion over the earth and its resources.

The environmental challenges of today have moved Christians to reexamine their scriptures and traditions in search of truths that might help this generation to save the earth. Creation theology has been retrieved through a reexamination and reinterpretation of both testaments. Renewed emphasis has been placed on the sacredness of nature in the Hebrew tradition, as well as in the life and teachings of Jesus Christ. The churches are awakening to the fact that amid their ancient treasures there are truths that are desperately needed in order to sustain the earth. A new ecological spirituality is emerging that views God as a saving and loving Creator who calls all people to be aware of their oneness with all God's creation and reminds them of their responsibility to act as images of a loving and creative God.

Discussion Questions

1. Interview some of the science professors in your college or university with regard how they see the relationship between science and religion. Discuss these interviews in class.

2. In what specific way might the theories of evolution and "the big bang" threaten some traditional religious beliefs?

3. How do you personally reconcile scientific perspectives with any conflicting religious beliefs in your tradition?

4. Point out some of the shifts that have gone on in both science and theology. Discuss how these shifts have affected the relationship between the two disciplines.

5. List some ways in which some religious beliefs may have contributed to the ecological problems that we have today.

6. Name and discuss some key Christian teachings that might be used to move people to get involved in sustaining their environment.

Suggested Readings

Bernhard Anderson, *From Creation to New Creation*. Minneapolis: Fortress Press, 1994.

Bryan Appleyard, *Understanding the Present: Science and the Soul of Modern Man*. New York: Doubleday, 1993.

Emily Bins, *The World as Creation*. Wilmington, DE: Michael Glazier, 1990.

David B. Burrell and Bernard McGinn (eds.), *God and Creation*. Notre Dame: University of Notre Dame Press, 1990.

Fritjof Capra and David Steindl-Rast with Thomas Matus, *Belonging to the Universe*. San Francisco: HarperSanFrancisco, 1991.

Denis Edwards, *Jesus and the Wisdom of God: An Ecological Theology*. Maryknoll, NY: Orbis Books, 1995.

Christopher Kaiser, *Creation and the History of Science*. Grand Rapids: Eerdmanns, 1991.

Sallie McFague, *The Body of God*. Minneapolis: Fortress Press, 1993.

Jürgen Moltmann, *God in Creation*. San Francisco: Harper & Row, 1985.

Rosemary Radford Ruether, *Gaia and God*. San Francisco: HarperSanFrancisco, 1992.

Dorothee Soëlle, *To Work and to Love: A Theology of Creation*. Philadelphia: Fortress Press, 1984.

Kathryn Tanner, *God and Creation in Christian Theology*. New York: Blackwell, 1988.

4.

Jesus of Nazareth

Framing the Question

My name is Ted and I grew up in Portland, Oregon. I am a journalism major, and my ambition is to write for a newspaper somewhere in the Pacific Northwest. I have been a Catholic all my life, but I honestly know little about Jesus. I heard some bible stories about him when I was a kid, and they talk about him a lot in church; but I have never come to see Jesus as a real person. Don't get me wrong, I admire Jesus. He has always seemed remote, however, and not someone to whom I could relate. I see Jesus as though he was God walking on earth. Even though Jesus appeared to be human, I have never felt that he really went through the things I experience in life. I would like to hear more about how he was in real life. Was it as hard for him to make decisions? Did he have the same kinds of highs and lows that I have? What was it like when he was alive, and what kind of role models did he have? Why did he wait so long until he got started with his career as a preacher, and why did he make so many enemies? If I knew the answers to questions like this, then maybe I would see Jesus as a real person, someone who could be my friend and share my life.

Many young people are like Ted and find it hard to see Jesus as a real person. Jesus often seems to be someone from the remote past, a person from some other "zone" that is foreign to everyday life. Because of this, people often find it difficult to relate personally to Jesus. This chapter will describe Jesus as a real historical person, a person of flesh and blood who led a human life like ours. We will begin by discussing some of the difficulties inherent in developing such a portrait, and looking at several different approaches used in the search for a clear understanding and appreciation of Jesus as a genuine historical figure. Then, using the information available today about Jesus' times, we will attempt to present a portrait of Jesus of Nazareth.

The Historical Jesus

We know very little about the life of Jesus of Nazareth. We have no pictures or descriptions of him, so we have to guess what he might have looked like. Jesus left no writings of his own behind, so we have no personal accounts of his inner thoughts or feelings.

There are few historical references to the life and ministry of Jesus. Josephus and Philo, Jewish historians, make mention of Jesus and his followers, and several Roman writers including Pliny the Younger, Tacitus, and Suetonius make passing remarks about Jesus and his movement.

The four gospels (Mark, Matthew, Luke, and John) are the main source of information about Jesus, but they were not written until thirty to sixty years after Jesus' death. While the gospels are often based on what Jesus said and did, they are highly colored by the beliefs and theology of the communities in which they were generated. They are intended to be statements of belief, not biographical accounts. The gospels tell us little or nothing about the first thirty years of Jesus' life. They focus on a period of about one year during which Jesus conducted a ministry of preaching and healing, which ended abruptly in his arrest and execution. The other books of the New Testament express the beliefs and concerns of the early Christian communities, but say little about the life of Jesus.

The challenges in discovering facts about Jesus should not be surprising. Many of the great figures of the past are merely names in history. We have little certain biographical knowledge about such notable figures as Aristotle, Socrates, Hillel, Cleopatra, or Alexander the Great. These were famous public figures about whom public records were kept, yet we still know very little.[1] It is not surprising that historians made little mention of a carpenter-turned-preacher who ended up being crucified.

We should not be surprised that it is difficult to develop a clear picture of what Jesus was like. Even with major modern historical figures it is difficult to obtain an accurate portrait of who they were. We have enormous amounts of materials on Abraham Lincoln, John F. Kennedy, and Martin Luther King, Jr., yet there are many conflicting accounts about their personal lives. Mother Teresa of Calcutta is known and revered worldwide, but the public knows little about her personal life. The inner selves of people, both ancient and modern, usually remain a great mystery.

The Search for the Historical Jesus

Since the beginning of modern biblical scholarship in the nineteenth century, much effort has gone into the search for the historical Jesus. The term "historical Jesus" refers to a portrait of Jesus gained by sifting through the various layers of the gospels to find the authentic words, actions, and personal characteristics of Jesus of Nazareth.

This search is based on the assumption that the gospels are faith documents produced in various Christian communities. The gospels represent memories of Jesus of Nazareth from the perspective of post-resurrection faith and early Christian theology. The biblical scholar attempts to dig beneath these theological perspectives in order to locate the words that Jesus actually said and the things that Jesus actually did.[2]

The historical Jesus is a construct of biblical scholars. This understanding of Jesus must be distinguished from the "earthly Jesus" or "real Jesus," who grew up as a Jew with his family in Nazareth, worked most of his life as a carpenter, preached both to crowds and to intimate groups of disciples, brought healing and forgiveness to many, and died on a cross. That figure will always elude us. Jesus can be re-created in fiction, theology, homilies, film, and in our personal imaginings, yet his true personality and identity will always remain a mystery. Only a few people were privileged to be able to touch him, know him, look into what must have been the piercing look of his dark eyes, and enjoy the warmth and intensity of his personal presence.

Different Approaches to the Search

The search for the historical Jesus has taken various approaches. Those who view the gospels as historical biographies have often "harmonized" the gospel stories. The various versions of what Jesus said and did were placed side-by-side in one account, which was thought to be the whole picture of a given incident. For instance, the two nativity stories (Luke chapters 1-2 and Matthew chapters 1-2) were blended together to make one account of what really happened at Jesus' birth. Even today the crib scenes in our churches place the Magi of Matthew's version next to the shepherds of Luke. A number of Catholic scholars, in particular, took this approach and published their findings as "The Life of Christ."[3]

Other scholars have approached the scriptures as rationalists. Denying the possibility of the supernatural and insisting that the biblical stories are mere myths, rationalists construct portraits in light of their own biases. H.S. Reimarus (d. 1768) is an example of such searchers. He maintained that Jesus was nothing other than a failed revolutionary who died on a cross crying out in anger and despair. Jesus' followers, in an effort to start a religious movement, stole the body and concocted stories about the resurrection and miraculous cures.[4]

Reimarus's theories were countered by other biblical scholars who had their own theories about the historical Jesus. Researchers like Strauss (d. 1874), Renan (d. 1892), and Harnack (d. 1930) attempted to strip away what they considered to be the dogmatic teaching of the early church from the "vintage Jesus," and then paint their own portraits. Albert Schweitzer (d. 1965) brought this kind of search to an end by showing that these portraits were more projections of these scholars and their times than they were accurate pictures of Jesus. After saying this, however, Schweitzer proceeded to sketch his own portrait of Jesus as a heroic but deluded preacher concerned about the end of time, who died hoping that somehow his death would usher in the kingdom.

Rudolph Bultmann (d. 1976), one of the most influential biblical scholars of modern times, denied the possibility of securing a portrait of Jesus. He viewed the gospels largely as myths and anecdotes used by the early Christians to convey the gospel message (kerygma) of Jesus Christ. Bultmann did not believe it was possible to recover any historical material about Jesus, other than that he lived and died. What was important for Bultmann was to recover the gospel message, and learn from it how to live an authentic human life. In later life Bultmann conceded that there might be some historical basis for some of the words attributed to Jesus in the gospels, but he still held to his position about the lack of historical material in the gospels.

It was one of Bultmann's disciples, Ernst Käsemann, who claimed in 1953 that the gospel writers based their proclamations of faith on historical material and real memories. He initiated a new search for this historical Jesus, grounded neither on devotion nor rationalistic assumptions, but on solid biblical scholarship. As a result both Protestant and Catholic scholars continue to carry on the search for the historical Jesus. Contemporary researchers like Günther Bornkamm, E.P Sanders, James Mackey, Edward Schillebeeckx, Walter Kasper, and Gerard Sloyan have made significant contributions in the ongoing search for the historical Jesus. More recently, John Dominic Crossan and John P. Meier, in markedly differing approaches, have developed their theories about the identity of Jesus of Nazareth.[5] Obviously, the search is still going on.

Additional Resources in the Search

Until recent times, the search for the historical Jesus focused largely on the four gospels. Now the list of resources has broadened to include historical, sociological, and political studies of the times in which Jesus lived. Modern researchers have pieced together what the cultural scene was like during the time of Jesus. They know more about what life was like in the eastern Mediterranean area where Jesus and his disciples lived. They also have a deeper understanding of the province of Galilee and the town of Nazareth where Jesus was raised and worked, and of Capernaum where he lived as a young adult and where he found many of his apostles and disciples.

Archaeological, religious, and cultural studies of Jerusalem have given a more accurate picture of this great city where Jesus taught and died on a cross. Judaic studies have revealed a complex picture of the many currents of Jewish life and thought at the time of Jesus. Studies of the Pharisees, Scribes, healers, and revolutionaries of Jesus' period have helped the contemporary scholar to understand better the context in which Jesus lived.[6]

In 1945 over 50 documents, including the so-called Gnostic gospels, were discovered in the Nag Hammadi region of Egypt. Some scholars propose that some of these documents should be accepted along with the traditional four gospels and used as a valid source for discovering what Jesus said and did. Others see these gospels only as being derived from the original four gospels and having sparse significance in the search for the historical Jesus.[7] On one side, John Dominic Crossan incorporates the Gospel of Thomas and other sources into his portrait of Jesus, and with the scholars of The Jesus Seminar, uses this gospel along with the traditional four to ascertain the authentic words of Jesus.[8] John Meier, on the other hand, accords these documents little importance in his study of the historical Jesus.

The discovery of the Dead Sea Scrolls in the late 1940s and early 1950s also had an impact on the search for the historical Jesus. These documents, apparently hidden in caves by the Essenes in the first century to protect them from Roman destruction, offer a glimpse into some of the customs and concerns prevalent during the time Jesus lived. Although there is disagreement about the origin and nature of these documents, studies of the Essenes provide comparisons and contrasts to some views regarding the historical Jesus.[9]

Contemporary Biblical Studies

The primary sources in the search for the historical Jesus are the four canonical gospels (that is, those gospels that were accepted by the universal church as being accurate and authentic). For the most part contemporary biblical critics have moved beyond the rationalism of the nineteenth century. Many have also set aside Bultmann's view that the gospels offer little historical information about Jesus. Most respected Catholic and Protestant biblical scholars believe that there is a core of historical material in the gospels where one can discover what Jesus said and did.

What might be described as a "layer cake" might be helpful in discussing how the gospels developed on a foundation of memories and authentic Jesus material.

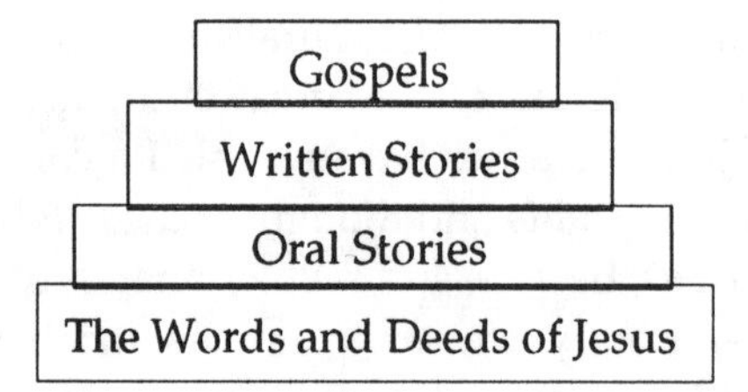

This model indicates that the gospels are based on what Jesus of Nazareth actually said and did. The story has its origin in the real person of Jesus living an authentic human life. This is the story of the man Jesus who taught, healed, and who died a horrible death on a cross. Many people knew him. Some saw him as a preacher on a distant hillside or as a healer on the crowded streets of tiny villages. Others shared a friendship with him, shared meals with him at table, and followed him from town to town.

The foundation of the four gospels is Jesus' parables, teachings, and healing miracles. They include the everyday events of his ministry as well as the torturous hours he spent dying on the cross. Memories of all this were riveted in the minds of his listeners and his closest followers, the recipients of God's powers that worked through Jesus.

Resurrection Faith

As awe-inspiring and unique as were the sayings and deeds of Jesus, none of this would have remained with people if his life had ended on the hill at Calvary. Jesus' arrest and death were a shock and disappointment to many of those who had perceived that Jesus was a prophetic figure, one who was profoundly gifted with the truth and power of God. Some had even hoped that he was the messiah who would usher in a new Jewish kingdom of peace and freedom. Some of his apostles and disciples had ambitions to be in high positions in a new and powerful movement led by Jesus. All of these hopes were dashed to the ground when Jesus died. Their "messiah" had been executed as a criminal and was now only a naked, limp corpse on a cross.

What made the profound difference in the future of the "Jesus movement" was the virtual explosion of faith that occurred when Jesus' followers began to experience Jesus as raised from the dead. Jesus had returned from the dead, now raised and glorified. As he had promised, his Spirit now revealed to them in dazzling light the true meaning of who Jesus was, and the meaning of all that he had said and done. They recognized the risen Jesus as the Christ, the anointed messiah of God, the savior. This faith ignited a pentecostal fire that spread from Jerusalem to Antioch, Rome, and throughout the Gentile population of the Roman Empire.

Oral stories of what Jesus said and did began to be repeated in these early communities. These tales, however, reported his words and deeds through the lens of resurrection faith. Theological interpretation, doctrinal concerns, and local cultural and religious struggles colored these accounts of Jesus' sayings and action. Eventually, the demands of catechesis, liturgy, and the need to preserve the authentic teachings of Jesus led the early Christian communities to put these stories into writing. And, of course, as the stories were written, new elaborations and nuances were added.

The canonical gospels began to appear several generations after Jesus' life. The first was the gospel of Mark, a simple yet profound account of Jesus' life and death. Some think this gospel came from the early Christian community in Rome around 70 C.E. The next gospels to appear were those of Matthew and Luke (c. 80 C.E.), both of which were influenced by Mark's gospel, a mysterious collection of the sayings of Jesus (also referred to as the Q source or *Quelle*), and other sources. The final gospel, that of John, was finished after a long and complicated process of development around 90 C.E.

Each of these gospels presents us with a slightly different portrait of Jesus, and differing accounts of what he said and did. At the very core of these gospels, nonetheless, is the person of Jesus of Nazareth, now revered by the gospel writers and their communities as the Christ, the anointed one, the savior and messiah.

Jesus and His Times

This section will use contemporary resources to reconstruct what Jesus of Nazareth might have been like. We will look at some of the places and peoples that might have influenced him. We will also examine some of the unique dimensions of his mission: his teaching career, healing miracles, and his prophetic positions. This chapter will then conclude by putting together a composite portrait of Jesus.

Palestine

People are shaped by the places where they grow up, and Jesus was no exception. By looking at the region of Palestine where Jesus lived, as well as his province of Galilee, his village of Nazareth, and Jerusalem—the city central to the Jewish faith—we can come to a better understanding of what the young Jewish preacher was like.

Jesus lived and died in the ancient area of Palestine. The Hebrews had lived there for thousands of years, going back to the time of the patriarchs Abraham, Isaac, and Jacob. The Hebrews had conquered this area and established a glorious kingdom there, only to be eventually conquered by a succession of nations—Babylon, Persia, Greece, and Rome. Throughout history, many nations with imperial designs have wanted to control Palestine because of its strategic location on the Mediterranean and its access to the major trade routes.[10]

During Jesus' lifetime this country was occupied by the Romans. The Roman Empire had enveloped Palestine about fifty years before Jesus was born. The Romans repopulated the rich and strategic coastal regions, and pushed many of the Jews back into the hinterland, where they had to work as landless peasants and day laborers.

Jesus probably experienced the fear and resentment that people feel when their country is occupied by a foreign power. He experienced feelings toward his oppressors similar to those felt by the indigenous peoples of the Americas, or by the Africans who have known colonization since the last century; by the people in Gandhi's India, or by the Catholics in Northern Ireland. Jesus had to watch what he said and be careful of where he went. He always had to be wary of the presence of the brutal mercenaries hired by Rome to keep their subjects in line.

Jesus also grew up amid a great deal of hostility toward the so-called Jewish rulers of his country, the corrupt Herodian family that had been installed as puppet sovereigns by the Romans. Jesus had surely heard stories of Herod the Great, a despot who killed his own wives and children when they threatened his power, and a ruthless tyrant who taxed his people mercilessly so that he could build luxurious palaces, theaters, baths, fortresses, and even cities in his own honor, and shrines to honor the emperors who kept him in power.[11]

Galilee

Jesus was a Palestinian Jew from the northern province of Galilee. The synoptic gospels (the gospels of Matthew, Mark, and Luke—so-called because they seem to view the events of Jesus' life from the same perspective) placed Jesus' ministry in this area. All of Jesus' apostles, with the possible exception of Judas, also hailed from this province.

Galileans had a reputation for being hardy and independent types. They lived far enough away from Jerusalem to avoid the direct authority of the Jewish leaders. They were often hard-working shepherds, farmers, and fishermen who did not always have time for all the niceties of the sabbath and purification laws. The rich harvests and the abundant fish of the Sea of Galilee also gave these northerners a sense of pride and autonomy. At the same time it gave them the reputation for being country types with strange accents and poor educations. Galileans were also criticized for being too closely associated with the Gentiles, among whom they lived and worked.

Jesus' many parables about rural life, his down-home wisdom, and his openness to people from all walks of life and backgrounds seem to reflect his Galilean roots. He was a hard-working man, who spent most of his life as a craftsman and carpenter. Far from being the willowy, blond figure we often see in Christian art, Jesus was muscular from years of hard work, his hands callused and scarred from working with wood and tools. His face must have been leathered and dark from working in the sun, and from traveling from place to place plying his trade.

The occasional terrorist actions that broke out in Galilee also gave the Galileans a reputation for being rebellious. Around the time of Jesus' birth there was an uprising that resulted in the crucifixion of thousands of Galileans. When Jesus was about ten, there was another uprising to protest the heavy Roman taxes. In 66 C.E. a Galilean named Menachem led a massive uprising against Rome, which continued off and on for decades, and which ultimately resulted in the destruction of Jerusalem and the leveling of the Temple.

Jesus, of course, was not a violent man, but he certainly rebelled against the hypocrisy and oppression that he saw around him. At times he confronted some of the learned Scribes, those among the Pharisees who were hypocritical, the merchants in the temple, and even the Roman procurator, Pilate. Ultimately Jesus would pay for his defense of the oppressed and for his confrontations with the corrupted leaders of his time. He would be executed as one who allegedly conspired against both the Jewish and Roman leadership.[12]

Nazareth

Nazareth, the village where Jesus is thought to have been born and raised, had little significance in Jewish history. It is not mentioned in either the Hebrew scriptures (Old Testament) or the Talmud (sacred Jewish writings from later centuries). Situated in the hills of southern Galilee, it was a Jewish ghetto village with a population of about 2000 at the time of Jesus.[13] The lifestyle was simple for some and somewhat impoverished for others. The dirt streets were lined with square one-room houses, each having an adjoining yard for a few animals. The houses were clustered close together so that the limited resources could be shared. This closeness no doubt helped develop ties among extended family groups. Perhaps Jesus' sensitivity toward neighbors and his affinity for the poor began in that little village.

The dark side of such closeness was the frequency of disease and the strain on the people's limited resources. The weak and the sick were often neglected and even expelled lest they contaminate the community. In caring communities, systems for looking after the needy were developed. Could it be in such an environment that Jesus learned compassion for the disabled and the outcast? Could it be that such situations helped him discover his amazing powers of healing and forgiveness?

Jesus the Craftsman

The gospels tell us that Jesus was a "*tekton,*" the Greek word for craftsman. Craftsmen were more skilled than carpenters and could therefore be contracted to build houses, furniture, and farm implements. They even were able to construct the small bridges needed to cross the streams of Galilee. Jesus probably learned his trade from his father, Joseph. From his early teens to age thirty, Jesus worked at his trade in Nazareth, and perhaps also labored on building projects in neighboring cities like Tiberias or Sepphoris. Jesus may also have worked in Capernaum, the city where he took up residence as a young adult.

Jesus of Nazareth was a young and vigorous workman. He traveled long distances on foot and often slept on the ground. He spent years cutting, hauling, and fashioning wood with primitive tools, often working outside in the hot Palestinian sun. Jesus most likely had the appearance of one who was a rugged outdoorsman.

Jesus' Education

Education was a priority for the Jews, even in a small village like Nazareth. Jesus probably attended the village school daily from early childhood until the age of twelve or thirteen. There he learned the teachings of the bible and the other basic knowledge needed to live as a devout Jew. As a teen Jesus might have studied with a local teacher of the law, and joined the adults who studied the Torah while working in the fields or on the rooftops in the cool of the evening. At the village synagogue, Jesus learned liturgical prayer, as well as the meaning of the sacred texts. To grasp all this, Jesus needed to understand Hebrew, the language of the scriptures, as well as Aramaic, the living language used for conversation and discussion.

The depth of Jesus' understanding of his tradition, as well as the unique originality and authority with which he taught, indicate that he must have spent many long hours of study and discussion with the learned of his community. Later he exhibited a unique gift for connecting this learning with everyday life.

Students today are often struck by this insight that Jesus had to study and learn just like all other human beings. Listen to Carrie, a sophomore from Tampa, Florida.

I always had the impression that Jesus knew everything simply because he was God. That made it difficult for me to relate to him, because learning comes so hard for me. I have to study for hours before a test, and then often don't do well. The idea that Jesus had to study hard helps me to realize that he was human just like I am. I bet he also got bored at times with his studies. I know I do.

Jerusalem

The Jerusalem of Jesus' time was at the center of the civilized world, the crossroads where nations converged. For the Jew, Jerusalem was the heart of Judaism, the city of David, the Holy City where Yahweh dwelt in the temple, the seat of Jewish authority and learning.[14]

It is not known how many times Jesus went to Jerusalem. The Gospel of John indicates three visits as an adult; the synoptics refer to only one such visit. Jewish law required that male Hebrews make a pilgrimage to Jerusalem three times a year for the feasts of Passover, Pentecost, and Tabernacles. It is doubtful that this law applied to the distant Galileans, but it is still possible that a Jew as devout as Jesus would have made the trip numerous times.

A trip to Jerusalem was no small matter for Jesus. It involved three or four days on foot over rough terrain. Terrorists and robbers roamed the hills, preying on pilgrims bringing their tithes and taxes to Jerusalem. Wild animals also posed a danger for travelers in those days.

Going to the "big city" must have been a striking change for a rural craftsman like Jesus. In Jerusalem he witnessed the luxurious villas and the sumptuous lifestyles of the rich landlords who enslaved and overtaxed so many of his fellow Galileans back home. No doubt Jesus was troubled by the slave auctions in the marketplace, by the fights to the death in the arena between naked criminals and slaves, or by the crudeness of some of the pagan dramas at the theaters. The chariot races, the exotic shows of Arabian wild animals, and the gymnastic exhibitions at the Hippodrome were quite a contrast to the quiet village life he knew.

At the magnificent temple of Jerusalem, Jesus saw thousands of priests slaughtering the animals of sacrifice. He observed the wealthy and powerful Sadducees ruling over the Sanhedrin; the learned Scribes holding forth with their students at the temple; the intense Pharisees mingling among the common folk. He observed the moneychangers and sellers of doves and sacrificial animals, people often known for their corruption and disregard for the sacredness of the temple. The gospels tell us of an occasion when Jesus was so disturbed by them that he trashed their displays and drove them out of the temple area (see Mt 21:12–13; Mk 11:15–17; Lk 19:45–46; Jn 2:13–17).

After looking at some of the places that influenced Jesus of Nazareth, it is time to look at some of the religious groups that were contemporaries of Jesus to see how they compared to the Jesus of the gospels.

The Essenes

The Essenes were a group of sectarian Jews best known for the Dead Sea Scrolls, the documents that were discovered in the late 1940s and early 1950s in Qumran, near the Dead Sea. There were perhaps thousands of Essenes in Jesus' time. About 300 lived at the monastery in Qumran; the others in communities in villages throughout Palestine.

The Essenes broke off from mainstream Judaism around the time of the Maccabean revolt (second century B.C.E.). They did not recognize the legitimacy of the temple or its priesthood, and established their own priesthood and rituals. They believed that they were the true remnant of Judaism, the last generation of Israel to whom the "messiah of Aaron" would come to announce the endtime.

The Essenes lived in exclusive communities that followed strict Sabbath practices and other laws of the Torah, as well as the teaching of their mysterious leader, the Teacher of Righteousness. Their membership was limited to male celibates who had no physical disabilities. Community members were expected to live an ascetic life with a daily routine of prayer, work, common meals, and charitable service to the needy among them. They were taught disdain for those outside their group, especially the wealthy, and harbored hatred for all their enemies.

The Essene community at Qumran was annihilated by the Romans during the revolution in the 60s C.E. There is some evidence that a number of them fled with the zealots to Masada, where they died in a mass suicide. Most of the historical information about the Essene tradition lay buried in the caves where they hid their scrolls to protect them from the marauding Romans, and which were only discovered in the middle of this century.[15]

Jesus and the Essenes

The Essenes are not mentioned in the gospels, but it is likely that Jesus encountered some of these austere figures in white robes as they traveled from one community to another. He shared many of their Jewish beliefs and their devotion to the Torah, although Jesus was more flexible in his attitudes toward observance of the law. Jesus sharply disagreed with the Essenes' rejection of the temple and the priesthood, as well as with their exclusivity. Women and men of all walks of life, married and single, and from all social strata were welcome as Jesus' disciples. In direct opposition to the Essenes, Jesus held those who were disabled or outcast in special esteem. He taught hatred of no one, not even of enemies. His was a doctrine of universal love and forgiveness that was to be preached as good news to all nations.

The Zealot Movement

Most scholars today agree that although groups of Jewish extremists and even terrorists existed in Palestine in Jesus' time, they did not organize into a formal party until the time of the revolution in the 60s C.E. These zealots who fought to free Israel from Roman occupation ranged from ardent patriots and prophets to gangs of disillusioned slaves and criminals. They vigorously rejected any cooperation with the Romans, and opposed paying taxes to the Empire. They believed in a God of vengeance. These violent revolutionaries wished to help God bring redemption to Israel through their violent terrorist actions. They saw themselves as instruments of God's destruction against the Romans and against those who cooperated in the occupation of Palestine. The stabbing of Roman soldiers in the crowded marketplaces, and the looting and torching of businesses and residences of Romans and their collaborators were all part of the zealot strategy to sustain terror and build toward violent revolution.[16]

Jesus and the Zealot Movement

Jesus may have been in sympathy with the zealot desires to gain freedom for Israel and to remove the Romans from their land. Jesus also was dedicated to promoting the reign of God among his people. Jesus, however, vehemently opposed the violent methods used by those in the zealot movement. Jesus did not teach about a God of vengeance, but about an "Abba" (gentle Daddy) God, who loved and forgave. Jesus was confrontative and aggressively opposed to oppression and abuse, yet he maintained a nonviolent opposition toward those with whom he came into conflict. Revenge, wanton destruction, and brutal terrorist tactics were never part of Jesus' mission. Although he opposed Roman domination, he admired and befriended individual Roman military personnel. Despite his objections to giving Caesar any honor and worship, Jesus did allow for the paying of taxes lest his people be severely punished by Rome.

Sadducees

The Sadducees were the wealthy aristocracy of Jewish society in Jerusalem. Included in their number were the chief priests, elders, and the lay nobles of the Hebrew community.[17] The Sadducees saw themselves as the guardians of the written Hebrew tradition, the Torah, and had no use for teachers who added their oral traditions to this tradition. This put them at odds with many of the Scribes and Pharisees, and obviously with Jesus. The Sadducees objected to oral teachers for presumptuously adding to revelation, and to interpreting the teachings so as to appeal to the masses. Josephus described the Sadducees as heartless individuals who strictly obeyed the written law and imposed harsh punishments on those who did not.

Ironically, in spite of their devotion to the Torah, the Sadducees were extremely materialistic and secular. They did not believe in divine providence, the resurrection of the dead, or in any specific messianic beliefs. The here-and-now was all important to these religious elite.

They interpreted their opulence and material success as a sign that they were blessed by God.

Politically the Sadducees were quite conservative and opportunistic. They held that collaboration with the Romans was the most effective way to maintain their powerful and sumptuous lives. The Sadducees controlled the Sanhedrin, the highest political and religious body in Judaism. The high priest, chosen by the Romans on the basis of his loyalty and cooperation, was selected from the Sadducees to head up the Sanhedrin.

Jesus and the Sadducees

Of all the groups in Jesus' time, the Sadducees stand in the starkest contrast to him. Jesus was a relatively poor commoner who placed little importance in material things and even warned that riches could endanger one's salvation. He was a simple layman with no formal higher education, yet he spoke his own powerful oral tradition with a unique personal authority. He exposed hypocrisy and self-righteousness and was known to be liberal in his observance of the law when there was an occasion to help others. Moreover, Jesus appealed to the common folk, especially outcasts, assuring them that they were beloved by God and blessed. In other words, all those whom the Sadducees shunned as unclean were welcomed by Jesus as friends, and even disciples.

Jesus' emphasis on afterlife, his deep faith in divine providence, and his messianic and prophetic concerns were all unacceptable to the Sadducees. These aristocrats had many reasons to hate Jesus, and in fact were the most visible group in the gospel accounts of Jesus being handed over to Pilate.

The Scribes

The Scribes of Jesus' time were the learned theologians and scholars. Since they had no party of their own, many of the Scribes belonged to the Pharisee sect. A good number of them were priests. The Scribes saw themselves as master teachers, and the successors to the prophets. Each Scribe gathered a select group of bright young aspiring scholars around him. The Scribes would pass on their secret and intricate teachings, and in return their students would act as servants. The Scribes were held in great esteem, and were hailed as rabbi or master as they strode through the streets in their long scribal robes. Anytime a Scribe appeared at the synagogue or at a feast, he expected to be given the highest place of honor.

Jesus and the Scribes

Jesus easily made enemies among the Scribes. He did not belong to any sect, never sat at the feet of any of the famous Scribes, and had no official teaching credentials. Generally he did not refer to any of the learned scribal interpretations of the law. Jesus preferred to teach his own insights. He also had the audacity to gather disciples of his own, both men and women, rich and poor and outcasts. It infuriated many of the Scribes to hear their titles of rabbi and master used by followers of this upstart carpenter from Galilee. They were scandalized at how freely Jesus forgave sins, and how flexible he was with the sabbath and the purification laws.

Unlike the Scribes, Jesus did not expect his disciples to act as his servants. He said he preferred to think of them as friends. Toward the Scribes themselves, Jesus was often critical of their pomposity and heavy-handed way of dealing with people. He granted that they had authority, but he pointed out that they were too close-minded and exclusive in their teaching.

Scribal hostility toward Jesus was evident in the gospels. They slandered him and attempted to trick him in debate. Scribes were among those in the arresting party in Gethsemane; they were also in the group that presented Jesus to Caiaphas for judgment; they accused Jesus before Herod, mocked him on the cross, and persecuted his followers (see Mk 14:53; Mt. 26:57; 27:41).

Hostility toward Jesus was not universal among the Scribes, however. One Scribe addressed Jesus as "Teacher" and offered to be a disciple. Another complimented Jesus on his answers to the Sadducees who tried to embarrass Jesus. Jesus commended that Scribe and told him that he was not far from the kingdom of God (see Mk 12:28–34). These stories pointed to memories of Scribes who were indeed supporters of Jesus.

The Pharisees

Pharisees have unjustifiably been given a bad reputation among Christians. They are considered to be hypocritical and self-righteous. Much of this comes from the negative images that they receive in the gospels, where they are described as blind guides, frauds, whited sepulchers, and even as those who do the work of the devil. Even among the Jewish people, the Pharisees have not fared well. Rabbinic literature painted disparaging pictures of Pharisees: Some pompously parade their good deeds; some have false humility and cower before an avenging God; others are just downright foolish.

There is a growing consensus among scholars that these negative views about Pharisees are of a later vintage than Jesus' times. While Jesus may have had disagreements with some Pharisees, the portrait of the Pharisees that we find in the gospel seems to be taken from the era after the destruction of Jerusalem in 70 C.E. These later Pharisees ruled Judaism, usually quite harshly, and often persecuted Christians.[18]

The Pharisees during Jesus time were not so politicized as their later successors. Actually they were looked upon as the party of the common people; they often distanced themselves from the high priests and Sadducees. Many of the Pharisees were commoners who worked at a trade and lived a simple lifestyle in open communities. The fact that Jesus is described as dining at the house of Simon the Pharisee (see Lk 8:36–50) indicates that their table ministry was open, even to a rural preacher. They were popular among the common people, because they preached conversion of heart, and acted with love and justice. Jesus apparently befriended some of the Pharisees. Recall that it was a Pharisee who warned Jesus to watch out for Herod, and that another, Nicodemus, came to Jesus in order learn about salvation.

Jesus and the Pharisees

Jesus had more in common with the Pharisees than with any other Judean types of his day. Like most of the Pharisees, Jesus was a layman who had to support himself with hard work. He also valued simplicity of lifestyle, community life, and service to the poor. Like the Pharisees, Jesus often felt himself separated from the priestly and aristocratic leaders of his religion.

Still, Jesus had differences with the Pharisees. He often bypassed the treasured scribal opinions about the tradition, preferring to offer his own teaching. He was more liberal in his views on the law than even the Pharisees. Jesus' own table fellowship went beyond the openness of the Pharisees because he even included sinners and the unwanted. The story of the sinful woman showing up while Jesus was dining at Simon the Pharisee's table is certainly a moving example of how Jesus was uniquely free in his association with others. Jesus extended the love of God beyond Judaism to all people, and he radically commanded his disciples to love all, even their enemies.

Jesus also went beyond the Pharisees in his teaching that God's forgiveness was available even to those outside observance of the Torah and the scribal laws. Eventually his teaching replaced the Torah, and his followers broke with Judaism. It was at this time that the Pharisees violently persecuted Christians and alienated the gospel communities.

In actuality, the pharisaic tradition of Judaism is one of the most outstanding in the history of that religion. It is quite likely that Jesus held many of these men in high esteem, and was perhaps profoundly influenced by some of them.

A Portrait of Jesus

After looking at the places and people that influenced Jesus, it is time to look more closely at the gospel narratives to determine the characteristics of Jesus. His actions along with his words, when seen in the faith-context in which they were written down by the believing Christian communities, provide a clear and rather complete image of the Jesus of history.

Jesus the Healer

In the gospels Jesus is often portrayed as a healer. Nearly one-fifth of the literary material in the synoptic gospels alludes to miracles of healing and exorcism. Similarly a large portion of John's gospel is concerned with miraculous signs. Many biblical scholars maintain that there is a strong historical basis for many of these miracle stories.[19]

Jesus' healing ministry is unique, and offers important glimpses into his personality. Healing miracles were not all that common in the ancient world. In the thousand years of the Hebrew tradition, there are only a handful of miracle stories, and only a few of these were concerned with healing. There were some rabbis during Jesus' time with miraculous power, namely Hanina ben Dosa and Honi the Circle Drawer, but these men were more rainmakers and wonder workers than persons with a ministry of healing. The magicians of Jesus' time claimed to have secret and mysterious powers, but their magical formulas and sensational actions were quite different from the compassionate acts of Jesus.[20]

There was also not a strong miracle tradition among the pagan religions. There were some stories of Roman emperors who could perform cures, but generally Roman stories of wonders were concerned with portents, omens, and dreams. Many cures were recorded at the Greek city of Epidaurus, but these were attributed to the god Asclepius and not to individual healers. Apollonius, a contemporary of Paul the Apostle, was described as a divine man because of his curative powers, but his cures were due to natural therapy and special insight rather than the powers of the merciful Abba-God about whom Jesus preached.

The rabbinic tradition generally was suspicious of healing miracles.

Many thought that sickness and disabilities came as a punishment from God and were deserved due to one's evil actions. Others thought that such misfortunes were the work of the devil, and that healers were thus conspiring with the powers of evil. Jesus himself was accused of such evil conspiracy (see Mt 12:22–29). Later rabbinic documents point out that he was executed for sorcery.

Acts of Power

The uniqueness of Jesus' healing miracles came through in a number of ways. Unlike other miracle workers, Jesus was neither trying to confirm his authority nor trying to prove personal divinity. He was not involving himself with evil spirits or with secret powers and formulas. Nor was he doing spectacular things to draw attention to himself, gain a following, or prove that he was divine. If anything, Jesus often tried to hush up the beneficiaries of his cures (see Mk 7:31–37; Lk 8:56).[21]

For the most part Jesus' healings were done simply and publicly. They were primarily demonstrations of the presence of God's healing power in the world and God's love for all people. These healings countered the belief that sickness and disabilities came as a punishment from God or were the work of the devil. Jesus revealed a God who wanted people to be whole. Healings were signs that God's reign of love and salvation were near at hand. This reigning power was accessible wherever faith was present. This message was at the very heart of Jesus' ministry.

Luke portrays Jesus reading from the Book of Isaiah in the synagogue in Nazareth and then identifying himself with the prophecy at hand: "The Spirit of the Lord is upon me, because he has chosen me to bring good news to the poor. He has seen me to proclaim liberty to the captives and the recovery of sight to the blind, to set free the oppressed" (Lk 4:18–19). Matthew refers to this prophecy in his story about the followers of John the Baptizer asking Jesus if he is the one to come. Jesus answers: "Go back and tell John what you are hearing and seeing: the blind see, the lame can walk, those who suffer from dreaded skin diseases are made clean, the deaf hear, the dead are brought back to life, and the Good News is preached to the poor" (Mt 11:4–6). Jesus' healings were clear signs of the good news of God's healing and saving presence among all God's people, especially among those who traditionally had been excluded from the community and the kingdom.

There is sound historical reason to view Jesus as a compassionate man who brought people into touch with the power of God through healing. Even though the miracle stories are post-resurrection accounts written primarily to proclaim faith in the risen Lord, they are based on treasured memories of Jesus as one who brought many to physical, mental, and spiritual wholeness.

Jesus the Teacher

All four gospels give accounts of both the friends and enemies of Jesus addressing him as "teacher." Although this may be a post-resurrection title for Jesus, possibly even influenced by later Greek and Jewish models of teachers, it points to memories of Jesus' mission of teaching.

Jesus certainly did not qualify as an official teacher in his day. He did not attend any of the rabbinic schools or academies, nor was he an ordained Scribe with authority to transmit and create the Jewish oral tradition. Jesus received only a modest education in his village school and synagogue, so many of his insights must have come from "the school of hard knocks," from years of personal experience, and from prayer. Jesus' major point of reference seems to be what he had learned from his extraordinary experience of God as Abba, and from his observations of the reign of God's power and truth in everyday life.

In many ways Jesus' teaching resembles that of other sages of his time. He often teaches within the rabbinic tradition. Jesus' golden rule about treating others as you would want to be treated, about self-respect, the urgency of the present time, and on not being judgmental are similar to the teachings of Hillel, a prominent Jewish sage of Jesus' time. Some have also pointed out that Jesus can be compared to the so-called Cynics of the time. These Greek teachers were detached from material things and went about sharing their wisdom on such matters as how simplicity can relieve anxiety and why it is necessary to challenge the traditional value of honor and power.[22]

A Unique Teacher

Jesus' uniqueness as a teacher becomes clear when we compare and contrast his style and content with those of his contemporaries. Jesus was resented by some of the learned members of his religion. They were angry that he had not paid his dues by spending long years in arduous study as they had done as students and servants of an established Scribe. The scholars of the time diligently memorized every word of their master Scribe, and carefully learned to imitate his every action. They mastered the complex body of scholarly opinions of the Torah and earned their designation as teacher. Yet, here was this young upstart workman from the northern backwoods challenging them, debating with them, and even upstaging them with the masses.

Others resented Jesus for the way he boldly shared meals with all kinds of folk, and brought his teaching to the poor, the sinners, and the rejects of society. Some became enemies of Jesus and began to give him a reputation for being a "glutton, drunkard, and friend of tax collectors and sinners" (Lk 7:34).

Jesus was unique as a teacher in other ways. He did not start a school or select an elite group of young male scholars to follow him, as did the other sages of the time. Instead he selected a rag-tag group of followers from the waterfront fishing docks, the money tables of tax collectors, and the back alleys where the diseased, disabled, and street-walkers lived. Not all of his followers were from the lower classes, however. Jesus was all-inclusive in his selection of disciples. He called the well-to-do and the learned as well as the poor.

The gospels mention that Jesus had followers among the Scribes, the Pharisees, the Samaritans, and the Romans. It was a wealthy member of the Sanhedrin, Joseph of Arimathea, and a Pharisee, Nicodemus, who took the risk of securing Jesus' corpse from Pilate, and then anointing and burying it in a new tomb (see Jn 19:38–42). It was Mary Magdala, a woman of independent means, who first encountered the risen Lord and was sent to tell the others the good news. Jesus called all these followers "friends," rather than servants.

Kazunori, an exchange student from Japan and a Buddhist, was impressed by the friendliness of Jesus the teacher. He observed:

The best teacher I ever had was also a friend to me. He did not talk down to me or act superior, but always treated me with respect and kindness. When I struggled with my studies he was there for me as a friend and mentor. I will never forget this teacher. I can see why people still remember Jesus and pass on this teachings.

Jesus and Women

Radically breaking with his tradition, Jesus selected women to be his disciples. Many of the gospel stories present individual women as symbolic of the central role women played in Jesus' ministry and in the ministry of the early communities. Jesus did not honor the patriarchal taboos of his time that women were inferior, unclean, or seductive. He freely taught and healed women in public and in their homes. He allowed women and their children to come round him for instruction; he opposed the unjust divorce laws of his time that favored males, and taught that respect was due to mothers as well as fathers. Jesus placed discipleship and mission over the traditional roles of wife and mother.

He taught that all people were children of God and spoke of the kingdom as a community of sisters and brothers and friends, not masters and slaves.[23]

Throughout the gospels Jesus is portrayed as having profound respect and love for women. He defended and tenderly praised a woman with a bad reputation who came to him at a dinner at the house of Simon the Pharisee (see Lk 8:36–50). He praised the woman who anointed him, and confronted Judas for objecting to her waste of precious oil (see Jn 12:1–8; Mk 14:3–9). He asked for water from a Samaritan woman and then allowed her to bring her town to conversion (Jn 4:4–42). He saved a woman about to be stoned to death for adultery (Jn 8:1–11). Jesus defended widows against those who oppressed them (see Lk 20:45–47), praised their donations of a few coins over the large offerings of the rich (Mk 12:41–44), and on one occasion brought a widow's only son back to life (Lk 7:11–17). He ignored the taboos of his times as he allowed himself to be approached by a hemorrhaging woman in public (Lk 8:43–48), and as he put his hands on a dead girl in order to restore her to life again (Lk 8:49–56).

Jesus' teaching stories often balance male and female images. In the judgment scene in the gospel of Matthew both women and men came together for reward or punishment (Mt 25:31–46). In the parable of the wedding feast (often a symbol of the kingdom), the women who acted wisely enjoy the celebration with the bridegroom (see Mt 25:1–13). The gospel writer paired the parable of the sower (a man) with that of the woman putting yeast into the dough (see Mt 13:1–9, 24–30, 33). The story comparing God to a good shepherd was paired with the story of the lost coin where God is strikingly portrayed as a woman celebrating the recovery of a silver coin (see Lk 15:1–10). All of these are ample evidence that the early communities had vivid memories of Jesus as one who treated women with high regard.[24]

Women in the Gospels

Key portraits of women in the gospels further reveal memories of how Jesus uniquely called women to learn from him, and share in his teaching mission. Jesus' own mother, Mary, was described as the Lord's servant, the central image for discipleship in the early communities. Her prayer of Magnificat was not one of domesticity, but rather was a free and open proclamation of her share in God's mission to overcome the oppression of the lowly by the rich and mighty (Lk 1:46–55). At Cana, Mary played a "sacramental role" in the highly symbolic miracle at the wedding feast (Jn 2:1–11). She was present at Calvary, faithful and courageous to the end, and in John's gospel joined the beloved disciple in mission (Jn 19:26–27). In the pentecostal scene in the upper room she was recognized as part of a community that carried on the mission of the risen Lord (Acts 1:14).[25]

Mary Magdala was clearly a close disciple of Jesus. There are no biblical grounds for thinking of her as a prostitute or as one who was in love with Jesus. There is ample evidence that she was a woman of means who helped support Jesus' community. In several gospels she is placed at the foot of the cross, and she is prominent in the resurrection stories. Mary Magdala has been and remains an important role model for equality in ministry.[26]

Other women in the gospels also help us realize that Jesus taught women and called them to carry on his mission. The Samaritan woman stands for all women viewed as outcasts by the community, but called by Christ to authentic discipleship. There is Martha, who is reminded by Jesus that domestic roles for women are not as important as listening to the Word. It is she who was "minister" at the dinner in Bethany, a central figure in the resuscitation of Lazarus, and the one to whom Jesus revealed himself as "the resurrection and the life." There is her sister, Mary, who is a "hearer of the Word," instructed by Jesus in her own home. It is this Mary who later anointed Jesus in an action that mirrors Jesus' action at the Last Supper before his death. And there is Joanna, the wife of Herod's minister of finance, who left the sumptuous luxury of the palace to follow Jesus and eventually became one of the first witnesses to the resurrection. All of these figures demonstrate Jesus' unique respect for women and indicate that women played key roles in the early church.

A Prophetic Voice

There is a prophetic dimension in the teaching of Jesus. He was a teacher who spoke for God; one who proclaimed that God was a saving power in the midst of the world. Similar to the prophets of old, Jesus brought a sharp critique to the abuses of his day. He called people to convert to a new vision of life both now and in the time to come.

Jesus was aware that something significantly new was breaking through in his words and deeds. He made this clear in the synagogue in Nazareth when he identified himself with the liberating mission of Isaiah (see Lk 4:21). On another occasion when his authority was challenged in Nazareth, Jesus answered: "A prophet is respected everywhere except in his own hometown and by relatives and his family" (Mk 6:4).

Even in his prophetic role, Jesus is unique. Unlike other prophets, he did not attempt to offer credentials or speak with phrases like: "Thus says the Lord." Nor did he claim to have ecstatic states, visions, or mysterious calls from God in the manner of other ancient prophets. Rather, Jesus spoke with his own personal authority. Instead of bringing a message from God, Jesus was more intent on describing his experience of intimacy with God and making this available to others.

At times the gospels have Jesus speak of judgment in the language of the older prophets, but more commonly Jesus described the constant and eternal love of God, and the unlimited forgiveness of God. He warned of possible destruction, but this was more the self-destruction that came from the rejection of God's mercy and love than the punishing action of a wrathful God. As the final prophet, Jesus proclaimed a new creation and a new era of hope for sinners, for the poor, and for the marginalized.[27]

Many prophetic figures have had to pay with their lives. Jesus was no exception. He set his prophetic teaching down as though it was God's own word, and he refused to withdraw it even if it meant sacrificing his life. It was his hope that his disciples would carry on this mission of spreading the good news of God's saving power to all nations.

The Complete Picture of Jesus

Research into the social, political, and religious background of Jesus' times, archaeological digs, and close study of the deeper layers of the gospels help us put together a composite portrait of Jesus of Nazareth. The sketch of what such a portrait might look like includes the following essential elements.

Jesus of Nazareth was a real human individual, a flesh and blood person who lived for about thirty years in Palestine. He was a person who shared the same emotions, pleasures, thought processes, and ability to choose that are common to all people. Jesus had the same human limitation of intelligence that we all share, and thus had to struggle to learn and discover the truth. Like all of us, Jesus had to deal with confusion and doubt. All of these human characteristics are reflected in the gospel stories. Underlying what is often myth, theology, liturgical prayers, and other literary forms, the four canonical gospels contain the actual memories of Jesus as he was known by his followers and other observers.

Jesus was a Jew who accepted and cherished the religion of Israel as the will of God for him and for his people. He devoutly participated in his religion by learning the Torah, attending the synagogue, making pilgrimages to the temple, learning from the priests and teachers of his time, and following the laws and religious customs of the Jews. Jesus' life was shaped by the Jewish culture, by his family, by his life in Nazareth and other areas of Galilee, and by nearly two decades of hard work as a craftsman.

In a manner uncharacteristic of the times, Jesus left the familiar environs of his village and the financial security of his trade to enter public life as a preacher, teacher, and healer. His training for this was modest. He had studied the Torah in his local synagogue and participated in the usual dialogues that went on among adults in the villages of Galilee, but it does not seem likely that he attended any of the prestigious rabbinical schools or studied under any of the well-known teachers of his time.

Jesus was a follower of John the Baptizer, a prophetic preacher of the time. When John was executed, Jesus began his own public life, which lasted for perhaps a year or more. His teaching bore some similarity to other sages of his time, but he also had his own unique style and message. Rather than establishing a school, Jesus opted to be an itinerant preacher delivering his message in open fields, by the seashore, or at table. He taught with an authority that was distinctive, and seems to have confined his work mostly to the smaller towns of Galilee. Instead of the traditional manner whereby followers chose to follow a teacher, Jesus recruited his own followers. Most of his close disciples were commoners, both women and men.

At the center of Jesus' teaching was the notion of the reign of God. This was a common theme in Israel, but his version of it was uncommon. He experienced an unprecedented intimacy with God, whom Jesus uniquely called Abba. He invited "all who had ears" to hear the good news that they too could share such friendship with God.

Jesus perceived the world about him, both natural and human, as the creation of this loving and saving God. He taught that God's love and compassion was extended to all, even to sinners before their repentance. Jesus saw himself as being in radical solidarity with all outcasts and as a liberator of the oppressed. He extended his friendship and his table fellowship to people of all kinds, rich and poor, virtuous and sinner. Jesus offered the love of God to all, both Jew and Gentile. He promised his disciples a time of future fulfillment when the righteous would prevail and evil would be overcome.

Jesus called people to a radical conversion. He told them to prepare themselves to accept the reign of God in their lives. In both his own words and deeds, Jesus became the personification of this loving, saving presence of God in the world. He struggled against the religious legalism that put the law in the place of this loving God, and that distorted God's image into that of a fearsome and manipulative taskmaster. To demonstrate his rejection of such legalism, Jesus was liberal in his views and practice of Sabbath and purity laws, especially when legal observance got in the way of serving others. Jesus was dedicated to freeing people from anything that prevented them from experiencing the love and compassion of God.

Jesus performed miracles, especially healing and exorcisms. Through these miracles he demonstrated that the power of a caring and loving God was active in the world. He did not use these miracles to prove divinity, for he never claimed to be God, nor did he explicitly claim to be the messiah.

The initial response to Jesus' mission was enthusiastic. Amazement and high hopes were in the air. Gradually, however, Jesus' words and deeds put him into conflict with some of the religious and political leaders of the time. He was threatened, but refused to abandon his message or mission.

Jesus was arrested in Jerusalem and crucified as a seditionist. He faced death with courage and persistent fidelity to his mission, and died naked on a cross outside the city. After his death, Jesus' followers began to experience him as being raised from the dead. They came to have faith in him as the messiah, savior, and as the Son of God. These disciples established a new community within Judaism. Eventually this group became separated from Judaism, took on the name of "The Way," and then became known as the Christian Church.

Conclusion

At the beginning of this chapter, Ted spoke for many young people who seek to know Jesus more personally. This chapter assembled a composite portrait of Jesus of Nazareth by looking at the places where he lived, the kinds of figures who lived during his time, and Jesus' own mission as a healer, teacher, and prophet.

In many ways Jesus of Nazareth was unique. As Fulton Oursler wrote years ago, the story of Jesus is "the greatest story ever told." It is the story of a young carpenter turned preacher, who eventually came to be recognized as the Son of God.

This chapter has explored the historical Jesus. The next chapter will teach more about Jesus by exploring the gospel stories of his birth, death, and resurrection. The following chapter will conclude this section with a discussion of Jesus as the Christ, the savior, and the liberator of the poor and oppressed.

Discussion Questions

1. Is it valuable for you to know more about the historical Jesus? Explain your answer in some detail.

2. Modern biblical scholarship maintains that the gospel writers are often using "stories" to interpret what Jesus said and did, as well as to proclaim the beliefs of the early Christian communities. Discuss what you understand by this position, and whether or not you accept such a scholarly approach to scripture.

3. List and discuss some of the ways an understanding of the places where Jesus lived can help us understand him as a real person.

4. Compare and contrast Jesus of Nazareth with some to the figures of his time (Essenes, revolutionaries, Sadducees, Scribes, and Pharisees).

5. Discuss ways in which Jesus was unique as a healer, a teacher, and a prophet.

6. Compose a written portrait of who Jesus of Nazareth is for you.

Suggested Readings

James H. Charlesworth, *Jesus Within Judaism.* New York: Doubleday, 1988.

John Dominic Crossan, *The Historical Jesus.* New York: HarperCollins, 1991.

Sean Freyne, *Galilee, Jesus and the Gospels.* Philadelphia: Fortress Press, 1988.

Brennan Hill, *Jesus the Christ: Contemporary Perspectives.* Mystic, CT: Twenty-Third Publications, 1991.

Walter Kasper, *Jesus the Christ.* New York: Paulist Press, 1976.

Bernard J. Lee, *The Galilean Jewishness of Jesus.* Mahwah, NJ: Paulist Press, 1988.

John P. Meier, *A Marginal Jew: Rethinking the Historical Jesus.* New York: Doubleday, 1991.

Pheme Perkins, *Jesus as Teacher.* New York: Cambridge University Press. 1990.

John Riches, *The World of Jesus: First-Century Judaism in Crisis.* Cambridge: Cambridge University Press, 1990.

Anthony J. Saldarini, *Pharisees, Scribes, and Sadducees in Palestinian Society.* Wilmington, DE: Michael Glazier, 1988.

E.P. Sanders, *Jesus and Judaism.* Philadelphia: Fortress, 1985.

Edward Schillebeeckx, *Jesus: An Experiment in Christology.* New York: Crossroad, 1979.

Gerard Sloyan, *Jesus in Focus.* Rev. ed. Mystic, CT: Twenty-Third Publications, 1994.

5.

The Mysteries of Jesus Christ

Framing the Question

My name is Holly. I was raised in Wilmette, just north of Chicago, and went to public school. I have been a Catholic all my life, mainly because my mother is a Catholic. My father is a strict Baptist, and that has caused some tension in our family, especially when the topic of the bible comes up. My father reads the bible everyday and is certain that it contains the exact words of God and that everything in the bible happened as it is described. When I was in high school CCD, they began to teach that much of the bible was myth, and my Dad got really upset. He believes that Catholics are wrong in thinking that the stories of the bible are not exact history and that the gospels aren't word for word what Jesus said.

I am not sure what to say to him, so we just don't talk about the bible anymore. I need to know more clearly what is historically accurate and what is myth in the gospel stories. If you look at the main events in Jesus' life, his birth, death, and resurrection, what really happened? Were a lot of these stories just made up by the early Christians?

Different Approaches to Understanding the Bible

Holly puts her finger on a problem that is dividing Christians of different denominations as well as within individual churches. Some, like Holly's father, are fundamentalists who take a literal approach to the scriptures. In their view the scriptures are the exact, precise "words of God" dictated to the evangelists who wrote the gospels and to the writers of all the other books of the bible. In this view all the words of the scriptures are true and thus the gospels are accurate accounts of what Jesus said and did.

Many other Christians, including most Catholics and mainline Protestants, adhere to the findings of modern biblical criticism and accept the fact that the scriptures are written in a variety of literary forms. To understand the truth and the authentic meaning of the scriptures, one must understand the individual literary forms. These forms include parables, myths, historical narratives, miracle stories, prayers, theological interpretations, and many other literary styles. In this context scripture is viewed not as the exact words of God, but as the Word of God conveyed through the use of form and story.

From this perspective the four canonical gospels are understood to contain a base of historical material (what Jesus said and did) that is seen through the lens of resurrection faith. The gospel stories profess the faith of the early communities. Thus the accounts of the birth, death, and resurrection tell both about who Jesus was when he was alive, as well as how he was experienced in a risen and glorified state. We hear about Jesus of Nazareth (the historical Jesus) as well as about the Christ of faith and what the early followers believed about him.

This chapter will explore the three central events of Jesus' life, often called the mysteries of his life. These are his birth, his death, and his resurrection. These gospel stories contain important information both about Jesus' earthly life and about what the early disciples believed about Jesus Christ.

The Mystery of Jesus' Birth

What most Christians think of as the Christmas story is actually a blending of two distinct stories: one from the Gospel of Matthew, the other from Luke. These stories were developed many years after Jesus' death and offer theological interpretations of Jesus' birth; they are not so concerned for the facts about what actually happened. Both stories establish the identity and integrity of Jesus' parents, make clear the Jewish heritage of Jesus, and profess Christian faith in the power of Jesus Christ. As noted scripture scholar Raymond Brown points out, these nativity stories are the "gospel in miniature," summing up early Christian faith in the person and message of Jesus Christ.[1]

There are some similarities in the two nativity stories: the names of the parents, Mary and Joseph; reference to a virginal conception (although this is not as explicit in Luke as in Matthew); the designation of the place and time (Bethlehem during the reign of Herod); a name designation by an angel; mention of the Davidic line; the eventual settling in Nazareth.

There are, however, many notable differences between the two stories. Matthew's gospel, written around the year 80 C.E., possibly in a Syrian community of both Jews and Gentiles, focuses on Joseph, the plot of Herod to kill the child, the visit of the Magi, and on how Jesus is the fulfillment of many Hebrew prophecies. At the time of Jesus' birth the parents seem to be already married and living in Bethlehem. After the birth, Jesus is given gifts and paid homage by the Magi. The family moves to Egypt to escape the wrath of Herod, and upon his death settle into a new area at Nazareth.

Luke's gospel, which was written about the same time as Matthew's, possibly in the community of Antioch, focuses on Mary, the mother of Jesus. It explains that the parents of Jesus are engaged but not yet married. They live in Nazareth and go to Bethlehem for a census, arriving to find there is no room for them in any of the regular lodgings. Mary gives birth to Jesus in a manger, and shepherds come to pay homage.

Beyond this basic outline it is necessary to examine the stories in greater detail to see what these two ancient communities were saying about the meaning of Jesus' birth.

The Gospel of Matthew

Matthew's nativity story begins with a listing of Jesus' family tree that leaves no doubt that Jesus had good genes going back from Joseph, his father, to David and as far back as Jacob, Isaac, and Abraham. Jesus is portrayed as descending from a long line of people who had their weaknesses, but who were still able to further God's plan for salvation. Joseph and Mary, of course, are described as individuals who are utterly faithful to God's will.[2]

The author of Matthew's gospel places Jesus' foster father, Joseph, at the center of the narrative. Knowing little about Joseph, the author seems to rely on the patriarch Joseph (he of the multicolor coat) for his model (see Genesis 37–50). Like his namesake of old, Jesus' father is described as a man of forgiveness and compassion, one who is willing quietly to divorce his betrothed rather than denounce her for apparent infidelity. Also similar to the Joseph of old, Jesus' foster father is a "dreamer." Joseph learns of the divine origin of Mary's pregnancy from an angel in a dream and accepts this as the word of God. He later learns in a dream of the need to travel to Egypt.

The forced exile of the Holy Family in Egypt and Joseph's faithfulness to God's word and his dedication to his family also mirror the Joseph of the Hebrew scriptures. This "mini-Exodus" indicates that Jesus is a modern-day Moses figure who will lead his people out of exile. Herod's threat on the life of the infant Jesus also parallels the ancient Pharaoh's efforts to kill Moses as an infant. This, coupled with Matthew's demonstration of how Jesus fulfilled many of the Hebrew prophecies, had strong appeal to the Jews of Matthew's community. The gospel proclaims the early Christian belief that Jesus was indeed a savior sent by God. His life would ultimately be saved by God who would raise him from the dead.

The mysterious Magi from the East also provide rich symbolism in Matthew's nativity story. A great deal of legendary tradition has built up around these men over the centuries. They have been called "three kings," although the gospels never designate them as such. It is more likely that the Magi were Persian priests or astrologers, who make decisions and help others do the same by reading the stars in the heavens.[3] In this story the stars lead them to seek Jesus and pay homage to him, in contrast to the chief priests and Scribes who ignore the significance of the birth, even though they know the prophecies of its coming. The irony is quite evident.

The Magi are also contrasted with Herod, who treacherously wants to kill Jesus and other "innocents." While Jesus escapes the slaughter of the innocents ordered by Herod, he will later be humiliated before his crucifixion by Herod's son. The gifts of these sages from the East are also highly symbolic: gold for a king, incense for worship, and myrrh to symbolize how the cross would be part of Jesus' destiny.[4]

Some scholars have suggested that Matthew's story about the Magi and the slaughter of the innocents points to the later phenomenon where many Gentiles accepted Jesus as the messiah and came into the church, while many Jews rejected Jesus and even persecuted the innocent disciples who followed Jesus. This points out how the gospel stories often tell more about what is happening in the early Christian communities than they do about what actually happened during Jesus' time.

The Gospel of Luke

Luke prefaces his nativity story with an account of the birth of John the Baptizer. In a story that closely parallels the story of the birth of Isaac to his aged parents Abraham and Sarah (see Gn 17:15; 21:1–7), Elizabeth, the mother of John the Baptizer, is a barren older woman who becomes pregnant by the power of God. An annunciation scene with an angel attempting to convince the skeptical father, the priest Zechariah, signals that this birth is indeed from God.

In the sixth month of Elizabeth's pregnancy, an angel comes to another maiden, Mary, and announces that she too will conceive a son by the power of God's Spirit. Mary, though she has not "known man," accepts God's will with complete faith. She then sets out to visit her relative Elizabeth, apparently to assist her with the birth of her son.

The meeting of the two women is memorable. Elizabeth, filled with the Spirit, proclaims the blessedness of Mary and the child to be born, and then experiences her own infant leaping for joy in her womb. Mary, on the other hand, makes a proclamation that echoes the one made by Hannah, the mother of Samuel (see 1 Sm 2:1–10; Lk 1:46–55). She joyfully praises the power, the holiness, and the mercy of God. Her God scatters the proud, strikes down the rich and mighty, and lifts up the lowly. Today this passage is used by many as an indication that Mary supports the liberation of the oppressed.

The two annunciations in the Gospel of Luke prepare the way for Jesus' birth. There is a marked contrast between the two infants. The angel tells Zechariah that his child will be a great man, an ascetic, and a prophet who will reunite families and bring people back to God. His role will be one of getting people ready, of preparing the way for the messiah who is to come. In contrast, Mary is told by the angel that her son, Jesus, will be the Son of God, a king. This gospel thus makes it quite clear to the disciples, especially to those in the early church who were still following John the Baptizer, that Jesus was indeed the messiah, the savior, the Son of God. John's role was to open the way and then decrease. There was but One Lord and he is Jesus Christ.[5]

After the dual annunciation accounts, Luke's nativity story opens in Nazareth with the betrothed couple, Joseph and Mary, required to travel south to Judea to enroll in a census decreed by Caesar Augustus. They go to Bethlehem because Joseph is of the house of David, and while they are there Mary gives birth to their baby in a humble manger because there was no room in the inn. (This is the Christmas scene with which we are familiar, and not Matthew's, where Jesus is apparently born in the family home in Bethlehem.)

In contrast to the exotic Magi of Matthew's infancy narrative, Luke depicts lowly shepherds on the hillside listening to angels proclaim from the heavens that the messiah and Lord has been born. The shepherds seek out the manger, tell what they had heard from the angels, and then return to their flocks glorifying and praising God.

The shepherds are richly symbolic. David, from whom Jesus descended, was a shepherd. Jesus identified his own mission with that of the good shepherd. These lowly mountain folk might also represent the marginal people and outcasts for whom Jesus showed so much care and compassion.[6] There is also a kind of universal "everyman" quality to the shepherds, as the angel of the Lord proclaims to the "good news of great joy that will be for all the people" (Lk 2:10). The angels' song from the heavens indicates that this birth is indeed of divine origin and has cosmic implications.

Luke's account also establishes that Jesus' origins are from God. As in Matthew, the Angel Gabriel, one of the "angels who sees the face of God," announces that the conception will occur as a result of the overshadowing of the power of the Most High. The child will be the Son of God. This imagery echoes the creation scene in the Book of Genesis where the Spirit creatively hovers over the waters. The post-resurrection faith of the Antioch community reverberates throughout the Lukan nativity story. Jesus is from God. He is the Son of God, the messiah for the Jews and for all people.

The Historical Event of Jesus' Birth

Although belief in Jesus as the Christ clearly underlies the story of Jesus' birth, it is possible to detect historical actualities related to the birth of Jesus of Nazareth. The feistiness of the maiden Mary questioning an angel, her faithful acceptance of the will of God, the concern for justice that is in her Magnificat, and the self-sacrifice of her visit to Elizabeth are all characteristics that she passed on to her son.[7] The compassion, faith, courage, and protectiveness of Joseph are later reflected in the public life of Jesus. Jesus' outreach to those beyond his community—to Romans, Samaritans, and Syrians—is symbolized in the presence of the Magi. His concern for the poor and for those not able to practice the intricacies of the Torah is manifest in the recognition given the humble shepherds. His common roots and simple lifestyle are vividly symbolized by the manger in which he was born.

The infancy narratives portray Jesus as bursting on the scene like a new Moses offering freedom to his people. He came as a prophet challenging the abuses of his time, predicting dire consequences for those who oppress others, and promising a future of eternal life to the faithful. The Herods, Caesars, and Pilates of the world threatened his life and made him subject to their laws, but Abba saved his Son and evil was overcome. Jesus and many of his later disciples were innocents who were slaughtered, exiled as refugees, and ordered about by Roman authorities. Despite this, the God of love, forgiveness, and compassion reigned. Ultimately the mighty would be brought down from their thrones and the humble would inherit the earth. Rich and poor, Jew and Gentile, women and men share in God's kingdom, now and in the time to come. This was the hopeful vision of the early Christians, and it is proclaimed as they reflected on the meaning of the birth of Jesus.

College students often are surprised to hear the two distinct versions of the Christmas story. Some are shocked, others seem relieved because they had a difficult time accepting some of these stories as having actually taken place.

Craig, a junior English major for Lima, Ohio, has this to say in his reflective essay about the Christmas stories:

When I first heard this scholarly analysis of the Christmas stories, I was stunned. I never realized that there were two birth stories, that they were different, and that much of this writing was symbolic. Now I have come to accept this approach. It fits with so much of my other literary study. I can see now that the gospel stories are really literary forms that profess the beliefs of early Christians. Some are based on history, some not, but the main purpose of the stories is to profess faith. I get more out of reading these stories now than I did when I thought they were accounts of what really happened.

The Mystery of Jesus' Death

All four gospels reveal that the early Christian communities were struggling with questions about Jesus' crucifixion. Why would such a good man who spent so much time healing and teaching about love be scourged and crucified as a criminal? Who was responsible for a such a horrible injustice? How was this death carried out? This section will seek answers to these and similar questions.

Four Accounts of the Passion

Although there can be no doubt about the historicity of Jesus' crucifixion, there is some uncertainty about exactly what took place at this horrible event. Each of the four gospels deals rather extensively with the events surrounding the crucifixion, but they provide few details of Jesus' experience of suffering and death.

The gospel stories are like four "plays" about the passion and death of Jesus. While there is a historical core in each, the passion narratives are primarily literary creations. More often the writer is more concerned with the theological meaning of the event, rather than with giving an accurate account of what actually happened.

Each of the four gospels gives us a different portrayal of Jesus going to his death.[8] Mark's gospel, the earliest written, views Jesus as a man knowingly entering into his fate. At a dinner in Bethany, Jesus acknowledges that the woman who anointed him with precious oils was indeed preparing him for burial. He predicts that one of his own will betray him and hand him over. In Mark's drama Jesus appears to be resigned to his death. It is something he must do to fulfill the scriptures and bring about the kingdom of the Father. Jesus dies alone and abandoned by his followers. They had fallen asleep during his agony in the garden, and ran away when he needed them most. As the end draws near, Jesus silently accepts his fate. During the two late-night sessions before the Sanhedrin, Jesus has little to say but does admit that he is the messiah. Jesus stands resolutely as he is mocked, spat upon, and beaten. He seems even to be abandoned by God as he cries out from the cross: "My God, my God, why have you forsaken me?"(Mk 15:34).[9]

Matthew's account of the crucifixion is quite similar to the one given in Mark's gospel. Jesus is abandoned by his disciples, and is even denied by his prime disciple, Peter. Where Peter earlier had recognized that Jesus was the Son of God, he now says that he does not even know Jesus. Jesus goes to his death alone and sorrowful, yet always accepting that this is the will of God. At his trial he stands totally innocent of the charges leveled against him, and yet he remains silent before his accusers.[10] As in the Marcan account, Jesus is ridiculed as he suffers on the cross. He dies with the same loud cry of anguish that is heard in Mark.

The author of Luke's gospel presents a picture of the passion that differs considerably from the other two synoptic gospels. In Luke's account, Jesus is neither isolated nor deserted by his followers. True, he is betrayed by Judas and denied by Peter, but most of the other disciples remain faithful. Although his followers fall asleep several times in the garden scene, it is more out of sorrow than out of indifference. Even more strikingly, the disciples are present at the crucifixion itself.

In Luke's passion story Jesus is neither troubled nor resigned to his fate. Instead he is filled with peace and compassion. In the garden scene, Jesus heals the ear of the high priest's slave that is cut off by one of his disciples. When Jesus catches the eye of Peter after the denials, he moves Peter to repentance. Both Herod and Pilate recognize the innocence of Jesus, and he rather curiously is able to heal the enmity that previously existed between the two men.

In this passion play there is no brutal mocking by the soldiers. Rather, the soldiers seem to follow along with the crowds, actually lamenting the suffering of Jesus. The women of Jerusalem come out to weep for Jesus, and in return he tells them of his concern for the future of their children. On the cross Jesus does not cry out in anguish, but asks his Father to forgive his enemies because they have acted out of ignorance. Jesus promises the criminal on his right that he will be with Jesus in paradise that very day.[11] For Luke, the cross stands for mercy, healing, and atonement. Jesus dies peacefully, saying: "Father, into your hands I commend my spirit" (see Lk 23:46).

John's passion narrative is strikingly different from the other three. Here Jesus dies as the divine savior. He is a strong, majestic figure who goes to his death fully aware that he will live again. Here Jesus is the all-knowing Son of God who goes through the passion completely in charge of every scene. When they come to arrest him in the garden, Jesus is standing proud, not prostrate in grief. Those who come to arrest him are so struck down in awe that he seems almost to have to pick them up, dust them off, and assist them in arresting him. Ever in charge, Jesus firmly makes it clear that he wants his followers to go free, and that no harm is to come to them.

At the interrogation before Annas, the former High Priest is obviously out of his depth in dealing with Jesus. Likewise, Pilate, the fearsome Roman procurator, seems deferential when speaking to Jesus, and even seems to ask for instruction on truth at one point. After the scourging, Jesus still stands majestically before the crowds as Pilate all but intones "Behold the man." On the way to Calvary, Jesus does not need help from Simon to carry the cross. While hanging in agony on the cross, Jesus reigns as an authentic king of the Jews. The sign on the cross proclaims this to the world in three languages.

In this account of the passion Jesus is neither abandoned nor alone; a number of followers are actually gathered beneath the cross. Before Jesus dies, he leaves behind a family of faith as he tells his mother and his beloved disciple to care for each other. At the end, Jesus decisively completes the mission given him by God. He says: "It is finished," and then gives up his spirit. Joseph of Arimathea, a member of the Sanhedrin and a secret disciple of Jesus, along with Nicodemus the Pharisee, take the body, anoint it in kingly fashion with an enormous amount of spices, and bury Jesus in a new tomb.

The Reason for the Crucifixion

Scholars differ on the question of why Jesus of Nazareth was executed on a cross. Some follow the lead of Rudolph Bultmann and maintain that Jesus was killed by the Romans who mistook him for a rebel. Thus the crucifixion was simply a tragic and senseless killing of an innocent man. The death is thus unrelated to Jesus' life and ministry, removes Jesus from having any choice in the matter, and renders the death devoid of any significant meaning.[12]

Those of the more literal persuasion attempt to harmonize the gospels and show that Jesus was condemned by the Jewish leadership and then handed over to Pilate to be killed. This approach ignores the many textual difficulties in the passion stories. Close scrutiny of the stories shows that it is hard to ascertain whether there was a trial or a mere hearing, or to discover what the actual charges were, or how Jesus responded to the accusations.

Traditionalists have also tended to project later theological interpretations back into the historical event. They conclude that Jesus had to die to fulfill a divine plan and to ransom humankind from sin. This approach not only bypasses the actual historical situation, but implies that Jesus went to his death passively accepting his fate with little choice in the matter.

Other scholars have attempted to show that Jesus was executed because of his support of sedition and violent revolution.[13] There are also those who maintain that the gospel accounts of Jewish condemnation of Jesus were simply fabricated by anti-Semitic Christians. From this perspective, the Romans were solely responsible for the crucifixion.

Neither of these last two approaches is supported by careful study of the gospels or the background of the times. There are no indications in the gospels that Jesus either taught or practiced violence. As for who was responsible for the death, there was so much collusion among the Romans and the Roman-appointed Jewish leadership at that time, that one must conclude that both groups bear responsibility.

At the same time, it must be vigorously stressed that no Jew, past or present, should be held accountable for the hateful actions of some Jewish leaders two thousand years ago. The notion of the Jews as "Christ-killers," which resulted so often in the persecution of Jews, is preposterous and should be viewed as completely alien to the Christian tradition.

The Catholic tradition holds that Jesus' death was the culmination of his life and was freely accepted by Jesus as an act of self-sacrifice. Jesus' death came about because of what he stood for and what he did for others, as well as for his relentless refusal to back off from his prophetic positions when threatened with death. Jesus' mission and message brought him enemies. For various reasons, those who hated him schemed to rid the world of him. Ultimately they achieved their goal and had him publicly humiliated as he died naked on a cross outside the city of Jerusalem.

Executed Because He Was Unique

E.P. Sanders points out that it is unreasonable to think that Jesus was executed simply because he taught mercy and forgiveness or because he was a formidable debater about the law.[14] Some of Jesus' contemporaries proclaimed teachings similar to his, and some even performed healings, and yet these individuals were not arrested, beaten, or executed. What was it about Jesus that generated such rejection and hatred, such determination to do away with him?

The answer might be connected with the uniqueness attributed to Jesus. As a teacher, he took the radical position that God's reign was not one of fear, but one of love, justice, and forgiveness. From his own unparalleled experience of Abba, the divine parent of all, Jesus had come to believe that intimate friendship with God was extended to all.[15]

Against those who saw sickness, poverty, and disabilities as signs of God's punishment, Jesus brought the power of a God who wanted wholeness. This was a God who blessed the poorest of the poor, the outcast, and the marginal in a special way. This empowerment of victims, this awakening of the oppressed to their dignity was viewed by some as dangerous. Jesus died because the oppressors and tyrants wanted to eliminate individuals who bless and enliven their victims![16]

At the same time Jesus was building up the marginal, he was challenging the corrupt of his society. He called for a radical conversion (*metanoia* or repentance) from the prejudices, self-righteous judgments, and exclusiveness toward people who were considered to be unclean. He attacked greed, hypocrisy, pride, and the abuse of power. Jesus made it clear that salvation was a call to detachment, humility, self-sacrifice, compassion, and love of all God's children.

Killed Because He Was "Dangerous"

Jesus' call was a call to freedom, and he urged the oppressed to struggle for the freedom that was theirs as children of God. Sinners were to free themselves of their corruption and restore their own human dignity. With this attitude Jesus was inciting a nonviolent revolution that started in the hearts of both the oppressor and the oppressed. In the long run, this kind of revolution was more subversive than that of a terrorist. Small wonder that those who held the wealth and the power through their political or religious domination over others saw Jesus as a serious threat.[17]

Jesus' enemies felt that he had a dangerous attitude. He was a rather poorly educated Galilean, a manual laborer lacking ordination and scribal credentials; yet he had the nerve to teach the people with authority. Moreover, he did not refer to the traditional scholarly rabbinic teaching. He didn't even quote scripture very often. They saw Jesus as a peasant upstart who spoke from his own personal experiences, fashioned his own parables, and taught with an authority all his own.

Jesus' message was startling to many of the religious leaders of the time. He told the people that the primary requirement for salvation was to follow a way of love and self-giving. Salvation did not come by adhering to the scribal laws. He also taught that God could be worshiped in spirit and truth well beyond the boundaries of the temple, even in people's own hearts.

Resented for Arousing the Crowds

Those opposed to Jesus were probably alarmed by the response of the masses. The gospels say that the people came in great numbers and that they were amazed at his teachings and healings. Some thought he was one of the prophets returning to bring God's word for a final time. Others wanted to make him the new king of Israel and restore the glorious days of the past.

Men and women were willing to leave their families and their professions to follow him. Fishermen with established businesses in Capernaum left their boats and nets to become his disciples. Tax collectors left their lucrative agencies and the security of working for Rome to follow him. Prostitutes, many of whom may have been abused sexually since their childhood, found in Jesus a man who offered respect and who cared about their self-worth. Women of independent means chose to support Jesus' cause and became his followers. Soon his following began to include lepers, shepherds, Romans, Samaritans, Scribes, Pharisees, and even a member of the Sanhedrin. Rich and poor, the well-established and the outcast, women, men, children, Jew as well as Gentile all seemed to be attracted to this young Galilean with the open hands and the loving heart.

Jesus' entrance into the city of Jerusalem indicated just how popular he had become. Jesus was received with excitement by the many people who had gathered for Passover. He came not as a conquering hero might come on horseback proclaiming victory. Instead, Jesus came humbly on a donkey, with a calm and deliberated power that was extremely threatening to his enemies. John's gospel places this event at the very beginning of Jesus' last week of life and connects it with the raising of Lazarus. In this account the Pharisees appeared to be extremely distraught at the acclaim given to Jesus, and they murmur about themselves: "Look, the whole world has gone after him" (Jn 12:19).

The broad acceptance of Jesus' unique message and authority caused some people to turn against him. The religious and political leaders of the time had much to lose if the masses suddenly realized that they had dignity and that their plight was the result of oppression. Those who thought they had legitimate authority and who expected submission and obedience from those under them reacted negatively to a rustic peasant who spoke with such conviction and authority.

The Jewish leaders had two choices when facing someone as prophetic as Jesus. Either they had to accept his teaching (and thereby forfeit a profitable and comfortable way of life), or have Jesus declared a false prophet worthy of death. Apparently some of the leaders of the time felt there was just too much at stake for them to give any semblance of credibility to Jesus.[18]

The primary concern of Roman leaders in those days was subjugation of the Jews with a minimum of resistance. Any person like Jesus, who brought the masses a message of affirmation and freedom, was marked as dangerous. A teacher who made his listeners aware of corruption, injustice, and hypocrisy was not well received by Rome. Any person who challenged the integrity of the Roman-appointed Jewish leadership was considered a seditionist.

Rejected for Ignoring the Jewish Law

Jesus' method of healing might also have been a way in which he made enemies. Jesus healed as he taught, with his own unique way and with his own authority. Calling on powers unique to himself, Jesus brought sight to the blind, sound to the deaf, and wholeness to the crippled and infirm. At times he performed these miracles on the Sabbath, which angered the more conservative Jewish leaders.

Jesus also forgave sin freely, audaciously, and as though the power to forgive the most heinous sin came from within his own person. To add insult to injury, Jesus freely associated with and befriended sinners. He dined with sinners and even called them to be his disciples. Jesus' behavior in healing and forgiving was considered to be blasphemous in some influential circles. Important people in high places came to hate Jesus and wanted him destroyed.

The cleansing of the temple also played a crucial role in bringing on Jesus' execution.[19] Mark's gospel explicitly points out that it was after this event that the chief priests and scribes began to plan Jesus' death (see Mk 11:15–18). John's gospel places the scene at the beginning of Jesus' ministry and links it with Jesus' statement that if they destroy this temple, he will raise it up in three days (Jn 2:13–22). This statement refers to the resurrection and will come up again in the charges made against Jesus by the Sanhedrin in Mark's gospel.

In cleansing the temple Jesus reacted violently against the long-standing custom of selling sacrificial animals and exchanging foreign money in certain areas of the temple grounds. The action did not seem to be a spontaneous outburst of rage, but rather one that was carried out with great meaning and symbolism. Jesus confronted the Jewish elite who had made a profitable industry off the thousands of pilgrims who came to Jerusalem each year. The required animal and bird sales and the money exchanges were often occasions when many Jewish pilgrims were cheated. These swindles were a part of what Jesus described as the heavy burdens that Jewish leaders laid upon the people.

Jesus' action in the temple challenged the narrowness, corruption, and exclusivity of temple worship. It stood in the face of Jewish cooperation with the Romans, and the sharing of the bounties of the temple. It confronted the autocratic authority of the Sanhedrin over the Jewish people, and indicated that the corruption and hypocrisy of the leaders would bring devastation to the people. Since much of the gospel material was written after the destruction of Jerusalem, Jesus' prophetic words had enormous significance.

There were many reasons why people wanted Jesus out of the way. Animosity toward him had developed gradually. Matthew's story of Herod's attempt to kill the infant Jesus symbolically indicates that the shadow of the cross hung over Jesus' head throughout his life. In Mark's gospel, Jesus is portrayed as a prophet without honor in his own town of Nazareth. Early on in this gospel Jesus cures a man on the Sabbath. This enrages the Pharisees to the point where they meet with the Herodians to see how they might kill Jesus. Luke reports that Jesus' own townsfolk attempted to throw him off a cliff for his criticism of their lack of faith. The same gospel describes a debate between Jesus and the Scribes and Pharisees about healing on the Sabbath. His opponents become outraged and began to discuss what they might do to Jesus.

All this hatred and rage among Jesus' enemies festered and finally came to a head during that last fateful week of his life. His enthusiastic welcome into the city and his challenge to the corruption at the temple were the last straw for Jesus' enemies. They began to look for a weakness among his followers and found Judas to be the one who was willing to provide them with the opportunity to snatch him at prayer and lead him off to his death.

Who Was Responsible for Jesus' Death?

There has been much debate over what people should be held responsible for Jesus' death. Naming the Jewish people "Christ-killers" has spawned a great deal of unjustified anti-Semitism over the centuries. The so-called blood-curse has been wrongly thought to have commenced when the people shouted to Pilate: "His blood be upon us and upon our children" (Mt 27:25). This "curse" has been used to justify abuse and persecution of Jews through the centuries, culminating in the horrendous Holocaust during World War II.

Anti-Semitism cannot be justified by the gospels. The statement, "His blood be upon us," is a traditional Jewish acceptance of responsibility by certain people at a particular time. This phrase does not carry the intention of extending a curse to future generations.

It should also be pointed out that even the individual Jews who were responsible for Jesus' death are exonerated in the scriptures. Luke portrays Jesus as saying "Father, forgive them for they know not what they do" (Lk 23:34). In Acts, Peter points out that the Jews acted out of ignorance of who Jesus was (Acts 3:17). Paul also says that the Jewish leaders did not realize who Jesus was (Acts 13:27). The strong statements that are directed against the Jews in the gospels, especially in John's gospel, seem to reflect early Christian animosity toward those Jews who persecuted them, and not toward the Jews of Jesus' time.

Even though the gospels' negative opinion of the Pharisees came from a later time, Jesus did have enemies in this party. It is quite possible that some Pharisees, possibly scribal Pharisees tried to do away with Jesus and failed. In the account of Jesus' last days, especially in the synoptics, the blame for Jesus' death is aimed much more at the High Priests and Scribes than at the Pharisees.[20]

The Sadducees had more motivation to kill Jesus than did other groups. They were the wealthy elite who held control over the Sanhedrin and who were most challenged by Jesus. They were conservative, secular, often corrupt, and very much in collusion with the Roman occupiers. The Sadducees were not eager to allow some upstart preacher from Galilee to disrupt the people or challenge the status quo that enabled them to satisfy their expensive tastes. Most especially the priests and High Priests among the Sadducees resented Jesus and wanted him eliminated.

Some Jewish scholars have proposed that the crucifixion was solely the responsibility of the Romans.[21] They also maintain that the implications regarding the guilt of the Jews were fabricated by Christians who had antipathy toward Jews and wanted to slander them. They believe that it was the Romans who viewed Jesus as a dangerous man, even as a revolutionary, and who wanted him to die.

There are a number of reasons why this argument is not convincing. First of all, there is no evidence that Jesus or his followers advocated violent rebellion. At his own arrest Jesus dissuaded his followers from resistance. If Jesus had been perceived by the Romans as a dangerous seditionist, moreover, his followers also would have been arrested and killed.

When assessing blame and responsibility for the death of Jesus, it is vital to remember that both the Jewish and Roman leadership were in collusion in those times. Herod was a puppet leader, appointed and controlled by Rome. The High Priests who led the Sanhedrin were Roman appointees. Given all this complicity, it seems reasonable that both sides had their reasons and that both groups connived to do away with Jesus.

As for who had the authority to execute, in some instances the Jews could execute. Crucifixion, however, fell under the authority of the Romans.[22] Although the truth cannot be known with certainty, it is possible that all of Jesus' enemies, Jewish and Roman, worked out the plan for his demise.

The Agony of Crucifixion

Death by crucifixion was considered to be the most horrible way to execute a person in the ancient world. It was so brutal that there is little mention of crucifixion among ancient pagan authors, even though its use was widespread. The most detailed account of a crucifixion occurs in the gospels, and even here it is not explained in all its gory details. These accounts have been verified by excavations of ancient cemeteries which produced skeletal remains of crucified people.

Crucifixion was once a widespread means of execution. The Hebrews used this form of capital punishment in some of the older kingdoms when dealing with traitors or sorcerers. The Mishna mentions the crucifixion of 800 Pharisees in the Hasmonean Kingdom. The Jews stopped this form of execution once it became associated with the brutality of the Roman occupying forces.

The Romans used crucifixion frequently, especially in the punishment of rebellious slaves, dangerous criminals, and those involved in insurrection against the State. In the famous rebellion of Spartacus, 7000 rebels were hung on crosses alongside the road as far as one could see. Roman leaders believed that the sight of men writhing in agony and being picked apart by birds of prey and by wild animals would be an effective deterrent against further rebellion.

One indication of the horror of this form of capital punishment is that Rome would not sentence any of its own citizens to crucifixion, no matter how serious the crime. That seems to be the reason why the apostle Paul, a Roman citizen, was beheaded in Rome and not subjected to crucifixion, as was the apostle Peter.

Crucifixion was a long process whereby the victim would be humiliated, tortured, and then allowed slowly to suffocate.[23] It was done in full view of the public to allow them to vent their hatred and express their desire for vengeance. Crucifixion appealed to blood lust and other primal feelings. It also was designed to arouse fear in those who might be thinking of rebelling against the Empire.

Jesus' crucifixion has been so idealized and given so much theological interpretation that the horrors he endured are often overlooked. He first faced brutal beatings at the hands of soldiers known for their cruelty. Scourging was an integral part of this process. The victim was flogged senseless in order to insure that he would make no effort to escape or to resist the execution. For the scourging the prisoner was stripped of all his clothing, and his hands were stretched out and bound to the top of a post that was upright in the ground. This position exposed the back, buttocks, and legs for the whipping. The whip consisted of tongs of braided leather that contained small iron balls and sharp pieces of animal bone. Two muscular soldiers stood just behind the victim, one on the left, the other on the right. Then with a building rhythm of alternating blows, the soldiers tore at the victim with their whips. As the beating progressed, the iron balls made deep contusions, and the leather tongs and bone fragments cut deep into the skin. Eventually the blows tore through the flesh into the muscles causing tremendous pain, loss of blood, and usually shock.

The scourging left the victim in a severely weakened condition. At this point, he was cut down and forced to stand while a hundred pound crossbeam was placed on his shoulders. The arduous march to the place of crucifixion then began. This march was part of the public humiliation, and gave the crowd further opportunity to show their derision toward the victim. Along the way the victim was poked and prodded by the soldiers. One soldier carried a sign, bearing the prisoner's name and his crime. This sign was later be affixed to the cross for all to see. John's gospel tells us that Jesus' sign read: "Jesus of Nazareth, King of the Jews."

Once at the place of execution, the crossbeam was placed on the ground and the prisoner was thrown down on it. He was then nailed to this beam through the forearms with six-inch spikes. Four soldiers then lifted up the crossbeam to which the victim had been nailed, and affixed it to an upright beam that was permanently in the ground. The victim's feet were then nailed to the upright beam. Study of the bones of crucified victims reveals that the one foot was placed over the other and then a large nail was driven down through the heel bones. In order to prolong the suffering, a crude seat was provided for the victim on the upright beam, so that he could rest between gasps of breath.

Generally the crucified person died of slow asphyxiation. The hanging position so constricted breathing that the victim had to rise up and strain for each breath. In the process of raising up, the victim experienced excruciating pain from the severed nerves in the hands and feet. Eventually he became so weakened that he could no longer rise up to get air. The end came when the victim collapsed from exhaustion and died. Before being taken down, his legs were usually broken to insure that he could rise no more for breath. At times a spear was pushed through the heart to guarantee death.

The crucifixion of Jesus left many of his disciples confused, afraid, and even hopeless. How could their leader have come to such a humiliating death? Only after they began to experience Jesus as raised from the dead did they began to understand. It took some time before they gave meaning to such a horrible event. The next section of this chapter will discuss the disciples' experience of Jesus' resurrection. Chapter six will review the meaning that was later attached to Jesus' death on the cross.

The Mystery of Jesus' Resurrection

The gospels tell how some of Jesus' disciples anointed his mangled body, put it in a tomb, and then closed the tomb and withdrew. If that had been the end of the story, Christianity would not exist and there would be no need to explore the teachings of Catholicism. What made the difference was that Jesus' disciples soon began to experience him as "raised from the dead" just a few days after the burial. These experiences of the risen and glorified Lord began the movement now called Christianity. Resurrection faith in Jesus as the Christ burst forth in Jerusalem, spread first to Antioch and then gradually throughout the Empire.

The resurrection of Jesus as the Christ is at the heart of the Christian tradition. Paul told the Corinthians that their faith was in vain if Jesus Christ had not been raised from the dead. Yet, ironically, this mystery has been often neglected. The great ecumenical councils of Nicea (325 C.E.) and Chalcedon (451 C.E.) were so focused on the incarnation that they had little to say about the crucifixion or resurrection. Even in modern times there has often been so much emphasis placed on the cross that the importance of the resurrection has been obscured.[24] Only since the middle of the twentieth century has the resurrection been restored to its proper significance and reintegrated with other mysteries of Christ's life.

Resurrection from the dead was not unfamiliar to the Jews of Jesus' time.[25] The Hebrew Scriptures refer to Elijah being whisked into heaven (see 2 Kgs 2:11), and there are other references to life forever in the Books of Daniel, Wisdom, and Maccabees from our Hebrew scriptures. Still, belief in life after death only gradually developed among the Jews. During Jesus' time it was not accepted by the Sadducees. Even those who believed in the resurrection of the body expected it to take place at the endtime, after the Great Judgment. The immediate appearance of Jesus after his death, therefore, was unexpected and without precedent.

Early Christian Resurrection Statements

The earliest Christian witness of resurrection appears in brief teachings and liturgical formulas. (The appearance stories developed later.) Paul's brief statement to the Corinthians typifies such early testimony. Paul writes: "For indeed he was crucified out of weakness, but he lives by the power of God" (2 Cor 13:4).

The classic and perhaps most foundational statement can be found in Paul's First Letter to the Corinthians. This passage was written about 15 years after Jesus' death, and its source goes back about 10 years earlier. It speaks of Jesus being raised from the dead and then appearing to Peter, to the Twelve, to 500 people at once, to James, to all the Apostles, and then to Paul himself (see 1 Cor 15:1–11).

In what might be an even earlier tradition, Paul tells the Thessalonians that Jesus was raised from the dead and delivered people from bondage to sin. Here and elsewhere Paul proclaims the resurrection as an act of God that vindicated and glorified Jesus Christ. Paul mentions the appearances, but makes no effort to narrate them the way the gospels do. Neither does Paul attempt to describe the resurrection itself or mention the empty tomb.[26]

The Resurrection Event

The appearance stories are difficult to categorize. They are efforts to describe the indescribable: faith experiences of the risen Jesus. Mark's gospel makes no effort to give narration to these experiences, and the stories in the other three gospels differ in many details.

Matthew's account of the resurrection scene occurs at dawn on the first day of the week when two women come to anoint the body. They experience an earthquake and then encounter an angel outside the tomb who tells them that Jesus is raised and that they are to tell the disciples that Jesus is going to Galilee. On the way, they meet Jesus, grasp his feet, and worship him. Subsequently, the Eleven meet Jesus on a mountain in Galilee.

Luke speaks of three women who bring oils to the tomb and find it empty. Two men in the tomb tell them that Jesus is raised. On hearing this the women tell the disciples, but the women are not believed. Peter runs to the tomb to see for himself, and he arrives to find only the burial cloths. Peter returns home amazed. Later the risen Lord appears to Peter, accompanies two disciples on the road to Emmaus, and then appears at a meal his disciples are sharing in Jerusalem.

John's narrative is typically unique. The story opens in the darkness, before first light. Mary Magdala and possibly one other woman find the tomb empty. Thinking the body had been stolen they go to tell Peter and another disciple. The two disciples run to the tomb, find it empty, and return home. Later Mary Magdala looks into the tomb, sees two angels sitting there, and tells them that she thinks someone has moved the body of her Lord. Jesus then appears to her, and she recognizes him when he calls her by name. She attempts to embrace him, but is told by Jesus not to hold on to him since he has not yet ascended. Jesus later appears to the disciples (except Thomas) at a meal, then to the disciples with Thomas, and finally to seven disciples at the Sea of Tiberias.[27]

What Really Happened?

The discrepancies in these appearance stories indicate that this is not so much actual history as literary narratives pointing to another set of experiences. Obviously, none of the gospels attempts to describe the resurrection itself. In these appearance stories, however, there seems to be an effort to express the mysterious faith experiences that the disciples had of the risen Lord.

Naturally there have been hostile explanations of the appearance stories. The enemies of the early Christians spread the rumor that Jesus' followers stole his body from the tomb and then concocted the idea of his resurrection. Matthew's story of the posting of the guard might well be an early Christian apologetic against such slanders.[28] Celsus, who wrote scurrilous attacks on Christians toward the end of the second century, maintained that these appearances could be explained by hallucinations or hysteria. He was answered effectively by Origen (d. 254), one of the most brilliant of the early Greek Fathers.

In modern times H.E.G. Paulus proposed that Jesus merely fainted on the cross, was actually put in the tomb alive, and when he awoke came forth as raised. Most scholars give little credence to such a theory. It is based on the unlikely assumption that the Romans were careless in the execution, and that the disciples could mistake a beaten and half dead man as their glorious messiah.

Somewhat more widely accepted and certainly less bizarre is the theory that the resurrection experiences were solely subjective. Bultmann and many of his followers believe that the resurrection was a faith event with the disciples, but that nothing necessarily happened to the dead Jesus. From this perspective the appearance stories are simply myths that affirm the faith of early Christians in salvation through Jesus Christ. These myths signify that a new understanding of Jesus' message was grasped after his death, and that perhaps a unique conversion went on among the early Christians. Such conclusions are rejected by Catholics and also by many Protestants, who believe that Jesus was truly raised from the dead and is now present in the sacraments, scripture, people, and in the world itself.

A Subjective and Objective Event

There are a number of arguments for the position that the resurrection brought about both an objective transformation in Jesus as well as a subjective change in the disciples. A radical change took place in the disciples after the resurrection. They were transformed from a group of frightened and demoralized women and men to a faith community of disciples who were willing to risk everything, even life itself, to witness to the risen Lord.

Consider the change that took place in Paul. He was converted from a Pharisee who sought to destroy Christians to an apostle who underwent extraordinary suffering and eventually death to spread the gospel. Moreover, the witness of the early disciples was accepted by an ever-widening group of people who were diverse in their religions and cultures. This hardly could all come about simply because the disciples had an inner conversion.[29]

Other factors lead to the conclusion that the resurrection was more than a subjective experience of the disciples. Christianity spread rapidly throughout the Empire, and then grew into one of the strongest religious movements in history. Could such growth and development over two millennia be the result of a mere subjective conversion on the part of a handful of Jews? Could such a phenomenon as Christianity owe its origin to a mere subjective awakening? Is it likely that the foundational Christian belief in the afterlife is simply the result of the disciples gaining new insights into the death of Jesus?

Perhaps the strongest argument for the objectivity of the resurrection is that the gospel writers seem to be stressing that very point over and over again in the appearance stories. The appearance stories point to mysterious aspects of the disciples' encounters with Jesus, but there is no doubt that Jesus was real and once again alive.

The Post-Resurrection Encounters

The original experience of Jesus as raised from the dead was in a unique category all its own. It was an experience known exclusively by the faithful followers of Jesus as a profound personal and communal experience of Jesus, now transformed into a new mode of existence. The disciples met Jesus as the Christ, a person no longer subject to time, space, suffering, or death. They could now see him as the savior, the messiah, and the Son of God. With their new resurrection faith, they could look at their memories of Jesus' life and teachings, and see them in an entirely new light.

The encounter with the risen Lord was very different from those that the disciples had before Jesus' death. This was not a case of Jesus being "back in town." The meetings with him were indeed real, perhaps the deepest experiences of the real that they had ever had, but nonetheless on a different plane of reality.

The post-resurrection experiences of the risen Lord were not the kind of experience to which the general public had access. The Sanhedrin could not bring Jesus to trial again; Pilate could no longer sentence him; he would never again be subject to the brutality of the Roman soldiers. Jesus no longer walked along the dusty roads of Galilee, taught in the temple courtyards, or sat at table chatting with his friends over a glass of wine. Those days were over. As vivid as the experiences of the risen Lord were to the disciples, they could produce no visible proof that Jesus was once again alive.

Deidre, who is majoring in African-American Studies, made some insightful observations in class discussion about the resurrection appearances. She said:

The idea of Jesus not being "back-in-town" makes sense to me. I always had the understanding that Jesus sat up in the tomb and just walked out like he was. If that was the case then everyone would have seen him and there could be no challenging the resurrection. He could have been arrested again, and would have to die again. Now I see that the risen Christ was completely transformed, and could only be seen by the eyes of faith. Isn't that how we see him today?

Additional Post-Resurrection Appearances

The appearance stories witness both to marvelous experiences of the risen Lord and to the distinctiveness of such encounters. On one level the appearance stories confirm that this raised person was really Jesus of Nazareth. Jesus comes among them with the same peace, forgiveness, and compassion that was characteristic of Jesus of Nazareth. There is a definite element of recognition in the stories that point to the fact that this is Jesus.

In John's gospel,[30] Mary Magdala eventually recognizes him in the garden and embraces him. The disciples see Jesus and talk with him, and Thomas is invited to touch Jesus' wounds. The women in Matthew's account grasp his feet and worship him. The Eleven see Jesus on a mountain in Galilee, and they worship him in spite of the doubts that still seem to plague them. In Luke's account, Jesus comes to the disciples insisting that he is not a ghost, but is truly "flesh and bones." He shows them his hands and his feet, and then sits down for a fish dinner with them.

The gospel stories make it clear that these experiences go beyond a reappearance of some prophet or the dream-like sightings of pagan literature. This was no ethereal phantom as the Gnostic Christians would maintain. This was Jesus, the man from Galilee, who had been crucified, and yet was able to come before his disciples as the risen and glorified Christ.

Jesus Appeared Changed

Although the gospels stress that the disciples were indeed experiencing Jesus, they also show that the risen Lord was in a glorified state of existence. There is a degree of non-recognition in many of the appearance stories. Mary Magdala at first thinks Jesus is the gardener. The disciples on the road to Emmaus spend an afternoon with Jesus and even have a meal with him before they finally come to recognize him. In another appearance story the disciples think that they are seeing a ghost. This indicates that Jesus in obviously in some other "zone" of existence.[31]

Jesus' new form of existence is also brought out by showing that he is no longer limited to time or space. Jesus appears in a locked room and then just as abruptly disappears. He is with his disciples and then suddenly disappears into the heavens. (The ascension story may be a way of indicating that the resurrection experiences came to an end.) Only Paul seems to have a post-ascension experience of the risen Lord, and he uses this to lay claim to an authentic apostolic mission.

The letters of Paul underline the reality of the risen Lord somewhat differently than do the gospels. Paul is not so physical in his description, and points out that Christ's risen body is not flesh and blood. In his accounts, the risen Lord lives a spiritual existence and has a spiritual body (see 1 Cor 15:42–43). Paul teaches that in the resurrection all of creation has been somehow transformed. The resurrection reveals a "new creation" whereby the entire world has been radically changed.

Paul also sees Jesus taking on a cosmic dimension in resurrection. Jesus now exists in the world with a unique presence, and is a force driving creation to its fulfillment in God. Teilhard de Chardin, a controversial Jesuit theologian and paleontologist, developed this theology in our modern scientific era, and spoke of union with the cosmic Christ as the goal of the cosmos.

Experiencing the Resurrected Savior

The appearance stories speak of "seeing" and "hearing." Scholars debate whether or not this is a sensible seeing, or the experience of new insight. Thomas Aquinas seemed to interpret this in the latter way, for he spoke of the disciples seeing Jesus "with the eyes of faith." A contemporary theologian, Walter Kasper, indicates that the disciples experienced Jesus with a "believing seeing," rather than with physical sight.[32]

The insight gained in the resurrection appearances helped the disciples connect the risen Lord with the Jesus they had experienced on earth. As Edward Schillebeeckx observed, the resurrection made it clear to the disciples both who Jesus was all along, and the person he had now become. The life, death, and resurrection came together for them in a new revelation. The resurrection shed a new light of faith on the meaning of the life and teachings of Jesus of Nazareth.[33] They had perceived God acting in Jesus before; now they could see that there was such a close identification between Jesus and Abba that they could indeed worship Jesus as their Lord and God.

The Resurrection Continues

Christians today might wonder how the resurrection encounters of the past relate to their own experiences of the risen Lord in the Word, sacraments, people, and world about them. While contemporary experiences of the presence of God are similar in many ways to the disciples' experiences of the risen Lord, they do not seem to be identical.

The fact that the original resurrection experiences brought Christian faith and the church into existence indicate that there must have been a distinctive intensity in the first encounters with the risen Lord. It was such a profound encounter that it transformed a motley group of confused disciples into a fearless community of missionaries. This unique and unrepeatable encounter commissioned hand-picked disciples to start a new movement of faith. Encounters with Jesus Christ today are most certainly experiences with the same risen Christ. Although there seems to be a difference in purpose and intensity, both kinds of experiences are at the very heart of the Christian tradition.

Conclusion

Now that this chapter has examined the gospel stories about the mysteries of Christ, it is easier to see the blend of fact and faith in the scriptures. In the case of the birth stories, little seems to have been known about the historical facts of Jesus' birth. The event of his birth becomes surrounded with Hebrew prophecy and imagery, as well as with early Christian myth and symbol. The nativity stories proclaim resurrection faith in the Christ, as he is experienced in the early communities.

The passion and death of Christ, on the other hand, was a public event witnessed by many people. There are many more historical details available. From the historical event of the crucifixion, the early disciples developed dramas that portrayed their struggle to find meaning and purpose in the execution of the Master.

The resurrection of Jesus is in still another category. The risen Lord's appearances to the faithful were unique and without precedent. They were beyond description, and yet these experiences of the risen Lord were defining events that initiated the Christian movement. The disciples shared these experiences as best they could to capture the profound mystery that characterized these "meetings" with the risen Lord.

All the gospel stories related to the mysteries of Jesus Christ are multi-leveled. There are, on the deepest and most treasured levels, memories of Jesus of Nazareth. On another level, the early disciples told these stories to proclaim their experience of and belief in the risen Lord. Taken together these stories are foundational for the Christian tradition and stand as crucial elements to the witness of the Christian faith today.

Discussion Questions

1. Read the Christmas stories of Matthew and Luke. Compare and contrast the two stories.

2. List some of the symbols used in these two stories (e.g. star, manger). What meanings do you think these symbols carried for the early Christians? What might they mean today?

3. Read the Passion "play" in Mark's gospel and the one in John's gospel. Compare and contrast the portraits of Jesus in these two dramatizations.

4. Read carefully Luke's account of the Passion. What characteristics of Jesus stand out in this account? Cite specific passages to demonstrate your position.

5. Why is the resurrection of Jesus Christ so important for Christians?

6. The appearance stories show us the risen Jesus was similar to the way he was before, and yet also different. Cite specific appearance stories that deal with these contrasts.

Suggested Readings

Raymond E. Brown, *An Introduction to New Testament Theology.* New York: Paulist Press, 1994.

Raymond E. Brown, *The Birth of the Messiah.* rev. ed., New York: Doubleday, 1994.

Raymond E. Brown, *The Death of the Messiah.* New York: Doubleday, 1994, 2 vols.

Reginald H. Fuller, *The Formation of the Resurrection Narratives.* Philadelphia: Fortress Press, 1980.

Richard Horsley, *The Liberation of Christmas.* New York: Crossroad, 1989.

Gerald O'Collins, *Jesus Risen.* Mahwah, NJ: Paulist Press, 1987.

Pheme Perkins, *Resurrection: New Testament Witness and Contemporary Reflection.* New York: Doubleday, 1984.

Donald Senior, *The Passion of Jesus in the Gospel of Mark.* Wilmington, DE: Michael Glazier, 1979.

6.

Jesus the Christ

Framing the Question

My name is Kevin. I am a senior and I'm ready to get going with my life in May. School is getting a bit old for me at this point, and I want to get out into the real world. I am eager to begin working in my father's real estate business and to start building a life. Where religion will fit into all this is still an open question for me.

I consider myself a Catholic—sort of. I went to a Catholic grammar school and a Catholic high school. I learned all about many doctrines, but I still have to sort all this out for myself. Right now, I feel fairly comfortable believing in Jesus, but accepting the present state of the church is another matter. I find myself disagreeing with the church on many issues, so I don't know whether or not I will ever feel that I really belong.

As for Jesus, I can relate to him as a unique guy from Nazareth who lived 2000 years ago. I really believe that he existed and that he was a great man. Where I have trouble, is relating to all the doctrines and titles that have been attached to him over the years. How can a carpenter be divine? And if Jesus was divine, could he really have led a human life? I know Jesus is called our savior, but I really can't relate to that. I don't feel the need to be saved at this point in my life. Finally, I'm not sure what relevance Jesus has for today. The world is in such a mess with all the poverty, homelessness, violence, and destruction of the environment. I'm just not sure where Jesus fits into all this.

Kevin's concerns are shared by many Christians (both Catholics and Protestants) who see Jesus as someone who lived long ago, but who do not connect this Jesus with the contemporary world and its problems. For Kevin and many other people, Jesus is merely a historical figure, not a dynamic presence in the world today. This chapter will consider how the understanding of Jesus the Christ has developed over the centuries. We will look at some of the first controversies and see how the early councils of the church dealt with these issues. We will also probe the various interpretations that the Christian tradition has given to Jesus as savior. Finally this chapter will look at the contemporary trend of viewing Jesus as the liberator of people and of the earth.

Jesus Christ—Human and Divine

The early controversies about Jesus often focused on how he could be both human and divine. The gospels themselves often seem to emphasize one of these dimensions over the other, probably in answer to those who raised questions about the nature of Jesus. The gospels certainly portray Jesus as truly human. There are memories of him having to learn; times when he admitted not knowing; occasions where he was surprised at the faith of others. He enjoyed dining with friends, found peace in getting up early to pray, and welcomed little children who gathered around him. Jesus cried when a friend died. He was angry with the hypocrisy of some religious leaders, fearful in the garden before his arrest, and felt abandoned on the cross. The excruciating suffering and the horrible death that he endured showed beyond any doubt that he was indeed human.

While the memories of Jesus' life convinced the disciples that Jesus was human, his being raised from the dead and glorified indicated to them that he was divine. The New Testament demonstrates that the early communities openly proclaimed that Jesus was the Christ, the anointed one of God. (While some people assume that "Christ" was Jesus' last name, it was not. "Christ" is a term that means "the anointed one of God.")

In the minds of the disciples, Jesus was the Son of God, and thus worthy of their worship. The Gospel of Mark, the earliest of the four gospels, opens with the story of Jesus' baptism and proclaims the pristine Christian faith in the words from heaven: "You are my beloved Son; with you I am well pleased" (Mk 1:11). In Matthew's passion story the centurion is portrayed as saying: "Truly, this was the Son of God" (Mt 27:54). Luke celebrates the nativity of Jesus by having the Angel Gabriel announce to Mary: "He will be great and he will be called the Son of the Most High" (Lk 1:32). In John's gospel the proclamation of Jesus' divinity comes to a climax. In the prologue Jesus is acclaimed as having "the glory as of the Father's only Son" (Jn 1:14). In the appearance story, doubting Thomas eventually accepts Jesus as "My Lord and my God" (Jn 20:28).

The Letters of Paul also reflect the early Christian belief that Jesus was God's Son. Paul reminds the Colossians that Jesus "is the image of the invisible God, the first born of all creation" (Col 1:15). Similarly he writes to the Galatians that "God sent the spirit of his Son into our hearts, crying out, 'Abba, Father!'" (Gal 4:6).[1] This same conviction that Jesus is divine also comes through clearly in many of the writing of the Early Church Fathers (important Christian thinkers and writers) of the first and second centuries. Even the Romans seem to be aware that the Christians held Jesus in such esteem. Pliny the Younger writes about how these "Christians" gathered before sunrise to sing "a hymn to Christ as though to a god."[2]

These early sources demonstrate the people's faith in both the humanity and divinity of Jesus. It was a belief to be proclaimed far and wide. Little consideration was given as to how this could be possible. Such explanations began only later as early Christian "apologists" (theologians who defended the faith) attempted to thwart various heresies regarding the humanity and divinity of Jesus.

Early Controversies

Some of the earliest challenges to the divinity of Jesus arose as Jewish Christians struggled to follow their new beliefs while remaining faithful to the Hebrew traditions. This was exemplified in the position of the Ebionites—Jews who accepted Jesus but did not put him on a plane with their God. For them, Jesus was the elect of God and a true prophet, but not the pre-existing Son of God. They held that the Son of God was created as an archangel, and in time descended upon Jesus the man. They saw Jesus as a man with special powers who had a unique mission and who served as a good example for others.

Many Christians who had been raised as Jews struggled to be faithful to monotheism while believing in Jesus. Those Christians who had come from Hellenistic backgrounds tried to keep their faith in the absoluteness and unchangeableness of God, and at the same time believe in Jesus. These conflicts were apparent in early heresies such as Monarchianism and Adoptionism. The former stressed the "monarchy" of God and denied any distinction between the Father and the Son. As a result, the individuality and humanity of Jesus were given little consideration. The Adoptionists tried to preserve the oneness and unchangeableness of God by maintaining that Jesus was the adopted son of God and not truly the eternal, only-begotten, divine Son. Here the divinity of Jesus was denied.[3]

The Gnostic sect was one of the most significant and challenging movements in the early centuries of the church. It was a vast and diverse movement that existed both inside and outside the Christian communities. The Gnostics were dualistic in maintaining that God created and ruled the spiritual realm, but that the material world was the evil production of some errant spirit. The material world, including the flesh, led away from salvation. The body, therefore, was viewed as a repugnant prison that held the spirit from its true destiny. If that be true, it is obvious why the Gnostics would find the incarnation repugnant. Their God simply would not take on flesh.

For many of the Gnostics, Jesus came to save us from the flesh, not to become flesh. If Jesus came to free us from the prison of the body, why would he take on the same incarceration himself? Some Gnostics described the human Christ as a shadowy figure who accompanied the true Christ. The true Christ was exempt from birth, suffering, and death. For other Gnostics, the human Jesus was a mere phantom: The authentic Christ only seemed to have a body; only appeared to suffer and die. Flesh was an illusion, and the humanity of Jesus was likewise an illusion.[4]

Jesus, the Word of God

One of the early Christian apologists' first attempts to counter claims against the true and complete humanity and divinity of Jesus came with the notion of the "Logos." This term is found in both Jewish and Greek sources. For the Jews, the Logos was generally the "Word," the reality through which God was active in history. The Word was the creative agent in the Book of Genesis, the prophetic agent given to the prophets, and the source of Wisdom in the Jewish sacred literature. The Word was the means whereby God was operative in history, the mode through which God exercised divine power and presence.

The Greeks were more metaphysical in their notion of Logos. The Greek Logos is not so much a means of functioning as it was a principle of order and rationality. This principle of rationality was the link between God and rational creatures. This Greek notion goes back 500 years before the time of Jesus. The philosopher Heraclitus initiated this concept, and then it was developed in Platonism and Stoicism. Such thinking was often dualistic, and placed higher value on eternal essences than it did on the physical world.

The philosophical terms used to deal with early christological questions were often a blend of various versions of Greek Platonism and Hebrew thinking. For instance, the early Church Fathers used the notion of Logos to link the Son of God with the humanity of Christ. Greek and Hebrew thought melded as the man Jesus was seen as the incarnation of the divine principle of creativity, revelation, and reason.[5] Precisely how such melding occurred would be a matter of debate for centuries. The notion that the Logos is created constantly haunted the discussion, and remained the crux of the monumental struggle with Arianism.

While the understanding of the Logos was an effective way to link the divine and the human in Jesus, the Logos often seemed to fall short of being divine. This failing was evident in the writings of some of the great Church Fathers, although it was usually presented on such an abstract and Platonic level that it did not seem to be heretical. For Justin, an outstanding teacher in Rome in the mid-second century, the Logos was a derivative of God, but not the first and ultimate deity. Irenaeus (d. 200), the bishop of Lyon and a brilliant apologist, concluded that the Son was not quite equal to the Father. For Origen (d. 253), a remarkable teacher and scholar in the catechetical school at Alexandria, the Logos was indeed an image of God, but clearly not God.

Arianism

The teachings of Arius (d. 336) created a major christological upheaval. This tall, austere priest of Alexandria put the metaphysical language of the Logos aside, and baldly declared that Jesus was a creature. Arius was eclectic in his views, borrowing from earlier scholars. He had the charisma to give these views notoriety. Arius was also somewhat of a literalist, and accepted the account of creation as explained in the Book of Genesis. He reasoned that if God created all things in the world, then the Logos was part of creation. God was indivisible and unchangeable, and consequently, anything outside of God must be in the creature category.[6]

Arius made attempts to keep the Logos (and thereby Jesus) close to the divine. He viewed the Logos as a kind of demi-God, a superior creature, but a creature nonetheless. Jesus Christ, therefore, was a creature made to intercede between God and the world. Jesus was not the eternal Son of God, because, as Arius put it, "There was a time when he was not."

There were strong reactions to the views of Arius regarding Jesus. The bishop of Alexandria called a meeting of his priests, and they demanded that Arius recant. When he refused, all the bishops of Egypt and Libya gathered and voted to condemn and exile Arius. Arius fled to Palestine where he continued to make converts to his position.

The Emperor Intervenes

The Roman Emperor Constantine, a convert to Christianity, was determined to use his new religion as a means of unifying the Empire. The controversies over the understanding of the Logos made the emperor impatient and frustrated. He did not see the issues as being of much consequence, and was distressed that the dispute was causing riots in the streets of Alexandria and seriously dividing his people. Constantine made several futile efforts to settle the matter, and then finally decided that only a solemn church council could solve the problem. He convened what turned out to be one of the most significant councils of the church, the Council of Nicea.

Thinking of himself as representing the divinity on earth, the emperor hoped that he could guide the bishops in the same way that he influenced the Roman Senate, and thus resolve the Arian debate. About 250 bishops gathered in the city of Nicea, which today is the site of the insignificant village of Isnik in Turkey. This initial gathering of bishops demonstrated how far the church had spread and how extensive and varied its leadership had become. There was great enthusiasm as the emperor gave the opening address.

The main agenda item for the council was Arius' position on Jesus Christ. After much heated debate, Arius' view on the created nature of Jesus Christ was condemned, and the council formulated a creed that is still recited in many Christian churches. The Nicene Creed proclaims: "We believe in one God, the Father almighty, creator of all things both visible and invisible. And in one Lord Jesus Christ, the Son of God, the only-begotten born of the Father, that is, of the substance of the Father; God from God, light from light, true God from true God; begotten, not created, consubstantial with the Father, through him all things were made...." (This translation is a bit different from the one used during the liturgy in Catholic Churches, but the meaning remains the same.)

It is clear from this credal statement that the bishops believed that Jesus Christ was not created, and that he was of the same "substance" as God the Father. It is important to note that the bishops went beyond the scriptures and used Greek philosophy to settle the issue of Jesus' divinity. The Greek term for "same substance" *(homoousios)*, however, proved to be a slippery one and more controversy ensued. Still, a council had given a solemn definition with regard to the person and nature of Jesus Christ. In so doing, it established a high christology (i.e., one that started with the belief that Jesus was fully God) that led to a decided neglect of the humanity of Jesus for many centuries to come.[7]

Differences Between Antioch and Alexandria

The controversy over how Jesus could be both divine and human continued after the Council of Nicea. Two major schools of thought developed, each of which was centered in a large city: Antioch in Syria and Alexandria in Egypt. The two cities were divided in their understanding of the nature of Jesus Christ.

The Antiochenes stressed the full humanity of Jesus, and maintained that the Word (Logos) dwelt in Jesus as in a temple (the Word dwelt in a man). This indwelling was such that in no way did it diminish Jesus' humanity. These scholars were criticized for setting up a duality in Jesus, and even of coming close to losing touch with the true divinity of Jesus. Today this school of thought appeals to theologians who favor a low christology. From this perspective one starts with the life of Jesus of Nazareth rather than with a pre-existing Logos, and views Jesus' life as an ongoing opening to divinity.[8]

The Alexandrian school developed a high christology, and stressed the descending of the Logos in its understanding of incarnation. Here the accent was on the divinity of the Logos and Jesus. This approach emphasized the Word becoming flesh, and the oneness in union between Jesus and the Father, but tended to neglect the humanity of Jesus. Appolinarius represented the extreme position in the Alexandrian school. For him, Jesus was a kind of "heavenly man," who did not have a human soul.

The struggle between the schools of Antioch and Alexandria continued throughout the fourth and fifth centuries. Athanasius (d. 376) fought valiantly for the Alexandrian position, even after being banished by the emperor. The dispute reached a new climax in the confrontation between Cyril (d. 444), the Patriarch of Alexandria, and Nestorius (d. 451), the Patriarch of Constantinople. Nestorius maintained that the two natures in Jesus had to be kept absolutely distinct or else there would be a change in God because of the incarnation. Nestorius also concluded that Mary was the mother of Jesus, but not the Mother of God. Nestorius was condemned and exiled, but the dispute was not settled. A series of local councils followed, but they resolved little. When the tensions rose to the point of occasional violence, the emperor called for another council to settle the christological dispute once and for all.

The Council of Chalcedon

In October 451 the Council of Chalcedon opened with hundreds of bishops and dozens of nobles and papal legates in attendance. Amidst shouting matches and even an occasional fist fight, those in attendance eventually made some final definitions. Any view that taught a double sonship in Jesus, or the mixture of his human and divine natures, or that saw Jesus' humanity as a mere pretense was condemned. The bishops declared that Jesus Christ was the Son of God, and that he was "truly God and truly man." They stated that Jesus was of the same substance as God, as well as the same substance as man. It was defined that Jesus had two distinct natures, human and divine, both concurring in one person.

The Council of Chalcedon put to rest many of the heresies of that era. Its teachings stand forever as official Christian doctrine. Yet, there were many areas left unsettled: How could someone who was God suffer and die? How could divinity be united to humanity without the godhead undergoing some form of change? Was it really possible to apply a term like *"ousia,"* which means "stuff" or "substance" to both God and man? How can Jesus be understood as a human person?

Modern shifts away from ancient Greek philosophy, the contributions of biblical studies, and the modern psychological awareness of "person" have all led to new perspectives and new understandings of the issues that fueled these early christological controversies.[9] While the basic belief that Jesus is fully God and fully human is not questioned, Christians of every age struggle to explain adequately the essential understanding of this central mystery of the Christian faith.

Jesus Christ—Lord and Savior

After the resurrection the disciples revered Jesus as the anointed one of God, the savior. Empowered by the Spirit, they vigorously went forth to preach the message of Christ's salvation to others. The early disciples believed that God had truly saved them through Christ. They also believed that Jesus would come again soon to bring salvation to its fulfillment.

Since Jesus did not return swiftly, the Christian community has had centuries to ponder what it means for Jesus to be the savior and the Lord of the kingdom. The church has used many themes and images to convey this belief, but has never settled exclusively on any one of these explanations or formulated a single universal doctrine of salvation.[10] The Christian theology of salvation has been expressed differently in each period of time and each part of the world. This section will survey the development and different expressions of the basic belief in Christ as savior.

Scriptural Images

The notion of salvation appears in most of the world's major religions. The belief seems to arise from the experience of being safe under the protection of God, and of being rescued in times of danger or need. For the Hebrew people, the central event of their history and their belief system was the Exodus, the time when they were saved from slavery and oppression in Egypt. After this mighty deliverance the Hebrews viewed themselves as Yahweh's chosen people. They continued to see Yahweh as their rescuer despite their long history of exile and persecution. Their repeated liberations from slavery and captivity produced a strong tradition in Judaism that confronted oppressors and looked forward to a future time of complete salvation. These saving experiences also brought forth a tradition of prayerful confidence in God's saving power and thankfulness for God's protection.[11]

Jesus took this Hebrew tradition of salvation to a new and higher level. He restored the best of the tradition wherein salvation was viewed as a covenanted relationship with God. Then he taught people that God loved them unconditionally and was their Abba. Jesus preached that all people were to be included in the reign of this God; all were offered forgiveness for sin and eternal life in the kingdom of heaven. Jesus lived out this message in a life of love and self-sacrifice, surrendered himself in the ultimate sacrifice on the cross, and then was manifested as the savior through the resurrection.

Many salvation themes are woven through the gospels as the stories of Jesus' life are retold in the light of Christian faith. Jesus saves the sick from the despair of mental and physical suffering. He saves the disabled from isolation and abandonment, and rescues sinners from the degradations of evil. In each of these actions Jesus manifests God's saving power and its availability to all, especially the outcasts. Jesus is portrayed as the good shepherd, the new Moses, and the lamb of God sacrificed for his people. John's gospel proclaims this salvation clearly and universally: "For God did not send his Son into the world to condemn the world, but that the world might be saved through him" (Jn 3:17).[12] In the Pentecost scene in the Acts of the Apostles, Peter proclaims that Jesus has been made Lord and Messiah. Peter then invites his listeners to repent and be baptized in the name of Jesus so that they may save themselves "from this corrupt generation" (Acts 2:40).

The early Christians used many themes and images from their Jewish beliefs to convey this message. Redemption, justification, ransom, atonement, sacrifice, reconciliation, liberation, and other similar terms were used to indicate the many facets of salvation. Each theme relied on slightly different biblical texts and theological understandings to express this basic belief.

Redemption *Through* Christ

Arland Hultgren points to a number of ways in which Jesus Christ is described as redeemer in the New Testament. In Mark and in some of the epistles of Paul redemption is spoken of as "in Christ." Here God is at the center and accomplishes the divine plan of salvation by sending the Son. Jesus seems to be obeying a divine decree as he takes on the "curse" of human sin and obediently gives himself in the sacrifice of the cross. The cross and resurrection manifest the saving power of God, mark the end of an era of sin, and open a new age of oneness between God and the entire human family.[13]

The gospels of Matthew and Luke and the Acts of the Apostles often speak of redemption as being "through Christ." God is the initiator of salvation, but Jesus is the one who carries out the will of the Father. In this perspective there is more of an identification of their wills, and less emphasis on the role of Jesus' death in the redemptive process.

In Matthew's gospel redemption is brought about by an exalted and royal Christ who could avoid suffering and death, but who accepted them to fulfill the divine purpose. Although his blood is poured out involuntarily, Jesus freely gives up his own spirit at Calvary. As the risen Lord, Jesus Christ extends redemption to his followers, and commissions the disciples to spread the good news of salvation to all nations.

In Luke's gospel and in the Acts of the Apostles, Jesus is portrayed as the redeemer who brings people out of slavery and death to a new land that is safe and happy. This is done according to a plan whereby Jesus brings forgiveness to many during his life, and then must suffer, die, and rise to extend forgiveness to all. Luke does not use the ransom image, but instead sees redemption as an ongoing process. This process begins with God's design, is acted out in Jesus' ministry and death, and now offers forgiveness and the promise of final redemption to those who repent.

Redemption *By* Christ

Jesus is portrayed as a redeemer in his own right in the later Pauline letters (which seem to have been written by authors other than Paul), as well as in the Johannine tradition and the pastoral epistles (the New Testament letters of James, Peter, and Jude). Here Christ is pre-existent and, rather than being sent, comes by his own power. He comes as a vigorous redeemer who dynamically and deliberately sacrifices himself, and then draws all people to himself so that they may be redeemed. In this perspective Christ, himself, is the redeemer. He is the "image of the invisible God" (Col 1:15), the very agent of the process of creation who redeems not so much by deeds as by his very nature. This is the cosmic Christ who reigns at the right hand of God, and who is the very source of salvation and the promise of eternal victory in his final coming.

John's tradition incorporates the role of mediator into Christ's mission and speaks of redemption by Christ. Jesus comes from above with authority from the Father to give eternal life to those who accept him. The cross is not so much a sign of pain as a throne from which the divine Jesus reigns as he establishes his community and sends his followers to finish his mission. In this approach, the God who is love sends his Son, who lives and dies out of love for others.

Ransom

Most Christians are familiar with seeing redemption as a ransom or a buying back of salvation for all. This notion appears in the Gospel of Mark: "For the Son of Man did not come to be served but to serve and to give his life as a ransom for many" (Mk 10:45). Mark also weaves this theme into the liturgical formula of the Last Supper where Jesus' blood "is to be shed for many" (Mk 14:24).

Paul reflects what might be even an earlier version of this image when he writes to the Corinthians: "For you have been purchased at a price" (1 Cor 6:20). In the pastoral letters, the ransoming notion becomes part of a well-developed redemptive theology: "There is also one mediator between God and the human race, Christ Jesus, himself human, who gave himself as a ransom for all" (1 Tim 2:5–6).

The New Testament does not discuss who receives the ransom. This is left to some of the patristic writers who bring Satan into the transaction. Instead of God being the one who both gave and received the ransom, the devil becomes the one who holds humanity captive until the ransom is paid. This caricature of redemption prevailed for many centuries until Anselm of Canterbury put it to rest in the Middle Ages.[14]

Atonement

Ancient religions often used the notion of atonement to describe the process of purifying what was sinful so that it will be made pleasing to the gods. For the Hebrews, atonement meant being purified of that which separated them from God. It meant restoring the covenant with

God after their infidelity. They offered sacrifices to expiate their sins and to make them once again pleasing to God.

The purpose of the sacrifice was not to appease an angry God, but to stand as a symbol of radical change in the person. The transformation of the animal was an outward sign of the person's inner conversion, as well as an act of intercession to God for forgiveness and reunion.[15] The Jewish feast of Yom Kippur is the annual feast of this repentance and atonement. The English word "at-one-ment" clearly describes this notion of unity being restored.

The New Testament writers often turned to the Hebrew imagery of atonement when they wrote of Christ as the redeemer. Paul writes to the Romans about how justification occurs: "They are justified freely by his grace through the redemption in Christ Jesus, whom God set forth as expiation, through faith, by his blood" (Rom 3:24–25). The author of the Letter to the Hebrews uses temple imagery and describes Jesus as a faithful and merciful "high priest" who expiates the sins of the people (Heb 4:14—5:1–10). The Johannine tradition speaks of God sending his Son to be an expiation for sin (1 Jn 4:10).

This view of expiation or atonement does not mean, as is commonly thought, that Jesus dies to appease an angry God. Rather, a merciful and loving God both initiates and carries out this act of atonement. The sinful people could not bring about such forgiveness and reconciliation on their own. God both provides the gift of the Son and accepts the gift of loving self-sacrifice from the Son.[16]

The Cross as the Symbol of Atonement

One of the earliest theological challenges in the church involved the integration of the suffering of the cross with the joy of salvation. The first Christians had to deal with the brutal execution of their leader. Their enemies could ridicule them for believing that a lowly commoner who came to such a scandalous end could be recognized as the savior. The Gentile world found it impossible to think that the death of a lowly criminal could expiate sin. The Greeks and Romans recognized that someone could die for the common good and even make atonement to the gods, but such acts were done by noble heroes. The Jews had their tradition of the suffering servant in the Book of Isaiah chapter 53 and of the people who were martyred during the Maccabean period, but it was unthinkable that atonement could come from someone who was considered to be a sorcerer and a messianic pretender.

At first, the early disciples looked on the cross as the symbol of Israel's rejection of the messiah. Only gradually did the cross come to symbolize redemption. Paul reflected one of the earliest traditions when he wrote to the Corinthians that "Christ died for our sins" (1 Cor 15:3). John described Jesus as "the Lamb of God who takes away the sins of the world" (Jn 1:29). Yet, Jesus was not viewed as a passive victim. He faced death with resolve and chose to sacrifice himself throughout his life and in his death, rather than back down to threats. It was Jesus' teaching and deeds that brought about his death, and he faced this fate believing that his death would have a saving purpose.

After the resurrection Christians came to realize the meaning of the crucifixion. Martin Hengel offers a valuable insight into the way that the early atonement theology developed. As he explains it, the crucifixion event plunged many of Jesus' disciples into confusion and fear. They also felt guilty for abandoning Jesus in his hour of need. Their encounter with the risen Lord and his offer of peace and forgiveness brought them atonement. A veritable explosion of resurrection faith arose as the disciples came to understand that through his life, death, and rising Jesus has atoned for their sins and made them one with God. They then saw Jesus, in his person and mission, as the culmination of the Jewish tradition of atonement. He was the incarnation of the loving and forgiving Abba, not a sacrificial lamb sent to appease an angry God. In this context Jesus' death on the cross was seen as a supreme act of love, climaxing the total life of love Jesus had offered to God. The cross was viewed as the ultimate symbol of self-offering and self-sacrifice. Jesus was both the model for a life of self-giving and a source of strength for those who aspired to follow in his footsteps.[17]

Justification

The Hebrews were extremely concerned with being justified. The most authentic tradition held that this could only be brought about by God. Jesus accepted this position and confronted those who rejected this in favor of a legalistic approach that taught people that by following the laws they could self-righteously declare themselves justified. A hypocrisy had crept in whereby some people stringently followed the scribal laws and declared themselves justified in the eyes of God, and yet were not loving and caring. This also led to an attitude of condescension toward those less observant, and to outsiders and outcasts. Jesus had strong words against such hypocrisy and self-righteousness.

The early Christians saw Jesus Christ as the just one. Jesus' person and cause had been justified before God through the resurrection: Following him was seen as the means of being justified before God. All those who accepted Jesus, therefore, received the gift of justification before God. Paul told the Romans of this gift: "But now the righteousness of God has been manifested...through faith in Jesus Christ for all who believe" (Rom 3:21–23). For Paul, justification was a gift from God that was won by Jesus in the shedding of his blood for sin. Those who believed were "justified freely by his grace through redemption in Christ Jesus" (Rom 3:24). It was in Jesus Christ that God was revealed as just, and through faith in Jesus that the disciples appeared just before God.[18]

Patristic Views on Salvation

The Fathers of the Church were primarily concerned with questions about the nature of Jesus Christ. For them, the incarnation was the central saving event. Clement of Alexandria (d. 215) typified this approach when he wrote: "The Logos of God had become man so that you might learn from a man how a man may become God." He believed that salvation was brought about primarily by human nature being fully united to God in Christ.

Irenaeus' theory of recapitulation is another example of how the incarnation brought about salvation. For him, the plan for salvation unfolded in three acts: creation, the Fall, and the restoration of the world by Jesus Christ. The very purpose of creation was the sharing of divinity with the world and humanity. The Fall of Adam and Eve disrupted this plan. Hence God was moved by compassion to send the Son to be the new Adam, and to restore or recapitulate the union of God and humans. Christ assumed our human nature and thereby restored it to its original integrity. Salvation came to human nature by what Christ achieved in his life, death, and resurrection. Irenaeus echoed the New Testament when he taught that the saving plan of God was "to sum up all things in Christ, in heaven and on earth" (Eph 1:10). This was a more spiritual approach to salvation than the legalistic approach that developed in the Western Church.[19]

The Fathers of the early church also described salvation in terms of Christ's victory over Satan. They often used Jesus' struggles with Satan in the gospels as an example of how redemption was brought about. In the patristic allegory of ransom as it was used in the theology of salvation, Satan was understood to have gained proprietary rights over human beings after the Fall. Origen, a leading proponent of this view, pointed out that in the Fall humans sold themselves into slavery under Satan. As the drama unfolded, the devil wrongly tried to take possession of Christ, but failed because Christ was without sin. Christ paid the ransom of his blood to liberate humankind from enslavement and thus defeated the forces of evil in the world. This explanation of the theory of salvation was often interpreted, not as an allegory, but as a very real struggle between Christ and Satan. This view prevailed into the medieval period until it was replaced by the salvation theory of the great theologian Anselm of Canterbury.

The Satisfaction Theory

The view that Jesus Christ made satisfaction for our sins was developed by some of the early Fathers, but it did not gain popularity until the twelfth century with the work of Anselm of Canterbury. Anselm's theory of satisfaction, still influential today, is often misunderstood. It is wrongly thought that Anselm viewed the crucifixion as being necessary to satisfy an angry and vengeful God and to make up for the sin of Adam. Nothing could be more foreign to Anselm's dispassionate and highly reasonable English mentality. Anselm was concerned with love and honor, not with holding back the hand of a wrathful God.[20]

In his famous treatise, *Cur Deus Homo* (Why God Became Man), Anselm accepted the medieval view that the universe was designed by God to be orderly and reasonable. Humans were created with a level of reason that enabled them to enjoy the beauty of such order, and have the capacity of sustaining this order by obeying God's will. God, ruling in the manner of a feudal lord, maintained public order and was to be held in high honor.

Anselm pointed out that sin clouded the human capacity to observe the beautiful and orderly universe. Sin also offended the honor of the God who created and maintained such order. Such sin against an infinite God was infinitely wrong, and could not be satisfied or atoned for by mere finite human beings. Proper satisfaction, that is, the complete restoration of God's honor and the renewal of the harmony and beauty of the world, could only be achieved by the actions of an infinite person. Only the Son of God could perform such satisfaction, and he did so by freely and lovingly sacrificing himself for us. Christ is the savior, not because he appeased an angry God or because he substituted himself for sinners, but because he restored harmony to the world and honor to God. Anselm's theology of salvation, often referred to as the satisfaction theory, prevailed in Catholic thought well into the twentieth century.

Contemporary Understandings of Salvation

Some college students today have a difficult time relating to the idea of "being saved." Kim, a math major from St. Paul, explains this problem.

I guess the problem for me is not knowing why I need to be saved at all. Right now I am fortunate to have a good family and lots of friends. I am getting a fine education in math, which I love, and I hope to have a career teaching in a university someday. I am not a bad person, and I really don't feel the need to be saved. I am sure that there are lots of people in the world who are not as lucky as I am. Maybe salvation is for them, but I don't think it's for me.

Many students as well as older adults agree with Kim's views. They live in a time when many people are autonomous and self-sufficient, and really don't see a need to be saved from sin or alienation from God. Theories based on ransom or satisfaction often have little relevance to people today. At the same time, there are many constraints and dangers from which contemporary people would like to be saved. Some feel a sense of helplessness in the face of debt or unemployment. Others long to be rescued from the threats of violence, drugs, diseases like AIDS, or from the grip of hunger, homelessness, or environmental hazards. Many struggle to be freed from the oppression imposed upon them because they are homosexual, a minority, or disabled.

Today's world is generally not perceived to be populated with evil spirits or sinister powers and principalities. It is not seen so much as a battlefield where God wages war with the devil, as it is a world plagued with addictions and oppressive structures. For many today the world is not a fallen world looking to be restored to a modern-day paradise; it is rather a world filled with injustices. It is a world that calls out for solidarity among the peoples of the world as the means to restore harmony and justice.

From this perspective, redemption is not a case of a remote God sending a Son from above, but of a God coming from within each person to support and sustain suffering people. This redeeming God is "part of" and "along with" the people who need salvation. This is the redeeming God who was personified in Jesus of Nazareth; a saving God whose Spirit acts in the risen Christ to free people from their struggles against injustice. As Schillebeeckx puts it, salvation that is not connected to human experience loses its meaning and usefulness. Although salvation is a gift from a loving and merciful God, it happens in the events of human life when it is experienced in nature, social life, cultural life, and religion. Creation and salvation, everyday life and redemption become linked in a continuing process.[21]

Jesus Christ—The Liberator of the World

The image of Jesus as liberator has emerged from Latin America, a continent which has known severe poverty, oppression, and violence for centuries. Liberation theology is a theology "from below," a theology arising from the poor in countries where plunder, genocide, deprivation, and persecution have been rampant since the time of the Spanish Conquistadores.[22] It presents an image of Jesus that is rooted in the historical Jesus; in his passionate struggle for the outcast, his confrontation with those who abused the poor, and his willingness to die in order to save others. Liberation theologians speak of faith in a Christ who today stands in solidarity with those who struggle for freedom.

Those who propose such a liberating view of Jesus Christ are often critical of much of traditional Western christology. Liberation theologians point out that much of the theology developed in Europe has ignored the sorry plight of the poor, and has not been actively involved in practical action *(praxis)* for peace and justice. In contrast, liberation theology often begins in action for the poor, and then develops through further reflection on the gospel teachings against oppression.

The modern understanding of Jesus as liberator was precipitated by the Second Vatican Council. This council, as will be explained in chapter eight, moved the Catholic church away from a posture of isolation from the world to one of solidarity with today's poor and suffering. The post-Vatican II church planted its feet firmly in the modern world, and let it be known that it was in solidarity with the marginal and the oppressed. This commitment subsequently inspired the Latin American bishops who gathered at two historic meetings in Medellín, Colombia in 1968 and in Puebla, Mexico in 1979 to declare that their church was in solidarity with the poor of the world. A worldwide Synod held at the Vatican in 1971 also pointed out that a commitment to justice was constitutive of the life of faith.[23]

Liberation theology found its initial formulation in the now classic book by Gustavo Gutiérrez, *A Theology of Liberation*.[24] This was followed by an avalanche of writing about how the gospel of Jesus was linked with action for the poor. At first, these liberation theologies concentrated on critiquing traditional theology and on the urgency of reclaiming the gospel commitment to the poor. Gradually these theologians developed a positive christology that was consistent with the liberation perspective.

A New Search for the Historical Jesus

Liberation theology generally shifts the focus away from the classic "Logos" christology of the early councils to a concentration on the historical Jesus. Many liberation theologians hold that the Logos theology of Nicea and Chalcedon is too heavily stamped with ancient Greek philosophy to be relevant to today's problems. They argue that these classical views can be so preoccupied with the nature of Jesus that they neglect his mission. They propose a return to the memories of the historical Jesus, and a study of this flesh and blood person who struggled against injustice. Such memories are then linked to contemporary understandings of Christ who empowers people today to stand up for their rights and the rights of others.

The liberation perspective emphasizes the humanness of Jesus. Jesus' humanity is seen to be very real, and representative of a God who stands with all people struggling for justice. Jesus represents the incarnation of a personal God who is passionately involved in life; a God who enters into human suffering and reveals how people can be victorious over those who persecute them. This is a God who gives people the power to overcome the suffering and death that is so much a part of their lives. This Jesus is portrayed as one who is intensely involved in the human scheme of things, one who had to live like any other person amid ambiguity and even darkness. In his fidelity and unswerving commitment to people, Jesus revealed the possibilities that exist for humans. He offered a glimpse of what people can be when they are at their very best. He showed people that to be fully human is to be divine.[25]

This emphasis on the humanness of Jesus in no way denies his divinity. Rather, it sees divinity revealed in the history of a human life. Jesus comes into the fullness of divine sonship, and thus serves as a model for all who aspire to be one with God. Jesus' story becomes a human story, and serves as an inspiration for others who experience suffering, pain, and even death as a result of their opposition to tyranny.

A Theology for the Oppressed

Liberation theologians propose that one of the best ways to understand the historical Jesus as a liberator is to listen to the poor as they relate the gospels to their experience of oppression. Jesus is found in the voice of a peasant who tells of losing a loved one when the military massacred many people in his village. Jesus is met in the eyes of a mother whose son was kidnapped, tortured, and killed; his body left in an alley to warn the neighbors that they must not criticize the government.

Jesus is felt in the grip of a child whose mother was raped and tortured to gain information from her. This is a suffering Jesus, yet a courageous Jesus who is not afraid of death, and who is determined to go on with his mission no matter what. It is the steel-willed Jesus that many saw in Archbishop Romero, as this prelate stood up to the corruption of his government, knowing that his name was on a death list. It is the Jesus that many found in the bullet-riddled body of Fr. Rutilio Grande, and in the rising of this Jesuit's spirit among the people after his death.

At times individuals who have had personal experiences of oppression will share their experiences with classmates and friends. Ignacio is from El Salvador, and knows terror and cruelty first-hand. His father was arrested ten years ago for labor union activities. He was tortured to the point where he lost his mind and had to be put in an institution. Ignacio's mother belongs to a group of mothers and wives who work to stop terrorism and who seek to bring the military death squads and their civilian collaborators to justice. Ignacio spoke about growing up amid violence and seeing how it affected his family.

You would be amazed at the courage of my mother and the other women who gather in a dingy office everyday to gather evidence against terrorists. Many of the violent people whom they investigate worked as assassins for the government. During the war, the military made many attempts to terrorize these women, but the women were not scared off. They have no fear of death. They are gentle, forgiving women, but they are determined to bring permanent peace to my country. Every morning they start their work with a prayer to Jesus Christ. They believe that this gives them the strength and the courage to go on. I worry about my mother's safety. But I am proud of her.

Jesus and Politics—Then and Now

Since liberation theology is often concerned with political issues, the question arises as to whether Jesus was concerned about such matters. It seems apparent that Jesus was not politically militant in any direct way. The gospels give no indication that he engaged in disputes about the Roman occupation of his land, or that he engaged in any revolutionary activities. Even though Jesus was probably crucified for political crimes, there is no evidence that any of the charges made against him were true. His followers were not accused of being insurrectionists, and did not seem to get involved in the Jewish uprisings of the late 60s or the early second century.

Although Jesus did not engage in overt political activity, there is still a political dimension to his teachings and actions. Father Ignacio

Ellacuría, one of the Jesuits murdered in El Salvador for their efforts to bring about justice, once pointed out that "Jesus engaged in what was primarily religious activity; but it could not help but appear to be political to those who held religious and political power."[26]

It should be kept in mind that in Jesus' day the distinctions between the secular and the sacred, the religious and the political, were not as clear as they are in today's secular society. Many Jews longed for a theocratic form of government where religion and politics would be integrated. The Roman occupation of Palestine had political and religious implications for both Jews and Romans. Insurrection by Jewish rebels was viewed as a religio-political action, and was punished as such by Roman crucifixion. The blending of religion and politics in Jesus' day is also seen in the fact that the religious leaders in Jerusalem, the Sadducees, were appointed by the Romans, and were known to be collaborators with the Empire. In all this, religion and politics become so mingled that it is difficult to distinguish one from another.

Jesus was born and raised amidst a highly charged and oppressed atmosphere. Galilee was known for its rebellions. Displaced persons, migrant workers, and slaves were prevalent in Jesus' time, and he probably heard the murmurings of those who were burdened and at times terrorized by their Roman occupiers. It is logical to assume that Jesus himself resented the heavy taxation and domineering governance of the Roman authorities. It is quite unrealistic, therefore, to portray Jesus as a naive preacher, unaware of the oppression that went on around him.

The gospels reflect memories of Jesus as a conflictual person whose confrontations often had political implications. He is described as being in conflict with the people of his own synagogue, because he had identified himself with the prophetic tradition. His words must have been threatening indeed, if his own villagers were so provoked that they wanted to throw him off a cliff. On other occasions Jesus is portrayed as telling the crowds and his disciples not to follow the example of the Scribes and the Pharisees. He castigates these Jewish leaders for laying heavy burdens on people's shoulders. He calls these prestigious figures hypocrites, blind guides, and white-washed tombs—certainly inflammatory remarks toward the religious intelligentsia and the political leadership that had appointed them.

In Jesus' time, an attack on Jewish leadership was also taken to be an affront to the Romans, who wanted matters among the people they dominated to be uncontentious and calm. The passion narratives in the four gospels reveal that Jesus had built up tremendous animosity among the Sanhedrin, the Sadducees, and the high priests of the temple throughout his public life. Since many of these men were pawns of the Romans, Jesus' enemies were connected to each other through lines of power and pragmatic cooperation.

There are some passages in the gospels that underline Jesus' penchant for confrontation. He defiantly called Herod a fox, and he advised his followers to give Caesar nothing more than the coin of tribute. Jesus openly challenged the corruption at the temple, disrupted the marketing there, and predicted the ultimate destruction of the temple if such abuses continued. Jesus said that the hated Samaritan could be more compassionate and charitable than the priests and doctors of the law. He attacked the greed of the rich. He condemned the pompous self-righteousness of some religious leaders, and contrasted them with devout publicans and humble widows.

Jesus' message of inclusive love, forgiveness of one's enemies, and compassion for outcasts enraged those who advocated lives of secluded luxury, quick vengeance upon any adversary, and intimidation of the weak and defenseless. To call the poor blessed, and to set himself up as a model of meekness and humility rankled many of the corrupt pillars of his religion. Jesus' parables, teachings, miracles, and actions posed a definite threat to those who lived off the work and taxes of the poor. His teachings about a God of love and compassion were unacceptable to those who intimidated the masses by proclaiming a God of domination and destruction.

A Prophet of Liberation

Jesus never claimed to be an anarchist or a political revolutionary, yet his message about human dignity and the blessedness of the poor was considered dangerous by many. The freeing of Barabbas instead of Jesus stands as a symbol that Jesus' nonviolent confrontation was viewed by some as more threatening than the terrorism of a zealot. As Jesus stands before Pilate, the power of a kingdom "not of this world" overshadows the imperial power of Rome. Many were concerned that Jesus' message and ministry might set in motion an unprecedented religious and political upheaval. The quick spread of Christianity and its impact over the centuries show that their concerns were justified.[27]

Liberation theologians point to the prophetic dimension of Jesus' mission. In Luke, Jesus identifies with Isaiah in bringing good news to the poor, releasing captives, and freeing the oppressed (Lk 4:18–19). Similar to the prophets of old, Jesus lives austerely, holds no official position in the religious or political establishments, and does not belong to any of the parties of his time. In the tradition of Elijah, Jeremiah, and John the Baptizer, Jesus stands out as a charismatic figure who challenges corrupt leaders and institutions. Jesus attacks the conventional wisdom that riches were a blessing from God, and that poverty is a sign of divine retribution. He challenges those among the rich who live at the expense of others, and points out how wealth can result in self-destruction. Jesus declares the poor blessed before God, and explains that poverty is a result of oppression, not a punishment from God. In this way Jesus brings the prophetic tradition to a climax. With the finality appropriate for the last and greatest prophet, he proclaims the love and intimacy he has experienced from Abba, and offers the same to all people.[28]

The liberation perspective has moved many people in the Third World to believe that Jesus stands with them as they confront political corruption, oppression from the military, and injustice from the wealthy and powerful. They find courage and hope in the faith that Jesus is with them in their agonies, as well as in their resistance to such abuses.

A Preferential Option for the Poor

Jesus had a first-hand knowledge of what it was to be poor, having left the security of a craftsman's life to become a wandering preacher dependent on the offerings of others. His background as a Galilean put him in solidarity with the plight of the common folk. Jesus knew the frustration and anguish of tenant farmers who barely eked out a living and who stood in constant fear of reprisal if they fell behind in paying their taxes or mortgage. He witnessed the misery of many who had become displaced persons under the Roman regime. He knew of the suffering of the disabled and diseased who did not have adequate shelter, food, or health care.

In many places throughout the world the poor find parallels between Jesus' times and their own situations. Many of them live in dire poverty, and fear imprisonment or even death if they protest. They hold firm to the belief that Jesus has compassion on outcasts, and that his Spirit is with them in their trials. These modern-day outcasts are convinced that the risen Lord supports and strengthens them in their struggle for freedom.

Jesus' proclamation of the beatitude, "Blessed are the poor," still rings true deep within the hearts of the marginalized people of the world. They are well aware that there in nothing blessed about poverty itself, and yet they believe that Christ uniquely loves them and will be with them no matter what happens. This is one of the central beliefs of liberation theology: that the life of Jesus bears witness that God always has and always will be singularly present among the poor. As Dom Helder Camara of Brazil, a great bishop and supporter of the poor, has pointed out, the poor have a privileged position with God. God actually became one of them in Jesus, experienced their lot first-hand, and now dwells in their midst.[29] In Christ, God continues to struggle for justice with the poor; suffers with them, dies with them, and brings them to new life. In listening to the poor, one can often hear the voice of God and sense the power of the risen Lord.

Ministering With the Poor

Jesus chose many of his disciples from among the poor, and asked all his followers to be detached from material things. He asked the rich young man to divest himself of his riches and join in his mission (see Mk 10:17–22). A spirit of detachment enabled Jesus' earliest disciples to move about freely and spread the good news. A life of simplicity gave them the freedom to be critical of oppression, since they had nothing from which they could be deprived by the authorities. They had only their lives, and many stood willing to give up life itself for the cause of peace and justice.

Liberation theologians view simple living and identification with the poor as an essential aspect of following Jesus. Simplicity puts one in solidarity with the poor, helps one listen to the revelation that comes through them, and enables one to bear witness to their suffering to a larger world. Many believe that the church has always been stronger when the poor were at the center of its membership, and the prime object of its ministry. When the disciples became part of the establishment, they became comfortable, protective of their possessions, and disinterested in the plight of the have-nots. From a liberation perspective, that is a decided departure from authentic Christ-like discipleship.

Dedication to the Reign of God

Liberation theologians offer a profound and distinctive interpretation of Jesus' central teaching on the reign of God. They understand the reign of God to be the realization of a world free from pain, sin, violence, and death. In many ways, it is a world out of reach, and yet a world that can be glimpsed in the transformation of human hearts.

From the liberation perspective, the reign of God is sharply distinguished from social reform, revolution, and even from the church itself. Ultimately, the reign of God is a gift, the graced bestowal by Christ of freedom and justice on all God's children. The reign of God cannot be reduced to temporal progress, social contracts, or the overthrow of tyrannical governments. Any of these might help open people's hearts to the reign of God, but they are not to be identified with the kingdom.

God's reign, which is experienced through the presence of divine power and love, can be realized only in societies where there is equality and justice. Oppression, hatred, and violence are obstacles to the coming of this reign. God's work is done amid forgiveness, healing, and compassion. It calls for a purification of hearts, and for radical freedom on all levels of life—social, political, and religious. Jesus' mission of liberation is offered to the whole world, not simply to chosen followers. It is a mission to free all people from the evils that surround them, including those that are social and political. Homelessness, hunger, unjust salaries, and poor health care are viewed as situations where God's power needs to be focused. The divine presence and power that Christ brings is a creative, healing, serving power that promises a new creation both now and in the future.[30]

The Death of Jesus

Death is often more visible and more horrible among the poor of the world. It comes to an innocent child who is malnourished, to an elderly person without adequate health care, or to the victim of a soldier's bullet. Death can come from a nightime death squad or an afternoon bombing. Instantaneous, premature, undeserved death so often comes to refugees and the have-nots of the world. Many of these people have had to cling to the cross of Jesus to give meaning to their lives and their deaths.

Liberation theologians have learned much about the cross in listening to their people. They have discovered that God can be found in suffering and death. Christ is a fellow-sufferer, who has been there, and who walks in solidarity with victims.[31] Jesus' own death teaches that God does not will suffering or death, but instructs people not to fear death in their struggle for freedom. From this perspective, Jesus' death is not the result of a divine decree, but the action of those who could not accept his teachings. His death reveals a God who is with all people who die unjustly at the hands of tyrants. The presence of God's Spirit enables victims to die in peace and with forgiveness. Their death has meaning, for it gives hope and inspiration to other victims.

The Resurrection and Liberation

In liberation theology the resurrection often represents the vindication of Jesus' teachings and actions for peace and justice. When Jesus was raised from the dead, suffering and death were defeated, and his disciples got a glimpse of the new creation. The death of the innocent person in the struggle for freedom today is given ultimate meaning. The life given for others is glorified and exalted over the lives of those who inflict pain and suffering on others. The resurrection is seen as an eschatological event whereby the risen Lord reveals the final goal of all creation—ultimate freedom from suffering and death.[32]

Jesus, the risen liberator, becomes a source of hope to those who have lost loved ones in the struggle for justice, and who daily live with the threat of death. From early Christian times, the example of Jesus has enabled many of his followers to be free from the fear of death and have the courage to continue his liberating mission. The central Christian belief is that people will never die, and that the risen Lord will be present among his people in their quest for freedom. Archbishop Romero witnessed to this belief just before his own assassination. He pointed out that no matter what happened to him, he would rise up again in his people.

There is a song from El Salvador that captures this belief in the resurrection. As Christians sing their praises to God in church or in processions through the streets, a name is shouted out: Oscar, or Maria, or Tomas. These are the names of those who were killed in the cause of freedom. After each name is called, a resounding *"Presente!"* is sung to celebrate that the person is still present among the people through the mystery of risen life. Just as the resurrection glorified their Master, resurrection now validates their mission for justice.

A Costly Discipleship

Those called to follow Jesus the liberator accept a demanding and costly discipleship. They are called to detachment, confrontation, and vigorous but nonviolent action on behalf of others. Archbishop Romero spoke of such discipleship in his last homily, the day that he was gunned down offering the eucharist. He said:

> You have heard in Christ's gospel that one must not love oneself so much as to avoid getting involved in the risks of life that history demands of us. Those who try to fend off the danger will lose their lives, while those who, out of love for Christ, give themselves to the service of others will live. The grain of wheat dies,

> but only apparently. If it did not die, it would remain alone. The harvest comes about only because it dies, allowing itself to be sacrificed in the earth and destroyed. Only by undoing itself does it produce the harvest.[33]

Moments later a shot rang out from the back of the chapel, and the archbishop who had spoken for the oppressed bore witness to the truth of his own words.

A New Starting Point

The view of Jesus the liberator has given many Christians a new starting point. It places them firmly in the world in which they live, awakens them to the poverty and suffering around them, and gets them moving toward helping others. This perspective is enabling Christians all over the world to reclaim the authentic historical Jesus as the one who brings freedom and justice. Many Christians are realizing that the risen Lord is in their midst, giving the oppressed the courage to speak up, and inspiring the "haves" to assist the "have-nots."

This liberation perspective, grounded in the life of Jesus and founded on the gospels, has moved from Central and Latin America to Africa, Asia, Eastern Europe, the Americas, and many other areas throughout the world. Liberation theology has moved Christians to see the suffering in their world and to realize that they can do something to alleviate it. The perception of Jesus as liberator has moved many women toward gaining freedom within society and in their churches. It has awakened many to see that the earth itself is being oppressed, and it has moved them to struggle to save the planet from destruction. It is an image of Jesus that will continue in the future to move people to sacrifice themselves for the sake of justice.

Conclusion

After Jesus was raised from the dead a new level of faith appeared among his followers, whereby they proclaimed him to be the Son of God and their savior. As disputes arose about how Jesus Christ could be both fully human and fully divine, councils were called to define for all times that Jesus was indeed truly human and truly divine. The search still goes on, however, for adequate words, terms, and images to understand and explain such an incredible mystery.

Jesus' role as savior has been interpreted in a number of ways throughout the church's history, ranging from his ransoming us from the devil to his satisfying the Father with his death. Each age has had its own needs for salvation. Today people cry out to be saved from oppression, violence, and the destruction of their earth. For Christians, the risen Lord stands as one who can bring them hope and salvation from what threatens them physically and spiritually.

From those who suffer poverty and injustice in the developing countries of the world new insights about Jesus have arisen. A theology of liberation has developed "from below" to proclaim Jesus Christ as the liberator of the marginalized, and the Spirit that can help those struggling against violence and deprivation. This approach to Jesus is now spreading throughout the world, and will fuel more and more movements to free the oppressed of the world through the power of Jesus Christ.

Discussion Questions

1. What were some of the early challenges to the Christian belief that Jesus Christ was both human and divine?

2. What was Arius' position with regard the divinity of Jesus Christ? Why was this position condemned? How did the Council of Nicea answer the Arian heresy?

3. Discuss Chalcedon's formulation with regard the true divinity and true humanity of Jesus Christ. In what sense is this not a finished answer?

4. Many terms are used to describe the fact that Christians have been "saved" by Jesus Christ: redemption, ransom, atonement, justification, ransom from the devil, satisfaction, and liberation. Discuss what you understand by each of these terms, and comment on the strengths and weaknesses of each.

5. What does it mean to call Jesus Christ a Liberator? What do people today need to be freed *from*, and what do they need to be freed *for*?

Suggested Readings

Leonardo Boff, *Jesus Christ Liberator.* Maryknoll, NY: Orbis Books, 1978.

Gabriel Daly, *Creation and Redemption.* Wilmington, DE: Michael Glazier, 1989.

Leo Davis, *The First Seven Ecumenical Councils (325-787)*. Wilmington, DE: Michael Glazier, 1987.

Denis Edwards, *What Are They Saying About Salvation?* New York: Paulist Press, 1986.

Alfred T. Hennelly (ed.), *Liberation Theology: A Documentary History*. Maryknoll, NY: Orbis Books, 1990.

Arland J. Hultgren, *Christ and His Benefits: Christology and Redemption in the New Testament*. Philadelphia: Fortress Press, 1987.

Edward Schillebeeckx, *Christ: The Experience of Jesus as the Lord*. New York: Seabury Press, 1980.

Gerard Sloyan, *Jesus: Redeemer and Divine Word*. Wilmington, DE: Michael Glazier, 1989.

7.

The Church of Jesus Christ

Framing the Question

My friends call me Jobie. I was born in Japan where my father was stationed in the military, and right now we are living in San Diego. I am a junior, majoring in the life sciences.

I have a couple of questions about the church. First of all: Did Jesus really establish a church? I have heard that all he really wanted to do was teach about God's kingdom and reform his own religion. The church seems to come later. If that is true then why do we say that Jesus is the founder of the church?

Secondly, how did such a complicated and diversified group like this ever get started? I have heard that there are more than a billion Christians in the world; divided all different ways, with Catholics, Protestants, Orthodox, etc. Are we sure that all these different churches go back to the same beginning? How do we tell the real church from the pretenders? There must be some way we can go back and see how the original church operated, so that we can have some standard to measure churches today.

Finally, how do I know that I need a church? What can the church really do for me that I can't do for myself? I have many friends that don't belong to a church, and they seem to be doing just fine.

Jobie is right when she says that Jesus did not establish a church. It is true that Jesus did not set up a formal institution or a church organization with structures and officials like we see today. Strictly speaking, the church did not get started until after the death and resurrection of Jesus.

It might be more accurate to say that Jesus, through his teachings and actions, laid the foundation for the church that eventually developed over time. After the resurrection, Jesus sent his Spirit as he promised. From that day to today the Spirit of the Lord has helped Jesus' disciples to initiate, shape, and sustain the church.

Remembering Simple Beginnings

Jobie also makes a valid point when she states that we have to know something about the early church communities in order to see if the church of today remains faithful to its beginnings. Of course, it is no easy task to go back two thousand years and try to reconstruct what the early church was like. In fact, there is no consensus among our best scholars about exactly what took place during the earliest days of the church. We have only fragments of historical data, some archeological findings, and a few biblical passages that give us varying accounts of those early days of the church. At best, we can make educated guesses about the structure and activities of the early church. Many of these views come from biblical scholars who offer their opinions after thorough analysis of the New Testament passages that were often written in a highly stylized fashion.

There is a conviction among many in the Catholic community that if the church is to carry on the mission of Jesus faithfully, it has to remain true to its beginnings. The earliest beliefs and values must be the benchmarks against which today's church is measured. To be authentic, today's church must live up to its earliest foundations.

When Pope John XXIII initiated the Second Vatican Council, the pope said he wanted: "to restore the simple and pure lines that the face of the church of Jesus had at its birth." The image he used was that of the freshness and innocence of the face of a newborn infant. John XXIII apparently hoped that this council—which many think was the most significant religious event of this century—would recapture the original simplicity and purity that the church had at its inception.

In this chapter we are going to look at the role Jesus Christ played in the establishment of the church. Then we will discuss how the Christian churches actually got started. And we will look at some of the very first communities of believers in Jerusalem, Antioch, and Rome, along with other important churches described in the New Testament. We will close by summarizing some of the essential beliefs and practices of the early churches. These will stand as the standards against which today's church must be measured. In the next chapter we will see how the church must perennially struggle to hold onto these essentials through reform and renewal.

The Foundation of the Church

The traditional notion that Jesus is the founder of the church can be somewhat misleading.[1] First of all, one must recall that Jesus was a Jew, not a Christian. He seems to have been more intent on reforming his own religion than wanting to start a new one. Jesus of Nazareth identified himself with certain liberal Jewish perspectives of his time. His teachings sounded similar to those of Rabbi Hillel and some of the other charismatic teachers of his day. It is quite possible that John the Baptizer was Jesus' mentor. Like the Baptizer, Jesus took a prophetic posture against the corruption and hypocrisy that he saw among the religious leaders. Jesus called people back to the original Hebrew covenant through a radical change in their lives. He invited his followers to embrace the best of their Jewish tradition—worshiping their Father-God in spirit and truth. Jesus asked people to recommit themselves to the great commandments of Judaism by loving God, self, and others.

Deep within the layers of the gospels we hear echoes of Jesus as an apocalyptic preacher warning that the end is near, and yet on other occasions he admits that he does not know when the end will come. We see him bringing the healing and forgiveness of Yahweh, and the hope for salvation and eternal life to a people oppressed by foreign occupation, religious legalism, and a judgmental attitude that reduced many to the status of outcasts. The church that evolved after Jesus' death treasured these teachings and strove to emulate the actions of Jesus' that flowed from these beliefs.

The Uniqueness of Jesus

Although there are parallels between Jesus and the other teachers and miracle workers of his day, he stands in a category all his own. He experienced God with such oneness and intimacy that he could address God as "Abba," which was the familiar form of "Father," and is similar to our use of "Dad." This experience of God moved Jesus to preach, teach, and forgive sins with an authority all his own.

For a rustic Galilean carpenter with no scribal degree, Jesus did the unthinkable. He interpreted the law and even contradicted some of the religious leaders of his day. So often we read in the bible that Jesus said: "You have heard it said....But *I* say to you." He taught of love, compassion, forgiveness, and self-sacrifice for others. He extended his intense love to all kinds of people, especially the "untouchables," and then asked people to extend this same love to others. His community cherished and lived out Jesus' teachings about a loving and compassionate God. Many people, especially the common folk, experienced Yahweh's presence in the person of Jesus in a way that has never been felt before or since.

There was also a confrontational side to Jesus. He condemned oppression and injustice, self-righteousness, hypocrisy, and greed. He stood up for the "little people" against those who abused them. He lashed out at hypocrites, and drove the con artists out of the temple. He was a man of courage who held his ground to the end, even when it meant that he would have to have his body torn up with whips and be nailed to a cross where he suffocated and died.

Unlike his mentor, John the Baptizer, Jesus was neither a loner nor an ascetic living in the desert. Jesus valued having friends and experiencing a sense of community. His customary "table ministry"—where he dined with all kinds of folk, rich and poor—earned him the reputation for being a drinker and a friend of sinners. He selected twelve unique followers, as well as many other disciples—women and men who were with him as he moved about in his ministry. Like the rabbis, Jesus made a serious effort to prepare these disciples to carry on his teachings and his work of reforming Judaism.

Jesus' disciples carried on his mission and organized a church that witnessed to his message about the kingdom and lived according to his teachings about love, compassion, and self-sacrifice. His table ministry culminated in his offering his body and blood at the Last Supper. The celebration of the eucharist became the centerpiece of the community. As models of leadership evolved in the community they were based on presiding at table and serving the community.

The Kingdom of God

Most agree that Jesus' teachings about the kingdom of God, or reign of God, are central to his message and foundational for understanding the meaning of the church. Although this concept is seldom mentioned in John's gospel, it is mentioned over a hundred times in the other gospels. Jesus is portrayed in Mark, the earliest gospel, as beginning his mission with the words: "The time is fulfilled and the kingdom of God is at hand; repent and believe in the gospel" (Mk 1:15).

Teaching about the kingdom of God was not original to Jesus, although he did give it a newness in light of his own unique experience of God as Abba. The Hebrews believed that Yahweh was the Creator and sustainer of all reality. They called God "King" because of the divine power through which God guided, protected, and liberated them.

The kingdom of God was understood to be "the biblical expression for God's being: unconditional and liberating sovereign love insofar as this comes into being and reveals itself in the lives of men and women who do God's will."[2] The experience of the kingdom of God was that of God's powerful and saving presence. It was God's will and the basis of God's law that this presence should prevail in the world by overcoming evil, injustice, and oppression. At some established time in the future, God's rule will be accomplished, Israel will be justified, and all nations will recognize that God rules over all creation.[3]

Jesus' teaching regarding the reign of God stood as a rebuke to those religious leaders who used the concept of the kingdom to justify their dominance over people or to promote violent revolution in the name of Yahweh. The "power for" love and liberation can easily get translated by religious leaders as the "power over" others so that those who represent God feel that they can oppress others in God's name. Jesus clearly taught that God's power prevails or "reigns" as a power of healing and saving. This is the way Jesus exercised power, not in being greater than, but by being part of; not by reigning over, but by serving; not by being first, but by being last. In meeting Jesus and being loved and served by him, his followers experienced the saving power of God. They learned that the kingdom of God was at hand, and experienced the power of this kingdom in the actions of Jesus. He taught his disciples that God also could use them as instruments of this power, and that their lives could also tell the story of God's action in history.[4]

A Preference for the Poor

Jesus was convinced that through his words and deeds a new phase of God's power was coming to the poor. This reign of God was coming especially to the poor and the marginal. That is why the poor were "blessed"—because this powerful and loving God was with them. That is the reason Jesus taught them to stand up proudly as beloved children of God. The oppressed could depend on God to be part of their lives, and to be a liberating force in the world.[5] It was Jesus' mission, and the mission of those whom he chose as his disciples, to awaken people to the presence of the reign of God, and to open their hearts to the experience of it. As one catechist from Honduras put it:

God is not in heaven watching us. God is with us bringing about the kingdom. In the end, the power of God's love, forgiveness, and sense of justice at work in us will win out over death squads and ruthless leaders.

Already and Not Yet

Even though Jesus generally agreed with the Jews who thought that God's redemption of Israel would come sometime in the near future, Jesus also understood that there was a unique immediacy to the kingdom—a unique present dimension to the kingdom of God. God's love and compassion could be experienced now; the reign of God had already come. At the same time Jesus also spoke of a future dimension to the reign of God. The time of fulfillment was still to come; there was a "not yet" dimension to the reign of God. Jesus maintained that the time of this fulfillment was not known, even to himself. The Gospel of Matthew says: "But of that day and hour no one knows, neither the angels of heaven, nor the Son, but the Father alone" (Mt 24:36). Jesus' mission was to alert people to the presence of God's reign, and to prepare them for its final coming when Israel will gather all nations into God's reign. As the church developed, it carried on this mission first proclaimed by Jesus.

Evil and corruption stood as very real obstacles to the accomplishment of God's kingdom. The world then, just as now, was filled with evil, violence, and sin. Jesus taught that ultimately the power of evil would not prevail. Until this time of fulfillment, however, his disciples would have to struggle against evil as they prepared for the ultimate coming of God's reign. Jesus promised his followers that they could count on his power in their struggle: "And behold, I am with you always, until the end of the age" (Mt 28:20).

The Church Is Not the Kingdom

The kingdom of God, although related to the church, is not to be identified with it. The church bears witness to God's power and presence. It promotes the reign of God's loving and saving presence and is a living symbol of the reality of the kingdom. At the same time, the church consists of people and structures that may or may not witness to God's presence. The church has its weaknesses, its limitations, its sins. None of these can be equated with God's presence or with the kingdom of God.

The kingdom of God and its eventual fulfillment, like God's grace, is pure gift. It is the work of God and can neither be earned nor "built up" by human efforts. The power is only from God. The church's role is to be open to this power, to witness to it, and to do all it can to promote the kingdom always and everywhere.

Father Henry, a missionary to South Africa for a number of years who is now completing a graduate degree in theology, offers these comments on the church and the reign of God.

I experienced the reign of God in a new and profound way on the day we had the national elections in South Africa. You could feel the power of hope, forgiveness, and determination in the air. One of my parishioners, who had been a house-servant for fifty years, said: "Today I became a human being." I realized that there was something larger than any of us at work here. True, there had been the courage and the hard work of leaders like President de Klerk and Nelson Mandela. There was the willingness on the part of those imprisoned for years to come out of jail without a desire to be vindictive. And, of course, credit has to be given to the churches. Anglican Archbishops Trevor Huddleton and Desmond Tutu and others played enormous roles in bringing us to freedom. The Catholic church also played a key role in resisting apartheid. Archbishop Hurley and many priests and laity worked for years on behalf of the oppressed people. Religious orders kept their schools open to people of all colors, even in the face of great trials and threats. But beyond it all and deep within it all, it was God's reign of love, forgiveness, justice, and peace that prevailed. This was truly a sign of the kingdom of God already present in the world, and it was the churches that opened the way for this to happen.

Early Communities of Believers

It seems clear that Jesus did not establish a church. Instead he gave his disciples the essential ideas they would need when the time came for the church to begin. He gave them the teachings, the sense of community, and the rituals. He also conferred the authority they would need to establish a church. Most important, Jesus gave these disciples himself—his own Spirit—to guide and inspire them in their task of establishing a church.

The Church Born in the Resurrection

The church was born in the disciples' experience of Jesus as raised from the dead. These experiences gradually transformed the disciples from a confused and frightened group of followers to a faith-filled community of witnesses who accepted the truth that Jesus was Lord, God, and Savior.

The church of Jesus Christ has its beginnings in resurrection faith, in the acceptance of the amazing grace needed to believe that Jesus is the Christ. This beginning of the church is marked with a special sense of newness that extends beyond that of other beginning situations. There is within the Christian community an experience of a new Israel, a new covenant, and a new creation. Jesus is the first-born of his people. His disciples are filled with enthusiasm as they preach the good news that humankind is getting a fresh start with Jesus as their Savior.[6]

Luke's highly stylized story of Pentecost recounts the disciples' determined going forth and witnessing their faith to all nations (Acts 2:1–47). Matthew's account of the disciples' commissioning reflects the early church's awareness of mission (Mt 28:16–20). The church continues to happen as people listen to the teachings, accept Jesus as the Christ, and come forth to be baptized into new life.

A classic example of how the church develops is found in the Acts of the Apostles where Philip goes down to Samaria to preach to the people about the Messiah. They listen, experience the power of God in miracles, and "there was great joy in that city" (Acts 8:4–18). Then Peter and John come from Jerusalem, pray that these people will receive the Holy Spirit, and baptize and lay hands upon them. The people receive the Holy Spirit and the church is born in Samaria! Luke's account in Acts seems to be a model of the stages of Christian conversion and how the followers of Jesus formed local assemblies in those early days.[7]

What we see described in Acts is similar to the phenomenon that Jane, a non-traditional student from Kansas City, experienced in her parish catechumenate when she became a Catholic. She recalls:

We gathered in the parish hall in September, a motley crew of fifteen people, none of us quite sure where this was going to take us. I am married to a Catholic and wanted to go to church with my family, so I thought I would go to the inquiry class and find out how to join the Catholic church. I thought it would be like joining a club. As the months passed, we received instructions, listened to the gospels, prayed, sang, and shared our questions and our lives. Most of us could see that we were not simply joining an organization. Something was happening deep down inside of us. I know that in my case, I was beginning to have faith in Jesus and his teachings like I never did before. I was seeing my family, other people, and my world differently. At the Easter Vigil we were baptized. Now I know what church is. Church happens inside us. We are now bonded to each other as a community and we are working to find this in the larger community.

The development of the church, therefore, might be looked at as a process of faith-sharing and community-building. The process begins with Jesus' ministry to his people, Israel, and his calling them to reform. It involves his commissioning of the disciples to carry on his work, and empowering these followers with his Spirit after the resurrection. His disciples continue his mission to Judaism, and as that begins to fail, extend the mission to the Gentiles. The entire beginning of the process and its continuation is "the work of God," who is creating his eschatological people through Jesus Christ and the Holy Spirit.[8]

The Word "Church"

The word "church" is first used to refer to the Christian community in Thessalonica, a town in Macedonia where Paul established a community around the year 50 C.E., some 15 years before Mark's gospel—the first of the four—was written. The word "church" is a translation of the Greek word, *ekklesia,* a term that refers to the assembling or calling forth of the people to deal with political or juridical matters. The Hebrews have a similar word, "qahal," which refers to the assembly of people called by God. The English word "church" is derived from another Greek word, *kuriakos,* which means "belonging to the Lord." Putting this all together, we might say that the church is a gathering of those who are called to belong to God.

Beginning with the writings of Paul, the scriptures use the word "church" to refer to a local house church or to a cluster of these house churches, such as the churches in Galatia (Gal 1:2). Paul also refers to the church as Christ's body (1 Cor 12:27). Although each gathering of disciples was considered to be a church, a bond of unity existed among all the communities. Together these communities made up "the church of God" (Gal 1:13). The word was used to designate both the local gathering of believers and the union of all believers.[9]

Rather surprisingly, the word "church" appears only twice in the four gospels. Both times the word is used in the Gospel of Matthew (written around 80 C.E.). The often-quoted text: "You are Peter, and on this rock I will build my church" (Mt 16:18), probably reflects a later awareness of the meaning of church, as well as the prominence that the Matthean community gave to Peter. Matthew's other use of the word "church" occurs in the context of settling disputes among the faithful (Mt 18:15–17) and might be a later addition to the original sayings of Jesus.[10]

In all the gospels there is a keen awareness that there is a community of disciples struggling to live the gospel, and that this "Way" is in continuity with what Jesus established. But generally, the word "church" only gradually is used to identify that reality.[11] Paul seems to have been primarily responsible for applying the term to the Christian communities. Now let us look at how some of these individual churches originated and developed.

The Church of Jerusalem

We are not certain whether the disciples' experiences of Jesus as being raised from the dead occurred in Galilee, Jerusalem, or in both places. The gospels give us varying accounts of these resurrection experiences. Regardless, it would seem that the first gathering of Jesus Christ's disciples as the new family of Israel occurred in Jerusalem.

In the Gospel of John this initial gathering occurs on Easter Sunday evening, whereas Acts depicts it taking place on the feast of Pentecost. Both accounts are intended to express in a concrete manner how faith in the resurrection bonded the disciples and gave them a sense of mission to spread the word about the possibility of salvation in and through Jesus Christ.[12]

The church in Jerusalem had its beginning as a Jewish sect—a group of Jesus' disciples who accepted him as the Christ and their Savior, while continuing to attend the Jewish synagogue. One might expect that one of the apostles such as Peter or John would assume leadership of this community. As a matter of fact, a non-apostle, James, who is described as "the brother of the Lord," eventually is given the leadership role (Acts 15:13–23). It is interesting that a blood relative of Jesus takes precedence over the apostles. This may be due to the Jewish emphasis on clan, and the understanding that the church is like an extended family.

From the outset the primary community in Jerusalem was filled with the Spirit. The members were intently conscious of Jesus' commission to them to warn their fellow Israelites that they must repent before the coming of the Lord. In just a few short years this community had grown to include so many Greek-speaking Jews that the latter group formed its own worshiping community. This latter group was cosmopolitan enough to spread the good news beyond Jerusalem.[13]

One might expect that since Jesus was a Galilean the first church would appear in his native area. There were, however, certainly adequate reasons for the disciples to form the first community in Jerusalem. It was the city where Jesus held his last meal with them; the place where he was crucified, and the location where Luke placed the Easter Sunday appearance of the risen Lord. Jerusalem, in addition, was the heart of Judaism; the place for continual pilgrimage to the temple, and the seat of the learned Jewish leadership. It was widely held among the Jews, moreover, that the endtime would occur in Jerusalem. There Yahweh would establish the messianic kingdom, and call all nations to pay homage to the true God.

If the early followers of Jesus were effectively to carry out their commission to prepare Israel and all nations for the Lord's coming, Jerusalem was the place to be. It was here, too, that the idea of being an apostle developed into a notion broader than that of the original twelve, to include Paul and other female and male disciples who bore witness to the risen Lord. In Jesus' name they would cleanse the temple, and be the city on the mountain, the new Zion, proclaiming God's salvation in Christ.[14]

The Acts of the Apostles gives us much of our information on the Jerusalem community. Although Acts was written in the 80s when the focus had shifted away from the imminent coming of the Lord, the text still carried echoes of earlier concerns about the coming of the endtime. This explains why the Jerusalem community was so detached from material things that they sold what they had and shared it with the needy. If Christ was coming soon, why be acquisitive? Second, many were not aware of the need to spread the message beyond Jerusalem. If Israel would draw all nations to itself in the endtime, why go far afield on mission? They reasoned that they should remain faithful to the Torah and the temple because these were the main signs of Jewish fidelity. They wanted to be prepared when Christ returned. Expectantly they prayed: "Maranatha, Come, Lord Jesus!"[15]

In addition to their Jewish identity, the early Christian community in Jerusalem viewed themselves as being unique. They had their own treasured memories of Jesus, faith in his resurrection, and a mission to convert their fellow Jews to Christ. They gathered in the homes of believers where they said prayers, sang songs, celebrated the breaking of the bread, and baptized new disciples into the community. They shared in friendship and strove to live the gospel life, which they called "The Way."

It would be unrealistic, however, to idealize this or other early communities. The early churches were communities of human beings, people like ourselves, who had faults, limitations, and inclinations toward evil. There were tensions and conflicts. The story of Ananias and Sapphira, who were struck dead because they lied about the amount they were donating to the apostles, indicated in story fashion that there were deadly conflicts over financial matters (Acts 5:1–12). The story of the selection of deacons to serve the widows of the Greek-speaking Jews indicated early problems about leadership and ministry, including such mundane issues as who would serve at table (Acts 6:1–5).

Tensions appeared early on between the Jewish Christians and the Greek-speaking Christians (Hellenists). The latter were usually "diaspora Jews," and often more critical of the temple and traditional

Jewish practices. Their devotion to Jesus as the "New Temple" confused traditional Jewish Christians and outraged the Jews who rejected Jesus.

The account of Stephen, the first martyr, depicts some of these tensions and shows how they could erupt into violence. In the story Stephen has gone to the synagogues to preach the message of Jesus to the Hellenistic Jews. His attitude toward the temple and his commitment to Jesus as Messiah so outrage the Jews that they have Stephen arrested. Eventually, he is stoned to death by an angry mob. This story, which may have some historical basis, recounts a happening in the year 36 C.E., just several years after Jesus' death. The story offers us a glimpse into the very earliest days of the church.

Soon after Stephen's martyrdom, the Hellenist followers of Jesus were driven from Jerusalem, leaving the city in the hands of more conservative Christians. The departing Hellenists, however, were able to take a historic step and begin missions to the Gentiles. Many of these Hellenistic Jews were cosmopolitan, and their openness and ability to speak Greek made them ready candidates to spread Christianity beyond Judaism to the Gentile world. Even before Paul began his ministry of preaching and writing, these people served as the first "apostles to the Gentiles." This missionary activity is typified by the story of Philip heading north to Samaria where the good news of Jesus finds a welcome reception (Acts 8:4–25).

After hearing about these differences and disagreements among the early Christians, Ted, a senior from Spokane, who is often critical of the church, remarked:

I'm glad to hear that these early Christians had their problems, too. I always thought that the people in my parish were hypocrites. They say they are Christians, and yet where I work in the summer I see them cheating on their hours and putting each other down. I guess I might have been a little unrealistic in thinking that because they are members of a parish they should be living perfect lives. At least they aren't stoning each other!

The Church at Antioch

The Hellenist mission to Antioch in Syria had great significance in the spread of Christianity. Antioch was a thriving city, the third largest city—after Rome and Alexandria—in the Roman Empire. The church there began early, perhaps in the late 30s, and was composed of both Jewish converts and Greek-speaking Gentiles. It was in Antioch that the disciples of Jesus were first called by the name "Christian." The title seems to have arisen outside the community as a nickname or possibly even as a rebuke. The fact that the followers of Jesus were given a name indicates that the community was beginning to get an identity of its own, one that would ultimately separate it from Israel.

Many scholars think that the Gospel of Matthew emanated from the church in Antioch. This gospel, although not the first one written, was most influential both with the early Church Fathers and in shaping the beliefs and practices of the church throughout the ages.[16]

The prominence of Matthew's gospel has given the Christian community at Antioch a special significance. It is Matthew who explicitly links the church with the ministry of Jesus. Matthew's gospel, written in the 80s, reflects a community that had flourished for forty years. The mixture of Jew and Gentile is reflected in Matthew's nativity story. We find a moderate Judaism that blends the image of Jesus as the New Moses with the homage paid to the infant Jesus by the Gentile Magi. In this gospel strong Jewish figures like Joseph and Elizabeth are balanced by Roman centurions and the Canaanite woman.[17] The controversies over circumcision and kosher food and whether to spread the gospel more widely among the Gentile world also get prominent mention in this gospel. The variety of views on these issues are reflected in Jesus' dialogues throughout the gospel. At one time Jesus seems to think that he is called to save only the lost sheep of Israel (Mt 15:24), but later on he commissions his disciples to teach all nations (Mt 28:16–20).

The ministry in Antioch initially could be characterized as being charismatic and featuring apostles, prophets, and teachers. Paul, and more especially Peter, exerted an influence over the church of Antioch so that its ministry eventually took on a hierarchic leadership structure governed by a bishop who was assisted by priests and deacons.

By the time Matthew's gospel was written, several significant events had affected the community at Antioch. First of all, Jerusalem had been destroyed and its church no longer had control over Antioch. From then on, the church of Antioch enjoyed considerable autonomy. Second, after the destruction of Jerusalem the Jews had regrouped at Jamnia. Under the leadership of the Pharisees, hostility toward Christians was intensified. The followers of Jesus were routinely cursed during the prayers and synagogue services, and Christians were expelled from the synagogues. Paul's pre-conversion career demonstrated how Christians were being sought out for arrest and persecution. The destruction of Jerusalem also created an identity and authority crisis among the Jewish Christians. Matthew's emphasis on the headship of Peter arose as the people of Antioch searched for a strong and legitimate authority-figure who had continuity with Jesus.[18]

Any idealism about uniformity in the early church is quickly dispelled by an examination of the variety of groups in the Antioch church. There were Judaizers who insisted that Christians strictly follow the Jewish heritage, and who did not think that the church's mission need go beyond Israel. There were those who held the views of James, and who linked a strict observance of the Mosaic Law to a strict moral code that was traced back to the preaching of Jesus. Others opposed devotion to the Jewish law and favored a strong mission to the Gentiles. Among them, there were differing views on the moral code that should be presented to potential converts. In the commissioning by Jesus at the end of Matthew's gospel we see that the community ultimately resolved this conflict by agreeing to bring the good news to all nations.

The Church in Rome

Rome, of course, has always been a significant Christian community, and is today the center of Catholicism. The church in Rome was founded around 40 C.E., most likely by Jewish Christians from Jerusalem.[19] Long before Jesus' time, the Jewish community in Rome exercised considerable influence in civic and political affairs, and the rabbis in Rome were known for their education and influence. Cicero wrote about the Jewish political influence evident during the reign of Julius Caesar. Many of the Jews in Rome flourished financially due to the religious privileges that they received under the Roman regime. Even the Jewish rebellion and the fall of Jerusalem in the late 60s did not seem to affect Jewish privilege in Rome. Titus, who conquered Jerusalem and destroyed the temple, considered bringing Berenice, a Jewess, back to Rome as his mistress, where she would have become empress of Rome, but faltered under the pressure of public opinion.[20] Titus also faced pressure from the Roman Jewish community when he triumphantly brought vessels from the Jerusalem temple back to Rome.

Early Christian sources (the writings of Ignatius of Antioch and Clement of Rome) indicate that both Peter and Paul were held in high regard by the Christians of Rome. Peter came there around 60 C.E. when the Christian community was about twenty years old. He was martyred in Rome during the persecution of Nero around the year 65, probably by crucifixion. Paul was brought to Rome as a prisoner in 61, where he was greeted outside the city by Christian admirers. He remained in prison for several years and then was probably beheaded. It is possible that both were betrayed to the Romans by ultra-conservative

Jewish Christians who thought Peter and Paul were too lax in their fidelity to the law and possibly too "soft" on Gentiles.[21]

The fact that Nero executed both Peter and Paul and then killed many other Christians, possibly to suppress the rumor that he himself started a fire that destroyed much of Rome, is a clear indication that there was a large and identifiable Christian community in Rome at the time.[22] Tacitus refers to the "notoriously depraved group who were popularly called Christians." He also interestingly identifies their "originator" as "Christ, [who] had been executed in the reign of Tiberius by the procurator, Pontius Pilate." Tacitus, unintentionally and for all times, gives historical verification to the gospel accounts of Jesus' crucifixion.

Paul's well-known Letter to the Romans was written about 58 C.E. In the letter he greets a number of the leaders in the Christian community, apparently familiar with the reputations they had in Rome. Paul's letter indicates there is both a Jewish and a Gentile Christian population in Rome. At the time the letter was written, it seems that the Gentile element prevailed. In the 40s many Jews had been expelled from Rome for causing unrest by disputes over issues like whether Jesus was the Messiah or not.[23] To appease both Jews and Gentiles, and to be able to raise money for the church in Jerusalem, Paul assures the Roman Christians that he is an apostle. At the same time, he takes a rather polite and moderate view regarding the Jewish law, and appeals to their loyalty to the church in Jerusalem where they had been evangelized (Rm 7).

By the time that the First Letter of Clement (an extra-biblical text from the first century) was written from Rome in 96 C.E. the church in Rome had an established church order and looked back to Peter and Paul as "pillars of the church." This church order included presbyters and presbyter-bishops, and had the beginnings of apostolic succession. While Jewish cultic practices were prevalent among the Christians in Rome, the Roman organizational patterns and the stern Roman legal opposition to dissent and schism deeply influenced the formulation of church policies. These Roman models served as the foundation for future models of authority and for the subsequent Romanization of Christianity. This process came to its climax in the fourth century when Christianity was officially recognized and then made the official religion of the Roman Empire.

Other New Testament Churches

We have been examining some of the earliest and most significant Christian communities at Jerusalem, Antioch, and Rome. Now we will turn our attention to some of the other churches mentioned in the New Testament.

Modern biblical criticism has made us realize that often in the gospels we learn more about the particular beliefs and concerns of the church community that produced the gospel than we do about what went on during the time of Jesus. This perspective on the gospels gives us a rare opportunity to learn much about early church communities.

We have already dealt with the community behind Matthew's gospel, the church of Antioch. Luke's gospel, which also seems to have been written in Antioch, offers further insights into the struggles of the Gentile members of this community and their disputes with Jewish Christians, as well as a look at their questions about who should be included in their church.[24] The Acts of the Apostles gives some insights into the fledgling church of Jerusalem through Luke's stylized accounts of the early days of that community. The Gospel of Mark was the first written, possibly emanating from Rome around 60 C.E. Although scholars have not been able successfully to reconstruct the kind of community to which it was addressed, the gospel does give additional hints of the anxieties about persecution and about the repercussions upon the Christian faithful should there be a revolt in Palestine.[25]

The Community of the Beloved Disciple

Traditionally it was thought that the Gospel of John was written by the apostle of the same name. It was also presumed that John was the "beloved disciple" of Jesus who is mentioned throughout the gospel. Modern biblical criticism, however, has presented a much more complicated picture. Scholars tell us that we really can't ascertain the identity of the author of this unique and final gospel that seems to have been written around 90 C.E. As for the identity of the beloved disciple, he does not seem to have been John, or even an apostle.[26] Apparently he was a very close personal friend of Jesus. In his community he seems to have been a genuine hero who held an authority among his followers that was superior to that of Peter and the Twelve. Although the beloved disciple was probably the authority behind the Gospel of John, it is unlikely that he is the actual author.[27]

This Johannine community probably began with Jewish Christians in Palestine and later relocated to Ephesus in Asia Minor. The original members were most likely a mix of former followers of John the Baptizer, converted Samaritans, and Gentile converts. The gospel's hostile attitude toward the Jews reflects the strong feelings of alienation toward Judaism that were present in the community at the time this gospel was written. This may have been because many of the members of the community had been thrown out of the synagogues and persecuted by the Jews. Once separated from Judaism, the Christians no longer enjoyed the religious tolerance given to Jews, and were vulnerable to Roman persecution. This isolation and persecution might well explain the passages in John's gospel about the kingdom not being part of this world. Jesus' words at the Last Supper about how the world will hate his followers might well come out of the isolation and persecution felt by this community.

Love is the central concern of this church, and the long discourses on love by Jesus at his last meal are classic examples of the poignancy of their views. The glue that bound the Johannine community together was the experience of being loved by the Lord, and extending this love to others.

Rather than speak about the church or the people of God, or even the kingdom, this community used the organic image of the vine and the branches to indicate the strong personal bonds they felt with Jesus and with one another. The members of the community addressed each other as brother and sister, reflecting an equality in ministry that is neither patriarchal nor institutional, nor concerned with offices. The stories of Mary at Cana, the Samaritan woman, and the importance given to Mary Magdalene indicate that women played key roles in this community.

Anita, an ardent feminist who hopes to be ordained a priest in her Episcopalian community, is always in tune with women's issues. On the role of women in John's community she noted:

Just look at the importance that Jesus' mother and Mary Magdalene had in the minds of these early Christians. It seems like John's community "got it" as far as the great things women can contribute to the church. I just don't understand why the churches, particularly the Catholic church, can't allow women to use their gifts and talents for the Lord.

In the community of the beloved disciple, humble service to each other in the name of the Lord was considered to be sacramental. This was exemplified in the story of Jesus washing the feet of his disciples. In John's gospel this gesture was given central position at the Last Supper over the breaking of the bread. This community developed a "high christology," which stressed Jesus' divinity. This approach to understanding the person and nature of Jesus profoundly influenced the early church councils' definitions on christology, and has prevailed as the dominant perspective throughout the Catholic tradition for nearly two thousand years. It is curious that this community's charismatic and egalitarian approach to ministry did not have the same impact on the church's tradition.

In many ways this Johannine church is a paradigm for the church of Christ as a whole. It started simply with the intention of carrying out the memory of Jesus' love. It went through many difficult phases where it struggled to absorb different kinds of believers, engaged in difficult controversies, and carried on a love-hate relationship with the world surrounding it. Amid these divisions, this church continued to strive to be faithful to the Lord and his teachings. Its tenacity and constant awareness of the presence of the Spirit of the Lord in its midst serves as a useful model for today's church.

The Pauline Churches

We can learn a great deal about the development of the early churches from Paul's letters, most of which were written to address pastoral needs in these churches.[28] Here are thumbnail sketches of several of the major churches associated with Paul.

The Church at Thessalonica

Paul's earliest letter was written to the church in Thessalonica in Greece, a church that was established about 50 C.E. This church was composed mostly of Gentile converts who faced strong opposition from their Jewish neighbors. When Paul writes, the community is concerned about the delay in Christ's return. He encourages them to continue hoping in Christ's return, and urges them to live responsible and loving lives as they await the Lord's return.

Paul also encourages them to respect the leaders in their community. Paul's tone to the Thessalonians tells us a great deal about leadership. He preaches and then lets the church develop, fully aware that it will not be perfect. Being a member of the church, Paul says, involves being sexually moral, keeping marital fidelity, and not doing wrong to your neighbor. It also includes doing good for others and avoiding revenge. Paul encourages his listeners to find happiness in their discipleship. He writes: "Be joyful always, pray at all times, be thankful in all circumstances. This is what God wants from you in your life in Christ Jesus" (1 Thes 5:16–18). Paul expresses his concern in a compassionate, fatherly way, never threatening or coercing the people. He leads by inspiration and persuasion rather than by domination and control. He thus provides a model for all who aspire to be authentic church leaders.

The Church at Philippi

Paul wrote his letter to the church at Philippi while he was in prison at Ephesus. Philippi was a thriving Roman city where Paul, in spite of resistance from the Romans, was able to establish a small community of mostly Gentile converts to Christianity. This community gathered at the house of Lydia and eventually grew into a large church community. Paul gives us a view of its emerging ministry, using the words "bishop" and "deacon" to describe the people who carried out tasks of service.

In this letter Paul also reveals his irritation that certain Jewish Christian missionaries are trying to undo his work in that city. He tells the community that their life in Christ is a gift from God that cannot be earned by obeying the Jewish law. In this letter there is a classic statement about Jesus Christ. Paul writes: "He always had the nature of God, but he did not think that by force he should try to become equal to God. Instead of this, of his own free will he gave up all he had, and took the nature of a servant" (Phil 2:6–8).

The Church at Corinth

The church at Corinth must have been a lively and boisterous community. It had been established in a Greek harbor town that was known for its shipbuilding and its sporting events. Corinth is where Paul met Priscilla and Prisca, an extremely influential Christian couple who had been tossed out of Rome by the authorities. They owned a home in Corinth, and from there went about the town preaching the gospel to the local folks. Priscilla and Prisca were also responsible for establishing the church at Ephesus, which served as a major base for Paul, and from which he wrote some of his major letters.

Priscilla presents a good example of how women were active in ministry in the early church. There were others significant female figures in these early communities, women like Phoebe, Junia, Chloe, Euodia, Synteche, and Apphia. Few of these are household names, but Paul certainly gave recognition to them as significant ministers of the gospel of Jesus Christ in the early church.

Paul's later letters to the Corinthian church (the two contained in the bible are really the compilation of three or more distinct letters) reveal that there were many factions, conflicts, and scandals in that church. Some members held that Christian converts could still frequent the local houses of prostitution. Others were noted for being rowdy at the celebration of the eucharist, as though they were at some kind of party. The community also experienced conflict between those Christians who were affluent and those who were poor. And there were other points of division. Some members followed Paul, while others were loyal to those who spread the ideas first preached by Peter. Still others were beholden to Apollos, another missionary. Paul expresses his concerns about this, and reminds the Corinthians of their new life in Christ.

Paul feels that diversity, but not division, should characterize the Christian community. In a classic passage, Paul writes to the Corinthians about their basic diversity and unity:

> There are different kind of spiritual gifts, but the same Spirit gives them. There are different ways of serving, but the same Lord is served. There are different abilities to perform service, but the same God gives ability to everyone for their particular service. (1 Cor 12:4–7)

Paul also reminds the community that they are the Body of Christ, and that since they belong to Jesus, love must be the main thrust of their lives. In chapter 13, Paul writes one of the most inspired passages ever written on love:

> Love is patient and kind;
> it is not jealous or conceited or proud;
> love is not ill-mannered or selfish or irritable;
> love does not keep a record of wrongs;
> love is not happy with evil, but is happy with the truth.
> Love never gives up;
> and its faith, hope and patience never fail....
> Meanwhile these three remain;
> faith, hope, and love;
> and the greatest of these is love. (1 Cor 13:4–7, 13)

The situation in Corinth got so bad that Paul needed to write several more times, and even visit the church personally a number of times before things began to settle down.

The Church at Galatia

Galatia refers to an area that is located in modern central Turkey. This was a church that Paul himself established, and it was predominantly a

Gentile community. From the letter that Paul sent after he left, it appears that some Jewish-Christian missionaries had arrived and told the community that they should observe circumcision and some of the other requirements of the Jewish law. These preachers also questioned Paul's apostolic status. Paul vehemently protests that he is an authentic apostle, and repudiates the teachings of the Jewish Christian missionaries. He points out how he opposed Peter and James on the question of forcing circumcision on Gentiles, and seemingly questions their status, referring to them as the "pillars" of the Jerusalem church. Apparently, there were personality clashes even among the most prominent of the early church leaders.

In this letter Paul writes some of his most profoundly influential statements on the equality and freedom that should exist in the church of Christ. On equality he writes:

> You are baptized into union with Christ Jesus. You were baptized into union with Christ, and now you are clothed, so to speak, with the life of Christ himself. So there is no difference between Jews and Gentiles, between slave and free, between men and women; you are all one in union with Christ Jesus. (Gal 3:27–29)

On freedom Paul writes: "Freedom is what you have—Christ has set us free! Stand, then, as free people, and do not allow yourselves to become slaves again" (Gal 5:1). Those lines have empowered many over the centuries. Some heard these words on the underground railroad as slaves were being brought north. They have been heard in the barrios of Mexico and in the hillside rebel camps in El Salvador. They are on the lips of the Palestinians and the South Africans, the Irish and the people of Bosnia.

Other Views of the Early Church

In this section we will look at some of the other churches mentioned in the New Testament. We will also look at two letters, Colossians and Ephesians, that were probably written by disciples of Paul within a decade after his martyrdom. Then we will consider some of the notions of the church found in the pastoral epistles (Letters to Timothy and Titus) and in the First Letter of Peter. The themes of these add to our understanding of the fledgling church.

Colossae was a city in present-day Turkey, just east of Ephesus, the capital of that part of the Roman Empire. The perspective of the writer of this letter is not as intimate or "brotherly" as that of Paul. Little mention is made of the Spirit or of the institutional aspects of the church community. Where Paul had generally used the word "church" to refer to the local communities, here the word "church" refers to the universal collection of churches that is more than an earthly reality.[29] The expectation of Christ coming soon seems to have faded, and the church has a sense of "nowness" with the fulfillment of the resurrection being experienced in the present.[30]

The Letter to the Colossians reflects a high christology in which Christ is seen in cosmic terms. This perspective greatly affected Teilhard de Chardin in his thinking. It is also relevant today in considerations of reverence for the environment. One of the most moving passages reads:

> Christ is the visible likeness of the invisible God. He is the first-born Son, superior to all created things. For through him God created everything in heaven and on earth, the seen and the unseen things. (Col 1:15–16)

Here the author takes Paul's notion of the Body of Christ, applies it to the members, and then identifies the Body of Christ with the church itself. The church is thus viewed as a dynamic and growing entity that lives in harmony with the very life of Christ.

The Letter to the Ephesians sees the church as a universal phenomenon taking in all of creation. Where Paul had viewed Christ as the foundation of the church, this author describes the foundation to be the apostles and the prophets. Paul's notion of the Body of Christ being the various members now shifts to the perspective that the Body of Christ is the church. These may seem like subtle differences, but later they influenced people to see the church more as a corporate institution than as a group of people. This letter contains the well-known passage that parallels the relationship of Christ with the church to that of a husband and wife in marriage. Much to the dismay of feminists, the model of marriage is one that is characteristic of a patriarchal society. Finally, this letter indicates that expectation of the imminent endtime has waned in this community, and its members are urged to focus instead on living in the present power of the risen Christ.

Early Catholicism

Some who charge the Catholic church with being a triumphant and hierarchical institution see these early shifts away from communal and charismatic forms of leadership as a move toward "early catholicism." From this perspective, it was here that the church departed from its original values and its initial identification with the kingdom of God, and began to be an end in itself.[31]

In answering these charges, it should be pointed out that one should not over-idealize the early church. It is unrealistic to equate "pure" church forms with early institutional practices and presume that later changes were all illegitimate. The early church, as we have seen, was a diverse group of complex communities with a variety of organizational and disciplinary structures. This is not to deny, however, that the church can stray from its original and authentic character. As we will see in the next chapter, the church must be "always reforming." The church must be willing to go back to its roots and its original values and constantly be open to renewal.

The Pastoral Letters

The pastoral letters include the First and Second Letters to Timothy and the Letter to Titus. These letters were previously thought to have been written by Paul, but now are believed to have been composed by anonymous authors around the year 90 C.E. Their concern is pastoring (thus the title "pastoral") the churches that were already formed, and not with establishing new missions.[32]

These letters reflect later development in the church communities. Most notable is the appearance of more defined church structures and offices. There seem to have been a number of factors that contributed to the development of this more defined church order. First, the early apostolic witnesses had all died, and there was now a complete break with Judaism. Second, there was further confusion over the Jewish roots of Christianity after the destruction of Jerusalem and its temple. Then, the churches were often experiencing persecution by both Jews and Romans. Finally, the cultural and religious perspectives of the Gentile world were having an ever-increasing effect on the communities. These and other factors moved the churches to look for a stronger authority structure and stricter organizational patterns.

The pastoral letters reveal how this visible and stronger leadership had taken shape in these churches. The Letter to Titus calls for an elder-overseer to be appointed in every town to stave off false teachings, preserve the "deposit" of teaching, and provide the church with a stable administration. Paul is presented as the model of apostolic authority, and current leaders are exhorted to carry on his authority and his commitment to orthodoxy. Gradually the responsibility of teaching and pastoral care is relegated to a select group of appointees. We see the churches moving away from the earlier populist and charismatic notion of ministry to a more organized and more structured system of leadership.

These letters propose an exclusive view (Paul's view) that Christianity is the only acceptable religious perspective. They also endorse a return to patriarchal views toward the role of women in the church. While there are mentions of women office holders (the order of widows and deaconesses), the letters contain prejudicial attitudes toward women.

The Petrine Tradition

Biblical scholars speak of a Petrine tradition, a Christian perspective that can be traced back to the apostle Peter in Jerusalem. There is solid evidence indicating the influence that Peter had in Jerusalem, in the Matthean community in Antioch, and in Rome. The Acts of the Apostles and the letters of Paul give insights into this tradition, and the First Letter of Peter helps us further understand the Petrine tradition. This New Testament letter was probably written by a disciple of Peter from Rome about the year 90 C.E. to a community of Gentile converts.

Many of the converts in these communities were ostracized from their pagan neighbors and viewed as a secretive sect or as atheists who did not follow the Roman beliefs. The author points out to his readers that they are indeed God's people, and draws parallels between the Exodus story and their own liberation. God's people have survived, and will continue to survive! The author reminds them that in their church they have found a new home with Christ. United to Christ they experience a new dignity: "You are a chosen race, a royal priesthood, a holy nation, God's own people" (1 Pt 2:9). The leadership, which is now firmly established and in the hands of those identified as the elders, is urged not to be domineering and not to be greedy in getting paid for their services.

Characteristics of the Early Church

We have reconstructed from early scriptural writings what the church might have been like "when it was born," to repeat the image of Pope John XXIII with which we began this chapter. We can see from all that has been said that there was no ideal church at the beginning. Instead there was a complicated process of development beginning with Jesus and his life and teachings, and moving through different church communities that arose in various locales. By way of summary we can enumerate the essential characteristics that the church of Jesus Christ had at its beginning.

1. Centered in Jesus Christ. The early communities revered the memory of Jesus of Nazareth, the young carpenter turned teacher and prophet. Some were still alive who could remember the intensity of his love and the graciousness of his forgiveness, the outrage that he turned toward injustice, the compassion he showed to outcasts, and the courage with which he met his horrible execution. Others had heard the stories of his life and teachings from his followers and were able to put their trust in him. He had freed them to be intimate with their God, Abba, who promised them eternal life.

Besides memories of Jesus, some in the early communities had experiences of Jesus as raised from the dead. Jesus' disciples had unique faith-experiences of the risen Christ, and the early communities continued to experience him in story and symbol. The church was indeed born in resurrection faith and awaited his imminent return. Gradually those hopes shifted to the "now" experiences which they had of Jesus in their midst as he had promised.

2. Bonded in Community. The early Christians viewed themselves as being bonded to Christ and to one another. The community was noted for its lifestyle of loving and sharing with one another. The reality of community could be experienced on the local level in a house church, in a federation of churches in a city, and later in the more universal reality in which communities of believers existed throughout the Middle East and Asia Minor.

At first these tiny communities saw themselves as part of the Jewish faith community. As the church became more inclusive, it found itself influenced by many different cultures: Jewish, Hellenistic, Roman. The church had to adapt itself to the language, philosophy, and lifestyle of these cultures. Historical events also had their impact on the church. The destruction of Jerusalem, the massive fire in Nero's Rome, the martyrdom of the great apostles who were among the last alive to have personally known the Lord, and similar historical and cultural events helped to shape the evolution of these early communities.

As a community of believers they understood that they were to proclaim that the reign of God was at hand. They also were called to prepare for the final coming of the Lord and the fulfillment of the reign of God. Within a generation it became evident that the Lord was not coming anytime soon, and so the disciples came to realize that the church of Christ would become an ongoing entity.

The main ritual that bound these communities together was the eucharist. In the breaking of the bread the early churches carried forth the table ministry of Jesus in the ritual he had given them. Important also in their symbolic system was water baptism, whereby they initiated new members into their community.

3. The Gospel Message. The early church held to the tradition that had been handed on by Jesus. It centered on a belief in a loving and forgiving God, the saving presence of this God who reigned over all of creation, and the blessedness of the poor and the outcasts. Jesus had taught them that a life of humble service could lead after death to life eternal. The early disciples believed that Jesus was the Christ, their Savior. They saw the saving power of his death, and were convinced that he had returned in resurrection. As a community they were to be a living symbol of the presence of his Spirit, and to follow their calling to preach the good news of salvation to the world. This teaching was first proclaimed as a kerygmatic message and then storied in oral traditions about the life and preaching of Jesus. Eventually these oral stories were written down in gospel form.

4. Authority. Every group must have authority through which it can lead, teach, administer, and make decisions. The church is no exception. From the beginning there were controversies over circumcision, observance of the Torah, and attendance at synagogue. Some Christians were strict in their observance of Jewish law and customs, while others were more lenient. There were arguments among the churches over money, sexual ethics, the eucharist, the authority of the apostles and teachers, the sacredness of the body, and even the person of Jesus himself. Authority was needed to discern, to preserve the tradition, and to implement change and reform.

Prominent leaders emerged: people like Peter and James, Paul and the beloved disciple. On a local level many roles evolved: preachers, teachers, prophets, elders, deacons, priests (presbyters), and bishops. Women and men began churches and presided over them. While the Jerusalem church maintained its moderate views on Judaism, Paul took more radical views against circumcision and Jewish observance, and was eager to expand the Gentile churches.

From the start there were splits and divisions. The magnificent Johannine community eventually divided, with part going off to identify with the numerous Gnostic communities. Docetist groups, who could not accept the humanity of Jesus, left the main church. This action and similar situations accentuated the need for authoritative figures who could discern the truth from heresy. There was a need for leaders who could both reconcile and, if need be, exclude individuals or groups from the community of believers.

5. Service. From the beginning the disciples of Jesus Christ followed his example of self-sacrifice and humble service, especially to the poor. Ministry in his name was central to the Christian way of life. At first the ministerial forms seemed to be based more on calling forth those who were gifted by the Lord's Spirit. Gradually this charismatic and gender-inclusive approach to ministry gave way to more hierarchic and male-dominated clerical forms. From the beginning, Jesus' accent on the servant-leader was challenged by those who viewed leadership in terms of domination and control.

Christian ministry took shape differently in the various communities. Some churches stressed equality of the sexes and recognized the significant contributions that female members could make. Others favored more patriarchal patterns of that era and kept women in the background.[33]

Conclusion

When Jobie stated the initial questions that framed this chapter she asked how we might discern whether the church is true to its beginnings. From this overview of the development of the many early church communities, we have seen how complex a question this is. There is such diversity in the early churches, and there are many different yet authentic ways to follow Jesus. Still, we have shown that there are a number of essential characteristics that the early church sustained. These become the criteria for measuring how faithful the church is to the Lord who laid its foundations. These become the benchmarks for the church's ongoing commitment to reform and renewal.

Finally, Jobie raised the question about whether she needs the church. Each person has to answer that for herself or himself. As we have seen, the church has great treasures to offer in the person of Jesus Christ, his teachings, the caring community, and its leadership and service. To belong to that church involves both invitation and acceptance. For two thousand years countless people from every nation and race have chosen to walk with the Lord in the church. Why some do and others don't is somehow tied up in the mystery of God's grace and the variety of human responses to that grace.

Discussion Questions

1. Did Jesus set out to establish a church? Please explain your answer in detail.

2. Some say that Jesus laid the foundations for a church. What did Jesus say and do to lay such foundations?

3. Compare and contrast some to the early Christian churches: e.g., Jerusalem, Antioch, Rome, the Johannine community.

4. What were some characteristics that were unique to the Pauline communities? Please read several pertinent letters of Paul to help you formulate your answers.

5. Five essential characteristics of the church were listed in the chapter. Please discuss ways in which the church today still sustains these characteristics. List some ways in which renewal is needed with regard one of these aspects of the church.

Suggested Readings

Faivre Alexander, *The Emergence of the Laity in the Early Church.* New York: Paulist Press, 1990.

Raymond E. Brown, *The Churches the Apostles Left Behind.* New York: Paulist Press, 1984.

Francis J. Cwiekowski, *The Beginnings of the Church.* New York: Paulist Press, 1988.

Vincent Donovan, *The Church in the Midst of Creation.* Maryknoll, N.Y.: Orbis Books, 1989.

Helen Doohan, *Leadership in Paul.* Wilmington, DE: Michael Glazier, 1984.

Elisabeth Schüssler Fiorenza, *In Memory of Her.* New York: Crossroad, 1984.

Daniel J. Harrington, *God's People in Christ: New Testament Perspectives on the Church and Judaism.* Philadelphia: Fortress Press, 1980.

Gerd Lüdemann, *Early Christianity According to the Traditions in Acts.* Minneapolis: Fortress Press, 1989.

Ben Meyer, *The Early Christians.* Wilmington, DE: Michael Glazier, 1986.

Anthony Saldarini, *Matthew's Christian-Jewish Community.* Chicago: University of Chicago Press, 1994.

8.

Reform and Renewal

Framing the Question

My name is Connie. I am what they refer to today as a non-traditional student. I am not a typical undergraduate. I have been married for thirty-five years and have four grown children. After they all finished college, I decided that it was my turn to go back and get the education for which I never had the time or money. I may be a non-traditional student, but as far as my religion goes, I am a traditional Catholic. I was raised a Baptist, but I dropped out of organized religion after I left home. Then I met Lou, a Roman Catholic, and we married. After about three years I decided I wanted all of us to be the same religion so I became a Catholic.

I really took my conversion to the Catholic church seriously. When I first came into the church I got the impression that the Catholic church had been the same for two thousand years, just the way Jesus left it. The priest who gave me instructions said that it was not only the one true church; it was the only true church. I liked the way the church took strict positions and held to them. My church would be a "rock," the only unchanging thing in a world that was always in flux. I believed that once I joined it I could be saved. Change was not part of the church's vocabulary back in the days before the Second Vatican Council.

Well, in the 1960s things really changed a lot in the Catholic church. I couldn't believe how fast the changes were coming at me. It seemed that Catholics were becoming more like the Protestants I had left. Catholics were talking about the bible, and wanted to have closer communities. Lay people were getting involved in church activities. It was all pretty scary for me. Here I converted to find a rock to stand on, and it seemed to be crumbling.

Well, I reacted. I dug my feet in and decided to join those who did not want all the changes in the church. My family joined a small parish in the inner city that keeps things the way they used to be in the Catholic church. Our parish is definitely out of the mainstream, but because we are a poor parish no one seems to bother about us.

These days I have all kinds of questions about the church. Was Vatican II really necessary? It seems like a lot of the problems we have in the church now, like the priests and Sisters leaving the ministry, started with that council. Exactly what was the council trying to achieve? Why couldn't the church just stay like it always had been? Once the church started to change, it started to have problems. I wish we could go back to the way we were.

Connie, like many Catholics her age, is struggling with the phenomenon of a changing church. Some Catholics, like Connie, believe that the church should be the one part of life that does not change. It should be a rock to stand on in an ever-changing world. Others think that the church should keep up with the times and be a relevant and dynamic presence in the world of today.

This chapter demonstrates that change has always been a characteristic of the church. It also discusses the ongoing process of renewal within the church of Jesus Christ. We will begin with an overview of some significant examples of renewal, and then focus on the history-making renewal of the Second Vatican Council. Then we will look at the so-called marks of the church and see how the church has had to change in order to keep these distinguishing marks intact.

An Ever-Changing Church

There is an ancient Christian principle that the church must always be in the process of reforming. Even though the church is of Christ, and enjoys his presence all days as he promised, it is still a church composed of human persons. By that very fact, the church is finite and limited. A human church includes both success and failure; both virtue and sinfulness. The church's teachings and structures, although they look to Jesus in their origins and are sustained by his Spirit, are in part the product of human creativity and construction. They are born amid the events of history and are shaped by culture. The forms of the teachings and the structures can become distorted and corrupted, even to the point where they no longer effectively carry forth the message and mission of Jesus Christ. The structures can become oppressive and controlling. They can lose their very purpose, that of serving in the Lord's name. There is need, therefore, for constant reform and renewal within

Christ's church in order to assure that Jesus' original teachings and purpose are not lost amid outdated forms and structures.

Development and Persecution

As we saw in the last chapter, the church began in the enthusiasm of resurrection faith and pentecostal conversion. The early years of the church were a time of gradual development as Christianity spread from Jerusalem to other cities of Palestine, and then to Gentile areas throughout the Roman Empire. We saw how the early churches were house churches, often in urban areas. The leadership structures, ritual patterns, scriptural accounts, and rules of life gradually emerged in varying and differing forms throughout this loosely linked network of fledgling churches.

Wherever there is development and change there is controversy, and the early church was no exception. Since the first disciples were Jews who followed a Jewish Savior, the earliest controversies were over whether or not Jewish laws applied to the members of the Christian communities, especially in the case of the growing number of Gentile converts. There were also struggles over the identity of Jesus Christ, the criteria used to determine authentic teachers, the meaning and proper celebration of the eucharist, the role of women disciples, and the time of the second coming. The community also debated about charisms, offices and ministries, marital and divorce laws, the sharing of goods and money, sexual ethics, and even over such mundane matters as who should do such menial tasks as waiting on tables.

From the beginning, there was a strong determination among the disciples to preserve the truth of Jesus and his gospel and resist anything discerned to be an error or deviation. As new stories, images, and formulations developed, more debates ensued. As new forms of administration and authority evolved, added tensions and controversies appeared. It was Christ's church, but it was made up of fallible human beings.

Conflict with Outside Forces

Conflict came not only from within; it also came from outside the community. The early communities experienced persecution, both from the Jewish communities and from the Romans. To the Jews who rejected Christ, Christian Jews appeared to be idolaters in their esteem and worship of Jesus as the Christ. Eventually Jewish Christians would be excluded from their own synagogues and even hunted down as dangerous challengers to Hebrew orthodoxy.

To the Romans, Christians were considered to be "heretical" in their determined resistance to emperor worship, and in their opposition to violence. Moreover, Christian disputes with the Jewish community, their strange and secret rituals, and their persistent drive to make converts among Gentiles were often perceived by the Romans as being disruptive to order and control in the empire. As we have seen, most of the early apostles were executed, and many Christians were martryed, especially during the tyrannical imperial reigns of Nero and Diocletian. No doubt these persecutions made the Christians reconsider their beliefs, moving some to apostasy and others to even firmer convictions. For weal or woe, the persecutions deeply affected the ongoing process of reform and renewal in those early days.

Reform Efforts

Reform movements in the church came about for varying reasons. First of all, challenges to the central beliefs in the tradition had to be met with formal and authoritative definitions designed to settle the dispute and dissipate heresies. In the early centuries the major disputes centered on the community's understanding of Jesus Christ, and whether he was truly God and truly human. As we saw earlier, fourth-century councils, facing a spreading Arian belief that Jesus was not divine, clearly defined that Christ was both human and divine.

Reform movements also arose when leaders sought to gain better organization, discipline, and uniformity in the church. For instance, Charlemagne (d. 814), one of the most influential Western leaders in history, imposed on the church a strict code of ecclesiastical law, a sacramentary to be used for all worship throughout his kingdom, a uniform rule for monastic life, and a book of homilies that was to be used by all preachers.[1]

At other times, the church was challenged by those who thought that the institution was not being true to the teachings of Jesus. In the twelfth century Peter Waldo and his followers advocated giving all one's goods to the poor and went about preaching a radical gospel lifestyle. They called for a vernacular bible and encouraged everyone to read and interpret the scriptures for themselves. Official church authorities deemed these reform movements to be extreme and proceeded to have them condemned.

The Second Lateran Council (1129) opposed secular control of bishop appointments, forbade the marriage of clergy, and threatened excommunication to anyone inheriting the material wealth of a priest upon his death. It is interesting to note that a rule such as that requiring celibacy for the clergy was viewed at one time as an innovation, and was thus rejected by those who did not want such changes introduced into the discipline of the church.

Innocent III, one of the most powerful popes in history, held that the pope was the "Lord of all the World." He called the Fourth Lateran Council in 1215 in order to suppress heresies, make legislation for the appointment and responsibilities of bishops, establish sound training for clergy, reform the lifestyle of consecrated religious (monks and nuns), and separate Jews from Christians by having the former wear distinctive clothing and live in ghettos.

The Reformation

One of the most profound reforms in the church's history occurred three hundred years later, at the dawn of the sixteenth century. Many new abuses had appeared in the church, especially after the chaotic and often harsh times following the Black Death. The divisions became so marked, and the reforms so delayed, that those who called for reform, the "Protestants," separated themselves from the Catholic church. It was the Council of Trent (1545-1563) that belatedly attempted to answer the protests of the reformers. The council profoundly reformed the papacy, religious orders, the education and formation of priests, the selection process for bishops, and many other areas where abuses had built up in the church throughout the Middle Ages.

During the Reformation, the disputes centered on the issues of church authority, the interpretation of scripture, the role of faith in salvation, the sacraments, and other important doctrinal and disciplinary issues. In 1563 the Council of Trent answered the Protestants' calls for reform with harsh condemnations and firm doctrinal definitions. The Catholic church then began a reform that would indeed put its house in order, but which at the same time would leave deep divisions within Christianity.

The Pre-Vatican II Period

The reforms called for by the Council of Trent, once made, were strong and effective. The Catholic church took positions regarding its doctrines, rules, and rituals that prevailed well into the twentieth century. In fact, many of the decisions regarding the papacy, episcopacy, priesthood, sacraments, and church law that were imposed by Trent are still very much in place today. The *Catechism of the Catholic Church,* published in English in 1994, is modeled in structure and often in content after the Roman Catechism of the Council of Trent.

The First Vatican Council, the first worldwide church council to be convened in over 300 years, intended to reform the nineteenth-century church. Its original agenda was largely concerned with internal church matters. The definition of papal infallibility, which has become synonymous with this council, was not on the original agenda, but once it appeared it became the focal point of the gathering. The outbreak of the Franco-Prussian War forced the gathering to disband early, and the only doctrine that had been defined was that of papal infallibility. The council greatly strengthened the authority of the pope in Rome, which had been seriously weakened by the French Revolution, the growth of democracy, and the modern secularization of Europe.

Pope Pius IX (d. 1878), who organized Vatican I, reigned for thirty-two years (1846-1878). During his papacy, he shored up the heretofore embattled papacy, promoted devotion to the Blessed Virgin Mary, increased the numbers and influence of religious orders, and decreed that the one official and correct framework for doing philosophy and theology in church education was medieval thomism based on the writings of Saint Thomas Aquinas.

At the dawn of the twentieth century, the church had a strong identity and authority, but it was isolated and often hostile to the developing modern world.[2] This antipathy toward modernity increased with Pius X, who reigned from 1903-1922. He roundly condemned "modernism," and instituted strict policies to prevent Catholic scholars from employing the latest research in biblical criticism and historical-critical studies in theology. These condemnations and the ensuing oaths against modernism were aimed at protecting the church from the excesses of some of these fledgling disciplines. As a result, Catholic scholars were held back from pursuing biblical and theological disciplines in a scientific way for another half century.

A New Reform Movement

Efforts to update the Catholic church and bring it into dialogue with contemporary issue and global concerns began to arise after World War II. The liturgical movement's efforts to rediscover the rich history of Christian liturgy and bring Catholics into more active involvement with their rituals actually began in monasteries in Germany and France early in the twentieth century. This movement received official support from Pope Pius XII with his 1947 encyclical letter (an official papal statement) on the sacred liturgy.

Some venturesome Catholic scholars attempted to enter the emerging world of contemporary biblical criticism early in this century, but their views were found unacceptable by Vatican authorities. It was the scholarly Pope Pius XII, encouraged by Cardinal Bea, who finally issued Catholic biblical scholars their "magna carta" in 1943. His encouragement initiated an astounding period of Catholic biblical studies that continues to the present day and that has significantly altered the way Catholics interpret and understand their biblical heritage.

Theologians, unfortunately, did not receive the same approval to use contemporary approaches in their scholarship. In 1952 Pope Pius XII denounced the "new theology" of Father Yves Congar and others in France. Forward-looking theologians continued to grow in number despite the papal admonition, but they were kept in the shadows until the Second Vatican Council was underway in the 1960s. Eventually, these theologians were invited to serve as *periti* (learned consultants) during the council. As a result, the progressive theological thinking of Congar, Henri de Lubac, M.D. Chenu, Karl Rahner, Redemptorist moral theologian Bernard Häring, and American Jesuit John Courtney Murray found its way into the council documents. In addition, some of the more progressive views of deceased Catholic thinkers such as John Henry Newman and Teilhard de Chardin were also given currency.

Grassroot Reforms

Many things happened on the grassroots level that prepared the way for the Second Vatican Council. In the late-1950s new and more accurate English translations of the scriptures were completed, and people were encouraged to read the bible. There were increasing signs that people wanted to use their own language for the celebration of the Mass, rather that having everyone use the Latin language, which virtually no one understood. People were also encouraged to participate more actively in the Mass by reciting the responses and by following along with the prayers and readings in a missal.

In the United States, the laity assumed a more active role in such groups as the Catholic Action Movement and the Catholic Family Movement. Lay leaders such as Dorothy Day and Baroness Catherine De Hüeck inspired many Catholic lay people to minister to the poor and the homeless. Father Thomas Merton, a convert to Catholicism, wrote his inspiring autobiography, *The Seven Storey Mountain*, from his Trappist monastery in Kentucky and ignited new enthusiasm for religious life and contemplation.

The Second World War, despite its horrible destruction, had brought people of many faiths and religions together in a new atmosphere of dialogue and understanding. In progressive seminaries the works of contemporary European theologians were included in the theological training. The social teachings of the popes since Leo XIII (d. 1903) greatly influenced the social awareness and involvement of many Christians. Moral theology was undergoing a revolution, inspired by the precise and yet passionate scholarship of Redemptorist Father Bernard Häring. By 1960 the stage had been set for what many call the most significant religious event of the twentieth century, the Second Vatican Council.

The Second Vatican Council (1962-1965)

Pope John XXIII (d. 1963) cut a unique image as a pope. He was a rotund, jolly, friendly man who did not take himself too seriously. His work in many different parts of the globe had made him worldly wise. Pope John was deeply committed to Jesus Christ and he wanted the church to be the same. It was while at prayer that he was inspired to call religious leaders from all over the world to gather in an ecumenical council to once again reform and renew the church.

Pope John's announcement in 1959 that there would be an ecumenical council caught Catholics on all levels by surprise. Even many of his closest colleagues in Rome did not respond enthusiastically, possibly because they suspected that it would stir the waters and bring about many changes. Some no doubt feared that such a meeting might open the door to some of the contemporary theologians who were beginning to knock more loudly. Most were not sure how such a council would operate, since a council had not been held for nearly a hundred years. That council, Vatican I, had been interrupted by a revolutionary war. The last full-fledged council, Trent, had occurred four hundred years before. Undoubtedly, a long agenda had accumulated over a period of that length.

Tom, a junior from Indianapolis who plays guard on the varsity basketball team, finds this span between councils to be humorous. He remarks:

How can an institution as big as the church call its meetings only every several hundred years? The chairman certainly can't open the meeting by asking: "Was anyone at the last meeting?" All those who attended the last meeting are long dead. No wonder change takes so long in the church!

The Second Vatican Council was unprecedented in that for the first time in the long history of the Catholic church, leaders from every corner of the world were present. What Karl Rahner would later call a "world church" began to take shape, as representatives from most nations flew in and out of Rome for four major sessions over a period of three years. During that time over two thousand Catholic bishops tirelessly debated and voted on documents that dealt with many pastoral issues facing the modern church. It is no wonder that many consider this council to be the most significant religious event of the twentieth century, indeed in the history of Christianity. It was a gathering that not only had profound impact on the Catholic church, but also had an influence on many other churches and religions, and on the world as a whole.

The Purpose of the Council

When it was first announced that the pope was calling for an ecumenical council, many thought that perhaps the purpose of the meeting was to discuss unity with the Protestants. After all, the word "ecumenical" had generally been attached to the movement for Christian unity. It was soon discovered that in the context of this council, the word "ecumenical" meant "worldwide." Cardinals and bishops from every point on the globe were present at this council.

Pope John's purpose in calling the council was to provide for the updating of the Catholic church. His broad experience as a Vatican representative in many parts of the globe had taught him that the church was often closed to other churches and religions as well as to world problems. John liked to use concrete images. He said that the church should not exist as a museum. Rather the church should be cultivated as a "living garden" where people could enjoy a hopeful future. Pope John said that he wanted the council to "open the windows" in order to let fresh air into the church. He hoped that this great meeting would prepare the way for a "new pentecost," where the church would renew itself as a community of disciples of Jesus Christ, deeply committed to the gospel.[3] He wanted the church to show how the gospel was relevant to world problems, as well as to the struggles of all its brothers and sisters everywhere.

In order to bring about such a renewal, Pope John asked that this council be focused on pastoral rather than doctrinal matters. The pope, of course, had his critics and nay-sayers, but he waved aside these prophets of gloom who thought that changes in the church would be harmful to what they perceived to be an unchangeable tradition. John's conviction was that the substance of the gospel can remain the same, while the forms in which this gospel is presented can vary throughout history. He pointed out: "It is not that the gospel has changed; it is that we have begun to understand it better."[4]

The Council Is Convened

After two years of planning, the Second Vatican Council opened in 1962. Many members of the planning committee that organized the original documents for consideration hoped that the gathering would simply rubber stamp their traditional views and be done with it. Many of the European bishops, however, were trained in contemporary theological methodologies, and were looking for profound changes in both the way the church thought of itself and the way it related to the world outside itself. One cardinal pointed out early on that the church had become too triumphant, clerical, and legalistic, and that the council would have to address these tendencies and make serious efforts at reform and renewal.

A Change in Image

Vatican II described the church as the "people of God," a phrase that became synonymous with the profound change that took place in the church's self-image during the council. Previously the church's understanding of itself was reflected in images such as the "perfect society" or the "Mystical Body of Christ."

It was Saint Robert Bellarmine (d. 1621), the post-Reformation Jesuit theologian, who developed the notion of the church as the perfect society. By this he meant that the church was a society that was perfect unto itself, needing no other societies. This understanding was designed to preserve the church's autonomy, and to fend off the secular governments that were attempting to gain sovereignty over the church following the Reformation. It was a strong image of the church, a church that consisted only of those loyal to Catholic teachings. It gave Catholics a clear identity and sense of membership amid profound and even violent divisions taking place in sixteenth-century Christianity. At the same time, it indicated a posture that was closed and militant. It was perhaps an appropriate stance for the period of the Reformation, but it was hardly suitable in the modern era.

Another image of the church that was prevalent before the council was that of the "Mystical Body of Christ." Pope Pius XII had reclaimed this older image of the church, and gave it currency following World War II. It was an image that was more biblical and Christ-centered than the image of the perfect society. While it was more inclusive in its consideration of all church members, it equated the church with

Catholicism, thereby leaving other Christians and other religions on the outside. Other Christians churches somehow "pertained" to the church and could therefore offer salvation. As for the other world religions, however, their value seemed questionable at best.

The People of God

Vatican II's use of "people of God" to describe the church had a profoundly inclusive effect on its members, as well as on the church's relationship with those outside its membership. The phrase is deeply rooted in the biblical tradition and links the church with all people. It includes the first people in creation, those affected by the early covenants with Noah and Abraham, and the Hebrew people to whom Jesus belonged. Even though the council did not explicitly identify the "people of God" with all people, many leading theologians, such as Yves Congar and Karl Rahner, hold that the term "people of God" is co-extensive with all of humankind.

The inclusivity of the people of God is implied in other teachings of the council. In discussing its concern for unity, the council speaks of other (i.e., non-Catholic) churches and ecclesial communities with recognition and respect. In dealing with the questions of revelation and salvation, the council grants that God's truth and salvation can exist in other Christian churches, other religions, and even outside organized religion altogether. In the broadest statement on salvation in the history of the Catholic church, the council admits that salvation is possible to all those who sincerely search for God and who follow their conscience and lead good lives (*Dogmatic Constitution on the Church,* #16).

The most dramatic statements on the church's solidarity with all people come in the *Pastoral Constitution on the Church in the Modern World.* This document is unique in ecclesiastical history because of the relationship it proposes between the church and the world. Throughout the course of history the church has moved through different periods in its relationship with the world. In the early centuries after it began the church was persecuted by the world. Then the church grew to such stature that it dominated the Western world. With the advent of nationalism, secularism, and modernity, the church tended to withdraw from the world and took on a closed, often fortress-like posture toward the world. Vatican II, in contrast to the latter position, presents a church that is now open to the world, in solidarity with the struggles of all people, and ready to serve the world in the name of the Lord.

In this document the church indicates that it now intends to recognize the "signs of the times" and discern its calling in the modern world. It recognizes modern progress in all areas, and at the same time prophetically offers the model of Jesus and his teachings to help direct such progress. Poignantly, the church describes itself as being in solidarity with all the people of the world, especially those who suffer deprivation or oppression. The statement that has now become classic is:

> The joys and the hopes, the griefs and the anxieties of the people of this age, especially those who are poor or in any way afflicted, these too are the joys and hopes, the griefs and the anxieties of the followers of Christ.[5]

The church sees itself as a human community among other peoples, and stands with people in all their human experiences. Instead of condemning the modern world, the church now sees itself as a part of it, called to listen to and learn from its movements, as well as to bring the gospel to instruct, heal, and liberate. Most especially, the church opts to be concerned for the poor and dispossessed or the world.

A Movement for Liberation

The church's solidarity with the poor and its commitment to freedom spawned a liberation movement within the church that continues to have a profound influence on Catholics and other Christians throughout the world. In Latin America, it has taken shape as liberation theology and positioned itself as a people's church that aggressively confronts oppressive governments. In Eastern Europe the church's concern for the oppressed guided its struggles against the Communist regimes. In South Africa the church preached liberation as the driving force behind their struggle to overcome apartheid. Harking back to the early church, base communities (house churches) have reappeared where the gospel has been reinterpreted from the point of view of the voiceless, and where action against injustice is planned in prayerful and closely bonded communities.

The church's solidarity with the poor has at times been depicted by oppressive governments as revolutionary. As a result, numerous lay people, priests, Sisters, and a number of bishops have had to pay with their lives for their identification with the struggle of their people for freedom.

As mentioned earlier, Archbishop Oscar Romero of El Salvador (d. 1980) was one of the most outstanding examples of a church official who stood in solidarity with the poor and the oppressed. When elected to his office, Romero was a traditional churchman; pious, scholarly, and aloof from the political and social arena. He was rather perplexed to see some of his priests and catechists so active in the liberation movement. All that changed when one of his close priest-friends, Father Rutilio Grande, was machine-gunned to death along with an old man and a child on a country road.

Romero realized then that his people were being tortured and killed by a government that was corrupt and oppressive. When several other clergy and religious activists were killed Romero experienced a conversion and decided to join in solidarity with his people in their struggle for freedom. He became politically active, and began regular radio broadcasts across the country, condemning the violence and terrorism of the government. Shortly before his death, Romero stood in the pulpit of his cathedral and told the soldiers to disobey orders when they were sent on death squads to terrorize, kidnap, and murder. That sermon, in effect, sealed his death warrant, and a sharpshooter was sent out to kill him. While the archbishop said Mass in the chapel of the hospital where he lived, he was shot through the heart and died soon after. Along with other martyrs like Thomas Becket (d. 1170), the Archbishop of Canterbury who was killed after opposing certain actions of King Henry II, Oscar Romero stands as a symbol for those who stand up to repressive states and are willing to pay with their lives for it. Romero indeed is a dramatic incarnation of the Vatican II ideal of the church standing with the poor.

Along with Archbishop Romero on the list of martyrs for the cause are the six Jesuit priests and their housekeepers who were murdered in El Salvador, and the four women from the United States who were helping refugees and the poor in El Salvador when they were arrested by the military, brutalized, raped, and murdered.

Women's Liberation

The church's willingness to stand in solidarity with those seeking freedom has moved many people to take a stand for equality and human rights around the world. Many of the women of the church have also taken up the call for freedom. Feminist theologians and ministers have denounced sexism in all areas of culture and society, and have challenged the church to give them their rightful place on all levels of church government and ministry. Catholic women have demonstrated that they have the personal gifts as well as the level of learning needed to hold key positions in the church. Many Catholics hope that the church of equals enunciated at Vatican II will one day become a reality, and that the way will be opened for women to participate fully at all levels of the church community.

Laura, a criminal justice major, surprised the class one day when she said she honestly felt that she had a calling to the priesthood. She said:

Where do I go with this calling? I have done an internship in prison ministry and I know that I really could make a difference with the inmates if I were a priest. I do not understand why this is not possible in the Catholic church. From what I've read in scripture study and theology on the issue, it seems like it could happen. Why has the issue been closed?

Many Catholic women think there is not equality in the church. Given the shortage of priests, it is unfortunate that the church does not find more ways to use the talents of its female members. Their opportunities for participation in ministry and decision-making are seriously limited, and thus many believe that it is time for radical changes in this area.

We Are the Church

The song, *We Are the World,* is symbolic of a new awareness that all people are citizens of the world; that we are all somehow connected as brothers and sisters. From this perspective, the world is no longer out there as an object. The world is a subject and consists of many people who have individual human rights as well as responsibilities to look after each other. As the poet John Donne reminded us, no one is an island complete unto oneself. We are all linked with one another and dependent upon one another.

A similar awareness of participation and responsibility entered the church when "people of God" was used to describe the church. Previously, most Catholics thought of the church as a structure or an institution largely composed of the pope, bishops, and clergy. Suddenly the church was saying that first and foremost the church was a community of people. Many Catholics who experienced the exciting times of Vatican II can remember the first time they heard the expression "people of God." Catholics responded to this new awareness by saying: "Hey, I'm one of the people of God. I am truly part of the church!" This new awakening gave a tremendous impetus to many Catholics who now were being urged to participate more actively in liturgy, teaching, and ministry, as well as on all levels of the life of the church.

All Have a Voice

As a result of the Second Vatican Council, considerable attention was given to the notion of collegiality as a means of promoting a broader sense of participation in the church. This notion refers to the right that the bishops have as members of the college of bishops to teach with authority. It stands in contrast to the traditional centralized and monarchical mode of patriarchal authority that was prevalent in the church.[6] The concept of collegiality was soon picked up by the people at large as a way of describing the right they had to be consulted and to participate actively in the teaching and decision making of the church.

The authority of all church members had been acknowledged at other times by the church. Vatican I, in its definition of infallibility, said that while the pope enjoyed supreme authority, Christ had given authority to his entire church. Likewise, the church had always respected the "sense of the faithful" as an essential resource for locating and preserving Catholic beliefs. But still, these teachings were always seen in the context of a church of unequals where clergy held the positions of authority.

The Second Vatican Council returned to its members the kind of recognition they had lacked for many centuries. It acknowledged a church of equals, and declared that the Holy Spirit moves among all the people in the church. It recognized that the truth of the tradition can arise from the most unexpected places and people. Thus a new "listening" theology developed that acknowledged that the truth of God can be heard from below, especially from the cries and suffering of the poor and the victimized. As a consequence, a new and more vital sense of church and community was born among those who see Jesus as their liberator and the church as standing with them in their struggle for justice.

The Democratization of the Church

The contemporary populist emphasis in society and civil government has increased interest in the democratization of the church. This is not totally unexpected since the church has been influenced by many political and social structures over the centuries. It was born amidst the Jewish patriarchal structures; matured under the influence of Greco-Roman forms of thought, government, and law; and became a dominant force in Western civilization as it adopted monarchical structures of government. One would then expect that the modern church might adapt and adopt the now-prevailing democratic structures, especially in North America where freedom, independence, and the democratic process are so highly valued.[7]

In opposition to this, however, it is quite common to hear church leaders insist: "The church is not a democracy!" Granted the church is not an institution where the ultimate sovereignty rests with the people, or where decisions can be reached through a majority vote. This does not rule out the possibility that the church's governance include serious consultation with its people, authority exercised by representative groups, and a system of accountability from its leadership. Neither should voting be ruled out as a legitimate method of reaching decisions in certain circumstances. To this day the pope is elected by a vote of the eligible cardinals.

In the early church, and even at one time in the United States, voting was a way of selecting church leaders.[8] Some of this vested interest and personal ownership in church matters is being restored in the contemporary church. Today many parishes have pastoral councils with members elected by the parishioners. There are clergy associations whose members are elected by the priests they represent. Representative groups such as diocesan boards, school boards, and other associations are empowered to make decisions or at least to be consultative to those in authority. It is not impossible that someday there will be a consultative process whereby people can indicate their preferences for pastors and bishops. Like it or not, the monarchical days of the church are quickly passing away.

From the beginning, people were attracted to the church for the equality and freedom it offered. Authority in the community, as described by Jesus was not to be one of "lording over" people, but one of service. The first was to be the last. Church leaders are most effective when they lead by inspiration, example, and persuasion, rather than by intimidation or threat. The model of Jesus is one of compassion and forgiveness, not condemnation and exclusion. This seems to be the model to which Pope John XXIII was calling the church when he asked that dissenters be extended mercy instead of repression and condemnation. Most especially today, when the church is urging the recognition of human rights and is so seriously engaged in the struggle for justice, it must model these values in its own internal operations.[9]

The Church as Sacrament

Another dimension of the new self-awareness on the part of the church that arose after the Second Vatican Council is indicated in the description of the church as a sacrament. At first sight this notion can confuse Catholics who normally associate the word "sacrament" with seven symbolic rituals (baptism, confirmation, eucharist, matrimony, holy orders, penance, and anointing of the sick). In using the word "sacrament" to describe the church, the Second Vatican Council is reaching back to an earlier meaning. Here the word refers to God's plan of love and salvation for God's people, as well as to the sacred symbols of God's presence and power. In this context, the church ideally is a community of disciples who, in their lives and actions, make visible the presence and power of God. As a sacrament, the church proclaims in its teachings and work that God is a God of all people, one who loves, forgives, heals, defends, and saves those who are open to the power of salvation.

The idea that the church can be referred to as a sacrament can also be linked to the earlier discussions of how the kingdom of God is central to the teaching of Jesus. The church is not to be equated with this kingdom. It is mandated, however, to symbolize, promote, and nurture the kingdom. The church is to be a dynamic and productive symbol (sacrament) of the presence of God, inviting people everywhere to open their hearts to its power. What does this mean concretely? A priest recently explained it this way:

When we say that the church is a sacrament we mean that when one encounters the church, whether it be on a local level in a home or parish, or on a larger scale as a diocesan, national, or even international church, one should experience the power of Christ. It means that members of a parish serving in a soup kitchen can be a symbol of God's care and love, a sacrament of the kingdom. A basic Christian community in El Salvador that speaks out against injustice is a prophetic symbol that God does not will persecution of any of God's people. A diocese that takes a stand against pollution of its area's rivers and air represents God's protection of creation. When the universal church takes a strong stand against "ethnic cleansing" (a euphemism for the slaughter of innocent human beings), the church can be seen and heard as Jesus' protest against violence and oppression.

By professing that it is a sacrament, the church is saying: "When you meet up with the church you should also be meeting up with Jesus Christ. You should be experiencing his forgiveness, compassion, and saving power." Just as Christ was a visible and physical bearer of the mystery of God's saving grace, now the church carries that responsibility. The responsibility is not only carried out in the formal sacraments (baptism, eucharist, etc.), but also in all the church's works of service.[10] Sacramental symbols dynamically and productively bear the power of God. The church as sacrament proclaims Christ, his message, and his mission. It does this for its members and invites all people of the world to see, hear, and experience this saving reality.

The Four "Marks" of the Church

The ancient Christian creeds use four characteristics—one, holy, catholic, and apostolic—as ways by which the true church can be recognized. These marks are not extrinsic criteria, but are "intrinsically bound up with the very idea of the church as sacrament." They are imperatives that the church must constantly preserve; ideals toward which the church must strive. And yet, along with these ideals, the church fully realizes that there is sin and limitation within it.

Unless one keeps these characteristics in mind, the church can become a "countersign" to Jesus' redemptive work. To avoid such scandal, the process of reform and renewal is continually ongoing in the church. The fact that Jesus is always present in the church sustains such a challenging process. No matter how horrible the abuse or scandal, "his victorious grace is ever greater than the infidelity of his followers."[11]

We must now examine the church's struggle to sustain the "marks" that distinguish it as the true church of Christ.

1. The Church Is One

Oneness or unity has been an ideal of the church of Christ from the very beginning. Jesus of Nazareth preached and modeled a oneness with the Father as well as with one's neighbor. He extended his personal concern to all, especially those who had been excluded from ordinary human fellowship. Jesus also selected a group of disciples and told them to live as sisters and brothers, as friends with him and with each other. Jesus extended his friendship beyond traditional boundaries. He befriended publicans, prostitutes, lepers, and cripples. He flew in the face of taboos and selected women, revolutionaries, and illiterate fishermen for his disciples. The gospel stories of the Samaritan woman, the resuscitation of the Roman officer's daughter, and the curing of the Syro-Phoenician woman indicate memories of Jesus reaching out to those beyond the traditional Hebrew boundaries. For Jesus, all people were children of God.

Jesus envisioned a kingdom where all of God's creation and all God's children could be restored to the unity that God intended. The Johannine community emphasized Jesus' concern for unity in the familiar discourse on the Good Shepherd. After declaring his willingness to die for his people, Jesus says: "They will become one flock with one shepherd" (Jn 10:16). Jesus yearned for unity among his disciples and told them to carry forth this message to the world. His deep concern for this is poignantly reflected in John's account of Jesus' prayer at the Last Supper: "I pray that they may all be one, so that the world will believe that you sent me" (Jn 17:21).

Unity in the Early Communities

The unity that Jesus valued and prayed for was understandably important for the early communities. The brothers and sisters gathered in house churches that were closely affiliated. Even though there were disputes and divisions early on, Christians remained one in their faith in the risen Lord as their savior and one in their baptism into the mysteries of his life, death, and resurrection. They were known for their love for one another. In common they broke bread in memory of their Lord, and were firm in their resolve to announce the good news that Jesus Christ had died for all people.

Paul's writings reflect the reality of this oneness in the early church. He tells of coming to the awareness that in his persecution of individual Christians, he was indeed persecuting the church itself (1 Cor 15:9). He perceives a corporate bond among Christians with Christ. Christians are "the body of Christ" Paul writes to the church in Rome: "As in one body we have many members, and all the members do not have the same function, so we, though many, are one body in Christ, and individually members one of another" (Rom 12:4–5). So often Paul's letters are concerned with divisions in the communities. He urges a oneness with the teachings of Jesus Christ and does everything he can to discourage factions.

Paul recognizes that discipleship with Jesus effectively eliminates ethnic, social, and sexual divisions. In one his most significant statements he declares to the Galatians: "As many of you as were baptized into Christ have put on Christ. There is neither Jew nor Greek, there is neither slave nor free, there is neither male nor female; for you are all one in Jesus Christ" (Gal 3:27–28). The author of Ephesians writes to the church in Ephesus of a concern over the division between Jewish and Gentile Christians. He reminds the community that: "There is one body and one Spirit, just as you were called to the one hope that belongs to you all, one Lord, one faith, one baptism, one God and Father of us all" (Eph 4:4–6).

Many centuries later, after many tragic divisions in the church caused by questions of authority and doctrine, Thomas Aquinas still upheld the ideal of unity in the church. Commenting on the four characteristic marks of the church Aquinas pointed out that the church is a community that is one in faith in the Lord, one in hope for the future, and one in love for all people.

Authentic unity in the church is not an exclusive unity that rejects the world, other churches, and different religions. Rather, this unity should signal an inclusive oneness. The church's call is to bring the world together, not to contribute to its division. The church is commissioned to be an effective sign of Jesus' work to unify humankind and promote peace and reconciliation. Nurturing trust, mutual concern, and justice throughout the world is the mission of the church.

A Divided Church

Although unity is the will of Christ, the church has suffered deep divisions from its very beginning. The church, besides being "of the Lord," also consists of human persons. It experiences the breakdown and alienation so characteristic of humans. Early dissenting groups such as the Ebionites, Gnostics, Nestorians, and Arians broke off from the main body of the church. In the eleventh century a major split occurred as the Eastern church (centered in Constantinople) broke from the Western church (centered in Rome), largely over the issue of papal authority. In the sixteenth century a catastrophic division came upon the church as various groups disengaged from the Roman Catholic church during the Reformation to form what is now known as Protestant and Anglican churches. Divisions continued among these Protestant groups themselves, and now there are numerous sects and congregations that have broken off from the original churches. These divisions have brought much confusion and disruption to the Christian tradition. As the noted church historian Jaroslav Pelikan has said: "Everyone has lost something by the division of the church."[12]

The Second Vatican Council Calls for Unity

The reunification of divided Christendom was a major focus of Vatican II. Many signs of a deep desire for reconciliation were evident during the council. Representatives from Eastern Orthodox and Protestant groups were permitted to attend the council as observers, and from time to time were consulted about matters being discussed. In contrast to other councils, Vatican II expressed no condemnations. For the first time since the Reformation, the bishops at the council publicly admitted that the Roman church shared in the guilt of bringing about the divisions in Christianity. The council extended a friendly hand to its brothers and sisters who were members of other Christian churches.

The documents of the council reflect radical changes in thinking toward groups with whom the Roman church is alienated. The council proclaimed that all those who are baptized are incorporated into Christ, and it extended a friendly hand to all who were brothers and sisters in the Lord.[13] Eastern Orthodox communities, separated from Rome's authority, were recognized to be "churches," and Protestant groups, more broadly separated from the Catholic church on doctrinal issues, were referred as "ecclesial communities." It was acknowledged that these communities held the truth of the gospel and the grace of salvation, although not with the "fullness" present in the Catholic church.

Vatican II maintained that there is one church, but that there are different ways and degrees of being incorporated. Those who recognize the central doctrinal teachings and all the sacraments, as well as the ministry and authority of the church are "fully incorporated." Others are seen as being imperfectly united with the one church of Christ. Even though the union among Christian communities was acknowledged as imperfect, the council accented common ground and proclaimed that a true communion does exist among Christians. While there may be doctrinal and juridical divisions, there is still, on the level of faith, one church of Christ. The reality of the church transcends differences and divisions. This represents quite a departure from the days when the Catholic church excommunicated and condemned dissenters or detractors.

There were other signs at the council that it wished to establish common ground with all believers. The council renewed recognition of Christianity's Jewish roots and strongly rejected anti-Semitism. It also expressed an appreciation for the truth and salvation available in other religions. The council expressed its regrets that the many divisions among churches and believers hindered efforts promoting justice and "oneness" around the world. Vatican II also produced a landmark document on religious freedom, which recognized the right of personal religious choice and condemned religious oppression.

Ongoing Efforts for Christian Unity

As a result of the ecumenical and interfaith emphasis of Vatican II, there has been much dialogue and study intended to promote renewed understanding and unity over the past three decades. There were historical gestures of reconciliation. Pope Paul VI met with Eastern Orthodox Patriarch Athanagoras at the Jordan River, embraced him in friendship, and offered him a symbolic gift. Pope John Paul II walked side-by-side with the Anglican Archbishop down the aisle of Canterbury Cathedral. At the local level throughout the world a great deal of discussion and cooperation has taken place, not only among Christians of different churches, but also between Christians and people of other faiths.

In spite of marvelous gestures, the settlement of many points of disagreement in theological dialogue, and the mutual efforts at unity on the grassroots level, ecumenism seems to have stalled at the highest official levels.[14] Much of the common ground established in dialogue has not borne fruit in practice. The good will established through the sincere efforts of the Second Vatican Council has been lost in new entrenchments and regressive actions.

Ministry and liturgy have been two of the principal sticking points among the churches. Many of the Protestant churches now ordain women to the ministry, while both the Eastern Orthodox and Catholic churches have, at least for the time being, taken a firm position against this practice. Both the Orthodox and Protestant churches do not require celibacy of their clergy, while the Catholic church has resisted changes in this area. The permission given to a number of Episcopal married clergy who converted to Roman Catholicism to be ordained as married Catholic priests has caused considerable confusion and consternation among Catholics.

Eucharistic sharing (receiving communion in the church of another Christian denomination, sometimes called "intercommunion") has also been a matter of dispute. There are two Catholic views on the possibility of Catholics taking communion in a Protestant church or Protestants receiving communion at a Catholic Mass: one that eucharistic sharing with Protestants would help bring about unity; the other that unity must come before eucharistic sharing can be allowed. The second view prevails among Catholic church officials today. While there seemed to be movement toward eucharistic sharing for a time, at present there is a rigidity in this area of ecumenical activity.

Even with all these problems and limitations, ecumenism has come a long way. In earlier centuries wars were fought among Christian churches. Condemnations and anathemas were thrown back and forth. In 1919 Pope Benedict XV refused to participate in a World Congress on Ecumenism. The pope pointed out that Catholics constituted the one true church, and that if congress participants wanted to be reunited to the visible head of the church, he would receive them with open arms. At that time Christian unity seemed to be a question of inviting the "heretics" to recognize their errors and return to the one true flock.

Even in our own times there has been much division among the churches. Catholics in the not too distant past were not allowed to worship with Protestants or even enter their churches. So-called mixed marriages between Catholics and those of other faiths were strongly discouraged. If permission was granted for such marriages, they could not be celebrated in church.

In contrast to the closed attitudes of the past, serious ecumenical and interfaith dialogue now searches for mutual understanding, shared commitment, and united action. Even though the participants in ecumenical dialogue need to maintain strong commitments to their own tradition, there is a new openness to learn from one another, and to recognize that all churches and religions are pilgrims "on the way," and not exclusive possessors of definitive answers to the mysteries of existence. A new unity in understanding, fellowship, and action has been achieved in many areas: biblical studies, theology, shared liturgy and prayer, as well as joint action in such areas as peace and disarmament, social justice, and ecology. In North America today more than 50% of Catholics marry someone who is not a member of the Catholic church. Ecumenical dialogue and efforts at Christian unity allow these interchurch marriages (between Christians of different denominations) or interfaith marriages (between Christians and believers of other religions) to be celebrated in the church of either partner, and and be witnessed by a priest, minister, or rabbi, or even by both together.

Salvation Outside the Church

Traditionally the oneness of the church was interpreted in an exclusive fashion with regard to truth and salvation. The Catholic church saw itself as the one and only true church, and members of all other churches were viewed as being outside the church, locked in error with dubious access to salvation. Pope Pius XII granted the possibility of Protestants being saved, but only because they somehow "pertain" to the one true church.

Vatican II departed radically from these exclusive views. The council, rather than equating the church of Christ with Catholicism, observed that the church "subsists in" the Catholic church. At the same time, the council recognized the authenticity of other churches and ecclesial communities.

The Second Vatican Council established a milestone when it declared that salvation could be achieved within these Christian faith communities, in other religions, and indeed outside of organized religion altogether. In a statement unparalleled in Christian history, the council proclaimed an entirely inclusive position on salvation. To attain salvation people must "sincerely seek God and moved by grace, strive by their deeds to do His will as it is known to them through the dictates of conscience."[15] The council also acknowledged that the grace of salvation is not withheld from those who have no explicit knowledge of God, but who strive to live good lives. Indeed, the council acknowledged that God's grace for salvation is open to everyone, even the non-believer. As Father Avery Dulles, a noted Catholic theologian, put it: "Vatican II took pains to assert that the grace given in Christ is available to every human being, and that God is not bound to the sacramental and ecclesiastical structures."[16] Jesus' view that all people are God's children once again prevails.

The Challenge of Unity

Unity in the church of Christ is still problematic. The great historical divisions of East and West, Protestant and Catholic still remain stumbling blocks to full and complete unity. Even among Catholics there are serious divisions, ranging from the extremely conservative to the radical. Dissent from official church teachings is common among Catholics, and serious controversies concerning birth control, homosexuality, academic freedom, the role of women in the church, celibacy, and many other issues exist today. Some people estimate that possibly 60% of American Catholics are moving away from the institutional church.[17] Many want a pluralism in theology, liturgy, and moral standards, while others demand more uniformity.[18] How unity can be sustained in the midst of such diversity is still an open and challenging question.

2. The Church Is Holy

To say that the church is "holy" is not to propose that all of its structures and traditions are sacrosanct and unchangeable; nor is it to imply that the actions of any church—Catholic or Protestant—are beyond reproach. The many scandals throughout the church's history certainly indicate that to say the church is "holy" requires some serious qualifications.

Many people who admit that the church and its leaders are not perfect are nevertheless upset with the way the media treats scandal in the church. Cliff, a junior economics major whose brother is a priest had this to say:

I'm really fed up with all the bad publicity that priests are getting. Only about 2% of priests have sexually abused children yet the media makes it look like vast numbers of priests are doing this. Protestant ministers and other professionals who deal with children—doctors, teachers, and scout leaders—are charged with sexual abuse of children and teenagers, but you seldom hear about these cases. My brother says he is embarrassed to wear his collar in public. One night when he was out on a communion call, some guys yelled something about pedophilia at him while he was walking on the street. We have to be more supportive of our priests, and protest all this garbage that the media spreads about them.

The Elements of Holiness

The church's sole claim to holiness comes from the presence of Christ in its midst. Jesus Christ brings the very life of God to the church, and God alone is the truly Holy One. The church lives by the power of God's grace received through its Lord. Its life, protection, and goal are from above. Since Jesus Christ has promised to be with his followers all days, the church can have confidence that it will never lose holiness, nor the means to grow in it. The presence of Jesus in its midst offers the church a model of holiness, as well as a source of the healing, forgiveness, and grace needed to achieve it. Christ comes to each generation as the savior who died and was raised for them. It is he who offers people both the call and the means to be holy.

Other elements in the church that give it the claim to holiness are the scriptures and the sacraments. The scriptures are the living Word of God, the revelation of God that actively speaks to people of each age and offers Christ's followers a dynamic and powerful contact with his Spirit. The sacraments are symbols of Christ's presence that offer opportunities for being initiated into Christ's life; being fed, healed, and forgiven by his power, and being called to his service.

A People Called to Holiness

In his first letter to the Corinthians, Paul reminds them that they have been "called to be saints" (1 Cor 1:2). From the beginning, Christians have recognized that even though they are sinners, Christ has called them to a reconciliation with their God and with each other. We might say that the church is holy in that it is made up of people who are called to holiness. This, of course, is not to deny that some Christian faithful as well as some Christian leaders have been corrupt, greedy, violent, or oppressive throughout history.

To say that the church is holy is not to ignore the abuses and scandals perpetrated by both church institutions and individual members throughout its long history.[19] It is to say, however, that in spite of its sinfulness, the church will never lose the presence of the source and sustainer of holiness, Jesus Christ. The call to sanctity, as well as the grace to be forgiven and to strive for goodness will always be available to Christ's disciples.

All Are Called to Holiness

One of the key elements of Vatican II reform involved reclaiming the notion that all Christians were members of the church, and therefore that they were all called to holiness. Before the council, a notion prevailed that holiness was for the vowed religious and the clergy.[20] The prevalent Catholic spirituality was largely monastic, world-denying, and elitist. The council opened the way for a spirituality that is more inclusive, pluriform, socially concerned, in touch with people's everyday lives, and influenced by other world religions.

The council's call to all church members to seek holiness had profound implications. Religious life and its monastic spirituality came under scrutiny for its lack of contact with the world, its aloofness from everyday life, and its distance from peace and justice issues. As a result religious life underwent radical revision and reform immediately following the council. Many groups of women religious led the way in updating their education, lifestyle, and commitment to social justice. The spirituality and ministry of vowed religious communities now includes not only a personal and pastoral focus, but also political and social dimensions. Much of this renewal in spirituality has also affected diocesan clergy, introducing them to a variety of different prayer styles and a broader commitment to justice issues.

Some think that the call of all members of the church to holiness is responsible in part for the drastic decline in vocations to the clergy and religious way of life. Following the council, phenomenal numbers of men left the priesthood. Most got married, raised families, and joined the work force. In addition, significant numbers of religious Sisters, Brothers, and priests left their communities. At the same time, the number of young people applying to enter seminaries and religious life in North America went into a serious decline and remains that way at present.

No one has an adequate explanation for this sudden and drastic change. Has the call to the clergy or religious life lost its unique identity now that it is clear that all Christian believers are called to holiness? If marriage and single life are now viewed as genuine calls to holiness, can it be that the religious life marked by poverty, chastity, and obedience, and the requirement of celibacy for priests, no longer attracts many young Catholics? No definite answers are available. But one thing is sure, many young Catholics want to make a difference in the world. They welcome realistic opportunities to serve others and can be a rich resource for the Church.

Increasing Interest in Spirituality

In the contemporary church there is a strong interest in spirituality. Renewal movements are popular, prayer groups attract people of all ages, and small faith communities are springing up around the world. What was once of interest primarily to Catholics—and then mainly to its priests, Brothers, and Sisters—is now a topic of interest for clergy and laity of all Christian denominations. Spirituality books have become best sellers.

There are also significant shifts in how the disciples of Jesus Christ live out their call to holiness. Many bishops are simplifying their lifestyles, convinced that neither the princely nor the corporate image is appropriate for those called to be servants of the people. Some bishops and priests have entered into solidarity with the poor and the disenfranchised, and now live unpretentiously among the people. Many religious communities are on the cutting edge of social action, and have been formidable advocates in the areas of disarmament, the environment, housing, and prison reform. Perhaps most significantly, vast numbers of laity are seriously committed to spiritual renewal and involvement in social action issues as an outgrowth of their personal spiritual awakening.

3. The Church Is Catholic

The word "catholic" (with a small "c") means universal, widespread, or all-embracing. When the word "catholic" is applied to the Roman Church, it has multiple applications. First, the church is catholic in that Christ died to save *all*—the whole cosmos, the earth, and all its people. Christ's love and self-sacrifice are universal; they include people of every time and every culture. His risen presence is found in every Christian church including the smallest local church or Christian small faith community.[21]

The "catholic" church encompasses all Christian churches that carry the word of Christ's mission to all people. It has the responsibility of being a sign of love and salvation to all human persons, no matter what their age, color, ethnic background, or religious commitment.[22] There is a grand diversity among the disciples who are in unity with Christ.

For "catholic" to mean closed, triumphant, or intolerant is a contradiction. Christian churches are becoming increasingly aware that they must be concerned about the dignity and freedom of all people. By virtue of its catholicity, the church is an open community. It is not to be sectarian, elitist, or preferential to any one class of people. Following the example of its Lord, the church is to be especially open to and concerned about outcasts, the oppressed, and the marginalized.

A Global Church

Shortly after the Second Vatican Council, Karl Rahner observed that the church has evolved to the point of being a world church.[23] He pointed out how it moved through phases of being a Jewish church, then a Greco-Roman church, and then a European church that spread throughout the world. In the past, while the church was worldwide, it was a colonial church—a European church that imposed upon and was destructive of the cultures and religions indigenous to the areas that were conquered and colonized. According to Rahner, a new era has begun in which the church is more aware of national, ethnic, and religious autonomy. The modern church is now more inclined to adapt itself to the cultures where it dwells, whether that be in Asia, Africa, or Central and South America.[24]

The development of the world church becomes even more complicated with the collapse of Western Communism and the division of the Soviet Union. The map of Europe has been radically changed and no one can predict what structures will emerge.

A world church is one that is open to newness. It is open to all that is human, and it is willing to learn and change. Such a prospect presents a serious challenge to those who equate unity with uniformity, as well as to those who are accustomed to the centralization of church authority.

"Catholic" also means wholeness and fullness. The Catholic church maintains that it contains the fullness of the teachings of Jesus and the means of salvation. The Catholic church enjoys the presence of Jesus, the scriptures, a complete sacramental system, a local as well as global community, and a clearly defined authority system. The fact that Catholicism claims to have the Christian tradition in its fullness, does not rule out the possibility of the church neglecting or misinterpreting its tradition.

There are instances, however, when other churches and ecclesial communities, perceived as being "imperfectly" in union with the Catholic church, have been more faithful in preserving some elements of the Christian tradition. For example, it can be argued that many Protestant communities have preserved "catholic" elements such as the importance of the bible and the need to foster the growth of the community more effectively than has Roman Catholicism. The Quakers have been outstanding in their dedication to the Christian tradition of nonviolence. Pentecostal churches have contributed greatly by preserving an awareness of the Spirit and the gifts of the Spirit. Many Protestant churches have been leaders in environmental concerns. The Shakers have provided Christians with an inspiring model of simplicity and communal living.

Jeannette, a senior history major from San Diego, is very aware of the history of Christianity. Regarding the Quakers, she remarked:

We have a Quaker meeting hall near our house, so I have dropped in to get to know them. They are really a terrific group. Did you know that they opposed slavery long before other Christian churches did? They were very active on the underground railroad, bringing slaves from the South to safety on the East Coast. The Quakers also were active in the peace movement long before the Catholic or Protestant churches woke up and promoted disarmament and global peace. We Catholics can learn a lot from the Quakers.

Christianity still faces many challenges to catholicity. As the church moves toward being an authentic world church, it needs to move beyond the European theological perspective that has prevailed for so long. Already new Oriental and African views of Jesus Christ are appearing. Latin American models of community are developing. In many cultures there are growing feminine perspectives on the faith. If there is to be freedom for the inculturation of the Christian tradition in developing countries, there may have to be less foreign control. Church leaders have to realize that little respect will be given to authority that is exercised universally through repression and fear.

The Western church, which has for so long valued uniformity, will no doubt find it difficult to watch pluralistic churches emerge. The church of the future will be faced with the problem of preserving its essential elements while allowing these elements to be interpreted differently in a complex world.[25]

4. The Church Is Apostolic

The term "apostolic" entered the creeds in the fourth century. To be "apostolic" is to maintain continuity with the origins of the faith, be true to the teachings that Jesus gave to his early apostles and disciples, and be faithful to the mission of spreading the good news of salvation. Thomas Aquinas maintained that the church is built on two foundations: The first is Christ, and the second is the original apostolic witness to the resurrection.

The apostolic "mark" guarantees that the church remains in continuity with its beginnings. Some theologians, however, caution against interpreting the apostolic element of the church too narrowly. Being apostolic involves much more than the original twelve apostles handing on the tradition to the bishops.[26] After all, they reason, Jesus' authority and teachings have been given to the whole church. They also point out that the Christian tradition gives great importance to the "sense of the faithful," which holds that all the disciples carry forth the tradition authentically.

Who Were the Apostles?

In earlier times it was easier to ascertain the lines of continuity regarding the apostolic tradition. People understood that Jesus chose twelve apostles and gave them authority and a mission, which is now carried out by the bishops of the church. In reality the picture is not quite that simple. Modern biblical studies and a more precise awareness of history reveal a much more complicated situation.

The list of the names of the apostles varies from gospel to gospel. Luke includes a Judas, son of James, who does not appear in Mark and Matthew's listing of the Twelve. They both include a new name, Thaddeus. The Gospel of John does not give the names of the Twelve. The apostles seem to be a select group among Jesus' disciples, but they do not take on the role of apostles until they received their mission from the risen Lord. They elect Matthias to replace the traitor Judas Iscariot, but after that there are no efforts to replace the apostles as they die. In the accounts of the early church found in the Acts of the Apostles, only Peter is named. The apostles seem to be active in the church of Jerusalem, but we read nothing in the New Testament about any of them individually founding churches or assuming roles of leadership. In Jerusalem, the leadership is in the hands of James who is described as "the brother of the Lord." James was certainly not one of the apostles, and yet he holds an extremely important position. In this case, being related to Jesus seems to carry more weight than being an apostle.

Paul's apostleship creates even more problems. Paul strongly claims the authenticity of his own apostleship, when in fact he never met Jesus. Paul, moreover, distinguishes between the apostles and the Twelve. The Twelve take on a special symbolism in the early church as the symbolic heads of the tribes of the "new Israel." The word "apostle" has a broader meaning for Paul, however, as he speaks of "all the apostles," and includes leaders other than the Twelve.[27]

People who are clearly not members of the Twelve but who share Paul's apostolic work are considered to be apostles. Barnabas is called an apostle, as is Junia, whom many think was a woman. Phoebe, Priscilla and Aquila, Mary, Andronicus, and others have key roles in the founding and sustaining of some of the first domestic churches. Romans chapter 16 provides a clear description of these small Christian communities that met in people's homes. Both women and men served as elders and presiders over these early Christian communities that were linked in a collegial structure.

By the end of the second century, this more inclusive structure was replaced by an episcopacy consisting of men who were considered to be "successors of the apostles." Today the episcopacy is still considered to be an authoritative link with the apostolic tradition. Vatican II pointed out that the apostolic succession of bishops was divinely instituted. This does not necessarily mean that Jesus left behind a clear and precise church order. Rather, church structures and offices gradually evolved under the guidance of the Spirit of the Lord. Many hold that this evolution continues, and that present needs call for new authority structures.

What is at question is how narrowly the term "apostle" should be understood. Is the apostolic succession from the Twelve, and therefore only male? Does this office serve as the channel for priesthood and therefore limit the church to an all-male priesthood? Or might "apostle" be viewed more expansively as we see it in Paul, and might women assume such a role? If the latter be the case, then both priesthood and succession must be reconsidered in the future reconstruction of church authority and ministry.[28]

Conclusion

This chapter demonstrates that change has been present in the church from the beginning. Like the good steward in the gospel, the church has perennially brought forth things both old and new. The church has been a "conservative" institution in that it always carefully protected its treasured traditions. At the same time, the church has been open to new developments.

There was a point in the church's history when the diaconate was new, when priesthood was an innovation, when celebrating eucharist in churches was a notable change from gathering in people's homes. The papacy developed over a long period of time before it became the universal office that we know today. Individual confession was an innovation of the Irish monks, and it took centuries before it was acceptable. At one point in history celibacy was a new requirement of priesthood. The monastic communities came upon the scene as a new way of living the Christian life. The mendicant religious congregations, universities, and indulgences all appeared for the first time in the Middle Ages.

In our own time, communal penance and anointing services are new. There is a new universal Catholic catechism to replace the Roman Catechism of Trent and the more familiar *Baltimore Catechism* used in the United States for the past hundred years. Newness and change are integral to the church's life. Doubtless, there are many new, wonderful, and challenging things on the horizon for the church of the future.

Discussion Questions

1. List and discuss the various ways in which the church has related to "the world" throughout the history of the church.

2. What areas of the church were most in most need of reform at the time of the Reformation? Research the Council of Trent to see in what ways this council did much to reform the church at that time.

3. List and discuss some areas of reform and renewal that were going on in the period previous to Vatican II. Research some of the theologians who laid the groundwork for Vatican II renewal.

4. It has been said that the Catholic church changed its self-perception at Vatican II. Discuss some specific ways in which this observation might be accurate.

5. The church is to be one, holy, catholic, and apostolic. Discuss the meaning of each of these "marks" of the church. Please indicate specific areas where further renewal might be needed in our own time.

Suggested Readings

Eugene C Bianchi and Rosemary Radford Ruether (eds.), *A Democratic Catholic Church*. New York: Crossroad, 1992.

Denise Lardner Carmody and John Tully Carmody, *Bonded in Christ's Love: An Introduction to Ecclesiology*. New York: Paulist Press, 1986.

Dennis M. Doyle, *The Church Emerging From Vatican II.* Mystic, CT: Twenty-Third Publications, 1992.

Avery Dulles, *The Catholicity of the Church.* Oxford: Clarendon Press, 1985.

Avery Dulles, *A Church to Believe In.* New York: Crossroad, 1984.

Adrian Hastings (ed.), *Vatican II and After.* New York: Oxford University Press, 1991.

Michael G. Lawler and Thomas J. Shanahan, *Church: A Spirited Communion.* Collegeville, MN: Liturgical Press, 1995.

Lucien Richard and others (eds.), *Vatican II: The Unfinished Agenda, a Look to the Future by Professors of the Weston School of Theology.* New York: Paulist Press, 1988.

Edward Schillebeeckx, *Church: The Human Story of God.* New York: Crossroad, 1985.

Francis Sullivan, *The Church We Believe In.* New York: Paulist Press, 1988.

9.

Mission and Ministry

Framing the Question

My name is Matthew. I am a junior majoring in computer science. I grew up in Detroit, where I attended a Catholic high school. Right now I'm not much into faith or religion, but I do a lot of thinking in these areas. I guess I backed away from the church because I'm never sure what its purpose is, and I don't know where I fit in. So often when people talk about the church they mean the pope and bishops and priests. These are all distant figures for me, and I don't see myself conforming to their rigid standards.

I had an experience the summer after my junior year in high school that still has me thinking. One of our teachers invited me to go to an Indian reservation for a month. At first I was not too anxious. It sounded like one of those "do-gooder" activities and I didn't see what difference I could make. But I liked the teacher, so I went. The time there was really amazing. We did some clean-up and painted some areas, and that was okay. At night we hung out with the people who lived on the reservation. It was great getting to know them. Most of them were really great people, and they seemed to enjoy getting to know me. I think we were all surprised to see how much we had in common. I felt that when I played with the kids, they forgot for a time that they were poor and lived a hard life. When the time was up I was really sorry to leave. They did a lot for me; made me feel like a real person. And I felt that in some way I had made a difference.

When I got back home, I started to think. Where does the church fit into all this? What can the church do in the face of so much poverty and suffering in the world? And who is going to do all the work? There were no priests or Sisters on the reservation I visited. A priest came there once a month to say Mass. One of the men on the reservation taught the kids about religion, but that's about all he had time for. How can the church keep going in a situation like that?

Matthew raises a question that is discussed more and more in theology: What is the mission of the church? In past times it was easier to answer this question in terms of the church's responsibility to guard the faith of its members and send missionaries to spread the faith to "pagans." The church saw itself as a closed society, protecting its own doctrines and inviting others to join. The church today, in contrast, is very much part of the world, dedicated to dealing with the world's problems like over-population, hunger, war, violence, and destruction of the environment. In light of these massive problems the question is: What is the church's mission now? And who is going to accomplish this mission?

This chapter examines the mission and ministry of the church. We will examine the nature of the church's mission and how this is being carried out in contemporary society. Then we will turn our attention to the ministers, the people who work to achieve the mission of the church. We will look at the duties and responsibilities of clergy and laity, and focus on some of the more visible ministers of the Catholic church: the pope, bishops, priests, and deacons. We will end by looking at some of the key factors involved in planning the ministry of the future.

The Mission of the Church

The church has traditionally pointed to Jesus' commissioning of his disciples as a description of its mission. This commissioning appears in the last chapter of Matthew's gospel and indicates an awareness on the part of the Christian community in Antioch (from whence this gospel most likely originates) of its Christ-given mission. According to this passage, the disciples are told to go to a mountain in Galilee. There they meet the Lord and worship him, although they are still having their doubts about the resurrection. Jesus approaches them and says:

> All power in heaven and on earth has been given to me. Go, therefore, and make disciples of all nations, baptizing them in the name of the Father, and of the Son, and of the holy Spirit, teaching them to observe all that I have commanded you. And behold I am with you always, until the end of the age. (Mt 28:16–20)

The early Christian communities, according to the scriptures written fifty or so years after Jesus' death, already were aware that they had to carry on Jesus' mission to bring about the kingdom of God. Jesus had spoken so often of the kingdom, this divine order that the rabbis believed was in creation; this goal of peace and justice to which their God would ultimately lead them. Now the early Christians saw this reign of God's power personified in their risen Lord. This power had raised Jesus and glorified him as the Christ. Now his followers were given the power to co-mission with their Savior. The power of God that was so dynamically present in Jesus Christ could now be proclaimed to the world by his followers.[1]

The early disciples went forth with the Spirit of Christ in their midst, and witnessed to the good news. They proclaimed that Jesus Christ was the Savior who had died so that all sins could be forgiven. They also announced that through his resurrection Jesus promised eternal life to those who are faithful to God's law of love and compassion. The members of the early church witnessed to this good news primarily by their lives together. They tried to live humbly, simply, and generously in imitation of Jesus. In doing this, they believed that they were imitating the holiness of God as seen in Jesus. Their mission was to give the world a glimpse of the happiness that could be achieved by following Jesus. As Pope John Paul II has written: "The Church's fundamental function in every age, and particularly in ours, is to direct peoples' gaze, to point the awareness and experience of the whole of humanity towards the mystery of Christ."[2]

Going Forth

Pope John XXIII used to say that the church had done a lot of teaching, but that now it had to start "going forth" more. His vision of the church was that of a community of sisters and brothers who, by their example and their concern for others, helped make the world a better place. In his experience in World War II and in his work throughout Europe, he had seen a world filled with violence, hunger, poverty, and injustice. Pope John's vision of the church was of a community that goes forth into the world and works for peace and justice.

This going forth entails seeing other people as neighbors. This often stands as a challenge to our common prejudices and stereotypes. A local billboard put it this way:

> Your Christ is Jewish,
> Your car is Japanese,
> Your pizza is Italian,
> Your democracy is Greek,
> Your coffee is Brazilian,

You holiday in Turkey,
Your numbering is Arabic,
So why is your neighbor a foreigner?

There is a strange irony that in the global-village world of today with all its multicultural varieties, Jesus' notion of loving one's neighbor is often unfamiliar. His teaching is clear that all life is sacred and that all people are children of God. The church's mission is to spread this message, not only in Bosnia, Rwanda, South Africa, Guatemala, and Germany, but in the streets of cities and towns of every country including our own.

The Mission Is for All

Since the commissioning in the Gospel of Matthew was addressed to the eleven disciples, it often has been assumed that the church's mission is to be carried out only by some elite corps in the church. Yet if one looks at the early communities we see that the mission is carried out in different ways by all the disciples: women and men, poor and rich, Greek, Roman, and Jew.

It is the sacrament of baptism that gives everyone a share in Christ's mission. The discipleship that arises because of baptism carries with it both the privilege and the responsibility of acting in Christ's name. In this "church of equals," the Spirit of the Lord works through each member of the church in a unique fashion. Unfortunately, most followers of Christ have never been made aware of this, nor have they been given many opportunities to take part in this mission. As one theologian put it:

> A quarter of a century after the close of Vatican II the laity are in practice accorded little more than an ancillary role, and very little authority to appropriate their baptismal mission....Indeed, the chasm between some of our rhetoric and current ecclesiastical discipline and practice sometimes seems unbridgeable.[3]

Many Catholic women think that they are locked out of leadership roles and positions where key decisions are made. Many young Catholics also find that they are given few opportunities to serve. Listen to Paul, a French major from Pittsburgh, who is frustrated with his parish:

There are a lot of teenagers and young adults in my parish who have the tal-

ent and the willingness to be of service, but we don't have anyone who can organize us and get something going. Several years ago we had a youth minister. He organized a trip to Appalachia during spring break. The ones who went really got a lot out of it, but not much is happening these days for the youth in our parish.

A Call to Conversion

Jesus began his mission by calling people to conversion and to a radical change in the way they lived their lives. The Gospel of Mark, the first of the gospels to be put into written form, says that right after John the Baptizer was arrested, Jesus started his mission in Galilee. Jesus proclaimed: "This is the time for fulfillment. The kingdom of God is at hand. Repent, and believe the gospel" (Mk 1:15). When Jesus called people to repent, he wanted them to turn around and go in a new direction, to alter their lives and live in a new way.

The mission of the church and all its members is to call people to repentance. This includes regret for evil actions of the past, a firm resolve to change and improve one's life, and a desire to be reconciled with enemies. Bishop Desmond Tutu gave a stunning example of this when for years he called the people of South Africa to repentance. He called them to stop the racial hatred of white for black and black for white. He asked blacks to stop atrocities like using the "necklace"—a gasoline-soaked tire placed around a person's neck and then ignited—to torture and kill other blacks whom they hated. He pleaded for an end to tribal wars. He called upon the whites to stop their oppression of blacks, most of whom lived in squalor under the grinding system of apartheid. He asked people to stop the arrests, the terrorism, the executions. When the change came in 1994 with a free election, who can forget how the archbishop danced up and down on his porch for joy! He was witnessing the good news of conversion.

Conversion is always a two-way street. The very fact that we call others to change demands that we change ourselves. To call another to drop a prejudice requires that we do the same. To lead someone from violence involves rooting such inclinations out of our lives as well. To be on mission to others is also to be on mission to ourselves. That lesson was best taught to me during a visit to the Madres of San Salvador. These are the mothers of the "disappeared"—women and men who had been taken at night by death squads to face torture and death. Each day these sorrowing women search for evidence of what happened to their loved ones, always with the hope of bringing the killers to justice. The supervisor of the women's groups had been raped and killed.

Their offices had been bombed. But they persisted in their work; in their call for a stop to the violence, and for punishment of the murderers. Never in talking with them does one sense hatred or a desire for revenge. These remarkable women, their faces etched with grief and loss, have compassion and love for their persecutors. Although they want their oppressors brought to justice, they want even more to see them change their ways and be saved from their own hatred and violence. These women are formidable disciples, and no terror or threat can get in the way of their mission to go forth and teach the gospel of repentance and forgiveness to others.

The Church in the Modern World

The Second Vatican Council did much to help bring the church's mission back into focus. The council envisioned the church as a community of people intimately linked to the world and all its people. It described the church as journeying through history promoting the kingdom of God; present within the world and yet not identified with it. In order to accomplish this the council pointed out that the church has to be attentive to the "signs of the times." This involves discerning the "signs of God's presence and purpose in the happenings, needs and desires in our age."[4] Such immediacy to world events demands that the church be flexible and varied in its mission. At one moment the church might be called on to serve peasants in Guatemala; at another to help the oppressed in Haiti; or possibly to open clinics for unwed mothers in inner-city Cincinnati. It is the local needs that often determine the specific mission of the church.

A priest offered this explanation of the Jesuit Refugee Service.

I first arrived at the mission in Guatemala in the early 1980s. It was truly a baptism by fire. A month after I started working in the parish, the army came through bombing and burning the villages. Most of the people who were driven out or killed were Mayan Indians. The army said they were afraid of the build-up of a guerrilla movement. Hundreds of thousands became refugees, and countless men, women, and children were killed. In all 440 villages were burned to the ground.

Our mission was to stay with our people. We walked for days with them into Mexico, and then helped set up refugee camps there. In Mexico we set up clinics and a food-distribution center. We built a chapel where we could gather for eucharist and prayer. We organized groups to pressure the Guatemalan government to let the indigenous people return to their land. Things seem to be looking up in this regard and some people returned to their land. Some of our priests who stayed behind in Guatemala were killed. My friend wrote me: "Now they have begun to shoot us. Now we truly share the lives of the people. Now we know that we really belong to them."

Should the Church Get Involved?

Not everyone agrees with church groups like the Jesuits getting involved in social and political problems. Many still debate the question: "How does the church's concern for the political, economic, and social order fit into its world mission?" We know that the Second Vatican Council expressed a concern for world suffering, yet at the same time took a rather conservative view about actual involvement. It pointed out that Christ did not give his church a proper mission in these areas. The council maintained that Christ gave his church a religious mission, and out of this can come an energy to serve the human community.[5]

Catholic thinkers are divided on the question of the church's social mission. Some still see the church as a perfect society, that is, a society complete in itself and in need of no other human structures. They argue that the church's mission is supernatural, and thus concerned only with showing people how to get to heaven. The church, therefore, has no business meddling in political affairs or social problems.[6] The United States bishops encountered this mentality when they published their controversial documents on nuclear disarmament and on the economy. There were those who maintained that the bishops should attend to church matters and not meddle in secular matters. Many other bishops throughout Europe, Latin America, Mexico, and the Orient have found the same kind of resistance, and even violent persecution, when they entered what some people consider to be the political arena.

There still exists a dualistic mentality among many in the church. They see a dichotomy between the natural and the supernatural, the profane and the sacred, the religious and the political. Consequently this view generally opposes the church's involvement in secular issues and political action. In the United States the constitutional separation of church and state has often further separated religious concerns from political issues.

This dualistic approach is in marked contrast to the more holistic approach of Catholic thinkers like Rahner, de Lubac, Lonergan, and Teilhard de Chardin who see reality as one, with both natural and supernatural dimensions. For them, nature and grace, the world and the spirit, are integrally connected. It is this holistic view that leads many Catholics to accept political and liberation theologies. Both of these approaches take a radical, activist approach to the church's mission.

Social Action and Church Mission

Even among those who believe that the church should address social issues, there is a wide range of views. Some argue that the church may enter the world of social action only as a substitute for the state. In other words, when the state fails to carry out its responsibility to the needy the church can and should step into the breach. For example, if a given city fails to provide shelters for the homeless, it falls on the church to establish such facilities. The nature of the church's mission, however, does not ordinarily require the church to get involved with such services.

Others propose that the church should only serve the world "unofficially" through its laity. People who favor this approach see the official mission of the church as spiritual, but since the church is present in the world, it can take on tasks that are beyond its mission. This was the attitude of the Catholic Action movement popular in the 1940s and 1950s. In this situation lay people take on social responsibilities and are guided by church hierarchy in their application of Christian principles to social problems. In this way the official church can keep its distance from worldly controversies, and bishops, priests, and Sisters who do get directly involved in political issues can be pressured to withdraw. Conversely, the "worldly" laity are not encouraged to get involved in official church ministries.

This view is open to criticism for many reasons. It seems to take a narrow view of the church's mission, limits the activity of clergy and religious, and fails to recognize the laity's authentic call to mission, which is inherent in their baptism.

People who have been influenced by Avery Dulles' post-Vatican II explanation of the nature of the church in his widely read book, *Models of the Church*, allow for ecclesial effort in the world only when the church acts out of the servant model. This approach also has limitations as the understanding of social concern pertains to the mission of the church only in certain instances.[7]

Political and liberation theologies have gone beyond these views and see social action and the struggle for justice as integral to the church's mission. From this perspective, salvation history and the mission of the kingdom are integral to world history. Work for the kingdom, by its very nature, includes being in solidarity with the poor, and actively confronting those who promote injustice in political and social matters. As one theologian puts it: "Outside the world there is no salvation." Disciples of Jesus follow a master who was very much part of his world, and who was dedicated to promoting human dignity and social justice.

A Gradual Awakening

The church's awareness of the social dimension of its mission has come gradually. The modern popes were especially effective here. As early as 1893 Pope Leo XIII spoke up for a papacy and church that felt opposing forces pressing in on all sides. Leo saw the church as divinely instituted to provide the means of salvation. By virtue of its authority the church could tell the State how to provide the social harmony wherein salvation might be worked out. In this view the church does not have a direct mission to the world. The church does, however, have the true doctrine and authority to tell the State how it must carry out its worldly mission.[8]

In 1933 Pope Pius XI offered further solutions to world problems based on the sovereign authority of the church. He condemned liberal capitalism, now in a shambles and mired in the Great Depression. He also attacked the dangerous movements of Communism and Fascism that were violently oppressive in Russia and Italy. Pius was tough-minded and deeply concerned about social injustice, but his solutions were from a different era, and therefore did not bear much influence on the crises of the times.[9]

Pope Pius XII was in office during the critical times of World War II. Despite the complexity of the world's political and military situation he often spoke on behalf of human dignity, called for a reconstruction of the social order, and worked behind the scenes to assist and even rescue those suffering from the war. After the war Pius identified with the free world and encouraged democracies to lead the way in post-war reconstruction. He offered no ecclesiastically conceived solutions, as did his predecessors, but he presented a church deeply interested in social issues and committed to individual freedom and human rights.

It was Pope John XXIII who took both the church and the world by surprise. He called for radical reform within the church, and also showed his intense concern about economic oppression and the nuclear arms race in the world about him. His documents on world peace and social justice gained worldwide attention. The ecumenical council that he convened supported scientific and industrial progress, but also offered prophetic and critical responses to the abuses of the times.

Pope Paul VI traveled the world putting the questions of justice and peace even more in a global context. He wrote about the development of the people, the process whereby individuals and nations unfold their own potential and write their own histories. He called for bold and courageous reforms initiated by the victims themselves. Many maintain that his radical positions helped lay the foundations for liberation theology.

The Bishops of Latin America—in historic meetings at Medellín, Colombia (1968) and Puebla, Mexico (1979)—approved a liberation approach to the church's mission. They shifted the focus of Christian theology to human experience, especially the experience of oppression. The Latin American bishops supported liberation theology, which called for a conversion of both the powerful and the weak to change the sinful structures that bring about poverty, hunger, and starvation. Liberation theologians urged the church to see its mission in the light of Christ's mission to set all human beings free. To bring this about the church needed to be in solidarity with the poor, and to identify with their struggle for freedom and justice.

A world Synod on Justice in Rome (1971) reiterated that the church's mission was "to be present in the heart of the world by proclaiming the Good News to the poor, freedom to the oppressed, and joy to the afflicted." This synod explicitly placed justice as a "constitutive dimension" of the church's mission.

Pope John Paul II has consistently stressed themes of peace and justice in his many trips throughout the world. He has written numerous documents on social justice, and has been one of the most powerful voices for human rights in the modern world.[10] He also seems to have been a significant figure working behind the scenes in the movement to bring about the collapse of Communism and the break-up of the Soviet Union.

Foreign Missions

By virtue of their baptism all Christians share in the mission of the church. Some do this through organized efforts to spread the good news in lands that are "foreign" to the missionaries.

In the last several decades there has been a marked shift in the theology and practice of foreign missionary activities. Previously the church's foreign missions coincided with colonial expansion.[11] Many of the missionaries were in solidarity with the natives and ministered to them with love and generosity. Other missionaries, however, lacked an appreciation of the indigenous people and their native religions. In the European colonial expansion in the Americas during the sixteenth and seventeenth centuries, the church often tolerated, and occasionally participated in the mistreatment of the indigenous peoples. Native Americans were often viewed as savage heathens. The missionaries' goal was to convert as many as possible and replace their native religion with Eurocentric Catholicism.

In Latin America untold numbers of indigenous peoples were annihilated by disease or through slave labor in the mines. Many missionaries took the side of the Indians and protested the cruel atrocities. Others held that the subjugation of those they saw as sub-human creatures was permissable, at least so that they could be converted and thereby saved. At times conversion to Christianity was often forced upon the natives, sometimes at gunpoint. Bartolomé de Las Casas, a church leader from Spain, aligned himself with the Franciscans and Dominicans who took the side of the indigenous people of Latin America. He vehemently opposed the Conquistadores: "Tell me what right, with what justice, do you hold these Indians in such cruel and horrible servitude? On what authority have you waged such detestable wars on these people in their mild, peaceful lands?"[12] Las Casas is quite clear on how evil it was to plunder, enslave, and slaughter this gentle people. He wrote that such horrors contradicted the Christian faith because: "The Indians are our siblings, and Christ has given his life for them."

Insensitivity to native culture and religion was also apparent in the foreign mission efforts to the Orient. Matteo Ricci, an extraordinary missionary of the eighteenth century, tried to inculcate Christianity into the Chinese culture by honoring the beliefs and rituals of the Chinese people. His work was condemned, however, and the Catholic missionary thrust in China has been severely limited ever since.[13]

The theology that guided this style of foreign mission activity viewed baptism into the Catholic church as necessary for salvation. The task of the missionary was to proclaim the truths of the church, lead the candidate to faith and baptism, and thereby provide salvation for the souls of these individuals. The number of baptisms and marriages performed was important to missionaries, for they measured the success of their work by the number of souls they saved.

Foreign missions were generally established as safe-zones, places cut off from the native culture in order to provide education, worship, and pastoral care that was largely European in nature. The local culture was often disdained and, if possible, the convert was led from it to the more "enlightened" Western cultural perspective. Within this framework, many Catholic missionaries worked with deep faith and concern for the people to whom they brought the good news. The church often expanded notably in such areas but too often the church became associated with the colonial power that dominated and persecuted the indigenous peoples.

New Directions for Foreign Missions

In the last several decades there has been a change in both the theology and practice of Catholic foreign missionaries. This change has come about because of shifts in the understanding of the overall mission of the church. Catholics have renewed their sense of mission by reclaiming the gospel mission of Jesus, which was directed much more at enabling people than conquering them. At the same time the understanding of salvation and conversion has become much more holistic and inclusive. Theories guiding foreign mission activity are now seen in the context of a world church that values local cultures and religions, and is engaged in the global struggle for social justice.

The shift in attitude toward Catholic foreign missions has also been the result of many changes in the world scene. The collapse of colonialism, the rise of nationalism in the Third World, the disintegration of Russian Communism, the break-up of the Soviet Union, and the weakening of the European Catholic church have all been factors that have affected thinking regarding the foreign missions.

The shifts in both the church and the world have resulted in a number of interesting trends in the world of the foreign missions. Four significant trends can be detected.[14]

1. Inculturation. In recent times there has been a resurgence in interest among all the peoples of the world in their own cultural identity. On every continent a great value is placed on rediscovering cultural roots and reviving the customs, beliefs, and values of each particular tribe or national group. While this can have positive benefits for people, it has also contributed in no small measure to the cultural conflicts that have intensified in many parts of the world. The world has seen horrendous atrocities carried out in the name of "ethnic cleansing" in places like Bosnia and Rwanda.

For foreign missionaries, inculturation implies that the Catholic faith be integrated into the local culture in a respectful and sensitive manner.[15] This requires that the missionary learn the local language and customs, listen to local needs, and invite people to hear the gospel and integrate it into their lives. This often means that there will be some changes in the local culture, in that the gospel message always calls for conversion from sin, and has the power to transform culture. At the same time, however, inculturation calls for the gospel message to be adapted, re-interpreted, and connected to the everyday experience of the people. It is here that Catholicism is developing a pluriformity and going beyond the older uniform European models of the faith.

Where missionaries discover oppression and injustice in the culture, this new perspective calls for solidarity with those who are subjugated, as well as action against the oppressors. This kind of identification with liberation has put many missionaries in danger from repressive governments. As a result many missionaries have been murdered on account of their advocacy for the poor.

When Karl Rahner observed that the Catholic church is becoming a "world church," he did not mean, as was the case in the past, that a European version of Catholicism was being put in place around the world. Rather, today's world church is a church being born anew in many different cultures and peoples throughout the world. Control, the enforcement of uniformity, and absolute decrees by a central authority are increasingly more difficult to implement in such a church. New forms of global and local leadership that use persuasion and inspiration are more appropriate and effective in contemporary foreign missionary activities.

2. Respect for other religions and churches. The post-Vatican II church has gained a new respect for the truth and salvation claims of other religions and churches. The Catholic church has moved away from the position that "outside the church there is no salvation," and now more comfortably dialogues with and cooperates with other faiths.[16]

This openness to other faiths has radically changed the approach to foreign mission activity. First of all, there is no longer the urgency to convert and baptize, lest the person not be saved. Instead, the gospel message is proclaimed, and people are invited freely to accept it if they so choose.

Other religions are treated with respect, and the missionary might well end up nurturing membership in another faith, rather than insensitively proselytizing.

Productive dialogue between Catholicism and other religions has benefited all the participants. Partnership with other faiths on social, political, and more recently, on environmental issues has been effective. On ecological matters Catholicism has gained valuable insights on sustaining the earth from Native American religions, from the ancient religions of the Far East, and from some of more active Protestant churches.

Lisa, Marc, and Debby recently did a team research project on Native American religions and ecology. Listen to the comments of Lisa on their experience.

When we started this project we knew little or nothing about the Native Americans. We still called them Indians when we started our work. As we did our research we all noticed how much these religious beliefs spoke to us. The Native Americans hold all of nature sacred. For me the oceans, rivers, woods, and mountains have always been special. I never realized how much I have in common with these people and their religious beliefs. Their rituals also really move me.

3. Basic Christian Communities. Basic Christian communities first became popular in Latin America in the 1960s. Now throughout the world Catholics are gathering in small communities for faith-sharing, prayer, support, a more intimate sense of belonging, and for planning social action. It is as though Catholics are returning to the "house churches" that were so important in the early days of Christianity.

Small faith communities are a significant element of the foreign missions today.[17] Missionaries are not so set on the conversion of individuals, as they are on building small faith communities. The witness to the gospel way of living is what attracts new members. These communities stand as symbols of Christ's love and concern. The commitment of these communities to love, justice, and the service of others brings about conversions.

Missionaries are not expected to be greater than the local people, but part of the local faith community. Missionaries must truly be part of the these churches as equals, and share in the communities' simple lifestyles and struggles to survive. As one missionary put it: "It is the community that acts as the apostle, rather than the elite clerics from foreign lands."

4. Inadequacy of Ordained Ministers. Ministry in the Catholic church today is taking on a new look. The established churches of Europe and North America are beginning to look more like mission territories. There has been a massive exodus on the part of priests and religious. Many seminaries have closed, and those that remain train only a small number of candidates. Numerous parishes across Europe, Canada, and the United States are without priests. Of the 400,000 Catholic priests in the world, 68% of them are in Europe or North America. Only about one-third of the world's priests serve in the developing countries where the church's population is growing rapidly. It is estimated that by the year 2000 more than 70% of all Catholics will live in developing countries.[18]

While some people lament the decline in the number of active priests and long for what they remember as the good old days, many Catholic dioceses in North America are already training and making use of lay pastoral administrators and associates in parishes. They are calling forth lay people to exercise their baptismal ministry of service and mission, and offering appropriate training and education for many tasks previously handled by priests and nuns.

The foreign missions that have faced clergy shortages for decades are keenly aware of this crisis in ministry. Many missionary leaders have been strong advocates for a change in the requirement of mandatory celibacy for priests. In many areas of Latin America and Africa, such a requirement is not culturally acceptable. As the women's movement spreads from Europe and North American to countries where much of the church's missionary work is carried on by women, many of them are asking that they be given equality in church ministry and decision-making.[19]

New models of ministry are emerging from missionary lands and finding their way to North America. The role of the catechist has been a prominent ministry for some time in the foreign missions. Catechists have not only taught the faith, they have founded and led communities, and taken on many pastoral responsibilities. Many of them have been in the forefront of liberation movements and have paid with their lives for their commitment to justice. No doubt other creative models of ministry will emerge from the missions, where the needs have become so acute and where priests are in such short supply.

Finally, the shape of Catholic foreign mission activity will also change due to rapid growth in the non-Christian population. Where in 1970 the world population was one-third Christian, by 2020 Christians may be only one-fifth of the world population.[20] At that point, spreading the gospel will call for new and creative models of ministry.

Ministry in the Church

So far in this chapter we have discussed the purpose or mission of the church, especially as it relates to Jesus' command to proclaim the good news of salvation to all people. Now we want to turn our attention to the way that the mission of Jesus Christ is carried out, and especially to focus on the people who perform that ministry. We will examine the earliest forms of Christian ministry and note some of the significant developments throughout the church's history. We will examine the official ministerial offices: the diaconate, priesthood, episcopacy, and papacy. We will conclude with a discussion of the future of ministry and note how all the baptized faithful are being called to become more actively involved in the church's mission.

The Beginnings of Ministry

Christian ministry began in simple yet diverse ways in the early communities. By virtue of baptism, every Christian became a disciple of Jesus Christ, and by that very fact was held responsible to minister in the name of Jesus.[21] From the beginning there was a clear sense that all the members of the community were responsible for preserving the tradition and for sharing it with others.

The first disciples saw themselves carrying on the ministry of Jesus. Even though Jesus did not establish any specific church order, he lived and taught certain ideals of loving and compassionate service that became the model for authentic ecclesial ministry. Gifted with the Spirit of the Lord, the disciples went forth and served in Jesus' name, confident that Christ would guide them as their ministry developed.

Inspired by the memories of Jesus' own example, the early disciples were called to believe that the embrace of Abba took in all human beings, regardless of nationality, gender, religious background, or social status. Following their Master, the early disciples gave special preference to the outcasts of society. That explained, in part, why Christianity spread so quickly: The church had great appeal to the masses of poor and oppressed who had been without hope or dignity for so long.

Jesus taught his followers that authority was not to be exercised by "lording it over others." People in authority were to be the servants of the community. The early communities valued simplicity, shared responsibility with one another, and exercised the power of healing, forgiveness, and compassion, rather than the power of domination.

Even though there was occasionally some strife among the various groups in the communities, the ideal seems to have been one of equality. Even though ministry included the role of leadership, it was intended to be primarily a service among equals in discipleship.

The early communities saw their weekly gathering around the table of the Lord as a key meeting and bonding place. Here they followed the example of Jesus who valued a "table ministry" and often used this setting to teach or heal those around him. The person who was the leader, generally the host of the house church, also served as the leader of the eucharist.[22] This synagogue model is in marked contrast to the clerical model with which we are more familiar, where the one who has the "power" to consecrate eucharist is assigned to be the leader of the community.

The early house churches also kept alive Jesus' promise of freedom. Jesus said: "So if the Son sets you free, you will indeed be free" (Jn 8:36). In a similar way Paul reminded the Galatians of this new-found freedom: "Christ set us free, so that we should remain free" (Gal 5:1). This sense of freedom went beyond the Hellenistic notion of freedom only for the elite. The Christian community was free and open to all, rich and poor, saint and sinner.

The house churches enjoyed a certain liberty. Although loosely connected with other Christian communities and concerned about their welfare, the house churches nevertheless enjoyed considerable autonomy. As a result we find a broad diversity in regard to the forms and activities of ministry in these communities. In the Pauline churches ministry was based largely on how a person was gifted by the Spirit. Service was carried out in teams of workers who were not concerned about official titles. It is not until the later first-century communities described in the Pastoral Letters of the New Testament that we begin to see more formally defined offices emerge, and the authority to minister becomes more centered in elders and in the presbyterial council.

Ministry Based on Gifts

Christian ministry did not begin in institutional office or with those who had been formally ordained, but in charisms or "gifts of the Spirit" given to individuals for use in the service of the communities.[23] In communities founded by Paul and described in his New Testament letters, some people were gifted to witness to Jesus and the kingdom as prophets. The prophets' proclamation was radical in its nature, and was often so challenging to those who were corrupt that it could cost the prophets their lives. Others were gifted to be apostles and were called to carry the message of Jesus to other areas, where they would call the residents to conversion. Those gifted with the ability to live in solidarity with the poor were also considered to be authentic apostles of Jesus Christ.[24]

Those who were gifted by the Spirit as teachers had both a special understanding of the gospel message and the ability to teach it to others. Those gifted with the courage to be arrested and suffer for the cause of Christ were automatically considered to be ministers in their communities. Ministry in the early communities, then, does not seem to imply status or office. Rather, ministry was the performance of a certain service by virtue of one's giftedness from the Spirit. Paul describes this approach to ministry in his letter to the Corinthians. He writes:

> There are different kinds of spiritual gifts, but the same Spirit; there are different forms of service but the same Lord; there are different workings but the same God who produces all of them in everyone. To each individual the manifestation of the Spirit is given for some benefit. To one is given through the Spirit the expression of wisdom; to another the expression of knowledge according to the same Spirit; to another faith by the same Spirit; to another gifts of healing by the one Spirit; to another mighty deeds; to another prophecy, to another the discernment of spirits; to another varieties of tongues; to another interpretation of tongues. But one and the same Spirit produces all of these, distributing them individually to each person as the Spirit wishes. (1 Cor 12:4–11)

There seems to have been no shortage of ministers in the early days. As needs arose, the gifted responded. They were called forth without concern for office, gender, or marital status. The distinctions that are present today between clergy and laity, ordained and non-ordained, generally were not delineated in the early church. People forgave one another, anointed the sick, and chose from among themselves the individual who would preside at the eucharist when they shared the word and broke bread in remembrance of their Lord and Savior.

The Question of Leadership

The leadership roles in the early communities evolved gradually. Paul remained the chief authority figure in the communities he established and maintained, assisted by teams of fellow workers who were handpicked and proven disciples. About eighty names appear in Paul's letters of the women and men who were his closest fellow workers. They had no official titles, yet they were leaders with evident authority in the local Christian communities, as well as in the network that bound these small groups together. Theologian Edward Schillebeeckx maintains that all of this leadership "grew out of the pneumatic vitality and prophetic power of the Spirit."[25] The early disciples were convinced that the risen Lord was with them, and that he would provide the gifts needed to help them carry on his ministry.

The leadership in the communities was not a matter for claiming privilege or superiority. Leadership was manifest in simple service of the members of the community following the injunction that Jesus had given to his disciples that they not "rule over" or "domineer" others in the manner of worldly leaders (Mt 20:25–28). The one who wished to be first was to be the last.

Structure and Hierarchy

Toward the end of the first century, there was a clear shift in the form and structure of ministry. The domestic model of the small church community was replaced with the "household of God," which was modeled after the patriarchal Greco-Roman households. In this model, the presbyter (priest) or episkopos (bishop) was the head of the household, and the women were moved to the background. This shift marked the beginning of a more hierarchic model of Christian ministry.

The structure of the Roman Senate also came to bear on the development and ordering of ministerial offices. Prophets and teachers were replaced by official leaders, and there was a shift from charism (the spontaneous gift of the Spirit) to office (elected or appointed leaders) as the basis for ministry.

We will now examine offices of leadership that emerged in the early church, and which to this day provide the framework for leadership in the church.

The Diaconate

In 1964 the Second Vatican Council restored the diaconate as a permanent office of ministry in the Catholic church. For many centuries the diaconate had been simply one of the many stages that a seminarian passed through on his way to the priesthood. Now married men can be ordained to the office of deacon and serve the church in this official ministry.

The ministry of the deacon can be traced back to the very earliest Christian communities. The Acts of the Apostles relates a dispute that arose in Jerusalem when the Greek-speaking Christians complained that they were not getting their fair share of the common goods and that their widows were being neglected. When the apostles became aware of these complaints, they selected seven outstanding men to share in their ministry of service (Acts 6:1–7). One of these, Stephen, carried on a ministry of teaching that so upset the Jews that he was stoned to death, and is now considered to be the first Christian martyr (Acts 6:8–7:60).

In the Letter to Timothy the requirements for deacons are specified: They are to be serious and honest, live good lives, be good parents and spouses if they are married, and serve others well in the name of Jesus Christ (1 Tm 3:8–13). Paul recognizes the position of deacons and offers them special greeting in the salutation of the Letter to the Philippians (Phil 1:1).

It is doubtful that these early deacons were ordained in the full sense of the word, because formal ordinations did not begin until the second century. Nevertheless, these ministers were the pioneers who opened the way for new and unique ministries in the church. The Greek word "diaconos" means servant, and in that regard the original deacons were models of what Christian ministry should be: service to the needs of others in the name of Jesus Christ.

In some of the early documents of the Church Fathers, deacons were described as helpers of the bishops in the ministry of the word and in the service of the poor and needy in the community. As the priesthood became more established in the church the ministry of the deacon was taken over by the priest and the office of deacon faded out, except as a ceremonial office for seminarians on the way to priesthood.

Karl Rahner, one of the principle twentieth-century advocates for the restoration of the diaconate, points out that their chief role was to assist those in leadership positions in the church.[26] Since the order of deacon was restored after the Second Vatican Council, deacons have made a significant contribution to the ministerial efforts of the church. They assist in parish administration, liturgy, preaching, and teaching. Many deacons also minister as chaplains at prisons, hospitals, and shelters for the homeless and needy. Others have quietly exercised a ministry of witness and Christian service in the marketplace where they work in factories, corporations, schools, small businesses, and in many different professions.[27]

The permanent diaconate has not been without its problems and challenges. Some deacons have struggled with their identity, finding themselves in a vague role somewhere between the clergy and laity. Proper titles, garb, and appropriate lifestyle have also been problematic. Some of the laity do not take deacons seriously, and some priests do not recognize the level of learning and professionalism they bring to their ministry.

Jill, a sophomore Spanish major, tells of her father's experience as a permanent deacon:

My Dad was ordained a deacon when I was three years old. When I was small I can remember him preaching in church and baptizing babies. But he said that after a while he didn't really feel that he was needed in the parish. He stopped doing "churchy" duties. Now he goes off to the state prison every Saturday afternoon to work with the prisoners. I am really proud of what he is doing for those men. Sometimes I get worried about him there among all those criminals. That's not a job I'd ever want to do.

Deaconesses

In today's training programs the deacons' wives often participate in the classes and other activities with their husbands. As a result some women feel called to serve in the same roles of service as their husbands. Some have even asked to be ordained to the diaconate. While that is not possible today, this issue will undoubtedly have to be addressed in the church's future plan for ministry.

The office of deaconess may have existed at one time in the church. There is some evidence from the third century of deaconesses ministering in the church. Perhaps they had taken over the functions previously performed by widows. While deaconesses did not have the same prestige as the deacons, they nonetheless made important contributions to the community by visiting the sick and needy, assisting in baptismal rites, counseling women, and teaching.

The Council of Chalcedon (451 C.E.) required that deaconesses be ordained by the laying on of hands.[28] Both the *Didascalia* and the *Apostolic Constitutions,* important documents from the third and fourth centuries, show that deaconesses were an important ordained ministry in the Syrian church.[29] The deaconesses had an important role in the Eastern church from the fourth to the sixth centuries. Given the status of women in society at that time, this prominence of Christian women was both startling and revolutionary.

Why the order of deaconess disappeared is hard to ascertain. Perhaps social and political changes produced conditions wherein deaconesses were no longer needed. One can only conjecture from the few hostile papal and conciliar statements against deaconesses that some in patriarchal structures could not tolerate the presence and influence of these women. For whatever reasons, the office of deaconess vanished from Christianity in the early middle ages. Many hope that it will soon be restored.

The Priesthood

Throughout the history of the church the understanding of the priesthood has changed and developed. This office appeared gradually and has undergone numerous changes in interpretation and function with the passage of time. The word "priest" is often linked to the word "presbyter" in the New Testament. The Acts of the Apostles speaks of presbyters as leaders in teaching and preaching, but does not depict them as leaders of liturgy. There is also some mention of them in the later Johannine writings, as well as in the *Didache* (circa 100 C.E.) and in the writings of Ignatius of Antioch. The presbyters do not, however, seem to be central figures in the early Christian communities, and they are not mentioned in either the gospels or Paul's letters.

The connection between priesthood and Christian ministry arose gradually. In the New Testament, only Christ and the community were called priestly. The ancient church had difficulty calling the church leaders "priestly." The role of the minister was to be at the service of Christ and the priestly people of God.[30]

For the first three hundred years of the church, the bishops, and not the priests, were generally the leaders of the liturgy. It was only in the early fifth century, when the local communities had become so widespread and the pastoral needs so urgent, that presbyters assumed the leadership of communities. This leadership position gradually included the role of presiding at the eucharistic liturgy. It evolved to a role as local pastoral leader, a servant leader in all pastoral areas, including the conferral of the sacraments.

The Ordained Priesthood

By the early middle ages the meaning of ordination had shifted from a ceremony designating pastoral and liturgical ministers to a ritual wherein a person was "changed" into a priest. Discussions about the meaning of the priesthood shifted from the biblical notion of service and consecration to philosophical notions of powers. The priesthood came to be understood in terms of ontology, or in the order of "being." Once ordination was thought to change the person into a priest, the minister was separated from the other people in the church socially and even ontologically. The ordained priesthood was viewed as differing "not only in degree but in essence" from the priesthood of all the baptized faithful.[31]

A young priest, talking about what goes on in the seminary, was uncomfortable with the notion of the priest having a different "being." He told a group of college students:

Hey, I'm just like you. I went to college like you did, but instead of going to work for a company, I went to work for the church. That doesn't make me different than you. We all share in the priesthood of Jesus. My job as a priest is to remind people that to be a Christian is to be of service to other people, and then to help people use their gifts for others.

The Powers of the Priesthood

The notion developed in the middle ages that the ordained priest possessed a certain "sacramental character," an indelible mark that linked the person forever with the official ministry of the church. The priesthood came to be synonymous with "sacramental powers," rather than with the ministry of service. Ordination was seen to bestow special powers, in particular, the power to consecrate the eucharist and to forgive sins. Because of this the priest's main function shifted from the pastoral to the sacramental and liturgical.

When the sixteenth-century Protestant reformers denied the necessity of the ordained priesthood, the Council of Trent (1545-1563) reacted by re-enforcing the medieval model of priesthood with even greater emphasis. The clerical form of priesthood, with the accent on powers rather than on the servant-leader, became codified. Although this medieval, clerical model of priesthood was never dogmatically defined, it was the prevalent model in the Roman Catholic church for centuries. This Tridentine model of priesthood all but excluded the laity from official ministry, and made little mention of the common priesthood that is shared by all.[32]

A New Approach to the Priesthood

The Second Vatican Council attempted to revitalize the priesthood of the faithful by reminding all believers that they are called to ministry and Christian discipleship by virtue of their baptism. The council also encouraged priests to see their ministry as being linked more closely to Christ and his three-fold office of priest, prophet, and pastor.

The last fifty years have seen many models of priesthood: the worker-priests in France who lived and worked with the factory laborers; the so-called hyphenated-priests who combined priesthood with their work as chemists, writers, professors, psychologists, or workers in similar professions. Some priests pioneered in the labor movement, while other priests became involved in the civil rights movement and in social work. Many priests have risked and often lost their lives living and working in solidarity with the oppressed throughout the world. Many priests carry on the complex work of administering huge parishes; and there are those who struggle in Appalachia with the rural poor. In our era of individualism, many priests feel free to define the priesthood for themselves.[33]

With all these variations it seems clear that the priesthood has no fixed form. It does not seem appropriate, therefore, to speak of an unchanging definition or essence of a priesthood that has developed and changed so much over the centuries. The medieval and Tridentine models of ministry do not fit the complex needs of today's world, and they do not attract large numbers of young men to this way of life. Many in the church hope for changes in the priesthood that will represent a return to some of the earlier biblical values of ministry and service.

The Episcopacy

The office of bishop, which takes its name from the Greek "episkopos," gradually appeared in the early church and then evolved and changed as the size and scope of the Christian community grew and changed. "Episkopos" is mentioned once in the letters of Paul, but without any indication of the role assigned to the title. It is never used in the gospels. In the Acts of the Apostles the words "episkopos" and "presbyteros" are used interchangeably, but neither word is used to describe a successor of either the Twelve or the apostles. This connection was made later "outside and beyond the New Testament communities."[34]

The writings of Clement of Rome in the late first century indicate joint leadership of Christian communities by presbyter/episcopal figures. The writings of Ignatius of Antioch in the second century mention a college of presbyters led by one who is called an *"episkopos,"* or bishop. By the end of the second century these episcopal figures are in charge of local communities, functioning as overseers, teachers, preachers, and presiders over liturgy.[35]

As the itinerant missionaries and the charismatic ministries of teacher and prophet continued to vanish, the bishops of local communities gained more prominence. Often they became leaders of communities so vast and complicated that strong leadership was needed to safeguard the unity of belief and the purity of life against error and sinfulness. In the third century, Cyprian (d. 258), bishop of Carthage, was the first to mention Peter and the other apostles as episcopal leaders. He also began to speak of the current church leaders as "successors of the apostles," and pointed out that such leaders were collegially linked to each other.

In the fourth century, when Christianity became the required religion of the Roman empire, significant changes took place in the episcopacy. Bishops began to direct larger regions, which eventually came to be known as dioceses, and the expanding number of local communities were taken over by presbyters.

Bishops Acquire Wealth and Power

In the early days of the church the bishop was the "father of the poor," since he was the leader to whom the impoverished turned for help. This position was formalized in the fourth century when Christianity became the official religion of the Roman Empire. The church was given land and revenues to carry out these services, and the bishop's role evolved into one of economic administrator.

When the Roman Empire collapsed in the West in the fifth century, the bishops were the only authorities who still owned land and controlled large fortunes. As a result, the people turned to them for legal recourse, and for restoration of the cities after barbarian invasions. Some of the bishops also protected the people militarily, and thus became not only powerful financiers, but also commanders of armies and navies. The Patriarch of Alexandria, along with his spiritual duties as bishop, also had a fleet of thirty ships and controlled the entire grain trade with Constantinople.[36] The bishops had come a long way from Peter the fisherman! As the church became more institutionalized, the political model of church order became more prevalent, and powerful dioceses emerged, with the diocese of Rome in the ascendency.

During the medieval period the bishop's office became more regal, and the bishops came to be known as "princes of the church." Bishops gathered most of the key ministerial roles into their office. Priests often were reduced to mere helpers of bishops and "Mass readers." The priesthood of the faithful receded far into the background.

Bishops were described as teachers, spiritual fathers, healers, and shepherds.[37] They also carried such titles as the "father of the clergy" and the "father of the community." The growing power of the episcopal position created tensions with secular monarchs, as well as with the pope, priests, and monastic orders. Unfortunately, the laity became disenfranchised amid this struggle for power.

When the power and legitimacy of the episcopacy was challenged by the Protestant reformers in the sixteenth century, the office was strengthened by the reforms of Trent. Bishops were given even more control over the selection, training, ordination, and management of the clergy in order to bring about the needed reform of the church.

Modern Councils and the Episcopacy

After the Council of Trent, the centralization of authority in Rome diminished the authority of the local bishops. The First Vatican Council intended to address both the office of bishop and the papacy. The council was interrupted, unfortunately, so it gave attention only to the papacy, and left the office of bishop in an even more weakened position. Vatican I pictured the authority structure of the church starting with the pope as the supreme head of the church. Bishops were viewed as delegates of the pope, rather than leaders in their own right.

The Second Vatican Council strengthened the office of bishop by stressing that all bishops are "successors of the apostles." The council proclaimed that bishops have their own unique authority to build up and guide the church. They are leaders in their own right, and not just delegates of the pope. All bishops have authority to build up the entire church along with their brother bishops and the pope.[38]

The authority of bishops also has increased with a heightened awareness of "collegiality," the belief that the bishops are members of an authoritative body or college, and possess a unique authority when voting in unison with each other and with the pope. This authority was greatly exemplified by the Second Vatican Council (1962-1965) when over 2000 bishops from around the world debated, voted on, and issued decrees that profoundly changed the Catholic church. The pope, for the most part, stayed in the background during these conciliar sessions.

The importance accorded to synods (special meetings in Rome of representative groups of bishops from around the world to discuss specific issues of concern) and episcopal conferences (regular gatherings of all bishops from a country or a region of the world to discuss issues of particular importance to their area) has increased the responsibilities and duties of bishops. To the extent that these synods and episcopal conferences enlist the knowledge and experience of clergy and laity, the bishops demonstrate their recognition of the fact that collegiality pertains not only to themselves, but to all the members of the community. Consulting scholars, experts, and the faithful also represents a renewed recognition of the "sense of the faithful" and the crucial need for a mutual exchange between the "teaching church" and the "learning church."

Unfortunately the teaching authority of the bishops' conferences has been challenged by Rome, and the United States Conference of Catholic Bishops in its most recent annual meetings has not exhibited the same confidence it had during the 1980s when it issued major statements on nuclear disarmament and economic justice.

The Papacy

The papacy is an amazing office. Rooted in the primacy of position among the disciples that Jesus accorded to Peter, it is one of the few remaining institutions of ancient times. For nearly two thousand years it has survived persecution and scandal. It has had times of great glory and times of humiliating disgrace. Thanks to the integrity and diligence of recent popes, it stands as one of the most influential offices in the world today.

The papacy developed gradually. The title "Bishop of Rome" first appeared in the middle of the second century. Located in the capital of the Empire, it was the only apostolic see (diocese) in the west, as well as the place where both Peter and Paul were martyred. During the fourth and fifth centuries, a growing respect for the doctrinal and spiritual superiority of Rome developed. At the Council of Chalcedon in the year 451, during the pontificate of Pope Leo, the classic statement was made: "Peter speaks through the mouth of Leo."

During the papacy of Gregory the Great (d. 604) the title "servant of the servants of God" was applied to the pope and interpreted in terms of universal power. It was not until Charlemagne's reign in the ninth century, however, that we find the beginnings of Christian imperialism. This monarchical model with its trappings of palaces, crowns, coronations, and papal courts prevailed until modern times. Not only was the pope the supreme ruler, he was also the source of power for his fellow bishops.[39]

Pope Gregory VII (d. 1085) is an example of a pope who acted as an absolute monarch and claimed to have immediate jurisdiction over all Christians. He claimed the church's power to select bishops and sent his delegates to silence any bishops who opposed his decrees. He claimed the power to depose emperors, saying that "the pope is the only one whose feet are to be kissed by all princes."[40] Gregory maintained that the pope could not be judged by anyone, and that he was the head of a church that never had and never will err for all eternity. Pope Boniface VIII (d. 1303) raised the notion of papal sovereignty to even more exaggerated heights when he proclaimed: "We declare, state, and define that it is absolutely necessary for the salvation of all that they submit to the Roman Pontiff." Here, acceptance of papal authority was actually proclaimed to be necessary for salvation.

Attempts to Limit the Papacy

During the twelfth and thirteenth centuries the theory of conciliarism was developed by theologians and canonists in an effort to limit papal power by asserting the supremacy of general councils over the papacy. In the fourteenth century when the pope fled Rome for the relative safety of Avignon (in France), the cardinals made an effort to reduce the power of the pope and claim it for their own. When religious and political turmoil beset the papacy and three men claimed to be pope at the same time, the Council of Constance (1414-1418) resolved the chaotic situation and asserted the authority of the college of bishops gathered in a council.

During the Reformation the validity of the papacy was denied by the Reformers. In response, the Catholic church strengthened the legitimate power of the papacy and eliminated many papal excesses by promoting radical reform.

In seventeenth-century France, a movement called "Gallicanism" advocated that the Catholic church in France be free of papal control, that general councils be viewed as superior to the pope, and that the consent of the universal church be required to validate papal teaching on faith and morals. Napoleon, Bismarck, and other strong European rulers challenged the immense political power of the pope. By the end of the nineteenth century, the Papal States had fallen into the hands of Italian nationalists and brought an end to a thousand years of papal territorial rule. In an effort to stem the tide of the decline of the papacy, Pope Pius IX convened the First Vatican Council and gave it a mandate to redefine the modern papacy in terms of both sovereign power and infallible teaching authority.

The Modern Papacy

The First Vatican Council left no question about the completeness of the pope's primacy or jurisdiction. The pope was described as the supreme pastor of the flock, and the last court of appeals in all ecclesiastical matters. His supreme authority extended to teaching, discipline, and governance, and was not to be subject to any other judgment within the church.

This council explained papal infallibility to mean that when the pope defines a doctrine in faith or morality publicly from his papal chair, that doctrine is thereby free from error. Although this extraordinary power has only been exercised once since its definition (Pope Pius XII's 1950 pronouncement about Mary's Assumption into heaven) it has been a symbol of papal authority ever since.

Even though the doctrine of papal infallibility is misunderstood by many in the church and stands as a serious obstacle to ecumenism, the Second Vatican Council did not modify this teaching. The council did attempt, however, to restore a balance of power between the pope and the college of bishops. The council clearly stated that bishops, by virtue of their ordination, possess authority in their own right, not authority derived from the papacy. They are not mere vicars of the pope, but pastors in their own right who teach authoritatively within the college of bishops. The Bishop of Rome is seen as a member of the episcopal college, although he is the successor to Peter and therefore has the first place (primacy) among the bishops.

Even though Vatican II, both as a conciliar model of authority and in its documents, restored authority to the bishops, the 1983 Code of Canon Law reiterated that the Bishop of Rome is the supreme pastor of the universal church. He enjoys a power that is full, immediate, and universal, which he can exercise freely without checks or balances, since by law the pope can be judged by no one. This is a reaffirmation of an absolute model of papacy. Such a model of the papacy is, of course, unacceptable to both the Eastern Orthodox churches and the Protestant churches.

Recent popes have gradually set aside many of the royal trappings of the medieval papacy. No longer is the pope carried on a portable throne; the crown (tiara) and the elaborate pageantry once used to crown the pope are also gone. It is quite possible that a future pope will be from a Third World country, and that could bring about even further changes in this office.

Melanie, a junior who leads the student group that works with the homeless in the inner city, spoke about her trip to see Pope John Paul II in Denver in the summer of 1993.

It was a long trip by bus, and we spent most of our nights in Denver sleeping in a parking garage. But it was worth it. I had never seen so many young Catholics before, hundreds of thousands of them from all over the United States and other countries, too. Their faith was overwhelming. It was like you were in some "zone of holiness" when we stood in the field and listened to Pope John Paul talk to us. He is truly charismatic. I will never forget seeing him and listening to his words. I was amazed that he could get through to so many young people.

Ministry for the Future

While it is necessary to focus on the ordained ministers of the church (deacons, priests, bishops) the future of the church's ministry seems to be shifting to the laity. By virtue of the sacrament of baptism, all Christian faithful are called to share in Christ's mission. The decline in the number of ordained clergy and vowed religious Sisters, Brothers, and priests along with the heightened awareness of the importance of the laity will change the face of ministry in the twenty-first century.

Admitting that many of the present structures of ministry are woefully inadequate for effectively carrying out the mission of the church, here are five points that might be considered in planning the renewal of ministry for the future.

1. Emphasizing Jesus Christ as the Model Minister. Future ministry needs to reclaim the centrality of Jesus Christ. It is Christ who is the model minister and the one great high priest. All ministers—ordained and unordained, paid and volunteer, men and women—need to reflect on the message and actions of Jesus as found in the New Testament. Jesus' message of healing, affirmation, conversion, and salvation never grows old. Jesus' love of the poor and his insight that the greatest is the one who serves the rest should motivate all ministers.

The presence of the Spirit of the risen Lord is the source of power in the ministry of the church. The church and all its members emerge from and draw nourishment from the breaking of the bread, the reality of resurrection and pentecost, and the sending forth of the disciples to spread the good news. It is from this perspective that all followers of Jesus share in his ministry.

2. Utilizing Gift-based Ministry. The early church did not suffer from the shortage of ministers that we experience in the contemporary church. As needs were recognized in the community, those who were discerned to be appropriately gifted by the Spirit were called forth to serve.

A convincing argument can be made that the gifts of the Spirit are still generously given to the faithful followers of Christ. Unfortunately, many of these gifts go unused because of models of ministry that are too narrow and exclusive. In the future there is a need for a process whereby the gifted in the community can be discerned and called into service.

3. Developing an Inclusive Ministry. Christian ministry is for all to exercise in varied and different ways. Unfortunately gender, race, marital status, social class, or educational background often become factors that exclude many Catholics from service in the church. There is some movement to remedy this. For example, lay ministers in the Third World, often drawn from among the poor and illiterate, have revealed that Christ carries out his mission with all kinds of disciples, including those whose faith comes primarily from their heart rather than from theology courses. Future models of ministry must find a way to give women their rightful place in Christian ministry and leadership.

The idea that the call to ministry is universal draws strength from a consideration of the implications of the priesthood of all the faithful. Discipleship with Christ by virtue of one's baptism needs to be stressed, rather than concentrating on the ontological difference between the ordained and unordained.[41]

4. Accenting the Local Church. The appearance of small Christian communities and the new emphasis on the family as a domestic church provide new resources for ministry. When ministers rise up from among the members of the community, they are often better prepared to deal with immediate needs and issues, especially in the areas of social justice. Ministry arising out of the local community also recognizes more easily the equality and the giftedness of those who are called forth to serve the community.

5. Reclaiming the Value of Service. Clerical and monastic structures have often cut off and isolated ministers from the laity whom they are called to serve. This can lead those in power to view their ministry as "power over," rather than "power with." While future ministerial models will still hold a place for various offices and authority, these need to be arranged more properly for service rather than domination. Each of the official ministries in the church should be renewed in terms of servant-leadership and made more diverse and inclusive.

Conclusion

The church's mission begins with the work of Jesus and continues his commitment to love and justice in our own time. All disciples are called to share in this mission and to "go forth" both locally and abroad to serve the needs of others, especially the poor and oppressed.

We have seen how ministry has been an integral part of the living Catholic tradition. Like all aspects of the tradition, ministry has taken different forms depending on the needs of the community at the particular time in history. When priesthood was needed, it was developed. When there was a need for deacons and deaconesses, these roles evolved. Indeed all the offices and the laws surrounding these offices were designed by a church that believed that the Spirit of the Lord was present with it and guided it in its decisions.

Today there are critical needs for new models of ministry. There are a billion Catholics today, many of whom live in poverty and in oppressive conditions. Church authorities need to implement structures that encourage the action of present-day disciples who have the call to ministry by virtue of their baptism. These people are gifted by the Spirit and prepared to serve. What is needed now are new forms of ministry where factors like gender or marital status are not considerations in calling forth ministers to serve.

Discussion Questions

1. In our own time, are there new ways in which the church is "going forth" into the world with the message of Christ. Can you name areas of the world where the gospel is urgently needed? What are the needs in these areas?

2. Vatican II called the church to read the "signs of the times," that is, to look at our world and to listen to what God is calling us to do in our age. Discuss some the "signs" of our times, and suggest ways in which Christians might respond.

3. Discuss the gradual connection between faith and justice that came about in the church. What is your view on the relationship between Christian faith and concern for peace and justice?

4. What are some specific ways in which the Catholic church has changed its approach to foreign missions?

5. Compare and contrast the early Christian views on ministry with some of the views that prevail today.

6. What are the purposes for having official church leadership? How might these offices of papacy, episcopacy, and priesthood be more effectively exercised today? Discuss a local church leader who has affected your life in some way.

Suggested Readings

Anthony Bellagamba, *Mission and Ministry in the Global Church*. Maryknoll, NY: Orbis Books, 1992.

Paul Bernier, *Ministry in the Church*. Mystic, CT: Twenty-Third Publications, 1992.

Joan Chittister, *Women, Ministry and the Church*. New York: Paulist Press, 1983.

Robert Eno, *The Rise of the Papacy*. Wilmington, DE: Michael Glazier, 1990.

Patrick Granfield, *Limits of the Papacy*. New York: Crossroad, 1987.

Nathan Mitchell, *Mission and Ministry*. Wilmington, DE: Michael Glazier, 1982.

Marie Augusta Neal, *The Just Demands of the Poor.* New York: Paulist Press, 1987.

John P. O'Grady, *Disciples and Leaders: The Origins of Christian Ministry in the New Testament.* New York: Paulist Press, 1991.

Kenan Osborne, *Ministry.* New York: Paulist Press, 1993.

Pheme Perkins, *Peter: Apostle for the Whole Church.* Columbia, SC: University of South Carolina Press, 1994.

Edward Schillebeeckx, *The Church with a Human Face.* New York: Crossroad, 1985.

10.

The Sacrament of the Eucharist

Framing the Question

My name is Stacy. I am a convert to Catholicism. I came into the church with my father when I was twelve. Both of us wanted to be the same religion as my mother. It was our decision, and even though some of my relatives thought I was too young to decide something so serious, I have always been happy with my decision.

One of the things that attracted me to the Catholic church is holy communion. I was impressed with the way Catholics really believe that taking communion is somehow receiving Jesus Christ. It was hard for me to believe at first. I prayed hard that I could believe, and all of sudden, I don't quite know why, I was able to believe. My mother says it was her prayers that did it.

I have always seen Jesus as my friend, and I have often felt close to him, especially before I go to sleep and when I am at the seashore. But communion is something special. It is as though Jesus is really next to my heart talking to me. Communion also helps me to love other people better.

I do have some questions, though. Why do we call eucharist "the body and blood" of Christ? Is the bread really supposed to be "flesh," and the wine actually "blood"? I remember reading in a history book that some people have taken this very literally. I also wonder whether Jesus really intended that we have these big churches and all these fancy services. What did he really do, and what are we supposed to be doing in his memory?

Finally, I want to know why the church is not more attentive to young adults. At college the liturgy is great. It is informal, enjoyable, and easy to understand. The priest knows our concerns and addresses them. I go away feeling nourished and ready to take on all the problems of the upcoming week. But at my parish back home the services are quite different. There is a sameness each time, and the people are quiet and uninvolved. The sermons seldom seem to connected to real life, especially not to life as I know it.

As a convert Stacy does not take her Catholic faith or her belief in the eucharist for granted. Obviously she had to struggle to accept the gift of faith, and seems to have a special appreciation for the eucharist. Her realization that Mass is celebrated with varying emphases in different places is shared by many Catholics. In many typical parishes the celebration of the Mass and the homily are aimed at families with children. Young people often feel left out, and many simply drift away.

In this chapter, the first of three that will examine the sacraments, we are going to discuss the sacrament that is central to Catholic life, the eucharist. Before we begin to focus on the eucharist, however, we will situate this most prominent sacrament in the context of the seven sacraments, and consider the characteristics common to all sacraments. Then we will look at the origins of the eucharist, and the cluster of meanings that are attached to the celebration of this sacrament. We will also consider some of the controversies that have arisen over the understanding of eucharist, and how they have been dealt with through significant ecumenical dialogue. We will close with some projections about where Catholic thinking and practice might be headed. Along the way we consider Stacy's questions about the eucharist.

Sacred Symbols and Rituals

To understand the notion of "sacrament," we must begin with a look at symbols and rituals. As humans, we need concrete symbols and rituals to both express and receive meaning. For instance, words, both written and spoken, are symbols through which we are able to communicate meaning. Three simple words such as "I love you" can start a friendship or even seal a relationship for life. By the same token, a gesture such as a kiss, an embrace, or a handshake can convey a broad range of purposeful meaning. The ring given to a loved one at a wedding speaks of commitment. Sending flowers to a family who has suffered the death of a loved one expresses sympathy. A ritual such as gathering around a table for a Thanksgiving Day meal is a way of celebrating gratitude for the many blessings received. Birthdays are often celebrated with a cake brightly lit with candles that are to be blown out by the person whose birthday is being remembered. These visible symbols and rituals put us in touch with the invisible and even spiritual aspects of life, like friendship, love, sympathy, gratitude, and happiness.

Similarly, sacraments are sacred symbols and rituals through which we can uniquely be put in touch with the spiritual, indeed with the very power of God. Sacraments make it possible for the risen Lord to touch the lives of his disciples with many powers and graces. Through sacraments, Jesus welcomes, forgives, heals, and in many other ways touches his followers through such simple things as bread, wine, and oil, or through such simple gestures as the "laying on of hands."

Sacraments are both personal and communal. They are personal encounters with Jesus Christ, as well as ecclesial celebrations of his presence. As individuals we can be initiated into friendship with Jesus in baptism; we can be spiritually fed by Jesus in eucharist, forgiven our sins, healed in our suffering, prepared for death, called to service, or linked with spouse in marriage. At the same time sacraments are celebrations of the entire church community, the Body of Christ. They are "ecclesial events," wherein the entire community celebrates the presence of the Lord.

Jesus of Nazareth is considered to be the one who laid the foundations for the sacraments. Jesus was indeed himself a "sacramental" person. As a devout Jew, he came from a tradition that viewed all things as coming from the hand of a Creator God. The gospels tell of Jesus experiencing the reign of this "Abba" within all things. He taught that God could be experienced in the warmth of the sun, in the beauty of the birds, in the grandeur of the flowers, and even in a gentle breeze. Jesus could find God's presence in the face of a child, in the withered body of a leper, in the oppressed countenance of a prostitute. He could hear Abba in the cry of the cripple along the roadside, in the plaintive sobs of a mother who had lost her only son, and in the murmured request from a criminal next to him on the cross. Jesus heard the approving works of his God as he stood in the waters being baptized by John, as he prayed on a mountainside with his disciples, and as he anguished in the garden before his arrest. He passed this tradition for finding God in symbols to his disciples. The "reign of God" was within.

For Catholics, Jesus is uniquely a sacrament himself, in that he is a living symbol of a God who is loving, caring, and forgiving. Jesus told his disciples: "Who has seen me, has seen the Father" (John 14:9). An encounter with the risen Lord is indeed an encounter with the divinity and the amazing graces that flow from this mystery. Paul teaches this to the Colossians when he writes: "Christ is the visible likeness of the invisible God" (Col 1:15).

Similarly, the church is a sacrament in that the community of disciples is supposed to be a visible symbol of Christ's presence in the world. Locally, as well as universally, the disciples are expected to offer a powerful symbol that Christ is offering his love and forgiveness to the world through them.

As for the seven sacraments, each has its own history and its own theological meaning. They weren't actually numbered as seven sacraments until the middle ages. Each of the seven offers a distinctive experience of Jesus Christ; each is a celebration of his presence and power. While the presence of this same Christ can be experienced in everyday life, in people, in scripture, and in numerous other ways, sacramental celebrations of Christ's presence are distinctive and privileged. Each is an ancient and symbolic ritual where the fullness of Christ's presence is celebrated. Sacraments transform such common experiences as eating, washing, anointing, praying, storytelling, and placing hands upon one another into celebrations of Christ's presence and power. In the following we will consider how the eucharist is understood to be one of these seven sacraments.

Foundations for Eucharist

A proper understanding of the eucharist begins with Jesus' "table ministry." As a devout Jew, he valued the Jewish custom of fellowship meals. Jews gathered for these meals that included special prayers and the sharing of food. Bread would be broken and shared; wine would be passed and drunk; and through this ritual the Jews hoped to grow closer to their God and to each other. They would also have the opportunity to thank God for sharing all of creation with them, and for constantly showing them mercy.

Jesus put his own unique stamp on these meals. Where fellowship meals were often exclusive gatherings of Pharisees, Scribes, family members, or friends, Jesus gave such meals an inclusivity. He would sit down to eat and drink with people who were considered to be sinners and outcasts. He would dine with tax collectors, prostitutes, and with the oppressed and impoverished. This was so unusual that some of Jesus' self-righteous enemies used it against him. They whispered that this young preacher was nothing other than "a drinker and a friend of sinners."

At table Jesus would share his food and himself with these people in a gesture of love, compassion, and forgiveness. Their lives would never be the same after they sat down at table with Jesus. The gospels tell of many such meals, and raise these events to a level where they proclaim the Christian belief that the risen Jesus continues to minister to people at the table of the Lord.

Table Stories

Luke tells a story of Jesus stopping at the Bethany home of two sisters, Martha and Mary (Lk 10:38–42). As Martha serves the meal, she complains that Mary is doing too much listening and not enough helping with the meal. Jesus seems to chide Martha for her anxiousness and reminds her that listening to his teaching is the "one thing" that is important. Scholars have pointed out how this story proclaims Jesus' unique belief that women are worthy to be taught the Torah (the Law), as well as capable of being his disciples.[1]

John's gospel tells of another meal where Martha again serves Jesus, while Mary anoints his feet with precious oil and dries them with her hair (Jn 12:1–8). Martha and Mary of Bethany are indeed symbolic of women disciples whose lives were changed by Jesus at table. They both play a role in Jesus' resuscitation of their brother Lazarus. It is Martha who hears Jesus' proclamation of his coming resurrection, and in turn gives recognition to his messiahship. In John's account it is Mary who brings many to believe in Jesus (Jn 11:45). All these stories seem to signal the early Christian recognition of how Jesus' table ministry played a role in raising women to an unprecedented level in ministry and in the community of believers.[2]

There are many other gospel stories of Jesus' table ministry that seem to lay the groundwork for Jesus' Last Supper with his disciples. Jesus invites himself to the house and table of Zacchaeus, the hated tax collector of Jericho who had grown wealthy extorting taxes from the poor (Lk 19:1–10). Zacchaeus' life is turned around, and he resolves to give half of all he owns to the poor and to repay his extortions four times over.

One of the most touching stories in the gospels tells of a dinner that Jesus shares at the home of Simon the Pharisee. During the all-male feast, a woman with a bad reputation enters the room, kneels before Jesus, and proceeds to wash his feet with her tears and dry them with her hair. Jesus rebukes the whispers of his guests. Instead of being embarrassed by her presence, Jesus welcomes her and praises the repentance and love that fill her heart. He then raises her above Simon, his host, as an example of hospitality and loving care (Lk 7:36–50).

There are still other stories that tell of Jesus' ministry of feeding others. Matthew tells how tax collectors and sinners used to drop into

Jesus' house in Capernaum (Mt 17:24–27). On a grander scale, Jesus is portrayed as miraculously feeding enormous crowds. Luke's account of the feeding of the five thousand has echoes of Jesus' wondrous care shown both during his lifetime on earth and after his resurrection. In the story, Jesus sits the people down in groups of fifty and "then taking the five loaves and two fish, and looking up to heaven, he said the blessing over them, broke them, and gave them to the disciples to set before the crowd" (Lk 9:14–16). It is from the memory of instances such as these that the early communities came to place great emphasis on table fellowship.

Post-Resurrection Meals

The table ministry of Jesus and his gift of the eucharist to his disciples are also echoed in some of the post-resurrection stories. Luke tells a story of two disciples leaving Jerusalem after the crucifixion who meet Jesus, but do not recognize him as they walk on the road. Later Jesus joins them at their home and sits at table with them. He takes bread, blesses it, breaks it, and gives it to them. Only then are their eyes opened and they recognize the risen Lord (Lk 24:13–35). Later Jesus sits at table with his disciples in Jerusalem and instructs them on his messiahship.[3]

John's gospel comes to a climactic close with a story about the disciples who had returned to fishing in Galilee after the crucifixion of Jesus. From out in the boat Peter recognizes the Lord walking along the shore. With his typical impetuosity, Peter jumps into the sea and swims to shore to meet Jesus. The others follow in the boat, dragging a miraculous catch behind them. On the shore they encounter the risen Lord—cooking them breakfast. It is after this meal that Jesus touchingly asks Peter three times if he loves him (Jn 21:1–19).[4]

The Last Supper

These table and feeding stories are linked in meaning to the Last Supper, the fellowship meal that Jesus shared with his disciples the night before he died. The exact details of this meal are not available to us. The accounts given by Paul (1 Cor 11:23–26), and then decades later in the four gospels differ in many details. The words of institution vary, as well as the details of the sharing of the bread and the cup. Even the day when the meal was celebrated is not clear. The synoptic gospels place the meal at the time of Passover, whereas John's gospel places it before Passover. It seems that the memories of this meal had been influenced by theological reflection and liturgical practice by the time they were included in the scriptures. What is rather remarkable is that, after years of scrutiny by many capable scripture scholars, the accounts of the Last Supper are still viewed as substantially having their source in Jesus himself.[5]

Early Communion Celebrations

The earliest account we have of communion is found in the First Letter to the Corinthians (Chapters 10 and 11). This letter was written around the year 50 C.E. and reflects a tradition that Paul learned about in Antioch around the time of his conversion in the mid-40s. In other words, this eucharistic tradition is only a decade removed from the time of Jesus.

Paul is not attempting to write a theology of communion. In fact, were it not for the abuses that Paul found in the Corinthian community, we probably would not have this precious and early account of the commemoration of the Lord's Supper.

The main problem in the Corinthian community seems to be one of discrimination. The wealthier people, who provided the home for the celebration, apparently were not providing truly Christian hospitality to the poorer members of the community. The Lord's Supper, a full meal (sometimes called an "agape" meal, which resembled a modern-day pot-luck supper) with a communion service at the end, had become corrupted. Some were greedily eating and getting drunk, while others went hungry. Paul points out that the table of the Lord should be a place of unity. Communion is intended to celebrate the oneness and unity among the disciples of Jesus as well as their oneness with the Lord himself. Division, discrimination, and selfishness are contradictory to the purpose of this celebration. Paul informs the abusers that they are drinking a judgment against themselves (1 Cor 11:17–22, 27–34).

Paul tells the Corinthians what he had learned at the time of his conversion.

> The Lord Jesus, on the night when he was betrayed took a loaf of bread, and when he had given thanks, he broke it and said, "This is my body that is for you. Do this in remembrance of me." In the same way he took the cup also, after supper, saying, "This cup is the new covenant in my blood. Do this as often as you drink it, in remembrance of me." For as often as you eat this bread and drink this cup, you proclaim the Lord's death until he comes. (1 Cor 11:23–26)[6]

It is so simple and yet so profound. At a supper before he died Jesus identified his person (body) with bread, and his upcoming death (blood) with the cup of wine. He requested, moreover, that this action be continued in his memory. The early disciples quickly associated this ritual with Jesus' death, as well as with what was then thought to be his imminent second coming.

This passage in 1 Corinthians contains the core of the Christian tradition about communion. The Greek verb *eucharistein,* which means "to give thanks," is used here for the first time, although the ritual itself is not yet called "eucharist." The liturgical use of the term seems to appear initially at the end of the first century in the *Didache* (a collection of basic teachings about the faith), and in the writings of Ignatius of Antioch (d. 107) and Justin Martyr (d. 150).[7]

The commemoration of the Lord's Supper, as portrayed in the First Letter to the Corinthians, seems to be a fellowship meal intended to engender unity and concern for others. It is a meal in memory of Jesus which celebrates oneness in Jesus and in a common faith. Paul writes: "The cup of blessing that we bless, is it not a sharing in the blood of Christ? The bread that we break, is it not a sharing in the body of Christ?" (1 Cor 10:16).

In one of her reflective essays, Sabrina, a nursing student from San Diego, comments on what this fellowship aspect of eucharist means to her.

The Mass never meant a whole lot to me until I lost my father. I was devastated when he died just after my twelfth birthday. I remember that I did not even want to go to the funeral. When we got to the church, I saw many of my classmates and teachers and could tell from the expressions on their faces that they were hurting, too, and would help me get through this tough time. After church, one by one they came up to me and hugged me. This meant so much to me. From then on I felt very close to all these people.

The Gospel Accounts

The gospel accounts of Jesus' Last Supper reflect the theological and liturgical development that took place between the time of Jesus' death and the day when these words were put in their final written form in the individual gospels. There are some some obvious differences in the gospel accounts. Mark, the earliest gospel (written around 70 C.E., probably in Rome) has Jesus pass the cup to the disciples before he says the words, "This is my blood." Mark and Matthew (written about 80 C.E.) have Jesus refer to "my blood of the covenant," while Luke and

Paul both use the phrase "the new covenant in my blood." Luke's account differs from the others when he describes a ritual in which the cups of wine is shared twice.

In Mark, Jesus speaks of his blood being shed for the multitude. Matthew speaks of the blood being shed for the forgiveness of the sins of the multitude, while Luke merely has Jesus say, "my blood which is shed for you." Only Luke and Paul refer to Jesus' request to do this in his memory. And only Mark and Matthew quote Jesus as saying that he will not drink wine until the coming of the kingdom, although this eschatological notion seems to be captured by Paul's phrase "until he comes."

Even with all these obvious discrepancies, there is a remarkable consistency in the accounts of the Last Supper. In all the accounts the disciples are present and the meal is only for them. This is the only such meal in the gospel. In all of the accounts there is a meal-within-a-meal. There is an action of blessing and thanksgiving over both the bread and cup, with Jesus uniquely identifying himself with both. The command of remembrance, the association of the wine/blood and covenant, and the anticipation of a new kingdom seem to be unique to Jesus' ritual.[8] The passing of one cup to all is also extraordinary and seems to be original to the meal celebrated by Jesus and his apostles on the night before he died.

Two Cultic Traditions

Xavier Léon-Dufour, a noted biblical and liturgical theologian, maintains that there are two tendencies in the cultic tradition of the eucharist. The older of the two is that of Paul and Luke, called the Antiochene tradition because of Paul's links with Antioch. This tradition alone speaks of Jesus' command for remembrance. It also separates the actions of the cup from the bread by noting that the cup was passed "after the supper." It reflects a Hellenistic background more than one that is Jewish, and presents the eucharist as a personal gift of Jesus. It focuses on the eucharist as a sign of the covenant more than as a cultic ritual.[9]

The other tradition, which includes both Mark and Matthew's account, is called the Markan tradition. This apparently originated in Jerusalem or Caesarea and abounds in Semitic images. It draws a parallel between the words, "This is my body" and "This is my blood," and uses the familiar Jewish terms for blessings and "for the many." It contains notions of expiation, sacrifice, and covenant that arise out of a largely Jewish-Christian community. This tradition is also more liturgical with Jesus' gift of the eucharist being viewed as the fulfillment of Jewish sacrificial rites.[10]

John's Eucharistic Tradition

The differences in the tradition of the institution of the eucharist among the synoptics (Mark, Matthew, and Luke) and Paul present minor challenges compared to the difficulties that arise when one tries to match them with John's account of the Last Supper. In this gospel, Jesus' farewell meal does not include any reference to the eucharist. Does this mean, as some suggest, that the Johannine community was antiliturgical, or that there were early Christian communities that did not celebrate the eucharist?

Léon-Dufour maintains that the explanation lies in the fact that there were two ways in which the Last Supper tradition was presented. The one was a cultic tradition which speaks of table actions and the words of Jesus. This tradition is reflected in Paul and the synoptic gospels. The other tradition, which is found in John, is a testamentary tradition (as in "last will and testament"), where Jesus stresses his impending death, gives instruction to his followers about how to live in love and service, and then dramatically demonstrates this with the washing of the feet.

Over time there has been an interlocking of the two traditions. The cultic tradition stresses sharing and sacrifice and speaks of the fruit of the vine. The testamentary tradition portrays the washing of the feet in ritualistic fashion with Jesus presiding at table as a servant leader.[11] Taken together the two traditions give us a fuller picture of the early Christian eucharistic tradition.

The Meaning of the Eucharist

Many meanings cluster around the celebration of eucharist. The eucharist is a *meal* wherein the spirits of the faithful are fed, and which looks forward to the heavenly banquet. The eucharist is a *sacrifice*, in that it proclaims the sacrificial death of Jesus, and wherein is present the risen Lord, still offering himself in love for all. It is a *memorial* of Jesus' Last Supper and his crucifixion, shared in response to his command to continue the meal in his memory. The eucharist is also a *communion* with the Lord and with his disciples. And it is a *thanksgiving* for the saving events of history, especially for the powerful mysteries of Christ's life that continue to unfold. Let's look at each of these meanings in greater depth.

The Eucharistic Meal

The eucharist is in continuity with the unique table ministry carried on by Jesus, as well as with the last fellowship meal that he shared with his followers before he was executed. The eucharist is symbolic of eating and drinking, of sharing food, and thus of intimacy as well as nourishment.[12] Meals are events for bonding, sharing, and enjoying the company of friends and loved ones. They are often celebrations of special events. In gathering for the eucharistic meal, the community members signal their desire to share their lives in equality, love, and service. They come to gain nourishment from the risen Lord, and to "devour and imbibe" his spirit of unselfish service to the human community. The very transformation of the elements from bread and wine to Christ's body and blood symbolizes the community's prayer to be radically changed into disciples dedicated to love, peace, and justice.

The Christian taking food and drink at the Lord's table is also reminded of the hunger and thirst of so many throughout the world who suffer from famine and drought. As the believers gathered at the Lord's table to reflect on their own needs for spiritual and physical nourishment, they recall the desperate needs of others. It is at this table of abundance that disciples are called to confront the greed and injustice that brings want to countless others.[13] The eucharist should symbolize the deep emotional, psychological, and physical hungers of our day.[14]

On this point Carlos, a Puerto Rican student majoring in marketing, makes some good points. He recalls once how his class in high school worked for a summer in Appalachia among the poor. This is what Carlos had to say:

At first I felt strange visiting these people who lived in the backwoods in shacks that were surrounded by junk and garbage. They weren't neat and clean like my family. But one evening they invited us for dinner. It was a simple meal of soup, homemade corn bread, and vegetables. But the way they prayed before the meal; the way they shared what they had with us; and the wonderful songs they sang for us after dinner showed me that you can be happy even though you have few material possessions. That meal put me in touch with a whole new way of looking at life.

Anticipating the Heavenly Banquet

The New Testament eucharistic texts also reflect anticipation of the last days, the end of the world. In the synoptic gospels there are various versions of Jesus saying that he will not drink wine again until he shall drink it new with his followers in the final kingdom of his father. This remark is in continuity with Jesus' earlier themes about the heavenly wedding banquet (Mk 2:19), and how those who imitate his example of service at table will eat and drink with him in the kingdom (Lk 22:30).[15]

In the First Letter to the Corinthians, Paul remarks that in the eating and drinking, the communities "proclaim the Lord's death until he comes" (1 Cor 11:26). In the early communities the eucharist was seen in the larger context of expectation, even an immediate expectation of the second coming of the Lord. The covenant with God was understood to be past, present, and far-reaching into the future. Jesus' early followers believed that death and suffering will be conquered in resurrection, and ultimately in the final coming of the kingdom. The eucharist is a very real ritual celebration of this hope and the anticipation of the final banquet in heaven.

The Passover Meal

The synoptic gospel accounts of Jesus' Last Supper indicate that the preparations made for this meal are similar to those that were made for the Passover meal. We have seen that John's gospel, in contrast, refers to the Last Supper as a fellowship meal. It is very likely that the last meal that Jesus celebrated with his disciples during the Passover season was indeed a fellowship meal, rather than the actual Passover supper. The synoptics' emphasis on the Passover is perhaps more theological than it is historical. In the years immediately after Jesus' death, the liberation themes that are central to the Passover became an important metaphor for describing Jesus' saving acts. For Mark, the Passover is fulfilled in the event of the death and resurrection of Jesus.[16] As a result of this, the fellowship meal came to be described as a Passover meal.

The Eucharist as a Sacrifice

The understanding of the eucharist as a meal was the predominant theme during the period when it was celebrated in believers' homes and presided over by community leaders or by the head of the house where the celebration was taking place. As the liturgy moved from homes to basilicas—or large Roman meeting halls during the Constantinian period (fourth century)—the emphasis began to shift to that of sacrifice. While we see levels of sacrificial symbolism in the gospels and early documents such as the *Didache,* the notion became stronger as time went on. The table became an altar, and the time for the celebration shifted from the evening to the morning. Christians gathered more for a sabbath worship service than for a shared meal.

Ordinary bread, broken and passed, became unleavened hosts, consecrated and gazed upon.[17]

In the third century, some of the Passover language of the gospel was accented, and emphasis was given to metaphors of Jewish animal sacrifice. This was to serve as a "reminder of the saving offering of Jesus' own life and of the similar pledge which each Christian makes in the celebration of the ritual meal."[18] The Pauline notion of proclaiming the death of Jesus came to be understood as more explicitly sacrificial. Christians gathered for a worship service to celebrate their salvation through "the blood of the Lamb of God." The eucharistic liturgy was viewed as a genuine sacrifice insofar as Jesus' sacrifice continued to be efficacious in history.[19]

As early church councils like Nicea (325 C.E.) and Chalcedon (451 C.E.) stressed the divinity of Jesus, the liturgy took on the awesome transcendence of a cultic temple event. With the evolution of the priesthood and episcopacy, the presider's actions came to be interpreted more in terms of Jewish sacrificial offerings than with the sharing of food.

The notion of eucharist as a sacrifice assumed various levels of meaning. Eucharist as a sacrifice of praise and thanksgiving recalled God's gifts of creation and redemption. It was also viewed as a sacramental sacrifice of Christ's unique offering of self in life and in death. It is a sacrifice of petition, asking God to bestow the blessings afforded through the sacrifice of the cross. Eucharist is also a participation in Jesus' sacrificial intercession for his people.[20] Rather than the sorrowful cultic sacrificial ritual of old, it is the "grateful memory of the cross."[21] It is the joining of the people to Jesus, so that they sacrifice along with him and thus offer themselves to God.[22] In this context, Jesus and his disciples are not victims attempting to appease an angry God, but rather witnesses to the power of self-giving love and forgiveness.[23] The only cultic sacrifice they now need is a sacramental participation in the sacrifice of the risen Christ.[24]

A Memorial Meal

The disciples of Jesus Christ gathered regularly to commemorate the Lord's Supper in response to his command: "Do this in memory of me." This directive has to be seen in the context of Hebrew memorial customs. To keep in memory meant many things for the Jewish people. It meant reaching back into the past to recall God's redeeming actions. Remembering also entailed asking God to remember them now with the same saving power that was in the original event. And finally, such recalling gave hope that God would be with them in the future.

The memorial event celebrated the presence of God in the midst of the community, the God who is the savior of past, present, and future. The central saving event of the Passover was viewed by the early Christians as being intimately connected to the eucharist. This saving event was brought to fulfillment in Jesus' life, death, and resurrection, and now had power in both their present and future.

The Hebrew belief in the covenant was the basis for such memory. The covenantal relationship that God had established with people is the reason why God can be asked to continue to perform saving actions. God had promised never to abandon his people, and to be with them in fidelity and forgiveness. The God of history had never forgotten that vow, and could be counted on to remember it in the present. God's people could look forward, moreover, to the time when the covenant would be brought to fulfillment; when the kingdom will truly and fully come.

Athelia, an African-American student from Cleveland who is a varsity soccer player, explained how her Baptist congregation got a glimpse of this kingdom that is coming.

It was a sad day when an innocent twelve-year-old boy was killed by a stray bullet in a drive-by shooting. The whole community from the projects and the surrounding neighborhood gathered to sympathize with the family of this little boy and to celebrate his life. Our little church was full of hurting people. The spirit of concern and sorrow for this little boy and his parents and his brothers and sisters went far beyond the walls of that building. I truly believe that I had a taste of God's plan for oneness and peace that night that I will never forget. I know in my heart that I was treated to a little glimpse of what it must be like in heaven, when things are loving, peaceful, and where the hurts are no longer there.

For the early Christians, the eucharist was such a memorial. It recalled the saving events of Jesus' life, especially his death and resurrection. Mindful that this same risen Lord remained present to them, they celebrated the glorious events of their salvation with story, praise, thanksgiving, and intercession. Their eucharistic prayer united them to Jesus, their High Priest. Along with Jesus, they offered themselves to God, asking for a continuation of Jesus' saving power in the present day and in the times to come.[25]

Their covenant with Jesus was the basis for their calling upon God to remember them. They also looked forward to the final coming of the kingdom, when the Lord would come again in glory. The early Christians prayed "*Maranatha*" (Lord, come again).[26] Their hope focused on the present, as well as toward the heavenly banquet of the future.

The remembrance that takes place in the celebration of the eucharist is not a mere recital of the past. It is also a prophetic remembrance that promises a new future. Jesus added a prophetic dimension to the Passover when he promised a new covenant and a new creation wherein outcasts would be invited into the kingdom. He promised that the kingdom of God would stand in contradiction to present and future events of oppression and injustice.

Each celebration of the eucharist speaks to the events that contradict God's will, and empowers those in attendance to stand as prophets against exploitation and abuse.[27] It remembers the violence and suffering of today and calls upon God to empower the disciples to stand firm against it. The eucharist is a prayer that the worldwide Christian community will remember Jesus and take on the responsibility of carrying on his mission.[28]

Jake, a senior from Minneapolis who is a fine sculptor, had experienced violence in his home. When he was growing up he struggled to understand this situation. Eventually he was able to make sense of this problem in light of what he learned about the Mass.

My father was an alcoholic, and frequently he would come home drunk and in a mean mood. I saw him punch my mother and my older sisters many times, and I took some pretty bad shots myself. It was an awful time in my life, but something I had learned about the Mass as a youngster stuck with me and really helped when I was growing up. Whenever I would go to Mass I would think of the violence that Jesus experienced, and realize that the Lord knew what I was going through. That was a very comforting thought when I was growing up. Now I understand a little more clearly how the eucharist commemorates Jesus' sufferings and allows us to unite our pain with his. Sometimes I go to Mass during the week so that I can pray for people who are suffering violence, and join their suffering with Christ's death and resurrection.

Overcoming Forgetfulness

The opposite side of remembering is forgetfulness. It is here that infidelity and sinfulness reside. To forget to be thankful for forgiveness and salvation is to break the covenant and embrace evil and death. To remember is to ask for forgiveness and reconciliation. Remembering brings the creature back to the Creator. There is awe in the awareness that God carries the finite creature in memory and thought. The Psalmist prays:

> When I look at your heavens, the work of your fingers,
> the moon and the stars that you have established;
> what are human beings that you are mindful of them,
> mortals that you care for them? (Ps 8:3–4)

Memory for the Hebrew denotes the act of remembering God's care and saving action.[29] The eucharist is a remembrance of what Christ has done for us. At the same time, it recalls in wonder that Jesus always keeps us in mind; that he cares for us and blesses us. To be effective, these memories must be kept alive. The eucharistic liturgy, with its proclaimed stories of Jesus' life, and its commemoration of the Last Supper and Calvary keep this saving memory alive. Of course, the central element that keeps this memory alive is the presence of the risen Lord himself.

Do This in Memory of Me

Xavier Léon-Dufour points out that the word "do" in the phrase, "do this in memory of me" is an imperative, a command. Jesus urges his disciples to repeat the total cultic action that he has performed over the bread and wine. "In memory of me" is not merely a psychological act of remembering, but a concrete calling to mind, an action that causes remembrance. The term *"anamnesis"* (remembrance) when used to refer to the eucharist, the New Testament covenant meal, corresponds to the Passover remembrance mandated in the Book of Exodus: "This day shall be a day of remembrance for you. You shall celebrate it as a festival to the Lord; throughout your generations you shall observe it as a perpetual ordinance" (Ex 12:14). When Jesus tells the disciples to celebrate this ritual "in memory of me," the new saving Passover event is now identified with his person and his mission. His body and his blood symbolize the presence of Jesus and the mystery of his death and resurrection. This remembrance puts his followers in touch with the new life of the risen Lord. Léon-Dufour sums it up this way:

> The eucharistic liturgy places us collectively in the presence of Jesus who gives life for me and who asks me to act as he acted, or, more accurately, who gives himself to me as food and thereby asks me to act by means of his own power to act, which is now present within me.[30]

Communion

Communion, or "common union" with the risen Lord and with his disciples, is at the heart of the eucharistic celebration. Often this aspect has been blurred amid controversies about the real presence and the consecration of the elements. The denial by some Protestants of the real presence of Christ in the eucharist led the Council of Trent to place a great deal of emphasis on adoration and devotion honoring Christ truly present in the eucharist. Coupled with a moral theology centered on sin and unworthiness, it resulted in many Catholics seldom receiving communion. For many Catholics the climax of the Mass became the consecration and elevation of the host, rather than the reception of communion.

Pope Pius X in the early years of the twentieth century promoted the practice of more frequent communion for Catholics. By mid-century, liturgists emphasized that the Mass should be understood as "sharing food at a meal." These ideas were also emphasized by the Second Vatican Council so that the reception of the body and blood of Christ in communion has been restored as the culminating point of the eucharistic celebration. In addition, contemporary moral theology's stress on love rather than law, and on forgiveness rather than exclusion has resulted in Catholics receiving communion more freely and more often than in the past. The renewed emphasis on communion also brings out the social dimension of the eucharist and prevents the liturgy from becoming simply a private devotion.

Thanksgiving

The spirit of thanksgiving in the eucharist is not only for one's own personal friendship with Jesus Christ, but also for membership in his church, and for participation in his mission to the poor. At the liturgy the community gives thanks that the risen Lord is in its midst. The disciples express their gratitude for his life of self-sacrifice and for his death with its saving powers. They thank God for raising Jesus and for promising them eternal life as well. The Mass is in essence a celebration of all of God's gifts.

Eucharistic Controversies

A study of the controversies surrounding beliefs and practices related to the eucharist helps us understand some of its more difficult aspects and also sharpens our understanding of this mystery. We will look at some of the earlier dilemmas, and then examine the peak of debate regarding the eucharist that began in the medieval period and reached fever pitch during the Reformation. In the next section we will look at how ecumenical dialogue has attempted to resolve many of these older arguments.

Attacks From Outside the Church

Some of the first challenges to the eucharist came from those who were enemies to Christianity. Many Romans were outraged at the "atheism" of the Christians, who did not properly honor the Roman deities. Instead, they paid homage to a Jewish peasant who was crucified and whom they believed had been raised from the dead. Many Jews were outraged at the Christian claim that Jesus was the Messiah, and that he was worthy of worship. Mention of eating his body and drinking his blood was derided as cannibalism, and stories of sacrificing babies and bizarre sexual orgies at the Lord's Supper circulated against the Christian communities.

We know of these attacks largely from the apologetical writing of the time that answered them. Great apologists like Tertullian, Justin Martyr, and Athanagoras in the early centuries of the church answered these accusations and explained what was genuinely being practiced by Christians.[31]

Problems From Within the Church

The Gnostic communities, groups of Christians who placed a high value on wisdom and intelligence and who eventually were deemed to be heretical, held "matter" in contempt. Their dualism, which held that only the spiritual could be from God, prevented them from accepting either the incarnation or any sacramental approach to God. Out of this grew a belief that Jesus only appeared to be human and that Christians could not be joined to Jesus through material things like bread and wine. Other heresies, such as Arianism, which denied Jesus' divinity, and Docetism, which denied his humanity, also had implications with regard to the eucharistic presence.[32]

In these early denials that Jesus' presence in the eucharist was not "real," a pattern was started that developed further in the Middle Ages and the Reformation. For some, the real presence became so spiritualized that it had little sacramental value. By the same token, this over-spiritualized approach caused an ultra-realistic reaction in some medieval writers and even in Luther.[33] Such controversies also shifted the focus onto the elements of bread and wine, and away from the meaning of the Lord's Supper as a total event. The earlier belief in the presence of the risen Lord in the entire celebration and in both scripture and sacrament was blurred by this concentration on the elements. Believers were often distracted from the connection between this sacrament and their daily lives, as well as from the awareness that the total person, body and soul, was nurtured in the eucharist.

Controversy Over the Real Presence

Controversy over the eucharist shifted as the church moved into the medieval period. Whereas previous attacks had come from enemies outside, such as pagans and heretical communities, the division now began to come from within the main body of the community.

A philosophical shift played a role in the appearance of these new controversies over the real presence. The early Church Fathers had been largely Platonic in their philosophical perspective. Following in the tradition initiated by Plato they believed that true knowledge came as intuition perceived a world of abstract forms. The truly real was understood to exist in a "world of ideas." What appeared to be real materiality was a mere shadow of reality. From this perspective, reality was achieved by the mind's grasp of the essence of things, rather than through perception by the senses.

Applying this abstract approach to the eucharist, the real presence of the Lord was identified with the essence of eucharist. What was perceived by the senses—the appearance of bread and wine—had little bearing on the reality of the eucharist. This Platonic approach freed the believer from what appeared to be, and allowed for concentration on the true reality of the eucharist.[34] What was real—the essence—had been changed into the body and blood of Christ. It was Christ who transformed the bread and wine, and through contact with this Christ, the members of the community were transformed.

A Move Toward Realism

A number of factors moved Christian thinking from the Platonic way of thought, and brought new challenges to the understanding of the eucharist. First, as the Western tribes swept through Europe, they brought with them a stark realism about life. Everyday reality, what was seen and heard and felt, became the focus of life and thought, rather than a world of abstract forms. Second, the West's struggle with Islam brought it into contact with Aristotle's philosophy, whose writings had been preserved by the Arabs. This perspective, in contrast to the Platonic, perceived reality to exist in both matter and form, rather than just in a world of ideas. The Aristotelian world was perceived through the senses. Finally, Charlemagne's historic efforts in the ninth century to unify and reform Christianity brought about a scholarship that produced the first real treatises on the eucharist.

The Monks of Corbie

The first theological treatise on eucharist was written around 830 C.E. by Paschasius Radbertus (d. 860), a Saxon monk at the monastery in Corbie. Attempting to explain the Lord's Supper to his fellow monks, Paschasius used the same approach as some of the Church Fathers (Irenaeus, Hilary, and Cyril of Alexandria) to explain that salvation was brought about by the union of communicants with the risen body of Jesus. Just as Jesus' human nature was transformed by the divine nature, he taught that human nature was transformed by the body of Christ when a person received the eucharist. He insisted that this body of Christ which we receive is the same body born of Mary. He intended this as a simple explanation for ordinary monks, but it was often taken too literally, and led to an ultra-realistic approach to the eucharist. Some of his contemporaries maintained that Paschasius' teaching bordered on cannibalism.

Another monk of Corbie, Ratramnus (d. 868), wrote a treatise on the eucharist that was quite different from that of his colleague Paschasius. Ratramnus was not as realistic in his theology of eucharist. He held that in communion people received the body and blood of the Lord "in sign" or "in figure." He focused on the inner, spiritual reality of the presence of the risen Lord in the person who has received communion. In this way the real presence was not physical but spiritual. It was a presence perceived by faith.[35]

The question for future controversy had been set: Was the presence of the risen Lord real or symbolic? Paschasius had stressed the real, Ratramnus the symbolic. Yet the two monks were able to live together, and not much was made of their controversy for the next several centuries. For the most part, Paschasius' more realistic view seemed to be more acceptable to the prevailing mentality of the Western tribes.

Stephanie, a junior from Tucson, wrote a report on the Corbie controversy and had this to say about the realistic approach to eucharist:

When I was in second grade they told us we were going to receive the body and blood of Jesus. I was frightened. I loved Jesus and it sounded gross for me to be eating his flesh and drinking his blood. I remember asking my father to explain it to me, but he really did not know what to say. I think kids in the second grade are too young to receive communion. The church should wait until they are older and can understand what is going on.

Berengar of Tours

Controversy over the meaning of the eucharist increased during the eleventh century. A teacher named Berengar (d. 1088) revived the symbolic approach of Ratramnus. Berengar was a reputable scholar, well-versed in the grammar and dialectic of Aristotle. He believed that Christ was present in the eucharist only in a spiritual sense. He ridiculed those who said that bread and wine were changed into the flesh of Christ. He taught that the bread and wine remained just bread and wine, and were symbols of the reality of Jesus' spiritual presence.[36]

Berengar ignited a controversy that lasted for decades, and eventually official meetings would be called to settle the matter. The Roman synods of 1059 and 1079 required that Berengar sign oaths stating that he believed in the real presence of Christ in the eucharist. The first of these oaths took such a literal approach that the statement was later to become an embarrassment to the church. This oath maintained that after the consecration the true body and blood of Christ are present, and that "they are physically taken up and broken in the hands of the priest and crushed by the teeth of the faithful, not only sacramentally but in truth." This ultra-realistic view deeply influenced medieval theology, and was echoed by Luther. Fortunately the second oath given to Berengar was more nuanced. It used Aristotle's notion of substance, and said that the bread and wine were "substantially changed" into the body and blood of Jesus Christ. This laid the foundations for the development of the classical notion of transubstantiation. The term was first used in 1215 against the Cathars who, like the earlier Gnostics, disdained material things and thus challenged the real presence of Christ in the bread and the wine.

The Rise of the Universities

The rise of the universities in the eleventh and twelfth centuries provided a forum for scholars to write about the eucharist, and soon over a hundred treatises appeared. Hugh of St. Victor (d. 1142) and others began to develop a theology of the sacraments that could be applied to the understanding of the eucharist.

The approach of the medieval scholastics moved away from the realism of earlier times and dealt with the real presence more philosophically. Aquinas gave authority to the term "transubstantiation," explaining that the substance of the bread and wine changed, while the accidents remained the same. The literal approach, however, was still widespread among the common folk, who often dealt with the eucharist as a relic, or even as a charm to be carried in one's pocket on a trip.

The Origins of the Reformation

John Wycliffe (d. 1384), a theologian at Oxford and a fiery church reformer, argued that the scriptures should be the only source of authority for the church. He concluded that the papacy, priestly powers, and terms like transubstantiation had no validity because they were not found in the bible. He believed that holiness should be the requirement for liturgical leadership, not office, and he suggested that such leadership might well be carried out by the laity. Wycliffe's positions were condemned at Oxford in 1381, but he had laid the foundations for many of the Protestant positions that would appear at the opening of the sixteenth century. John Hus (d. 1414), a follower of Wycliffe, continued to preach reform in his native Bohemia, and proposed a moderate form of Wycliffe's views on the eucharist. Hus was censured, excommunicated, and in 1414, burned at the stake. The controversy then quieted for more than a hundred years.

Martin Luther

A century after the burning of Hus, another reformer appeared on the scene, a young teacher of scripture at the German university of Wittenberg. This professor was an Augustinian monk named Martin Luther, whose actions ignited the Reformation that tore Western Christianity asunder.

Young Luther was outraged at the scandals he witnessed in the church. The selling of indulgences, whereby people paid money to insure that their departed loved ones would enter heaven more quickly, had become a major industry. Unscrupulous monks and religious fund-raisers preyed upon the fears and superstitions of the populace. Luther also objected to the widespread corruption that he saw throughout the ranks of the clergy and hierarchy, all the way to the papacy.

In 1517 Luther called for a debate on these issues by posting his famous ninety-five theses on the cathedral door. Luther's call was heard all the way to Rome, and soon young Martin found himself at the center of a much larger conflict about church reform. In 1520 he raised a number of objections to the commonly accepted eucharistic theology of his times. He questioned the practice of having Masses said on behalf of the deceased, the theology of transubstantiation, the custom of the laity receiving the communion bread but not the cup, and the teaching that the Mass was a sacrifice.[37]

Accepting scripture as the sole authority for Christian beliefs, Luther eventually argued against the need for an ordained priesthood or for special priestly powers. He also protested against the belief that the celebration of the Mass transmitted the power of salvation.[38] He taught that the eucharist was but a sign of God's offer of salvation, and that faith and faith alone could actually save. Luther also called for the return to a service that more closely resembled the simplicity of the Last Supper. He maintained that transubstantiation was a pagan metaphysics, and he insisted on a literal approach to the real presence. Luther wrote: "Whoever eats this bread eats the Body of Christ. Whoever crunches this bread with teeth or tongue crunches the Body of Christ."[39]

Other Reformers

In the 1520s, Ulrich Zwingli (d. 1531), a Swiss priest and popular preacher, began his reforms in Zurich. Zwingli radically rejected the view that any material thing could play a role in salvation. This, of course, affected his view of sacraments and the eucharist. He agreed with Luther that only faith saved, but he went beyond Luther and had the Mass abolished. He also took the position that since the risen Lord was in heaven, he could not really be present in the eucharist.[40] In his view, the eucharist was a spiritual communion, but not a reception of the real presence of the Lord. Luther and Zwingli eventually debated this point, but never came to an agreement. Luther told his followers to avoid the "Zwinglian" way at all costs.

John Calvin (d. 1564) advocated a moderate version of Zwingli's teachings and laid the foundation for much of contemporary mainline Protestant eucharistic theology. Calvin insisted that the Lord's Supper could strengthen the faith, but denied that it could play any role in salvation. Both Luther and Calvin held that transubstantiation was perverse, and that adoration of Christ in the eucharist was idolatry. Calvin also taught that the Catholic consecration was sorcery, and that looking at the Mass as a repetition of Calvary was blasphemy. Calvin maintained that participation in the Lord's Supper was important to confirm one's faith.[41] Calvin understood the real presence to be a faith-union with Christ, not a result of contact with his body. He placed little value on the outward signs of bread and wine. He agreed with Zwingli that Christ's body was in heaven and not present in the eucharist.[42]

The medieval theology of the eucharist was profoundly challenged by the sixteenth-century Protestant reformers. The Council of Trent answered the Reformers with a strong definition that Jesus Christ is really, truly, and physically present in the eucharist. This historic council also reiterated the Catholic position that the Mass was a sacrifice, that its merits could be applied to the living and the dead, that the risen

Lord could be worshiped in the elements, and that transubstantiation was an apt term to describe what happened at the consecration. Trent set the views on the eucharist that guided Catholic liturgy, theology, and education for the next four centuries.

Contemporary Liturgical Renewal

Contemporary Catholic liturgical renewal began at the end of the nineteenth century in French and German monasteries, was given added impetus by Pope Pius XII in the mid-twentieth century, and came to fruition when the Second Vatican Council promulgated a historic document on liturgical renewal in 1963. The council hoped that such renewal would bring new vigor to Christian life, encourage liturgical adaptation to meet contemporary needs, and promote Christian unity.

The Constitution on the Sacred Liturgy described the eucharist as the action of Christ and the church, signaling a definite shift from the clergy-centered liturgical focus of the past. The council also promoted the use of the vernacular (the local language rather than Latin) in the prayers and readings of the Mass. Along with this the council called for the altar to face the people, thereby encouraging a stronger lay participation. Strong emphasis was placed on the Lord's presence in the Bible as the Liturgy of the Word was restored to a central place in liturgy. Singing was encouraged, frequent communion was strongly recommended, eventually under both species, and a new rite was drawn up to allow more than one priest to preside together at the celebration of the eucharist (concelebration).

Ecumenical Progress

Paradoxically, the sacrament that the Lord gave to help his followers express their unity with Christ and one another is actually the ground for division among the Christian churches. In an effort to deal with some of the tragic divisions between Christian communities, serious theological dialogues have been held since the Second Vatican Council between Catholics and Protestants. These are the first such discussions since the Reformation, and would not have been possible were it not for the outstanding breakthroughs in ecumenism achieved by the Second Vatican Council.

Lutheran-Catholic Dialogue

International Lutheran-Catholic dialogues began in 1965. In 1967 they produced an extremely important document called *Eucharist as*

Sacrifice, in which members of the dialogue commission expressed basic beliefs about the meaning of the eucharist that were acceptable to both Catholics and Lutherans. Common approaches to the methodology of biblical criticism and to basic theological principles opened the way for considerable progress on this and other important theological topics.

As discussions continued through the 1970s and 1980s, eucharistic sharing (receiving communion in the church of a different denomination) and the meaning of the ordained priesthood became sticking points for the Catholic and Lutheran scholars and pastors who met regularly to further their discussions. Over the past thirty years the dialogue has moved into those areas as well as into discussions about the papacy, infallibility, justification, and even Mary and the saints.

Lutheran and Catholic theologians came to an important agreement on the meaning of the real presence. In answer to Catholic queries as to whether they believe in the "real presence," the Lutherans explained that they believed that Christ was present in many ways: in people, baptism, scripture, and preaching. They also maintained that Christ was present "wholly and entirely, in his body and blood, under the signs of bread and wine" in the Lord's Supper. They pointed out that they affirm this presence rather than try to explain it, and that it takes place by the power of the Spirit through the Word.[43]

For their part, Catholics answered Lutheran concerns about the way that Catholics understand the eucharist as a sacrifice. Since the time of Luther, Protestants have objected to Catholic beliefs that the priest offers up the victim in sacrifice to God. Lutherans are concerned that this seems to add something blasphemous to the work of Christ at Calvary. Catholic theologians were able to come to agreement with the Lutherans that Christ's sacrifice is unrepeatable, that reconciliation exists only through the cross, and that we do not offer Christ, so much as Christ offers us at the celebration of the eucharist.[44] In later documents on the mutual understanding of the meaning of ministry, Lutherans and Catholics recognized that the real presence of the body and blood existed in each other's eucharistic celebration. They also recommended a cautious move toward eucharistic sharing (intercommunion). It must be noted, however, that these theological agreements have not resulted in any dramatic practical results.[45]

Anglican–Catholic Dialogue

The Anglican-Roman Catholic International Commission (ARCIC) has also been a significant force for increased theological understanding and unity since Vatican II. Traditionally the Church of England's views on the eucharist have reflected those of Calvin. Its Thirty-Nine Articles of Religion (1563) rejected transubstantiation, but avoided Zwingli's rejection of the real presence. Today Anglican views on real presence range from those whose views are similar to the beliefs of Catholics, to those that see Christ's body and blood to be alongside the bread and wine. Another obstacle to a common understanding of the meaning of the eucharist comes from Pope Leo XIII's declaration in 1896 that Anglican orders were considered to be null and void.[46]

Symbolic visits between recent popes and the archbishops of Canterbury—the head of the worldwide Anglican Communion—as well as high-level theological dialogue between the two churches have often raised hopes for greater unity. Significant agreement has been achieved on the question of real presence and the sacrificial aspects of eucharist in the *Windsor Statement* (1971) and its *Elucidation* (1979), yet many issues remain unresolved. The real presence in the elements, the permanence of this presence after communion, and the recognition of each other's ministers are all still problematic.[47]

The practice of Anglicans around the world—including the Episcopalians in the United States—to ordain women has put a chill on Rome's relations with these communions. In addition, thousands of Anglican ministers, including a bishop opposed to the ordination of women, have joined the Catholic church and been ordained as married Catholic clergy, while some Catholic priests have joined the Anglican church and now function as clergymen. Such movement and disagreement has made further discussion of unity problematic.

These two dialogues along with many other interchurch dialogues led to the publication of the document, *Baptism, Eucharist and Ministry,* by the World Council of Churches in 1982. This profoundly significant document still remains the centerpiece for future discussion.[48] Through these ongoing discussions the churches—both leaders and faithful—have come to realize that they share much in common. Through common biblical scholarship, a more accurate account of history, a united concern for social justice, and a greater desire for Christian unity, churches have made the first efforts to heal hundreds of years of scandalous divisions. Whether the churches will be able to continue implementing at a practical and pastoral level these agreements that have been reached on theological levels, remains to be seen.

The Future of the Eucharist

Catholic understanding and celebration of the eucharist has profoundly deepened in the decades following Vatican II. Modern biblical research and scholarship have provided a wealth of historical and theological insights into the early celebrations of the eucharist. Research into the writings of the early Church Fathers has given us information about the eucharistic tradition that was not available during the great debates of the Middle Ages and the Reformation. We now have a more accurate understanding of earlier beliefs about symbol, sacrament, ritual, sacrifice, priesthood, and real presence.

The reclaiming of a vigorous theology of resurrection has enabled both Catholics and other Christian churches to better grasp the meaning of the presence of the risen Lord in the eucharist. The increased emphasis on understanding the eucharist as a meal, and the central importance placed on the reception of communion have renewed Catholic celebrations of eucharist. The growing awareness of the importance of the eucharist in the faith life of all Christians is something to be shared, lived, linked to service, and connected to peace and justice rather than something to be argued over. It has given new vitality to this sacrament which is central to the life of Christians.

A Crisis in Ministry

The crucial questions for the future of the Catholic celebration of the eucharist revolve around ministry. There is a critical, worldwide shortage of priests. As a result, many Catholics do not have the opportunity to participate in the celebration of the Mass on a regular basis, and must settle for attending communion services.

As the clergy ages and declines in number, who will lead Catholic eucharistic celebrations? Will permanent deacons play a more significant role in liturgical leadership? Perhaps there will be a change in the celibacy law so that married clergy can officiate. Possibly women will be granted a more central role in liturgical leadership. Will Catholics return to the house churches of old, and might the "domestic churches" of families become the setting for eucharistic celebrations? Some envision combining many local parishes into mega-churches with clergy in the role of circuit riders going around to celebrate the eucharist, while others predict the spread of micro-churches with more leadership given to the laity.

Regardless of how often the eucharist is celebrated, it is likely that peace and social justice will remain central themes in the Catholic theology of eucharist. In the developing world, eucharistic liturgy will likely continue to be a base for nurturing the desire for liberation and justice.

Self-sacrifice, the lack of fear of death, and hope for a just future in this life and resurrection in the next will be central to any future understanding and practice of the eucharistic liturgy. Perhaps the eucharist will become more of a reality to be lived, rather than a theological topic to be debated; a personal encounter with the risen Lord, rather than a source of division among Christians. The eucharist is a living tradition that must be constantly renewed to remain the Lord's greatest gift of self to his people.

Conclusion

The eucharist is simple and at the same time unfathomable. It finds its source in Jesus, whose ministry at table culminated at the Last Supper. The eucharist is a living memorial of that supper as well as of Jesus' sacrifice on the cross. In the eucharist the risen Lord nourishes his disciples and binds them more closely with himself and with each other.

The eucharist has many facets: It is meal, sacrifice, remembrance, communion. Unfortunately, rather than being the supreme sign of unity, it has often been a source of division among the followers of Jesus. Perhaps the future will see Christians putting their controversies behind them so that they can join in communion and ministry to bring the good news to a hurting world.

Discussion Questions

1. Select some "table stories" from the gospels and discuss what they might teach us today about eucharistic celebrations.

2. Compare and contrast the Last Supper account in Mark's gospel with that in John's gospel. What do your findings tell you about how there were already various theologies of eucharist in the gospel communities?

3. Suggest ways in which these various aspects of eucharist might be better emphasized at liturgy: e.g., meal, sacrifice, communion.

4. What was the Jewish notion of liturgical "remembering"? In what sense are we "remembering" Jesus Christ at eucharist today?

5. Discuss some of the main controversies over the "real presence" of Jesus Christ in the eucharist. How is this understood by Catholics today?

6. Given the shortage of priests, what forms do you think eucharistic liturgies will take in the future?

Suggested Readings

William Crockett, *Eucharist: Symbol of Transformation.* Collegeville, MN: Liturgical Press/Pueblo Books, 1989.

Monika Hellwig, *The Eucharist and the Hunger of the World,* 2nd ed. Kansas City: Sheed and Ward, 1994.

Jerome Kodell, *The Eucharist in the New Testament.* Collegeville, MN: Liturgical Press/Michael Glazier, 1988.

Xavier Léon-Dufour, *Sharing the Eucharistic Bread.* Mahwah, NJ: Paulist Press, 1982.

Gary Macy, *The Banquet's Wisdom: A Short History of the Theologies of the Last Supper.* Mahwah, NJ: Paulist Press, 1992.

Raymond Moloney, *Eucharist.* Collegeville, MN: Liturgical Press, 1995.

David N. Power, *The Eucharistic Mystery.* New York: Crossroad, 1992.

John H.P. Reumann, *The Supper of the Lord.* Philadelphia: Fortress Press, 1985.

Philippe Rouillard, "From Human Meal to Christian Eucharist," in R. Kevin Seasoltz (ed.), *Living Bread, Saving Cup: Readings on the Eucharist.* Collegeville, MN: Liturgical Press, 1982.

11.

The Sacrament of Marriage

Framing the Question

My name is Jim. I was born and raised in Seattle, Washington. Right now I am trying to get my degree in dentistry so that I can go back home and set up a practice. I have some concerns about marriage. Frankly it scares me. My folks seem to have a good marriage, but what I see of marriage in our society has worried me. It seems to be falling apart. So many of the talk shows and the programs that I watch on TV are about affairs, divorce, and the problems of marriage. It almost seems that divorces have become more common than good marriages.

I am also concerned about making such a major commitment. I wonder if I can honestly say, "Until death do us part." Maybe my wife and I will get tired of each other. Then what? And then, too, marriage looks like a hassle; a loss of my freedom.

As a child I learned that marriage is a sacrament. I am not sure most Catholics know what that means. I know I don't. Does it mean that marriage is holy? Well, if that is true then why are so many marriages collapsing? I will have to think long and hard before I get married.

Jim expresses the apprehensions that many young people have about marriage. Marriage does seem to be in trouble today. It often appears threatening, awesome, and almost impossible to young people. Yet most people want to get married, and they hope that their marriage will last forever.

This chapter will look at how the Catholic tradition on marriage evolved over the centuries. We will begin by looking at notions of marriage in the Hebrew and Christian scriptures. Then we will discuss the various stages of development in the theology of marriage. Most important, we will look at modern views on marriage, especially the sacramental theology that has emerged in the last few decades. Then we will look at some of the key dimensions of marriage today: romantic love, friendship, marital love, gender and sex, the family, and the need for self-giving and service. We will end by looking at the shadow side of marriage and at some of the ways in which marriage can be a source of liberation. It is to be hoped that this information about the true meaning and sacredness of marriage will help people to make this vocational choice with greater hope and confidence.

Developing a Theology of Marriage

The Christian understanding of marriage has developed over two millennia amid many diverse periods of cultural and religious upheaval. This development has been deeply affected by the relationship that has existed between the church and the culture around it. In many ways Christians have found themselves to be counter-cultural, resisting and even protesting the norms and values of some cultures. The church's vision and values have often been in tension with those of society and culture, as the church walks the thin line between adapting to culture and giving up its gospel values. The followers of Christ in every era of history have maintained their mission to teach all nations in words and ways they can understand, but at the same time conserve an ancient gospel tradition that is unique.

Marriage is basically a cultural institution, which can and has been able to thrive without religion. Anthropology tells us that marriage in one form or another first appeared when humans settled into social groups. Once clans and tribes formed, marriage became a useful social structure for preserving blood lines, maintaining a home base, and raising offspring.

While it may appear that marriage was grounded in civil society, remember that religion was integral to most early cultures. Thus religious values and rituals often surrounded marriage. Since marriage was largely a family matter, the religious beliefs and symbolism of families generally affected the way marriage was understood and lived out. The initial Christian understanding of marriage was affected by the Hebrew belief that God had created marriage, as well as by Jesus' teachings about the unity and permanence of marriage. This understanding was the result of a blending of culture and religion, family and faith.

Early Christian notions of the sacramentality of marriage continued to evolve as the church encountered the cultures and religions of the Romans, Greeks, and many European tribes. This first section will overview some of the more significant stages in the church's understanding of the sacramentality of marriage. The second section will consider contemporary views with regard to this key Catholic sacrament.

Jewish Origins

The first Christian communities were composed largely of Jewish converts. In entering Christianity these first disciples brought their Semitic beliefs about marriage with them. They blended these beliefs with the teachings they had received from Jesus, and eventually a Christian theology of marriage began to take shape.

The Hebrew notion of marriage seems to have been a blend of religious and cultural values. For the Jew, marriage was a family matter. It was not associated with synagogue, temple, or priesthood. Yet, like all created things, marriage had come from the hand of God.[1] The Hebrew scriptures reveal that the Jews were quite aware that marriage was often the context for sin. Violence, abuse, incest, and infidelity were all associated with this institution. In light of this the Hebrews allowed divorce for a wide range of reasons, but generally restricted this privilege to husbands. The Jews had many laws to deal with these situations, and believed that somehow these laws had their origin in God.

The Jews had uniquely separated themselves from many of the views of other religions on marriage. The Jews did not accept the belief that marriage was a mirroring of the wedded gods with all their sexual antics. Marriage for the Jew was not "the Holy," but it was among the created "good things" of Yahweh. It was a place to experience God's blessings and participate in God's creative powers.

Hebrew beliefs about marriage are reflected in the two creation accounts recorded in the Book of Genesis. In the older of these two stories (written about 1000 B.C.E.), the Yahwist author describes God forming a man from clay, and then forming a woman from one of his ribs. The two are formed from the same flesh and bone, and in marriage cling to each other to "become one body" (Gn 2:24). For the Hebrew, all creation comes from God, including the ancient institution of marriage.

The other creation parable found in Genesis was written 500 years later by the so-called priestly author. Where the earlier tradition has man being created before woman, this account tells of human creation coming as the climax of all creation. After God has created the heavens, the earth, and all living things, God decides to make creatures in the divine image and likeness. The storyteller writes: "In the divine image he created him; male and female he created them." Then they are blessed and told; "Be fertile and multiply, fill the earth"(Gn 1:27–28). In this passage the author professes faith that both sexuality and the act of sexual intercourse are from the hand of God. The two sexes not only reflect God's image and likeness, they are also told to participate in the creative process.[2] These Genesis stories provide the foundation for later Christian understandings of marriage.

Jesus and Marriage

Jesus, being a devout Jew, revered the traditions of his religion. He was familiar with the way the prophets had used marriage as a metaphor for the covenant between Yahweh and his people. In the Hebrew scriptures, God's willingness to forgive the infidelity of his people was often paralleled with the unconditional love called for between husband and wife. Jesus knew how love and sexuality had been celebrated in the biblical book known today as the Song of Songs. The experience of his parents' Jewish marriage also gave him insights and inspiration about the value and meaning of marriage.

The Gospel of Mark tells a story in which some Pharisees approached Jesus and attempted to get him to take sides in the age-old dispute about divorce. In the story, Jesus seems to sidestep the traditional arguments for divorce. He reminds his listeners of the "two shall become one flesh" passage in the Book of Genesis, and then gives his own teaching regarding the permanence of marriage. He says: "Therefore what God has joined together, no human being must separate" (Mk 10:9). This passage has been used throughout the centuries by the church as part of its argument for the indissolubility of marriage.[3]

Matthew's gospel, written perhaps a generation after Mark's, tells a similar story. Here Jesus takes a stand against the divorce laws of his time and the double standard that discriminates against women. He again disallows divorce, but makes one exception: Divorce seems to be allowed if "the marriage is unlawful" (Mt 5:32). The actual meaning of this exception has been debated throughout the centuries and has been significant in theological discussions on the sacramentality of marriage, divorce, and the granting of annulments.

Other indications that early Christians recognized the blessedness of marriage can be drawn from the nobility given Jesus' family in the nativity stories. Both the communities of Matthew and Luke highlight the love, fidelity, courage, and dedication of Mary and Joseph. The Catholic tradition has also pointed to the wedding feast of Cana as an indication of Jesus' regard for marriage. John's gospel places Jesus' first miraculous sign at the wedding feast of Cana, an apparent indication that the Johannine community believed that Jesus paid special honor to marriage in his ministry. The role given Mary, the mother of Jesus, in this miracle is also significant.

The Pauline Tradition

Two principal sources in the Pauline materials reflect other early Christian attitudes toward marriage. In a very early letter, written about twenty-five years after Jesus' death, Paul attempts to answer a set of questions sent to him by the Corinthians. Since we do not have the actual questions that Paul is answering, the points that he makes are not always clear, and thus the content reflects only a partial theology of marriage. If anything, Paul, who himself was probably not married, seems to be merely tolerant of marriage as a means of avoiding sexual immorality.

In his remarks to the Corinthians, Paul reflects his Jewish belief that sexual contact is unclean, and indicates that he would prefer that people abstain as he now does. Paul is willing to concede, however, that people can marry in order to avoid immorality, and advises the unmarried and widows to marry if they cannot maintain self-control. In his classic concession to human weakness, Paul says: "If they cannot exercise self-control they should marry, for it is better to marry than to be on fire" (1 Cor 7:9). In general, Paul does not adopt the negative Gnostic attitudes that condemn marriage. But neither does he reflect a positive or inspiring theology of marriage.[4]

Paul also points out to the Corinthians that marriage makes ministry difficult because the spouses are too distracted by trying to please each other and too preoccupied with worldly affairs to be effective ministers (1 Cor 7:32–34). This passage has been used by many as a justification for the law of celibacy that prohibits priests from marrying.

One particular passage from the Letter to the Ephesians has been central to the church's tradition on the sacramentality of marriage (Eph 5:21–33). Many contemporary scripture scholars have concluded that this letter was not written by Paul, but by one of his disciples. If this be true, then questions must be raised as to how closely this reflects Paul's views, and also whether the classic passage should be given the weight it has held in the past.

This controversial passage likens the relationship between husband and wife to that which exists between Christ and the church. Reflecting the patriarchal structures of the times, wives are told to be submissive to their husbands, just as the church is subordinate to Christ. Husbands are told to love their wives with the same self-sacrificing and unconditional love that Christ has for his church. Husbands are to nourish and cherish their wives.

The author of the Letter to the Ephesians links his reflection to the passage from the Book of Genesis that mentions how "the two shall become one flesh." This union, like that of Christ and his church, is a "mystery," a part of God's hidden plan of salvation.[5] Although this passage had little influence on the thinking about marriage in the early centuries of the church, it later became foundational in the church's theology of marriage.[6] Ultimately it became the basis for understanding marriage as a symbol or sacrament wherein the couple can experience in each other the power of Christ's love. It also became an argument in favor of the permanence of marriage. This conclusion was drawn from the understanding that just as Christ's bond with his church was unbreakable, the same permanence applied to the marriage covenant.

The Beliefs of the Early Church

In the first few Christian centuries there was little reflection on the sacramentality of marriage. The marriages of Christians were simply "in the Lord," and their religious meaning seems to derive more from the baptism of the spouses than from marriage itself. The sparse theology that did exist on marriage in the early centuries was often designed to counteract Gnostic beliefs. The Gnostics could range from seeing sex and marriage as evils to be avoided, to promoting promiscuous lifestyles. Against these views and other pagan beliefs about free sex, the Christians stressed that both sex and marriage were part of God's creation, and that they belonged together. Marriage was viewed as a way to holiness, albeit one that was inferior to a life of dedicated virginity.

There has been in the Catholic tradition a long-standing belief that marriage, if a vocation at all, is for the masses of Christians who are not able to be celibate. Only in recent times has the church changed its views and recognized marriage as a genuine vocation, but still there are some who would prefer to see the earlier teachings extolling celibacy restored as the "official" teaching.

The Christian community came to an early awareness that marriage was a visible reality in which the presence and power of Christ was experienced. It was a life vowed to fidelity and permanency. The early church staunchly held this view in opposition to many Roman and Greek perspectives that held that marriages could be easily agreed upon and just as easily dissolved.

The early church also struggled with pagan views on orgiastic sex and promiscuity. The bizarre sexual behavior in Roman and Greek society led the early Christians to speak of a lower law of lust within sexuality. Sex seemed to be dangerous, and needed to be carried out with severe restraint. This attitude is evident in Tertullian's third-century writings on marriage where he vacillates between glowing idealism on partnership in marriage and disdain toward wedded life. At times he seems to consider marriage to be a blot on what might otherwise be a perfect Christian life.[7] This view is shared by other Church Fathers and culminates in the theology of original sin and concupiscence of Augustine in the fourth century. Augustine laid the foundation for the church's theology of marriage, and included in his theology a reluctance to permit sexual intercourse in marriage, unless it be for procreation.

The Influence of Augustine

Augustine's thought on marriage has had tremendous influence on Catholic thinking. Medieval councils, Thomas Aquinas, Vatican II, and several modern popes have repeated his teachings on marriage. Contemporary Catholic beliefs about the sacramentality of marriage and procreation are still heavily influenced by Augustinian thought.

Augustine, like so many other Christian thinkers, shaped his teaching in a defensive posture against what he perceived to be the errors of his time. Here and in many other cases, like the Reformation, the agenda is effectively controlled by protesters. This inhibits the theological scope of the arguments, and often gives a negative cast to the doctrinal positions.

Augustine developed his teachings on marriage to combat two groups that he held to be erroneous: the Manicheans and the Pelagians. The Manicheans were dualistic in that they divided reality into good and evil, spirit and matter. Sex, and of course, marriage were of the darker realities. The Manicheans instructed Christians seeking perfection to abstain from sex and marriage. Augustine opposed these negative positions by arguing that sex and marriage were essentially good, since they were created by God. He reiterated the teachings found in the Book of Genesis, but moved the argument forward by specifying the three "goods" of marriage: faithfulness, children, and sacrament. This laid the foundation for the position that Christian marriage requires promises of fidelity and permanence, and has the procreation of children as one of its purposes.

Augustine's writings on marriage are extensive and varied. It is easy to oversimplify his work, quote him out of context, or simplistically make him an easy target for criticism. Some of his writings on marriage are actually quite pastoral. At one point in his writings, Augustine adds still another "good" to marriage; that of companionship. Some theologians maintain that this perspective laid the foundations for the more personalistic contemporary approach to marriage.[8] Ultimately, however, it seems that Augustine had a limited and often negative perspective on sex, and his view has left its mark on the Catholic tradition for all times.

The Pelagians engaged Augustine on the question of original sin. It was their position that the "Fall" described in Genesis left human nature unaffected. After the Fall, women and men could perform the same actions as before without the help of God's grace. Augustine answered by stating that the Fall had seriously wounded human nature, and that humans required grace to live a good life. Applying this to sexual intercourse in marriage, Augustine taught that it was tainted with concupiscence as a result of the Fall. Sex, even in marriage, could be sinful by virtue of the disordered desires that exist in human beings as a result of the Fall. Augustine believed that since the Fall, human appetites were disordered, lustful, passionate, and against reason. Augustine concluded, therefore, that it was impossible for anyone to have sex, even in marriage, without sinning. The only motive that could justify the use of sex in marriage was procreation.

There are a number of problems with this perspective. First of all, modern biblical criticism, as well as studies in evolution and anthropology, generally rule out a historical Fall of the human race. The creation stories in the Book of Genesis are understood to be ancient epics, rather than historical accounts. There can be no doubt that sin and evil are integral to human life, but many suggest that this has been the case ever since evolution reached the stage where human beings could make free choices (including evil ones). It is thereby possible for humans to pervert and use in an evil manner any of the human capacities, including sexuality.

Contemporary studies of sexuality indicate that passion and desire are normal elements in the act of sexual intercourse, and not attributable to some "fall from grace." Sexual activity in the context of marriage is no longer viewed by Catholic theologians as being intrinsically tainted with sin. The sex act can and should be virtuous, loving, and life-giving. That is not to rule out the possibility that sex can be abused or sinful, even in marriage. The key point to be noted is that personal choice and intentionality are the source of evil. There is nothing intrinsic to human sexual activity that makes it evil.

It is broadly accepted today that married couples engage in sexual intercourse with their spouse for numerous reasons other than for procreation. It can be an expression of love, an enjoyable pleasure, or simply a comforting moment. The thinking in the Catholic community with regard to sexuality and marriage, while still influenced by Augustine, has moved considerably beyond his perspective.

Augustine and "Sacramentum"

Augustine wrote of marriage being a *"sacramentum,"* a term that for him had various meanings ranging from a symbol of the sacred, to a holy ritual, to a sacred vow.[9] All of these meanings affected Catholic thinking on marriage at one time or another.

Augustine initially developed a rich sacramental theology for baptism, eucharist, and ordination. In his view these sacraments were both signs of a clear participation in the saving actions of Christ, and powerful causes of grace. He applied these notions to marriage, noting that in marriage a sacred effect (a *sacramentum*) is produced in the soul. By virtue of this sacred effect, holiness is available in marriage. Through grace, couples can be moved to compassion toward each other, can forgive, and can find a relatively sinless protection from concupiscence. It is important to note that in this perspective marriage can provide helpful graces to the Christian, but it is not yet viewed as a vocation to holiness in itself. Augustine did not view marriage as being one of the sacraments. Still, he sees marriage as a permanent covenant creating a bond that cannot be broken.[10] This position survived through the ages and played a significant role in controversies surrounding the question of divorce.

The Era of Constantine

The year 313 was a landmark for Christianity, for in that year Christianity was proclaimed an acceptable religion in the Roman Empire. Toward the end of the fourth century, imperial orders went much further, and actually decreed that Christianity was now considered the official religion throughout the empire. All of this was a mixed blessing for the church. The horrible persecutions were over, and the church could carry on its mission with stability and safety. At the same time, large masses of converts entered the church out of obligation rather than through a sense of personal conversion or commitment.

The church's teachings, including those on marriage, were severely challenged by the concerns and cultural values of many peoples.

Powerful Teutonic tribes eventually crushed the Roman Empire and put new cultural pressures on the church and its teachings. Ultimately the church absorbed these masses, but was further challenged and influenced by the marital customs and beliefs of many diverse peoples.

Tammy, a senior who is majoring in English, makes some interesting observations about how even today culture continues to put pressure on the Catholic tradition.

It is difficult being a Catholic in our American culture. Today divorce and remarriage are widely accepted. One of my brothers and my sister are both divorced and have started second families. The use of birth control is routine for many Catholic couples. I want my church to uphold its traditional ideals because I believe that both marriage and sex are sacred, but I wish there could be some flexibility and some room for compromise. I want to remain a Catholic, and I want to raise my children Catholic, but I find it hard to accept some of the official Catholic church teachings.

The Theological Development of Marriage

From the time of the church's acceptance by the Roman Empire in the fourth century until the end of the first millennium, there was little theological development in the church's teaching on marriage. This was due to a number of factors: preoccupation with other more urgent doctrinal matters on christology, the Trinity, and grace; the prevalence of a neo-Platonic way of thinking that was not concerned with matters so "mundane" as marriage; the destruction of the centers of Christian learning by the European tribes; and the emphasis on monastic life as the Christian way of perfection.[11]

During the dark ages of the church's history, marriage was still largely viewed as a family matter that did not necessarily include a religious ceremony. Since marriage involved those who were baptized, however, it was the object of the church's pastoral and legal concern. During this period the church seemed largely concerned with issuing decrees and laws that protected Christian marriage against what were considered to be pagan or heretical views. Little advance was made during this era with regard to theological or spiritual insights about marriage. Religious views about marriage were drawn largely from a literal interpretation of the pertinent passages in the Book of Genesis, and a mere citing of the Pauline texts.

During this historical period marriage was still viewed as a state in life inferior to virginity. Sexual intercourse was still considered to be tainted, and was justified in marriage only because of procreation. The sacramental understanding of marriage was largely limited to seeing it as a sign of the relationship between Christ and the church that is cited in the Letter to the Ephesians.[12]

Marriage as a Sacrament

It was well over a thousand years after the death of Christ before the church finally counted marriage among its official sacraments. Why would there be such a delay when, as we have seen, Christians had believed that marriage was created by God and blessed by Christ? A number of reasons have been given for the church's long reluctance to list marriage as a sacrament. First, there was not a well-developed theology of marriage; second, marriage included a commercial element (brides were purchased and families exchanged gifts), which gave marriage a secular status; and finally, marriage involved sexual intercourse which was viewed by some theologians to be tainted with concupiscence and sin.[13] Noting the questionable status of marriage one theologian wrote:

> How can a man-woman relationship whose typical conduct is the carrier of hereditary sin, and in practice almost inevitably sinful, be an image of something sacred and an avenue of the divine grace that produces holiness?[14]

Amid these negative views on marriage, it must be realized that the church still taught that marriage was a created good, a remedy for sexual desire, and a way to fulfill God's command to procreate.[15] While marriage imaged the relationship between Christ and his church, it was still debatable as to whether marriage could be considered a symbol and experience of God's presence, and a place where Christian perfection could be sought. As we saw earlier, Augustine had suggested that marriage offered the couple the graces needed to be faithful, and kept the couple from sexual sin: yet he did not call marriage a sacrament.

The Medieval Contribution

During the medieval period a number of factors contributed to the church's move toward adding marriage to its list of sacraments. First, the thought of Augustine on marriage as a sacramental sign experienced a revival. Second, scholastic philosophy and the birth of the universities provided the church with the intellectual framework and the scholarship needed to develop a theology of marriage. Third, the negative dualisms of Gnosticism and Manicheanism, against which the church had struggled, were resurrected in the Catharist and Albigensian movements.

Both the Catharists and Albigensians condemned sex and marriage as fundamentally evil.[16] The church, reacting against such extreme positions, defended the holiness and goodness of marriage, and took over from civil authorities the legal and pastoral control of marriage. Marriage was first counted among the sacraments in the twelfth century, and solemnly defined to be one of the seven sacraments at the Council of Florence in 1439. There would be no doubt now but that marriage *was* a sacrament. What was left for the scholars to discuss, and that debate still goes on today, was determining *how* marriage is a sacrament.

A Variety of Approaches

Medieval scholars differed in their views as to how marriage might be a sacrament. Some suggested that it was the action of the priest during the marriage ceremony that made marriage a sacrament. That notion still prevails in the Eastern Catholic and Orthodox churches, which consider the priest to be the minister at the marital ceremony. This view is also common on a popular level and is reflected in a couple's asking a priest if "he will marry them."

Western (Roman Catholic) theology does not see the priest as the minister of the sacrament. Since mutual consent is essential for a marriage to occur, this consent comes from the spouses and not the priest. In the Western church, the bride and groom are the true "ministers" of the sacrament, and the priest is an official witness to their celebration of vows. The couple "performs" the ceremony and makes a marriage sacramental.

Since the middle ages there has been a debate as to whether the expression of consent or sexual consummation makes the marriage a sacrament. The Roman culture and legal system, which deeply influenced the Catholic church, maintained that it was consent that made the marriage. European tribes, on the other hand, held that the handing over of the bride as property, and the sexual consummation sealed the marriage. After much debate, the medieval church brought both these elements together. The classic understanding came to be that both mutual consent and consummation constituted the sacrament of marriage.[17] In the twelfth century this became the official practice of the church and still prevails in the church's canon law, as well as in the annulment process.

Medieval philosophers gave the sacrament of marriage an ontology and discussed its causality. Their debates considered when this sacrament was instituted, how the marital contract related to the sacramental nature of marriage, who was the proper minister of the sacrament, what kinds of grace were given by the sacrament, and what was the status of non-Christian marriages. With the decline in philosophy and theology in the fourteenth and fifteenth centuries, many of these questions were left unanswered. As a result the sacramentality of marriage was vulnerable to the attacks of the Protestant Reformers.

The Challenge of the Reformation

A number of factors led up to the Protestant challenge to the sacramentality of marriage. Followers of William of Ockham (d. 1349) in the fourteenth century challenged the existence of Platonic universals and the ontology of the scholastics. This laid open to attack the very essence or nature of marriage. In addition, Erasmus (d. 1536) took a more critical look at the scriptures, and challenged the literal understanding of the biblical passages on marriage. The Western mind wanted to be more realistic and more empirical about life. Humanists wanted to discuss the human experience of marriage, and not the essence or legalities of marriage. In a very different but equally challenging way, the troubadours and the new middle class praised the delights of romantic love and sexual pleasure and often scoffed at ecclesiastical teachings.

Martin Luther challenged the sacramentality of marriage claiming that marriage was created by God as a natural institution. He reasoned that Christ did not institute marriage, and thus it should not be under the jurisdiction of the church. As an Augustinian, Luther taught that marriage was created in original goodness and innocence, but that after the Fall, concupiscence infected sexual intercourse. He went beyond Augustine's position regarding the presence of concupiscence in acts of sexual intercourse not undertaken for procreation. Luther maintained that sexual intercourse is always tainted by concupiscence, but that Jesus' mercy covers over our guilt and excuses us.[18]

Luther was not consistent in his theological positions. At times he was earthy and bombastic in his discussion of marriage. On other occasions, he wrote enthusiastically on the sacramentality of marriage and waxed eloquently about the wonders of married love. Ultimately he rejected both the sacramentality and the permanence of marriage. These views were supported and further developed by other Protestant leaders such as Melancthon (d. 1560) and John Calvin. Once again, the Catholic church found itself in a defensive position and had to state its official position on marriage in confrontational tones.

The Council of Trent belatedly answered the reformers in 1563. Trent stated that God instituted marriage as indissoluble and that this was confirmed by Jesus. The council proclaimed that the sacrament of marriage confers grace upon the couple—grace that was merited by Jesus Christ. The council also asserted the church's authority over the sacrament of marriage. It decreed that all Catholic marriages were to be carried out in the presence of a priest and two witnesses.

Marriage in the Modern Era

The Council of Trent's position on marriage prevailed among Catholics for the next four centuries. Still there was much opposition. With growing nationalism, civil authorities, especially in France and Germany, claimed jurisdiction over marriage. Civil divorce separated the marital contract from the sacrament, and many came to view the latter as a mere ornament of marriage. Secularists denied that marriage had any religious origins or dimensions at all. The rise of biblical criticism in the eighteenth and nineteenth centuries challenged the traditional and literal interpretation of the biblical texts on marriage.

In reaction to those who opposed the church's traditional teachings about the sacrament of marriage, a series of papal documents were issued in the nineteenth and twentieth centuries that reaffirmed the official Catholic position on marriage.[19] Popes Pius IX and Leo XIII defended the divine institution, sacramentality, and indissolubility of marriage against the attacks of those who maintained that marriage was a mere human invention. Pope Pius XI, in an extremely influential encyclical, repeated the two-fold purpose of marriage: first, the procreation and education of children; second, the mutual help of the spouses and a remedy for concupiscence. Even though Pius XI wrote insightfully about the human element in marriage and even about marital love and partnership, the "two-fold purpose" prevailed as the dominant Catholic attitude toward marriage until Vatican II.

The Second Vatican Council

The bishops at Vatican II moved the church's teachings on marriage to a new and exciting level. They de-emphasized the legal and contractual descriptions of marriage and spoke of marriage in the biblical terms of a covenant. They also chose not to use the traditional two-fold purpose of marriage, which gave primacy to procreation. Instead, marital love was proclaimed to be the centerpiece, the ultimate goal of marriage. Procreation and the other ends of marriage were viewed in the context of the mutual fulfillment of the husband and wife.

The council described marriage as a community of love, an intimate partnership, and an authentic Christian vocation. It emphasized that marriage was created by the two partners through a mutual giving of love and sharing of life. The council stressed that marriage was a dynamic reality, created by Christ who enters into the union and remains with the couple enabling them to love and to be faithful. Grace is not, as it was described in the past, simply a help to avoid adultery and to control concupiscence. Grace is the living presence of Christ needed to carry out a genuine vocation and life of holiness. Grace in marriage is a unique sharing in the life of God. With this understanding, the sacramental and vocational dimensions of marriage have been brought to new heights.

The council also attempted to counteract centuries of fear and suspicion toward sexuality.[20] Council documents dealt positively with sexual intercourse, viewing it as integral to the nurturing of marital love. Children were viewed as the product of marital love, a unique love that is creative and nurturing.

Pope Paul VI continued and enriched this theology of marriage in the 1968 encyclical, *Humanae Vitae.* Unfortunately, his progressive views on marriage were overshadowed by the encyclical letter's strict teaching against artificial birth control. This latter issue is still divisive in the Catholic community.

The 1980 International Synod of Bishops held in Rome examined the theological and practical understanding of marriage. Pope John Paul II's exhortation following the synod carried forth the development of the church's theology of marriage. The pope noted that God calls all human beings to unity through love. Marriage is a sign of this creative love and embodies it in sexual love-making. John Paul also realistically recognized the lived experience of marriage with its pain and its crises.

The post-Vatican II theology of marriage was carried into the 1983 revision of the Code of Canon Law, although there are some regressions into legalism and contractual thinking. The *Catechism of the Catholic Church* also includes an enlightened (and enlightening) perspective on marriage. It speaks of marriage as a covenant, an intimate partnership of life and love, and an intimate communion of husband and wife.

Contemporary Views on Marriage

Catholic marriage today is viewed as a dynamic sign of the presence of Christ's love among us. Sacramental marriage symbolizes for both husband and wife, as well as for the community at large, a life-giving symbol of the power of Christ's life, death, and resurrection. This is not to say that the sacred dimension of life and love is not experienced by marriages in other religions, or even in the marriages of those who have no affiliation with religion. The sacramental marriage is a unique experience of the sacred in that the couple invites Jesus Christ to be part of their marriage.

If the sacramental dimension of marriage is to be effective in the lives of spouses it must be relevant to the everyday experience of married couples. The sacrament must be an authentic experience of Christ in the crucial areas of love, sexuality, and the everyday experience of family living. We will now consider how this integration of the secular and sacred is recognized in these three.

Falling in Love

It was common in earlier centuries and it remains the custom in some cultures even today, that marriages are arranged by families without much consideration for the feelings of the potential spouses toward each other. In much of the world today, people generally choose their own mates. Mutual love is of the essence, and it would be quite unusual to see couples marrying without such feelings.

In contemporary culture, the love that leads to marriage often begins in romantic love. Listen to Margie, who is in the graduate school of nursing and has been married for two years.

I remember the moment that I first "fell in love" very well. My roommate and I were shopping. I went into an art store to look for some paint, and at the counter I saw Tom. It was the strangest reaction. My legs went kind of rubbery and I almost thought I was going to have to sit down. We talked about painting, but we were looking at each other in the strangest way. I didn't even get the right color of paint that day, but it didn't matter. I had met the man I was looking for. We started dating and in six months we were married. I had fallen in love before, but never like that day in the art store!

The whole experience of romantic love is mysterious. It is in part connected with the senses: the way the person looks, sounds, smells, and feels to the touch. It is in part chemical: natural hormones and other natural narcotics flood into the system. The pulse races, the outlook on life can become very rosy, and there can be a burst of new energy. Suddenly the beloved seems lodged in the mind, memory, and imagination. Often there is a desire to be with the person every possible moment. There is a feeling that the person loved has been known for a long time. There is usually an intense desire to share things about oneself, and a sense of timelessness, completeness, and fulfillment in the presence of the beloved. There is often a deep desire to be with the person forever.[21]

What attracts us so magically can be a number of things: strength, beauty, kindness. Perhaps the other person enhances our self-esteem, or gives us a sense of security, or seems simply to be a good match for us. Whatever the reason, there is a tremendous drive to be close to the other person on many levels. This is romantic love, and whatever form it takes, Western people today seldom marry unless they share this kind of love.

Friendship

Romantic love can be simply a passing infatuation or an ephemeral attraction that heats up, cools down, and then disappears. On the other hand, romantic love can deepen and include another kind of love, that of friendship. Many young people today want their lover to be also their best friend.

There are various levels to friendship. Friends give us pleasure. They are the ones who are there when we need them, and the ones we want to help when they need it. Friendship includes trust, mutuality, respect, and continuity. The friend-lover relationship, of course, is unique. The friend-lover is a person that we both like and love. It is the one person that we count on in areas of need that we would not reveal to others.[22] There is a level of emotional and physical intimacy here that is not duplicated in any other friendship.[23] This is a friendship that longs for ongoing companionship. It is a face-to-face friendship with a high degree of exclusivity, yet one that must be open to others in order to thrive.[24]

Jesus uses the word "friend" to describe his relationship with his disciples. He tells them:

> No one has greater love than this to lay down one's life for one's friends. You are my friends if you do what I command you. I no longer call you slaves, because a slave does not know what his master is doing. I have called you friends because I have told you everything I have heard from my Father. (Jn 15:13–15)

Jesus' notion of being a friend involves giving everything, even one's life for the friend. Friendship embodies a love that includes self-sacrifice, sharing, and service. It is this love to which he invites his followers: "Love one another as I have loved you" (Jn 15:12). Jesus' symbol for this is washing the feet of his disciples.

For the Christian, Jesus is the role model for loving friendship. This modeling becomes even more dynamic when the couple begins to realize the presence of Christ in their relationship, giving them the power to build and sustain their love for one other. Until this point, each has walked with the Lord separately. Now they begin to think of walking together with Christ.

As romantic love and the love of friendship mature, a couple may begin to think about commitment, fidelity, and possibly even permanency. It is at this point that people of faith consider sealing their love with solemn promises or vows before the Lord and the church. It is a time for long looks into the future, for ultimate questions about whether this is the person with whom one wants to live one's life and work out one's salvation. It is a time to pray for guidance and help in making one of the most important life-decisions. This is the point when the lovers are moving toward a unique kind of love—marital love.

Marital Love

Love is at the center of marriage today. Many people marry both to receive and give a kind of love that goes beyond romance and even friendship. Married love involves a sharing on all levels; it includes affection, tenderness, passion, and empathy. Married love also signifies a permanent commitment that is intended to offer stability and security to both partners. Married love calls for a commitment to remain faithful to the union and to work out difficulties that might arise.

Marital love is also based on a profound trust. A husband and wife promise to be dependable and available for whatever need that may arise. Such love is a pledge of loyalty to one's spouse, and a promise of fidelity in all circumstances, especially in matters of sexuality.[25] This unique love involves a pledge to cooperate in decisions and in the manifold responsibilities that arise in family life. A married couple must move considerably beyond infatuation or romance. Such a deep and committed love is absolutely necessary if a husband and wife are to weather the inevitable storms that buffet married life.

Married Love and the Sacrament

The Second Vatican Council placed married love at the center of marriage. The council shifted from the traditional legal and procreational emphases to a personalistic approach to marriage that is more acceptable in modern times. The council documents point out that Christian marriage is a covenant that reflects Christ's own covenant with his church. Spouses, by their mutual love, fruitfulness, intimacy, and faithfulness, manifest to the whole world that Christ lives and loves in our world.[26] Thus Christian marriage is an authentic sacrament, a dynamic symbol of Christ's presence and power in the world.

In the sacrament of matrimony, the couple invites Jesus Christ to enter their marriage. The marriage becomes a "new creation," a union in which God is bestowed and revealed uniquely throughout the couple's life together.[27] The mystery of God, revealed through all of reality, now becomes uniquely revealed in a life of partnership and love. This love is strengthened and sustained by Christ. Moreover, the couple's love is open and reaches out to their children and ultimately to the service of others. Marriage, although uniquely exclusive, empowers the lovers to become inclusive of others.[28]

Mature love can also be redemptive. In marriage Christians have the special opportunity to develop just such a love. As Jared Wicks puts it:

> Marital love is sacramental when it is vowed by persons assimilated to Christ and consecrated by him in his priestly people. Each partner expresses to the other the self-forgetting and redemptive love that Christ manifested in going to death on our behalf. Because their love is such an engagement of their persons, it is sanctifying and enriching for a lifetime—as the partners prove responsive to each other's sacred commitment.[29]

Marital love can also expressed by the couple toward God. As Karl Rahner points out, the love of neighbor is the Christian way toward love of God. In marriage, the spouse uniquely becomes the neighbor, and this love between the spouses can become a singular way to God.[30] Seen in this way marriage is revealed as a genuine vocation, an authentic means for growing in the life of God. Marriage becomes "an event of grace"—the grace to grow in love toward others and toward the ultimate Other.

Faith and the Sacrament

The church considers marriage to be a sacrament when two baptized persons exchange vows. Such a union is not only personal and legal, it is also a union in faith. The husband and wife have joined their lives of faith and now consider Christ to be part of their marriage.

Many theologians and pastoral ministers wonder if some Catholics today have ample faith to enter a sacramental marriage. So often young people are in a searching stage of their faith or on a "leave of absence" from the church when they marry. One has to question whether they have ample faith or sufficient desire to have Christ be part of their marriage. Will such marriages stand as a living symbol of Christ's presence in the world? Are such marriages sacraments? Are we perhaps presuming too much of many young Catholics who come before the altar? Some would suggest that we are, and that it is time to allow for choices other than sacramental marriages for people who are unsure of their faith.

Faith is a gift from God, an invitation to share an intimate relationship with God. Faith requires the free acceptance of this gift and relationship. For Christians this involves the free acceptance of the gift of faith in Jesus Christ, and of discipleship in the church. Faith is a three-fold commitment to the code (laws), creed (beliefs), and cult (worship) of Christ's church. This is the faith that is shared in a sacramental marriage. It seems presumptuous to assume that a couple has such faith merely because they request a religious wedding ceremony and want "to do what the church intends to do."

The level of faith shown by the couple is important when we recall that the spouses are the ministers of the sacrament. It is the couple who vows to join their lives in faith. For this to be authentic, it seems reasonable to expect that they have faith and wish to enter a sacramental marriage. If we believe that sacraments are dynamic encounters with Christ, then we can expect nothing less of Catholic marriages.[31]

Marriage and Sexuality

Long-standing images and stereotypes are changing about what it means to be male or female today. These changes are affecting and challenging many of the traditional roles of husbands and wives and affecting marriages. Many women have become convinced of their equality and will not settle for the traditional patriarchal models of marriage. The majority of married women have also entered the work force, and no longer have the time, or perhaps even the interest to carry out the roles of wife and mother in the traditional fashion. Parenting, housekeeping, and even the role of breadwinner have become for many couples a mutual responsibility shared equally.[32]

Sally, a math major, talks about the differences in the three generations of women in her family.

It is amazing to look at how much things have changed for the women in my family. My grandmother never worked outside the home. Her job was to keep house and raise the children. She was a wonderful wife and mother. My grandfather never lifted a finger around the house, and still doesn't. He likes to be waited on. My mother stayed home until my two brothers and I started school. Now she is an officer in our local bank and works full time. She and my father split the cooking, and someone comes in to do the cleaning. As for me, I hope to be a jet pilot in the Air Force, and ultimately want to fly for a commercial airline. I intend to marry, but I want to maintain my career. I have little interest in cooking or housework, so I am looking for a modern guy who can deal with all that.

The Men's Movement

Profound changes are also taking place in how men understand themselves. Many men have moved away from the macho stereotypes of the past. They have attempted to become more in touch with their feelings, and their capabilities to nurture and parent. They freely exhibit sensibilities that were often expected to be kept hidden. This is evident as many fathers express a willingness to share in the parenting of their children, and in cooking, shopping, and many other tasks that once were considered to be "woman's work."

Changing Views on Sacramentality

How does all this affect the sacramental dimension of marriage? First of all, such equality and mutuality in marriage do not harmonize with the submissiveness or obedience that is asked for in Chapter Five of the Letter to the Ephesians. In the traditional interpretation where Christ's love for his church is seen as a model for married love, the role of Christ is taken by the husband, and the role of the church by the wife. As Karl Rahner points out, the metaphor need not be interpreted in the patriarchal context in which it was written.[33] He explains that the Christians of Ephesus are telling us that the love that Jesus has for his church is to be the model that spouses show *for each other.* The unconditional acceptance, fidelity, readiness to forgive, self-sacrifice, and compassion that characterize Christ's love for his disciples is to be the kind of love that both wife and husband manifest to each other.

Seen in this way, Jesus Christ is at the center of the marriage. He is not identified only with the husband. The couple in a sacramental marriage learn how to love and care for each other from Christ. From faith in Christ and a life of prayer, worship, and caring action the husband and wife learn how to be a "person for others." Two people joining such a sacramental union become a living symbol of Christ's presence for each other, their children, and many others.

Jesus Christ is more than a model for married love. In a sacramental marriage, Jesus is also the source of power and grace needed to be faithful to such a commitment over an extended period of time. With the changing of roles and the tensions between the sexes today, there will be times of crises and challenge. There may also be times of hurt, failure, and perhaps even of abuse or infidelity. There is the shadow side of marriage that comes from the limitations of the two human persons involved. With Christ in the marriage, however, the couple has available to them the healing and forgiving power of God. They have with them a Savior who bears the wisdom and kindness of the ages. They have with them a friend who has stood by couples for thousands of years, often helping them survive seemingly insurmountable difficulties.

Marriage and Sex

In developing its understanding of sexuality and sexual intercourse the early Christians rejected the ideas of those who said that sex was the creation of an evil God, or that it belonged in orgiastic rituals. The church, with its Judaic roots, insisted that sex was part of creation, made holy by a good and loving God as the means by which humans carried out the divine command to increase and multiply. At the same time, a literal understanding of the Fall coupled with Augustine's teachings about original sin led the church to teach that sex had become tainted and sinful. Sex was associated with the irrational passion and lustful desires that lurked in the human heart. It was justified only because it brought new offspring into the world. From this perspective, marriage and sexual intercourse between husband and wife were tolerated, but virginity or celibacy were preferable. Those who wanted to seek a life of perfection should forgo marriage.

Catholics and Sex

In general, Catholics today are more comfortable talking about and experiencing sex than they were in previous generations. They view it as a good and pleasurable experience; one that can express and nurture love, as well as procreate. Obviously Catholics realize that sex, like anything else, can be distorted, abused, and an occasion for evil. Catholics are quite aware of the prevalence of rape, child abuse, pornography, and immorality in today's world. The church, however, does not view this as the result of some historic fall from grace that tainted what had been a pure act. Instead, sex is seen as one part of the evolution of life. Sexual intercourse among humans is unique in that it is freely chosen, not simply a reaction to instinct or "heat." Human sex that is normal and healthy expresses love and commitment. In its free and healthy use, sex can be a source of spiritual growth.

Sex Is Life-giving

The phrase "making love" is apt for the act of sexual intercourse in marriage. Married couples share sex to express their affection, love, and care for each other. In a sacramental marriage, sexual intercourse can be an important way for the couple to express to each other the unconditional, unselfish, and caring love of Jesus Christ.

Intercourse is not an isolated action in marriage. It is shared in the context of the relationship and partnership that exists between the couple. Generally the satisfaction experienced is closely related to the level of love in the relationship. Intercourse is one way for the couple to share the love that exists in their union. Thus sex possesses the power to be creative and to generate deeper levels of love and bonding. It is also integral to the sacramental life of the marriage. Sexual moments can be sacramental moments, indicating the degree of the couple's physical and spiritual intimacy.

Sex, of course, can also be procreative. Many married couples will find that their love-making results in the beginning of new life. They will experience the amazing phenomenon of actually being party to a new person or persons coming into the world. Other married couples will not conceive a child, but this does not necessarily make their marriage any less sacramental or less sacred than the marriages of those couples that do have children. It is this awareness that not every married couple will have a child that has caused the Catholic church to focus equally on the procreative and unitive aspects of intercourse in marriage, where before the procreative purpose of intercourse was given prime importance.

Having a baby, or being there when the infant is born can be a sacramental experience. For the couple in a sacramental marriage it can be a unique experience of sharing in the creative power of Christ. When they hold their infant for the first time, they know that Christ is indeed with them as "the first-born of all creation." They can see the beauty and holiness imaged in this little face and body. They witness to the beginning of a life that can go on forever in eternity. In a very real sense, the product of their love-making can bring them to a unique experience of Christ's own birth and life. Similarly, those who adopt children often have the experience of giving "new life" to a child.

Likewise, the couple who loses a child through sickness or accident is plunged into the mysteries of Christ's life. They walk with Christ in the valley of death. It is at this point that many couples come to realize for the first time the meaning of the Cross. They pray to Christ hoping for resurrection for their loved one. And perhaps they look forward to one day being with their child in heaven. The life of faith in the sacrament of marriage can put people in touch with singular dimensions of the mysteries of life, death, and resurrection.

Christian Family Experiences

Knowing that Christ is a real presence in one's marriage can give new insight into the everyday experience of family living. The family has been called "the domestic church." This means that the family is the smallest, yet nonetheless real, unit of the church. We saw earlier how the Christian community began by meeting in homes. The church originally consisted of families who gathered in one another's homes to celebrate the Lord's presence in their midst. The family was often the most intimate and familiar experience of church.

The sacramentality of marriage and the notion of domestic church go hand-in-hand. The family is often the community where the presence of Christ is most needed. It is here that people need to learn to trust, love, sacrifice for others, and forgive. It is here that people most intensely come to know suffering and pain.

It is often in the context of one's family where people first face the death of a loved one. Faith in Christ and the awareness that he is present to the family give deep meaning to all these experiences. Christ becomes the model as well as the source of grace. Christ's courageous facing of suffering and death inspires and reveals the redemptive power that can be found in tragedy. When marriage and family are "in the Lord," the loss of a loved one holds up the hope for inner healing , as well as for life eternal for loved ones.

The family can also be a primary place for prayer and worship. The sacramental dimension of marriage can add new meaning to family life. It is in the family that many children learn their first prayers, the significance of the seasons of Advent and Lent, and how to celebrate great feasts like Christmas and Easter. Families often attend church together, especially when the children are small. They celebrate the special sacramental moments of their children's baptism, first communion, and confirmation.

As they gather around the dinner table, families can experience the "table ministry" that was so common with Christ and his followers. It is at table that so many of a family's struggles and pleasures are shared.

It is here that so many memories are created that will deeply influence the family members. At table, families have opportunities to "commune" with each other and with the Lord. Christ the eternal high priest is present to married couples and to families as they gather to tell their stories and break the bread of everyday life. Christ shares his priesthood with each member of the family, and invites all to pray and worship with him. There is indeed a "real presence," similar to that of the eucharist, that can be felt by families "breaking bread" around the family table.

Marriage Calls for Service

Ideally home is where spouses and children alike learn to become sensitive to the needs of others. It is here that we pick up our values; here that we learn how to serve others. Those who come from families that were abusive, insensitive, and selfish know well their liabilities and the challenges they face in building their own marriages and families. For others, however, the example of parents who were always willing to help people in need can be a lesson that a child never forgets.

Christ comes to each marriage and each family as a "man for others." The gospels recount how Jesus extended himself to the needs of others, especially to the non-persons and rejects of his society. He would go out of his way to speak to the crowds, heal a leper, give sight to a blind man, or get a cripple back up on his feet. He befriended and served prostitutes, Romans, corrupt Jewish leaders, good Scribes, and a widow who had lost her only son. He seems to have spent most of his life as a craftsman, laboring with his hands at carpentry. He knew the value of hard work, and for most of his life he labored to support himself and his mother. This is the Lord who shares friendship in a sacramental marriage and gives the perfect example of loving, caring service.

The Dark Side of Marriage

There is of course a dark side to marriage, which often hides inequality, abuse, oppression, and injustice. Women throughout the world are waking up to the fact that often their "sacramental" marriages do not give them the experience of Christ's love. They are becoming aware that sacraments are not automatic or magical. For a symbol of Christ's love to be present, both partners must be shaping that symbol with their lives. For many women today, the Christ in their marriage is a liberator who can free them from the cruelty, abuse, and oppression which they experience as wives.[34]

Families also experience oppression from without. Many live amid severe deprivation and poverty, and are oppressed by the wealthy. If the family lives in a Third World dictatorship and they complain or rebel, they may be subjected to terrorism, torture, and death. In so-called Christian countries, the family has become a place to experience horror instead of the love and compassion of Christ.

A married couple living in terror and deprivation, merely hoping to survive, often finds the sacramental theology of marriage difficult to understand. They ask: "Where are we to encounter the Lord in the midst of such horrors?"[35] It is here that the church needs to reach out to families and be in solidarity with them. These are also the occasions when families who enjoy security and abundance can defend and share their resources with less fortunate families.

Marriage as a Means of Liberation

Throughout the world we see new models of the church emerging. Once again, as in the early days, families are organizing into "base communities" in homes. These families give new meaning to the relationship between Christ and his church, the basic metaphor for the sacramentality of marriage. These people who know poverty, suffering, and death first-hand turn to Jesus the Liberator to empower them to resist injustice and condemn violence.

A new sacramentality of marriage emerges as families see themselves symbolizing Christ's will that all be free. This theology of marriage puts the symbol of Christ before oppressors. Many oppressed people see their families as symbols of the courage and confrontational style of Jesus. They view Christ in their marriages and families as One present to empower them to struggle, even at the risk of death, in order to free themselves, their families, and neighbors from unjust oppression.

Conclusion

We have seen the long evolution of the tradition of marriage in Catholicism. It is a tradition that has been influenced by other religions, cultures, and the pressing needs of the times. Today the Catholic tradition on marriage stands for the ideals of love, fidelity, permanence, and commitment in a world where the very fabric of family life is being torn asunder. The Catholic ideals can be a reason for hope among people preparing for marriage as well as for those who already face the challenges of marriage and family life. At the same time, if the Catholic tradition is to play a significant role in shaping the future of marriage as a social institution and as a sacrament, it will have to come to terms with some of the real challenges of our times: divorce and remarriage, family planning and population control, single-parenting, and domestic violence. Marriage, like all living traditions, continues to change, develop, and grow with "the signs of the times."

Discussion Questions

1. There seems to be much turmoil in marriages today. Have the growing numbers of divorces and marital problems affected your attitudes toward marriage? Do you think that some young people are actually wary of getting married because of the risks?

2. What were some of the Jewish teachings about marriage during the time of Jesus? What impact do you think Jesus' gospel teachings had on these Jewish beliefs?

3. What were some of the reasons why it took so long for marriage to be recognized as a sacrament of the church?

4. Why do you think friendship is such an important part of marriage for many people today? Do you think that your spouse should also be your best friend? If so, why?

5. From the text and your reading formulate a sacramental theology of marriage that would be understandable and appealing to young people today.

Suggested Readings

Aaron T. Beck, *Love Is Never Enough.* New York: HarperCollins, 1989.

Lisa Sowle Cahill, *Between the Sexes: Foundation for a Christian Ethic of Sexuality.* Philadelphia: Fortress Press, 1985.

Kathleen R. Fischer and Thomas N. Hart, *Promises to Keep.* New York: Paulist Press, 1991.

Walter Kasper, *Theology of Christian Marriage.* New York: Crossroad, 1983.

Michael G. Lawler, *Marriage and Sacrament: A Theology of Christian Marriage.* Collegeville, MN: Liturgical Press, 1993.

Theodore Mackin, *The Marital Sacrament.* Mahwah, NJ: Paulist Press, 1989.

Theodore Mackin, *What Is Marriage?* Mahwah, NJ: Paulist Press, 1982.

Ladislaus Orsy, *Marriage in Canon Law.* Wilmington, DE: Michael Glazier, 1986.

Challon O'Hearn Roberts and William R. Roberts, *Partners in Intimacy.* New York: Paulist Press, 1988.

12.

Initiation, Forgiveness, and Healing

Framing the Question

My friends call me Lindy. I was born in Alaska and came to the "lower 48" when I was ten. My mother is Eskimo and my father is Irish, so I am quite a combination of things. I was baptized when I was an infant, mainly because my father wanted me to be a Catholic like he was. I am not confirmed: partly because we have moved around a lot and never settled in one parish long enough for me to get instructions, and partly because I just never thought I was ready to say I wanted to be a Catholic for the rest of my adult life.

I really don't see the sense of giving sacraments to kids. Most of them don't understand what is going on, and a lot of them just drop out once their parents take the heat off them. I especially can't understand why little kids have to go to confession. After all, they really can't sin when they are so little. I have never gone to confession myself. When I am sorry, I just tell God and ask for forgiveness.

One sacrament that means something to me is the anointing of the sick. I was close to my grandma, and I was there when the priest anointed her before she died. She had been very afraid up until that time, but once we gathered around her and prayed with the priest, she calmed down. She had a very peaceful death, and I think that anointing really helped her. Now we never expected her to be healed from her cancer, so I'm not sure why the church connects healing to this sacrament.

Lindy, like many other Catholics, has had little opportunity to learn about and understand the seven sacraments. As she says, so often sacraments are celebrated with children, and there simply isn't enough maturity there to comprehend what is being celebrated.

Since we have already considered the eucharist as the central sacrament in the lives of Catholics (chapter ten), and the sacraments related to one's state in life—holy orders (chapter nine), and matrimony (chapter eleven)—this chapter will consider the remaining four of the seven sacraments celebrated in the Catholic church. First we will look at baptism and confirmation, which along with first eucharist, constitute the three sacraments of Christian initiation. Then we will discuss the church's rite of forgiveness, the sacrament of penance (also called reconciliation). Finally we will look at the ancient sacrament of the anointing of the sick, the ritual through which the church prays for healing of the sick and prepares the faithful for death.

Baptism

Water is the central symbol in baptism. Water is necessary to sustain human life, and essential for sustaining nearly all living things. Science tells us that life on earth began in water, and that it was from water that life first came onto land and commenced the long evolution toward the human species. Rain renews the land and nourishes life. Water brings refreshment, cleansing, and purification. Water can also save, for it can put out a raging fire. At the same time water can be associated with death and destruction. Floods can ravage the land, destroying life and property. Human life can be quickly snuffed out by just a brief time under water.

Given this elemental quality of water, it is easy to understand why it has been used as a powerful symbol in religious rituals. The Buddhists pour water over the head of the fledgling monk to indicate his entrance into a new mode of life. The Hindus cremate their dead and place the ashes in a sacred river. Native Americans revered the streams, for they sustained life and bore the remains of their ancestors.

Judaism, which was foundational in the establishment of Christianity, also uses water as a central religious symbol. In the Hebrew scriptures, one creation story depicts the Spirit of God hovering over chaotic waters to bring forth life. The myth of the great flood (Noah and the Ark) uses water to symbolize how evil people bring destruction upon themselves, while the same waters buoy up and save those who are faithful to God. In the Exodus, the central saving event in Judaism, God's people are brought from slavery across the Reed Sea into safety, and then set out on the journey toward the Jordan River and the promised land. At one point, as the Hebrews languish in the desert, Moses strikes a rock, and life-giving waters come forth to revive and sustain God's people. In each of these stories water symbolizes the saving power of God.

Considering this rich background of water symbolism, it is easy to see why the Jews performed ritual washings before meals and during their religious ceremonies. The Jews were also deeply concerned about the impurity derived from contact with blood, other body fluids, corpses, or persons "cursed" with disabilities. They performed ritual washings to cleanse themselves of impurities before they approached their God. The Jews also had a baptism-like ceremony for initiating converts to Judaism. This consisted in a ritual washing that was intended to cleanse the neophyte of past impurities and put the person in touch with the saving water events throughout the history of the Hebrews.[1]

The Baptism of Jesus

The baptism of Jesus by John serves as a bridge between the traditional Jewish washings and the new ceremony of Christian baptism. Most biblical scholars accept Jesus' baptism as a historical event that was pivotal in his life. The accounts of Jesus' baptism are key to the understanding of Christian baptism for they deal with the identity of Jesus and mark the beginning of his saving mission. All four gospels describe this event, each giving it a slightly different significance.

Mark, the earliest gospel, begins with the baptism of Jesus and moves immediately into the public ministry of the Lord. Mark presents John the Baptizer as a prophetic figure coming from a stark life of penance in the desert to preach repentance and prepare the way for Jesus. Great numbers follow him and confess their sins as they are baptized in the Jordan. Yet John the Baptizer makes it clear that one much more powerful comes after him, baptizing not only in water, but in the Holy Spirit. John's baptism is presented as a preparation for the baptism performed by the disciples of Jesus (Mk 1:1–11).

Matthew gives an account of the baptism only after recounting a magnificent birth story that clearly highlights Jesus' messiahship. Matthew stresses that the baptismal ministry of John is inferior to that of Jesus, and has John humbly remark that Jesus should be baptizing him. In Matthew's account, John's mission is closely linked with that of Jesus, in that John announces the kingdom of God and prophetically denounces the hypocrisy that he sees in Judaism. Where Mark has God's words addressed to Jesus, Matthew has God's words addressed more broadly to all those who are present: "This is my beloved Son. In him I am well pleased" (Mt 3:1–17).

Luke includes the birth of John the Baptizer in his infancy narrative, and portrays John as a kinfolk of Jesus whose mission is to prepare the way for Jesus, who alone is clearly "Messiah and Lord" (Lk 2:11). Luke begins his account of the public ministry of Jesus with a portrait of John calling his disciples to repentance, heralding the coming of the Messiah, and making clear that he and his baptism are inferior to that of Jesus (Lk 3:1–18). In Luke's gospel, only Jesus proclaims the kingdom. John the Baptizer is portrayed as a prophetic figure proclaiming the opening of a new period in Jewish history. It is in Luke that John is arrested, imprisoned, and then executed, opening the way for Jesus to follow in his mentor's footsteps.

The Gospel of John follows the opening Prologue with a scene wherein John the Baptizer denies that he is the Messiah or even a prophet, but is merely "a voice in the desert" called to prepare the way for Jesus. The Baptizer proclaims that Jesus is the Lamb of God, and turns his disciples over to Jesus, the Chosen One of God. Jesus is portrayed as the One on whom the Spirit rests. Although there is actually no account in John's gospel of the baptism of Jesus, the Baptizer does give witness that he saw the Spirit come to rest on Jesus (Jn 1:19–39).[2]

These accounts of Jesus' baptism indicate the meaning that the early Christians attached to baptism. For them it is a sign of repentance and a washing away of sin, but most important it links the disciples with Jesus, incorporating them into the life of his Spirit. It is a sacred sign that sets the disciple on a mission to proclaim the kingdom.

The Biblical Significance of Water

Additional symbolic water stories throughout the gospels provide further insight into the early Christian meanings attached to baptism. The Sea of Galilee provides an environment for Jesus to proclaim the power of God in miraculous catches of fish, walking on the water, and calming the storm.

The waters of baptism are linked with the cross as Jesus answers James and John's request to be at this right and left hand: "You do not know what you are asking....Can you drink the cup that I must drink or be baptized with the baptism which which I must be baptized" (Mk 10:38–39). The link is again made when water comes from the side of Jesus as he is pierced after his death on the cross.

John's gospel reflects a more sophisticated approach to baptism. The story of Nicodemus, the Pharisee who came to Jesus for instruction under cover of darkness, accentuates the themes of kingdom and Spirit. Jesus says to Nicodemus: "No one can enter into God's kingdom without being born of the water and the Spirit" (Jn 3:5). This story further links baptism with Calvary, faith, eternal life, and salvation. Jesus speaks of himself as being "lifted up" so that all who believe may have eternal life in him. He points out that God sent Jesus into the world so "that the world might be saved through him" (Jn 3:14–17). Further on, John's gospel reports Jesus promising that he will give "living water" to the Samaritan woman that he encounters at the well (Jn 4:7–14). The water motif appears again as Jesus proclaims: "If anyone thirsts, let him come to me" (Jn 7:37–39).

The First Baptisms

The gospels tell us that during Jesus' public life his disciples performed baptisms. It is difficult to ascertain the meaning of these baptisms. Clearly they form a link between the baptisms performed by John and the later Christian baptisms. They also seem to stand as signs of repentance as well as a way to initiate disciples.

It is not easy to determine whether Jesus himself performed such baptisms. The synoptic gospels are silent on the matter, and John's gospel presents varying traditions. At one point Jesus and the disciples are reported to be baptizing in the region of Judea (Jn 3:22), although later the gospel reports that Jesus' disciples, but not Jesus, were baptizing people (Jn 4:1–4).[3]

After studying these baptismal accounts it becomes evident that there is a gradual evolution from Jewish ablutions to the baptisms performed by John (climaxing in the baptism of Jesus), and then from the baptisms performed during Jesus' public life to the Spirit-filled baptisms of the early church.

Baptism After the Resurrection

The Gospel of Matthew, written fifty years after the death of Jesus, reflects the belief of the early Christians that the risen Lord had given them a direct mission to spread the faith and call others to baptism. The gospel depicts the risen Lord coming to the disciples on a mountaintop in Galilee. The disciples "see" Jesus and begin to worship him even though they still have their doubts about the resurrection. Jesus approaches them and says:

> All power in heaven and earth has been given me. Go, therefore, and make disciples of all nations, baptizing them in the name of the Father, and of the Son, and of the Holy Spirit....And behold, I am with you always, until the end of the age. (Mt 28:18–20)

The power of the risen Lord, a mission to proclaim the gospel and baptize in the Spirit, and a deep faith in the Lord's abiding presence are at the heart of Christianity.

Pentecost

The pentecost story related in the opening chapters of the Acts of the Apostles represents the commencement of the mission to make new disciples through baptism. The disciples had gathered in Jerusalem after the resurrection when suddenly the Holy Spirit came upon them and empowered them to proclaim the message of salvation to people from many parts of the world. Peter stepped forward and proclaimed that Jesus, though crucified, had been raised from the dead, was revealed as the Messiah, and now pours forth his Spirit. The people were touched by Peter's words, and they asked what they were to do. Peter directed them to repent of their sins, be baptized "in the name of Jesus Christ," and receive the Holy Spirit (Acts 2:1–41).

To be signed in the name of someone meant to belong to that person. Those accepting baptism now belonged to Jesus Christ.[4] The church of Jesus Christ was born as many people devoted themselves to the teachings, the communal life, and the breaking of the bread (Acts 2:37–47). From then on, proclamation, baptism, and the outpouring of the Spirit "constituted the integrity of initiation into the believing community."[5]

Paul's Theology of Baptism

Paul developed an elaborate theology of baptism for the fledgling churches. His letters interpret baptism as the entrance into the mysteries of Christ's death and resurrection (Rom 6:3–11). In the waters of baptism, the neophyte Christian dies to sin and rises to new life in the Spirit. The community's early baptismal rites reflect this theology. The candidate enters naked into the water, is momentarily submerged to symbolize entrance into the saving death of Jesus, and then rises out of the waters to be clothed in a white garment that is symbolic of new life in the Spirit of the Lord.[6] The candidate is born again and is now intimately bonded with Christ and his community.

The Development of the Baptismal Ritual

As with all the sacraments, the baptismal ritual developed gradually. An early church document, the *Didache,* recommends fasting before baptism, and states that baptisms should be performed in a running stream if possible, and if not, by pouring water on the head. The formula, "I baptize you in the name of the Father and of the Son and of the

Holy Spirit" is to be used. Here there seems to be no anointing or laying on of hands, as we find in the baptismal rituals of some other early Christian communities.

Justin of Rome, writing in the middle of the second century, describes baptism as being "made new through Christ." He describes how those who have accepted the teachings in faith are then instructed to pray and fast along with the other members of the community, and repent of their sins before they are brought to the waters "to be born again." Eucharist is then received for the first time.[7]

By the beginning of the third century, the writings of Tertullian and Hippolytus reveal a fully developed Greco-Latin ritual of baptism. It includes an extended period of instruction, an anointing and exorcism, the washing with water in the name of the Trinity, a laying on of hands, several additional anointings including a final "sealing," and the reception of the eucharist. Baptism is celebrated in the Roman Catholic church today using a similar ritual filled with many signs and symbols.

The Catechumenate

By the third century, an elaborate period of preparation for adult baptism had evolved. Persecutions, heresies, apostasy, and the danger of betrayal had made it imperative that each candidate be carefully checked out and instructed before being admitted into the community. In the Roman church of the early third century this preparation lasted up to three years, starting with a period of inquiry and then proceeding through a period of evangelization, prayer, and scrutiny. The catechumens eventually were initiated with the full ceremony of baptism on the vigil of Easter. This process involved the entire community, including a corps of teachers and sponsors, who accompanied the catechumens along their journey toward baptism. While the baptismal ceremony at the Easter Vigil was the climax of the preparation, should the catechumen be arrested for the faith and executed, he or she was considered to have been "baptized in blood."[8]

Changes in Attitudes Toward Baptism

Historical events deeply affect the church, its beliefs, and the understanding of its rituals. In the case of baptism, the legitimizing of Christianity by Constantine in 313 and the establishment of the Christian religion as the official religion of the Empire later in that century significantly changed the understanding of baptism.

Once Christianity was officially recognized and promoted as the religion of the Empire, its membership expanded quickly. Political and social pressures, along with the persecution of non-Christians motivated many to join the church. This heralded the beginning of the "cultural Christianity" that lasts until today, where vast numbers of people are Christian in name only, without ever truly experiencing conversion or instruction.

Baptism, which had formerly been a ritual of the community, gradually became privatized. By the seventh century, the West had been Christianized, and baptism largely became a ritual for initiating the babies of Christians, rather than the way of incorporating adult converts into the church. The elaborate period of preparation, the catechumenate, gradually disappeared, not to reemerge until after the Second Vatican Council in the 1970s.

Augustine and Original Sin

Augustine's teaching on original sin had a lasting effect on the church's understanding of baptism. This teaching was occasioned by Augustine's struggle with the Pelagians, who were optimistic about human nature and did not believe that people needed grace in order to perform good actions. Augustine insisted that human nature was corrupted by the sin of Adam, "the original sin," and that grace was necessary to perform good actions and to be saved.

Augustine also maintained that infants were born with "original sin," or the lack of grace, and could receive grace only through baptism. Logic told Augustine that people who were not baptized lacked grace and would go to hell if they died. In the case of unbaptized infants, however, hell was not a place of torturous punishment, but a place where individuals were deprived of being with God. (This was softened in the middle ages to "limbo," a place of natural happiness.)

Given the teaching of Augustine, one can readily see why parents were anxious to have their babies baptized as soon as possible after birth. This anxiety about unbaptized infants remains today among many Catholics, although not to the extent it once did. Fortunately, teachings about unbaptized children going to hell or to limbo never entered the official doctrines of the church. The *Catechism of the Catholic Church*, promulgated by Pope John Paul II in 1992, makes no mention of limbo, and advises that we can trust on the mercy of God to save unbaptized infants.[9]

Baptism Today

Contemporary discussions about baptism, as is the case with all the sacraments, begin with Jesus. Christ is the primary sacrament, the most powerful sign that God's power is with us—inviting, saving, forgiving, nourishing, and healing. The church, as the visible sign of Christ in the world, is also sacramental. All the Christian sacraments are celebrations of the communal nature of the church, and are not simply private or personal events.

Within this framework, baptism is a symbol of the redeeming Christ welcoming and, through the power of his Spirit, incorporating people into the church. Once bonded with Christ, we are beloved daughters and sons of God, the One whom Jesus referred to as Abba. Once empowered by the Spirit, we are gifted to share the good news and the ministry of Jesus. We are born to new life, and re-created in the image and likeness of Jesus. Through baptism our lives become irrevocably linked with the life, death, and resurrection of Jesus Christ.[10]

Beyond the effect of baptism on the individual being baptized, baptism also has a communal dimension. It is an action of the entire church, a celebration of the coming of the kingdom, and a saving event that is both personal and communal. Baptisms, both of infants and adults, are community celebrations.

Todd, a senior art major from San Francisco, comments on babies being baptized at Sunday Mass.

Baptisms at Sunday Mass used to anger me. I didn't even know these people and I have to watch their kid being baptized. Then when everyone clapped for the baby after the baptism I found myself getting really annoyed. I didn't see what all the fuss is about.

Now that we have talked about the baby being made a friend of Christ and new member of the community, it makes more sense to me. I guess the parents are proud that their new baby is a Christian, and I suppose the community does share their joy. I suppose I will want the same thing for my kids. I still don't know about the clapping, though.

Restoring the Adult Catechumenate

When the Second Vatican Council revised the procedure for celebrating the sacrament of baptism, it restored the formal period of preparation for adults seeking to be baptized. This process, known as the catechumenate, has become one of the most exciting and inspiring in the church today. The number of people wishing to join the Catholic church is growing throughout North America. In the catechumenate people enter into an extended process which, as in ancient times, involves evangelization, instruction, worship, and community building, guided by teachers, catechists, sponsors, and prayer leaders.

Throughout the process, the persons preparing for initiation are visible to the larger community, especially at the liturgies that mark the catechumens' rites of passage through the various stages of the process. The catechumenate culminates at the Easter Vigil with a welcoming into the church through the sacraments of baptism, confirmation, and first eucharist. Such events have become occasions of considerable inspiration to many Catholic parishes. After the initiation ceremonies there is another period of formation called the "mystagogia," which provides an opportunity to continue learning about the mysteries of the faith.

Confirmation

The celebration of the sacrament of confirmation can occur in several different settings. For Laura, a convert to Catholicism, is was part of her initiation into the church at last year's Easter Vigil. Laura had never been baptized. She spent the better part of a year in the local parish's catechumenate process. At the Vigil she was baptized, confirmed, and received the eucharist in a ceremony similar to that which was celebrated in the early church. It was an evening that she will never forget.

Joe's situation was slightly different. He had been baptized as a Methodist and was active in that Christian denomination for many years before he decided to become a Catholic. After his preparation in the catechumenate process, Joe was confirmed into full communion with the Catholic church and received the eucharist at the Easter Vigil. Because he had already received Christian baptism, there was no need to repeat the sacrament. For Joe, confirmation was an affirmation of his baptism, and the celebration of his entrance into the Catholic church.

Judy's story is different yet. She is what some might refer to as a "cradle Catholic." Her parents were both Catholic and brought Judy to be baptized when she was an infant. Judy attended Catholic schools from kindergarten through twelfth grade. During her high school years she participated in a two-year confirmation preparation program, and was confirmed when she was a junior in high school. For her, confirmation was an affirmation of the baptism she had received as an infant. It marked the beginning of a more mature phase of discipleship with Jesus.

Finally, there is Arthur, a second grader who was recently confirmed just before he received his first communion. This was done to indicate clearly that his confirmation and first communion are closely linked to the baptism he received as an infant. Arthur's initiation into the church followed the traditional sequence of baptism, confirmation, communion, and is now complete, although he will still have to make choices about how he will live his faith as he grows up.

We might ask how a sacrament can have so many different meanings. The answer is not simple, largely because of the ever-changing approach to this sacrament. More than any other sacrament, confirmation has evolved in ways that are complex and confusing.

Confirmation Linked to Baptism

The ceremony of baptism was celebrated in slightly different ways in the various early Christian communities. Baptism was sometimes accompanied by anointings with oil or by a symbolic "laying on of hands." The oil (also called "chrism") used in baptism was associated with Christ, who was "the anointed one of God." The laying on of hands symbolized the sharing of the Spirit of the Lord with the new members of the Christian community. Some communities emphasized that the Spirit came in the baptismal water bath; others held that the Spirit was received with the anointing and the laying on of hands.

By the year 215 a rite had been established whereby the bishop would baptize in water, extend his hand in prayer over the candidate, and then make the sign of the cross with oil on the forehead of the person being baptized. The initiation ritual continued as the bishop gave the new Christian the kiss of peace and the eucharist.[11] Although there were variations from one community to the next, for the most part this ritual of baptizing with water and anointing with oil became the standard form of the Christian initiation ceremony. The dual actions of bathing and anointing that later became the separate sacraments of baptism and confirmation began as two parts of a single initiation sacrament.

Confirmation Separated from Baptism

Confirmation became a separate sacrament as the anointing and laying on of hands was separated from the baptismal water bath. Scholars speculate on the reasons why such a separation took place, and on how confirmation eventually became a sacrament in its own right.

One factor that seems to have caused the separation of the anointing from the water bath was the rapid spread and de-urbanization of Christianity. The enormous growth and expansion of the church that began in the fourth century made it impossible for bishops, the ordinary ministers of baptism, to keep pace with the large number of conversions. Presbyters (priests) were put in charge of the outlying communities. They were responsible for leading the celebration of the eucharist and for attending to the initiation of new members. A practice emerged whereby the presbyters would initiate new members with a water bath, but postpone the anointing with oil and the laying on of hands until a later time when it could be done by the bishop.

There are medieval stories of bishops riding through the fields on horseback, and stopping to confirm the peasants working in the fields. In other cases people stopped at the cathedral when they went to the nearest large city, and were anointed by their bishop. Many of the baptized never actually got confirmed.

Another factor that contributed to the separation of the rite of initiation into the sacraments of baptism and confirmation was the increase in the practice of infant baptism. Since infants were incapable of making an act of faith at the time of their baptism, it became customary to have another ceremony several years later when the young person could give indication of a more mature desire to practice the Christian faith. Gradually this latter rite became a separate sacrament with unique theological interpretations.

By the fifth century the word "confirmation" began to be used, and by the ninth century theologians were designating this ritual as the time when the fullness of the Spirit was conferred. Medieval theologians, unaware of the history of the initiation rite, assumed that baptism and confirmation were always two distinct sacraments, and developed theological understandings of confirmation that had no reference to baptism.

Jerry is a "non-traditional" student from the Bronx. He drove an 18-wheeler for many years, raised his kids, and now has come back to get a degree in accounting. In a theology class discussion of confirmation he recalls his own confirmation many years ago.

I was in the sixth grade when I was confirmed. There was no mention of baptism at all. I was told that this sacrament would make me a soldier of Christ and that the Holy Spirit would bring his gifts to me. I remember hearing that the bishop was going to slap us on the side of the face during the ceremony. That sounded strange, and I did not know what to expect. Actually the bishop was a nice guy and he just gave each of us a friendly tap on the cheek, telling us to be strong adult Christians. Oh yes, I took a new name, Joseph, which I never used. Overall, I must say that I was not sure what was hap-

pening at confirmation. It was a pretty empty ceremony for me, although we did have a party and I got a gift from the uncle I had chosen as my sponsor.

Jerry was told that he was going to be made into a soldier of Christ through confirmation because of a long-standing belief that the sacrament was intended to strengthen the Christian and prepare the person for battle with heretics and other enemies of the church. This emphasis was developed by a sixth-century French bishop named Faustus. In a Pentecost sermon, Faustus proclaimed that the Holy Spirit came at confirmation and made Christians "soldiers of Christ." In the ninth century, some French clerics presented the "soldier of Christ" notion of confirmation as being an authentic church doctrine. These medieval perspectives about confirmation were affirmed at the Council of Trent, when it opposed the challenges of the Reformers who questioned the necessity and validity of the sacrament of confirmation.

Confirmation Today

The Second Vatican Council initiated efforts to reform the sacrament of confirmation. In 1971 a new rite of confirmation was promulgated which attempted to reconnect confirmation with the other initiation sacraments—baptism and first eucharist.[12]

Another significant development further influenced the celebration and meaning of the sacrament of confirmation. In the mid-1970s the ancient catechumenate was restored as the process of preparing adults who wish to enter the church. This move began a gradual shift in the church's focus from infant baptism to adult baptism. In the case of adults who are entering the Catholic church and who have never been baptized in another Christian church, baptism, confirmation, and first eucharist are celebrated together at the Easter Vigil as the rite of Christian initiation. Adults who have been baptized previously, receive confirmation and eucharist, and are thereby brought "into full communion with the church."

Restoring the Initiation Sequence

The present practice regarding the timing and celebration of the initiation sacraments for children is a matter of debate among liturgists, pastoral leaders, and religious educators.[13] Questions regarding the restoration of the original sequence of baptism, confirmation, and eucharist, and the proper time to celebrate these sacraments, are far from being resolved.

For children baptized as infants, first eucharist and confirmation are delayed until they are older. Most children receive first communion at the age of seven or eight, as has been done for most of the twentieth century. Prior to the start of the twentieth century both first eucharist and confirmation were received in early adolescence. Pope Pius X, a holy man filled with love for the eucharist, moved the time of first communion to "the age of reason," while leaving confirmation in the preteen years. As a result of his action, first eucharist and confirmation were separated from each other, as well as from any connection with baptism.

Following Vatican II, a concern for the religious formation of adolescents led educators to delay confirmation until the high school years. This precipitated a corresponding theology of confirmation that accented maturity and initiation into adulthood. Celebrating the sacrament at this time in their life allowed teenagers to affirm personally their acceptance of the faith. The process of preparation for confirmation gave religious educators the opportunity to catechize and minister to youth in ways that had not been available before. It also stimulated the adult members of parishes to mentor the young people, and make their communities more welcoming and hospitable to the young.

The move toward adolescent confirmation has not received the approval of all. Some church leaders and liturgists want the ancient initiation sequence of baptism, confirmation, and eucharist restored. There are several ways that this could occur. The Western (Roman) church could return to the practice of the Eastern church and initiate infants with baptism, confirmation, and first eucharist all together. This seems unlikely to happen.

It is possible, but unlikely, that infant baptism might be discontinued so that the three-sacrament rite of initiation could be celebrated at the age of reason or even at some later age. This would undoubtedly upset those people in the church—probably the majority—who cherish infant baptism. This would also distress those who still fear for the salvation of unbaptized babies.

For people serious about restoring the original order for the sacraments of initiation, the option that seems most advisable and least disruptive is to celebrate confirmation prior to the celebration of first eucharist when a child reaches the age of seven or eight. This puts these two sacraments together, and makes it possible to restore a semblance of the ancient sequence of baptism, confirmation, and eucharist. This option also allows the practice of infant baptism to continue and keeps first eucharist at the age of reason where it has been for nearly a hundred years. Only the timing and theological understanding of confirmation would have to be adjusted, and history indicates that this has been done before.

This initiation dilemma is not easily resolved. It seems clear, however, that these sacraments, whatever their sequence, are being celebrated with much more preparation, meaning, and fervor since their renewal after the Second Vatican Council. Each sacrament is now seen as a unique experience of the presence and power of the Spirit of the Lord, an experience that transcends all theological and pastoral controversies.

A Celebration of the Spirit

In spite of its checkered history, confirmation has been rather consistently understood as a celebration of the Spirit. Aidan Kavanagh, a highly-regarded liturgical scholar, suggests that the anointing was originally a mere dismissal rite, but that in the fifth century it took on the meaning of the completion of baptism and the coming of the fullness of the Spirit.[14] This makes baptism the complete initiation sacrament, signaling initiation into Christ, as well as into his Spirit and into the church. Confirmation then finds its meaning in intensifying this experience of the Spirit, and in giving it new strength and vitality as a person carries out Christ's mission.

As in all sacraments, the Spirit of Jesus is at the heart of the celebration of confirmation. The same Spirit that came upon Christ to fill his words and deeds with saving power is now intensely experienced in the confirmation rite no matter when or how it is celebrated.[15] This is the same Spirit that Jesus promised to send to his followers, and that was given to them in a profound way at Pentecost. This is the same Spirit that formed the church and sustains it for all time. The gifts and power of this Spirit of the Lord are experienced uniquely and specially in confirmation. Kenan Osborne therefore suggests that the controlling issue with regard to confirmation should "not be age, but the presence of the Spirit."[16]

Reconciliation/Penance

The sacrament of reconciliation (also called penance or confession) seems to have developed from the Christian belief in the saving power of God's forgiveness, which Jesus so uniquely extended to so many. From the beginning of his public ministry, Jesus called people to repentance or conversion from their sins. Repentance, or *metanoia,* is a turning around, a retracing of one's steps, a getting back on the straight and narrow.[17] To those who were mired in their sins, Jesus offered the good news that they were loved and forgiven by God. To outcasts who were led to believe that their disabilities or low social standing were signs that they were cursed by God, Jesus offered hope and healing. For those who were caught up in the guilt associated with a legalistic morality, Jesus brought freedom.[18]

Paul speaks of a "ministry of reconciliation" that is to be carried on by the disciples in Jesus' name. Paul writes:

> So whoever is in Christ is in a new creation: the old things have passed away; behold new things have come. And all this is from God, who has reconciled us to himself through Christ and given us the ministry of reconciliation, namely, God was reconciling the world to himself in Christ, not counting their trespasses against them and entrusting to us the message of reconciliation. (2 Cor 5:17–19)

The people of the church, therefore, are called to witness to the good news that God will forgive through Jesus any sins for which they are repentant.[19]

Penance Among the Early Christians

The early Christian communities continued some of the Jewish rituals that asked for God's forgiveness. The Hebrew scriptures teach that God will always welcome back sinful people if they but reach out with a sense of repentance. The Hebrews had many practices that symbolized their change of heart and their belief in the unfailing forgiveness of God. They fasted, wept mournfully, wore sackcloth, prayed, and offered sacrifices of expiation. Among Jewish people today, the Day of Atonement (Yom Kippur) still remains a solemn celebration of repentance and forgiveness.[20]

The disciples of Jesus learned about God's mercy and forgiveness in a new way. God was Abba, a loving Dad, who forgave even before the sinner performed the actions of repentance. Through Jesus the disciples experienced not a God of vengeance and punishment, but a God who extended mercy to all, especially the poor and the oppressed. They believed that Jesus' life, death, and resurrection brought ultimate reconciliation for all time. The proclamation of forgiveness became the central focus of their mission to call the world to repentance.

The Gospel of John relates the experience of Easter Sunday night when the risen Lord made his disciples aware that the divine power of forgiveness was in their midst. Jesus says: "Receive the Holy Spirit. If you forgive people's sins, they are forgiven; if you do not forgive them, they are not forgiven" (Jn 20:22–23).

The church's actions manifesting the power of forgiveness have evolved significantly through the centuries. Adult baptism is a dramatic celebration of conversion from sin and a reception of the grace of forgiveness. The celebration of the eucharist, which commemorates the events of Calvary and rejoices in the presence of the risen Christ, is also an occasion for forgiveness. Today's Mass concentrates on this in the calling to mind of one's sinfulness and the power of Christ's forgiveness that occurs at the opening of the liturgy, as well as in the petition for forgiveness in the Lord's Prayer.[21]

Matthew's gospel gives an account of an early form of reconciliation. It recommends that if a person has been offended, he or she should tell the offender. If that fails, the person should take one or two others along as witnesses. If there are still no results, the church community should be informed; and if there is no chance of repentance, the offender should be excluded from the community (Mt 18:15–20). Paul also speaks of setting serious offenders aside and then extending love to them once they have repented (1 Cor 5:1–5; 2 Cor 2:5–11).

Public Penance

The first public rituals of penance seem to appear in the second century. These rituals are concerned with serious sins such as adultery, apostasy, and murder. While some communities considered these to be unforgivable sins, most believed that such sins could be forgiven through public penance. Such forgiveness, however, could be received only once in a lifetime, and only after a prolonged period of rigorous penance.[22]

The rituals for public penance varied from one community to another. Generally they entailed a confession of one's sins to the bishop, enrollment in the "order of penitents," exclusion from the eucharist, and a period of three years or more of severe public penance. The community prayed for the penitent during this time, and once convinced that the sinner was repentant and reformed, the person was reconciled with the community. Obviously, only a small number of people ever participated in such extreme rituals, so this form of penance played no significant role in the daily spiritual lives of most Christians.

Individual Private Confession

Private devotional penance first found widespread acceptance among the sixth-century Celtic monks and nuns. At that time the church in Ireland had gained considerable independence from the Roman authorities, and was not hesitant to develop its own innovative rituals and traditions.[23] The tradition of penitential rituals had its roots in the earlier monasticism of the Egyptian desert monks, who confessed their sins and failings to spiritual directors, and then performed penances prescribed by the spiritual directors. These private rituals replaced the rigorous public penance that had been observed in many Christian communities throughout Europe.

During the sixth and seventh centuries, monasteries became the parish centers for the people of Ireland, and the monks and nuns became spiritual directors and guides for the people of the surrounding towns. The confession of one's sins to a priest or nun eventually became part of the regular practice of one's faith. Appropriate penances were assigned for each type of sin. For instance, a penance of fasting was assigned for overindulgence in food. Hard physical work was the penance prescribed for those who confessed to the sin of laziness. Eventually these penances were formulized into books called *Penitentials*, and through the growing usage of these books the practice of private penance became more widespread. It is important to note that the word "sacrament" was not yet applied to this ritual. This term was not applied to penance until the twelfth century. Nor was a formula of absolution used.

The Irish form of private penance spread to the European continent due to the missionary efforts of the Irish monks. Soon, however, this innovative form of receiving forgiveness was challenged by those who insisted on the use of the Roman forms of public penance. Local European synods condemned private confession and insisted that the public form of penance, which by the eighth century had become a ritual mostly for the dying, be enforced. The struggle went on for several centuries until the Fourth Lateran Council in 1215 endorsed private confession as the Western church's official ritual for penance. At this time, although some people were still confessing their sins to lay men and women, penance in its official sacramental form could only be administered by an ordained priest.

Medieval theologians provided a theological framework for the practice of private confession, focusing on such notions as contrition, satisfaction, justification, merit, and absolution. Eventually private confession once a year was required of church members who were in the state of serious sin.

Reformation Controversies

Controversies regarding the meaning and practice of penance set the stage for debates and divisions during the Reformation. One source of abuse was the custom of making a monetary offering instead of completing the often cumbersome penances. People would pay a set fee to the church instead of saying prayers or performing other acts of penance. This custom eventually grew into the selling of indulgences for what was called the "temporal punishment" due to sin. Monies that were originally given to the priest for the poor began to be used for other purposes. Abuses mounted until the selling of indulgences became one of the flashpoints for the Reformation.[24]

The sixteenth-century reformers staged a major assault on the sacramentality of penance. Using scripture as their resource, they denied that the sacrament of penance was instituted by Christ. From the Protestant perspective, only baptism and eucharist were instituted by the Lord. Luther, in many ways the most traditional of the reformers, saw a value in private confession, but insisted that it was faith that justified a person, and not absolution, penances for sin, or even merit.[25]

John Calvin also denied the sacramentality of penance. He saw some value in confessing one's sins to a minister of the gospel, but insisted that forgiveness comes from God in virtue of baptismal faith, not from the sacrament of penance. Knowing little of the history of penance, Calvin and the other reformers maintained that penance was an invention of the church. Today Anglicans (Episcopalians) and some Lutherans still maintain rituals of reconciliation, but most other Protestant denominations generally avoid such rituals.

Trent Reaffirms the Value of Penance

The Council of Trent issued decrees on the necessity of penance, its sacramentality, and its institution by Christ. It reaffirmed the importance of contrition, confession of one's sins, and satisfaction (performing the prescribed penance) as the proper means of gaining the forgiveness of sin. Trent adopted a juridic approach to the sacrament by focusing on the recital of list of sins according to number, kind, and circumstance. In this courtroom model, the priest acted as the judge ascertaining the disposition of the penitent, exacting a fitting penance as punishment, and pronouncing the judicial statement of absolution.[26] The medieval theology of the importance of the acts of confession on the part of the penitent, and the need for the absolution of the priest who exercises the "power of the keys" were given strong currency by Trent.

As a result of the tone set by the Council of Trent the reception of this sacrament became largely privatized and often mechanical. The communal dimension of the sacrament and its focus on conversion were generally neglected. The confessional box was established as a means of preserving anonymity, as well as an effective way to prevent abuses involving money and other immorality that at times had previously occurred between penitents and their confessors.

The Council of Trent's presentation of the sacrament of penance prevailed in the Roman Catholic church for the next four hundred years. In the first half of the twentieth century, confession played a central role in Catholic pastoral practice. For many Catholics it was a vital means for gaining counseling, forgiveness, and for maintaining spiritual growth. For others, confession was associated with fear and shame.

The Second Vatican Council

The Vatican II era ushered in new perspectives that changed the understanding and practice of the sacrament of penance. A careful historical review of the sacrament revealed the ever-evolving and diverse practice of penitential rituals. Since change was evident in the past, the bishops at the council felt secure in implementing changes that refocused the meaning of this valuable sacrament. A return to biblical sources led to a renewed consideration of the issues surrounding conversion, sin, grace, and justification. Emphasis on the communal nature of the church led to the restoration of the public and liturgical aspects of penance. Personalist and relational approaches to the nature of the human person challenged the legalistic approaches to sin and moral issues, as well as encouraged the use of individual conscience as a moral guide. The accent on the social dimensions of sin brought attention to issues of justice, peace, and care for the environment.[27]

A Communal Rite of Reconciliation

The mid-1970s marked a milestone in the evolution of the sacrament of penance. It was then that the Vatican promulgated the new rite, even giving the sacrament a new name—reconciliation. Reconciliation means "a restored state of harmony." Literally the word means "to walk together again." The word is more personal and relational, and it implies that the ultimate goal of the sacrament is not so much the confession of sins or the doing of penance, but renewed and growing intimacy with the Lord.

This new rite was received with a great deal of enthusiasm. It sounded more upbeat and positive than the old "confession." Comfortable reconciliation rooms were built in many churches as an alternative to dark, anonymous confessional boxes. A more welcoming atmosphere was promoted. Instead of mechanically listing their sins, people were encouraged to mention some area of their life where they had failed and wherein they wanted to grow spiritually.

One of the major shifts in the new rite was to move away from the former juridic model and back to one that was closer to the seventh-century spiritual direction model of the Irish monks and nuns. More emphasis was placed on the reading of scripture and the importance of prayers for conversion and forgiveness. The priest, rather than acting as a judge, adopted the model of the forgiving, healing Jesus and joined with the penitent in prayer for healing and reconciliation.

Reconciliation came to be seen more as a communal, ecclesial celebration with the priest representing the church community that had been harmed by the sins of each individual.[28] The sacrament, therefore, came to symbolize not only reconciliation with God, but also reconciliation with one's neighbor and with the church community. All members of the community were called to share in the ministry of reconciliation, and to assist one another in conversion and forgiveness.

As in the Vatican II renewal of all the sacraments, the theology of reconciliation placed the risen Lord at the center of the celebration. This is the same Lord who extended forgiveness to so many during his lifetime, who gave his life for the forgiveness of sin, and who is now present through his Spirit to bring healing, forgiveness, and growth in grace to his followers.

There are now three distinct ceremonies (rites) for the celebration of reconciliation. First, one can celebrate the sacrament privately, either anonymously behind the screen or face-to-face with the priest in a reconciliation room. Second, the sacrament of reconciliation is celebrated at communal penance services. Here the community gathers to proclaim the scriptures, reflect on their sins, and pray for forgiveness. At these celebrations priests are available for brief individual confessions and absolution. Finally, accommodation is made for general absolution given to large groups without the formal individual confession of sins. This latter form initially received a welcome endorsement from many Catholics who resisted telling their sins to a priest, but has since been surrounded with restrictions so that it is not commonly used at present.

The Fading Practice of Reconciliation

Amanda is a junior who has attended Catholic schools since kindergarten. Her family attends church regularly and tries to pray together as a family in their home, especially during Advent and Lent. But she admits that reconciliation is a sacrament she seldom receives.

When I was in grade school and high school I remember that we had reconciliation services several times each year. One priest would lead the service and then we would go to one of several priests and confess our sins. I remember thinking that this was pretty good. I'd feel sorry for the bad things I had done and I would really try to do better. I went to confession by myself a couple of time on a Saturday afternoon. I used the dark confessional box once and that was really spooky. A couple of other times I went to the reconciliation room and talked with the priest about what I had done wrong and how I could do better.

I haven't gone to confession for several years now, and I don't see a real reason to go. I haven't committed any terrible sins, and when I do something bad, I try to apologize to the person. I don't think I'm that unusual either. I know my folks don't go to confession except maybe one a year at a parish penance service. My grandmother tells these great stories about how when she was my age she went to confession every Saturday afternoon before going to communion on Sunday morning at Mass. But even she has changed. She rarely goes to confession but she always goes to communion, and I'm glad. She's a wonderful lady. Why should she need confession?

Amanda's experiences with reconciliation and her assessment of the sacrament are echoed by many Catholics. After the initial enthusiasm for the new rite of reconciliation in the 1970s, interest gradually declined. The sacrament of reconciliation plays a minor role in most parishes today, and the once long lines waiting for confession are no more. Many young Catholics have celebrated the sacrament only on those occasions when it was done at their parochial school or in a religious education program. Many Catholics think there is a need for further renewal and experimentation if the interest of the faithful in this sacrament in to be rekindled.

Some express discouragement at what seems to be a return of the church to more traditional attitudes toward this sacrament. Some official documents still refer to mortal and venial sins. The 1983 Code of Canon Law does not clearly address the social or ecclesial nature of the sacrament, and returns once again to the language of "confession" and "penance." Communal celebrations go unmentioned in canon law, and there are serious restrictions placed on the use of general absolution. Many theologians and pastoral leaders hold that such retrenchment has been partially responsible for the declining interest in this sacrament.

The Future of Reconciliation

If the sacrament of penance is to be integral once again to Catholic life, there may have to be more room for experimentation and adaptation. It is a normal part of human nature to reach out for healing, forgiveness, and reconciliation. Most certainly the church community can, as it has in the past, devise rituals that will effectively meet these needs according to the various levels of age, culture, educational background, and spiritual maturity. An accent on spiritual growth, theological reflection, creative prayer forms, and innovative communal celebrations will possibly bring this sacrament to the community's attention once again.

Anointing of the Sick

The sacrament of the anointing of the sick today focuses more on healing than it does on dying. In our contemporary society healing is a controversial topic. Charlie, a pre-med student from Tampa, offers his perspective.

One of the reasons that I want to become a doctor is that I believe in the need for healing. I believe that healing comes through good health care, expert surgery, and the proper medicines. The only "miracles" I believe in are the miracles of modern science. I get really turned off when I see one of those TV evangelists pressing his hands on some poor guy's head until the guy faints, and then claiming that the person was healed by the power of the Lord. Of course, the "miracle" is usually followed by a call for donations. I think these guys are modern-day snake oil salesmen and that they are duping a lot of innocent people.

As for all the miracle stories in the bible, I think they are just primitive myths that were written down before the days of science. Now that we know how diseases and the body work, we can explain cures rationally and through observable causality. As a doctor, my faith will be in skills and knowledge, not in healing power from God. If the church wants to make someone feel good by anointing them before death, that's fine. But I wish we could stop all this talk about healing and expecting cures to come from God.

Charlie, like many people today, has been turned off by the TV healers, and by all the commercialism that is associated with healing. In addition, he approaches the whole question of healing clinically and rationally, with little reference to the power of the Spirit in healing. Charlie certainly speaks for many people in our secular age, where science and technology seem to be all we need to solve our problems.

This section will attempt to offer people like Charlie some other ideas to consider with regard to healing and the sacrament of the anointing of the sick. We will start by looking at some ancient views of healing, and see how Jesus' perspective was unique in this regard. Then we will look at some of the factors that caused the church to lose its appreciation for healing. Finally we will look at the rite of the anointing of the sick and see how this sacrament can put people in touch with the power of the Lord.

Ancient Views on Healing

There is very little reference to healing miracles in Roman literature. Tacitus (d. 117 C.E.) reports that the Emperor Vespasian (d. 79 C.E.) was able to perform cures of the blind and the crippled, but most Roman references to the wondrous are concerned with portents, omens, and dreams.

The Greeks, by contrast, were more concerned with healing miracles. The city of Epidaurus was the favorite pilgrimage spot for the people of the ancient world seeking cures and miraculous healings. Excavated pillars from this region record many cures at this place. Asclepius was revered as the "healer god" from the time of Homer (eighth century, B.C.E.) until the time of Constantine (fourth century, C.E.).[29]

The Hebrews seldom speak of miraculous healings in their tradition. In the nearly two thousand years chronicled in the Hebrew scriptures from Abraham to Maccabees, stories of healing are rare. Among the few references to healing, mention is made of how Abimelech and his household are cured; King Saul is cured of an evil spirit; and several healings are attributed to Elisha (Gn 20:17–18; 1 Sm 16:23; 2 Kgs 4:18–37, 5:1–27).

Jesus and Healing

It was considered quite unique and amazing when Jesus of Nazareth burst upon the scene performing numerous healing miracles. About one-fifth of the literary units in the synoptic gospels allude to miracles of healing or exorcism, and a large portion of the Johannine gospel is concerned with miraculous signs. Many reputable biblical scholars hold that there is a firm historical basis for the healing miracles recounted in the gospels. These miracle stories, even though elaborated on and filled with the faith insights of the early communities, seem to have a factual origin and play a central role in the gospels.

The uniqueness of Jesus' healing ministry is evident throughout the gospel stories. Unlike other magicians and miracle workers of his time, Jesus healed many disabled people of blindness, deafness, dumbness, palsy, leprosy, withered limbs, menstrual problems, and dropsy. He did not use secret magical formulas or incantations as did some of his contemporaries. Nor did Jesus use these healings as a proof of his divinity or a demonstration of the validity of his message. Jesus adamantly denied that he conspired with evil spirits as did some of the sorcerers of his day. Jesus was not manipulative, sensational, or self-seeking in the healings that he performed.

Jesus healed out of compassion and love; out of a compelling drive to demonstrate that God (Abba) is a loving parent who wants all people to be whole. Jesus rejected the ancient and widely held belief that infirmities or disabilities are either sent by God as punishment for sin or are the work of evil spirits. His actions were empowered by a Creator-God who sends the Spirit to make people whole. Jesus' healings were "acts of power" *(dunemeis)* that clearly demonstrated the closeness of the reign of God.

The way Jesus brought the healing power of God to outcasts, the poor, and the oppressed was most extraordinary. In doing this he rejected the teachings of the religious leaders who said that the poor and disabled were to be ignored and set aside as unclean. It was Jesus' position that Abba blessed all people and wanted healing for them. This practice of caring for the lowly and the sinners was one on the main reasons why Jesus' enemies decided to arrange his demise.

Healing in the Early Communities

The early communities possessed a profound awareness that the risen Lord was in their midst, continuing to bring them the healing power of the Spirit. The gospels explicitly point out how Jesus entrusted the carrying on of this ministry to his apostles: "And he called to him his twelve disciples and gave them authority over unclean spirits, to cast them out, and to heal every disease and every infirmity" (Mt 10:1; see also Mk 6:7; Lk 9:1).[30]

Matthew points out that caring for the ill can be a means to inherit the kingdom and obtain eternal life. What is done for the ill (the least ones) is done for the Lord (Mt 25:36–46). The Acts of the Apostles gives accounts of this ministry being carried out in the Jerusalem community, where wonders and signs are performed by the apostles. Peter is portrayed as taking the hand of a crippled beggar and raising him up as healed. Later Peter heals Aeneas, who had been paralyzed and bed-ridden for eight years. Then Peter raises Tabitha from the dead (Acts

3:1–10; 9:32–43). Acts also records an ancient prayer of the community: "Enable your servants to speak your word with all boldness, as you stretch forth your hand to heal, and signs and wonders are done through the name of your holy servant Jesus" (Acts 4:29–30).

In the Letter of James there is an oft-quoted text which further reveals the healing tradition of the Jerusalem community.

> Is anyone among you sick? He should summon the presbyters of the church, and they should pray over him and anoint him with oil in the name of the Lord, and the prayer of faith will save the sick person, and the Lord will raise him up. If he has committed any sins, he will be forgiven. (James 5:14–15)

The ancient custom of anointing with oil—used by the Hebrews in the coronation of kings, the ordination of priests, and the care of the sick—now came to symbolize the healing power of Christ. (The name "Christ" means "chrismed," or "anointed One of God.")[31] The Jerusalem community's healing ministry and its custom of anointing provided the foundation for the later development of the sacrament of the anointing of the sick.

Carrying on the Healing Ministry

The tradition of anointing the sick in the hope of healing them was carried on in the church for many centuries. The *Didache* speaks of the blessing of oil. The *Apostolic Traditions* (c. 215 C.E.) along with fourth and fifth century documents mention the blessing of oil that can be used to restore health to the sick. A number of patristic sources, including the writings of Ambrose, Augustine, and Gregory Nazianzus also express concern that Christ's healing ministry remain alive in the church.

A bishop or priest often performed the actual anointing of the sick, but there is evidence that the laity also anointed the sick. Self-anointing and the anointing of family members also seem to have been a custom that lasted until around the year 800. The oil, also taken internally at times, was intended to restore the wholeness of the body, mind, and spirit. Such anointing was not regarded as a preparation for death, an emphasis which was to come later.

A Loss of Interest in Healing

Each sacrament has a history and has evolved over time. This has resulted in changes in both the ritual and the meaning of the sacrament.

In the case of the anointing of the sick, a loss of interest in healing coupled with an intensified focus on preparation for death and the requirement that the minister of the sacrament be ordained led to the decline in the use of this sacrament.

The loss of interest in healing was brought about by a number of influences. The holistic perspective toward the human person that was so characteristic of Jewish thinking was gradually replaced by the dualisms of Greek and Gnostic thought. In some Greek thinking there was a dichotomy between spirit and the body. In this perspective, the spirit was entrapped in the body, which is the grosser material and nonessential part.

Gnostics carried this even further, maintaining that material things were created by evil forces and were to be rejected as evil. Bodies, which were material things, were to be chastised through vigorous asceticism. This negative attitude toward the body brought on a rejection of the flesh, distorted the meaning of sex, and made even the Incarnation (God taking on human form in the person of Jesus) unacceptable to Gnostics and those influenced by them. Obviously, this point of view placed little importance on healing the body. The soul was of paramount importance, and therefore the sole object of salvation.[32]

The loss of interest in healing also was brought about by the gradual return to the notion that sickness was a punishment for sin. If sickness was indeed a punishment sent by God, then the emphasis should be on obtaining forgiveness, rather than escaping the just punishments for sin. The anointing of the sick began to focus on the healing from sin, and gradually came to be known as the "last rites," a preparation of the soul for death.

Another factor that diminished interest in healing was the desperate condition of life during the dark ages. The devastating invasions of barbarian tribes, the scourges inflicted by Moslem armies, and the ravages of disease brought on such widespread suffering and death that the hope of healing was all but lost. The common folk were more concerned with day-to-day survival than they were with healing. For many, life became a cross to bear, a trial to undergo in this "vale of tears." Escape from the body and all its sufferings, not the body's healing, became the focus for many Christians.

Medieval scholasticism with its Aristotelian philosophical framework also contributed to the loss of interest in healing. In this worldview the natural world was self-contained, with God's power in another realm. Thus Aquinas, following Aristotle's lead, generally avoided discussion of healing. When he treated miracles, Aquinas saw them largely as proofs of Christ's divinity. From the medieval time onward, any discussion of healing became largely associated with relics, pilgrimages, shrines, and the intercession of the saints. Theologians gradually lost interest in healing, and the anointing, which by now had reached sacramental status, was seen as a means of preparing for death.

Preparation for Death

The ninth-century reform of the church by Charlemagne provided a strong impetus to see the anointing as a preparation for death. Councils stressed that the anointing was for the forgiveness of sins. The anointing ceremony was held at the sick person's house and called the person to focus on his or her past sins. The sick person was asked to confess his or her sins, and then to wear a cross of ashes and a hair shirt as a sign of penance. Penitential psalms were recited and the five senses were anointed to cleanse them from past sins.

Gradually these rituals became known as the last rites and were reserved for the dying. In the twelfth century Peter Lombard (d. 1160) named "extreme unction" as one of the seven sacraments. In the next century, Thomas Aquinas provided a more developed theology for this sacrament. He saw it as a healing from sin and a preparation for eternal glory.

For the most part the Protestant reformers denied the sacramentality of extreme unction. They understood the healing miracles as unique events that occurred only in biblical times. In reaction, the Council of Trent strongly defended the sacramentality of the anointing. While Trent allowed the possibility that spiritual, psychological, and physical healing could result from the anointing, it decreed that this sacrament could only be conferred on those in danger of death. This sacrament was viewed as the last anointing, or extreme unction, until the reform that followed the Second Vatican Council in the 1960s and 1970s, when healing was once again emphasized.

The Minister of the Sacrament

As we have seen, until the ninth century the laity were permitted to anoint themselves and their loved ones. This practice was ended during the reform of Charlemagne, when it was decreed that only an ordained priest could anoint the sick. The anointing became one of the seven sacraments in the twelfth century, and then gradually became a private ceremony involving only the priest and a person who was dying. The loved ones and those who had been most intimately involved in caring for the sick person were excluded from this final spiritual ministry to the sick. The role of the community, so important in the early church, was neglected, and there was little anticipation of physical healing.

Vatican II Renewal

The sacrament of the anointing of the sick, like all seven sacraments, was renewed after the Second Vatican Council. The council reclaimed treasured traditions that enabled the community to rethink the celebration of this sacrament. There was a return to the scriptures and a renewed emphasis on the healing miracles of Jesus and the power of the Spirit. There was a deepened awareness that the risen Lord continues to bring divine healing powers to his disciples and all his faithful followers.

The council accented the presence of Christ at the heart of the Christian community, and recognized that the sacraments are ecclesial celebrations of the risen Lord's presence. The understanding of faith was broadened beyond intellectual acceptance of the truth to a personal openness to intimacy with God and the divine healing power. Coupled with this was a holistic approach to the human person that recognizes the interconnectedness among mind, spirit, and body. The material world was once again recognized as the creation of a God who wants the world and its people to be whole.

The official name of this sacrament was changed from extreme unction to the anointing of the sick. This change indicated a shift from preparation for death to a concern for healing. No longer a foreboding ritual announcing imminent death, the sacrament was to be approached with an expectant faith, hoping for healing of heart, mind, or body through the power of the Spirit of the Lord. The same Lord, who healed so freely and compassionately during his lifetime, could now be encountered among today's disciples, offering access to the same healing powers.

No longer a private ceremony, the sacrament is viewed today as a communal celebration. Loved ones, health care personnel, and local parish communities can celebrate the sacrament with those seeking healing. This sacrament can take place in homes, hospitals, and parish settings. Songs, readings from the Word of God, and prayers by the community are an important part of this powerful ritual of anointing and healing. All the people of God, with hope and expectant faith, join with the sick and pray for their healing.

The positive outlook and the broader use of this sacrament are major improvements. No longer does a person have to be at death's door to receive this sacrament. Anyone whose health is seriously impaired may ask to be anointed. This has been broadly interpreted to include those whose health is impaired not only by sickness, but by old age, a serious operation, mental illness, or even such diseases as alcoholism or drug addiction.[33] In all these cases there is a hope for healing on all levels–spiritual, psychological, and physical.

The requirement that the minister of the sacrament be an ordained priest has become a matter of special concern for some Catholics. In many places the population of seriously ill people is great while the number of priests available to administer the sacrament is few. Although the laity has been excluded from presiding at this sacrament since the ninth century, many call for a return to earlier traditions when laity did anoint one another and pray with them for healing. While the priest is the ordinary minister of this sacrament, many extraordinary situations call for deacons, as well as qualified women and men, to celebrate the sacrament of the anointing of the sick with those in need.

Pam, a nursing student, who already has several years of experience in the health care field, expresses her concern about the lack of pastoral ministry available to many sick people.

Our hospitals today do not provide adequate pastoral care. A stay in the hospital is for many people a time to consider seriously ultimate concerns about life and death. It is an extraordinary opportunity for the church to minister to people at this time of personal crisis. And yet often the sick and the dying languish without anyone to administer pastoral care or the sacraments to them. There is a need for creative church reform in this area. More people have to be trained and appointed to this crucial ministry.

Conclusion

Each sacrament has a unique history and is part of the living Catholic tradition. In the past, changing times created unique needs and demands for modifications in the meaning and celebration of the sacraments. The complexity of the contemporary world with the myriad needs of people indicate that this is a time for further change. The present rituals for initiation, reconciliation, and healing are all in a period of transition. Cultural diversity, a wide range of theological perspectives, and pastoral needs call the church to adapt its sacramental celebrations. In some circles, however, there is resistance to change and a clinging to older models. Some have grown indifferent to the importance and meaning of the sacraments, while still others desire a continuation of the reform and renewal of Vatican II.

The Catholic sacramental tradition is a living tradition. Its symbols must be vibrant and attractive, constantly focusing on Jesus Christ. The sacraments are gifts of the Lord to make accessible to the people of the world his welcoming, forgiving, and healing powers. Whatever changes are needed to make this more possible have to made with courage and with care.

Discussion Questions

1. Sacraments are said to be encounters with Christ. Discuss the differences in such encounters with the Lord in baptism, reconciliation, and the anointing of the sick.

2. Discuss the development from Jewish baptism to early Christian baptism to baptism today.

3. What age do you think appropriate for confirmation? Please explain your answer with some examples from your own experience of confirmation and your own observations.

4. If you were in charge of preparing third year high school students for confirmation, what would you emphasize? What would you do to help them see the celebration of this sacrament to be important in their lives?

5. What significance does the sacrament of reconciliation have in your life? Can you think of ways that would make this sacrament more attractive to young people?

6. Discuss the historical development of the sacrament of the anointing of the sick.

7. What is your understanding of the sacrament of the anointing of the sick? If you have ever been present for the celebration of this sacrament, discuss your impressions.

Suggested Readings

Gerald Austin, *Anointing with the Spirit.* Collegeville, MN: Liturgical Press/Pueblo Books, 1975.

Patrick Brennan, *Penance and Reconciliation.* Chicago: Thomas More Press, 1986.

James L. Empereur, *Prophetic Anointing.* Wilmington, DE: Michael Glazier, 1982.

Richard Gula, *To Walk Together Again: The Sacrament of Reconciliation.* Mahwah, NJ: Paulist Press, 1984.

Charles W. Gusmer, *And You Visited Me: Sacramental Ministry to the Sick & the Dying.* Collegeville, MN: Liturgical Press/Pueblo Books, 1984.

Monika K. Hellwig, *Sign of Reconciliation and Conversion: The Sacrament of Penance in Our Times.* Collegeville, MN: Liturgical Press/Michael Glazier, 1982.

Aidan Kavanagh, *Confirmation: Origins and Reform.* Collegeville, MN: Liturgical Press/Pueblo Books, 1988.

Aidan Kavanagh, *The Shape of Baptism: The Rite of Christian Initiation.* Collegeville, MN: Liturgical Press/Pueblo Books, 1974.

Arthur J. Kubick, *Confirming the Faith of Adolescents.* New York: Paulist Press, 1991.

Thomas Marsh, *The Gift of Community: Baptism and Confirmation.* Collegeville, MN: Liturgical Press/Michael Glazier, 1984.

Kenan B. Osborne, *The Christian Sacraments of Initiation.* Mahwah, NJ: Paulist Press, 1987.

Kenan B. Osborne, *Reconciliation and Justification.* Mahwah, NJ: Paulist Press, 1991.

Paul Turner, *Confirmation: The Baby in Solomon's Court.* Mahwah, NJ: Paulist Press, 1993.

Notes

Chapter 1: Does God Exist?

1. John Macquarrie, *In Search of Deity* (New York: Crossroad, 1985), pp. 18-19.
2. Harold Kushner, *Who Needs God?* (New York: Summit Books, 1989), pp. 45ff.
3. Hans Küng, *On Being a Christian* (New York: Doubleday, 1976), pp. 60ff.
4. Michael Buckley, *At the Origins of Modern Atheism* (New Haven: Yale University Press, 1987), pp. 1ff.
5. James Thrower, *A Short History of Western Atheism* (London: Pemberton Books, 1971), pp. 18ff., 45ff.
6. John Courtney Murray, *The Problem of God: Yesterday and Today* (New Haven: Yale University Press, 1964), pp. 78ff.
7. Louis Baldwin, *Portraits of God* (London: McFarland and Co., 1986), pp. 107ff.
8. Quoted in John F. Haught, *What Is God?* (New York: Paulist Press, 1986), p. 40.
9. Karl Rahner, *Foundations of Christian Faith* (New York: Crossroad, 1987), p. 47.
10. Hans Küng, *Does God Exist?* (New York: Random House, 1981), p. 287.
11. John Bowker, *The Sense of God* (Oxford: Clarendon Press, 1973), p. 121.
12. See Mircea Eliade, "Cultural Fashions and the History of Religions," in J.M. Kitagawa (ed.), *The History of Religions* (Chicago: University of Chicago Press, 1967), pp. 21-38. See also Hans Küng, *Freud and the Problem of God* (New Haven: Yale University Press, 1990), p. 73.
13. Küng, *Freud and the Problem of God*, pp. 159ff.
14. Murray, *The Problem of God*, pp. 86-90.
15. Denis Carroll, *A Pilgrim God for a Pilgrim People* (Wilmington, DE: Michael Glazier, 1989), p. 9.
16. Bertrand Russell, *Collected Essays (1943-1949)* (New York: Arno Press, 1972), p. 3.
17. See Alexander McKelway, *The Freedom of God and Human Liberation* (Philadelphia: Trinity Press International, 1990), p. 49.
18. Rahner, *Foundations of Christian Faith*, p. 50.
19. See Mcquarrie, *In Search of Deity*, pp. 32ff.
20. John Dunne, *A Search for God in Time and Memory* (Notre Dame, IN: University of Notre Dame Press, 1977), p. 35.
21. See Küng, *Does God Exist?*, p. 50.
22. Baldwin, *Portraits of God*, pp. 99ff.
23. Dunne, *A Search for God in Time and Memory*, pp. 63ff.
24. See Rudolph Otto, *The Idea of the Holy* (New York: Oxford University Press, 1958).
25. Küng, *Does God Exist?*, p. 439.
26. Paul Tillich, *The Courage to Be* (New Haven, Yale University Press, 1952), pp. 180ff.
27. Dunne, *A Search for God in Time and Meaning*, p. 35.
28. Tillich, *The Courage to Be*, p. 187.
29. McKelway, *The Freedom of God and Human Liberation*, p. 9.
30. Pastoral Constitution on the Church in the Modern World, #17, in Walter Abbott (ed.), *The Documents of Vatican II* (New York: Guild Press, 1966).

31. Dietrich Bonhoeffer, *Letters and Papers from Prison* (New York: Macmillan, 1967), pp. 202ff. See also Walter Burghardt, "Free Like God: Recapturing an Ancient Anthropology," *Theology Digest*, 26, no. 4 (Winter, 1978), pp. 358ff.

32. Quoted in Basil Pennington, *Centered Living* (New York: Doubleday, 1986), p. 72.

33. Quoted in Ana Carrigan, *Salvador Witness: The Life and Calling of Jean Donovan* (New York: Simon and Schuster, 1984), p. 113. See also Peter C. Hodgson, *God in History: Shapes of Freedom* (Nashville, Abingdon Press, 1989), pp. 42ff.

34. Bernard Cooke, *The Distancing of God* (Minneapolis: AugsburgFortress Press, 1990), p. 39.

35. Rahner, *Foundations of Christian Faith*, p. 53.

36. Bernard Lonergan, *Philosophy of God and Theology* (Philadelphia: Westminster Press, 1973), p. 9.

37. Lonergan, *Philosophy of God and Theology*, pp. 52ff.

38. Bernard Lonergan, *Method in Theology* (New York: Herder and Herder, 1972), pp. 103-104.

39. Cooke, *The Distancing of God*, pp. 19ff.

40. Dermot A. Lane, *The Experience of God* (New York: Paulist Press, 1981), pp. 2ff.

41. David Tracy, *Blessed Rage for Order* (New York: Seabury Press, 1975), pp. 43ff.

42. Edward Schillebeeckx, "Faith Functioning in Human Self-Understanding," in Patrick T. Burke (ed.), *The Word in History* (New York: Sheed and Ward, 1966), pp. 45ff.

43. See Kenneth Leech, *Experiencing God* (New York: Harper & Row, 1985), pp. 1ff.

44. Gustavo Gutiérrez, *The God of Life* (Maryknoll, NY: Orbis Books, 1991), pp. xiff.

Chapter 2: Who Is God?

1. Karl Rahner, *Foundations of Christian Faith* (New York: Crossroad, 1987), pp. 65ff. See also Catherine Momry LaCugna, "The Trinitarian Mystery of God," in Francis Schüssler Fiorenza and John P. Galvin (eds.), *Systematic Theology* (Philadelphia: Fortress Press, 1991), I, p. 156.

2. Quoted in John Courtney Murray, *The Problem of God* (New Haven: Yale University Press, 1964), p. 79.

3. See Sallie McFague, *Models of God* (Philadelphia: Fortress Press, 1988), pp. 29-40.

4. Mircea Eliade, *Myth and Reality* (San Francisco: Harper & Row, 1975), pp. 5ff.

5. See Ari L. Goldman, *The Search for God at Harvard* (New York: Random House, 1991).

6. Bernhard U. Anderson, *Understanding the Old Testament* (Englewood, NJ: Prentice Hall, 1986), pp. 29ff. and 103ff.

7. Anderson, *Understanding the Old Testament*, p. 65.

8. Walter Kasper, *The God of Jesus Christ* (New York: Crossroad, 1988), p. 235.

9. Lawrence Boadt, *Reading the Old Testament* (New York: Paulist Press, 1984), p. 545.

10. Ronaldo Muñoz, *The God of Christians* (Maryknoll, NY: Orbis Books, 1977), pp. 48ff.

11. Carlos Mesters, *God, Where Are You?* (Maryknoll, NY: Orbis Books, 1977), pp. 48ff.

12. See Rudolph Otto, *The Idea of the Holy* (New York: Oxford University Press, 1958), pp. 31ff.

13. Boadt, *Reading the Old Testament*, pp. 546ff.

14. Brevard S. Childs, *Old Testament Theology in a Canonical Context* (Philadelphia: Fortress Press, 1985), p. 41.

15. Peter C. Hodgson, *New Birth of Freedom* (Philadelphia: Fortress Press, 1976), p. 262.

16. Boadt, *Reading the Old Testament*, pp. 547ff.

17. Kasper, *The God of Jesus Christ*, pp. 137ff.

18. Elisabeth Moltmann-Wendel and Jürgen Moltmann, *God—His and Hers* (New York: Crossroad, 1991), p. 5.

19. See Kasper, *The God of Jesus Christ*, p. 139.

20. Robert Hamerton-Kelly, *God the Father* (Philadelphia: Fortress Press, 1979), p. 45.

21. David Tracy, "Approaching the Christian Understanding of God," in Fiorenza and Galvin, *Systematic Theology*, I, p. 33.

22. Kasper, *The God of Jesus Christ*, p. 140.

23. Brennan R. Hill, *Jesus the Christ* (Mystic, CT: Twenty-Third Publications, 1991), pp. 68ff.

24. Karl Rahner, "Trinity," in *Sacramentum Mundi*, Karl Rahner and others (eds.), (New York: Herder and Herder, 1970) VI, pp. 295ff.

25. See Rosemary Radford Ruether, *Sexism and God-Talk* (Boston: Beacon Press, 1983), and Sallie McFague, *Metaphorical Theology* (Philadelphia: Fortress Press, 1982).

26. See Joseph A. Bracken, *The Triune Symbol: Persons, Process and Community* (New York: University Press of America, 1985).

27. Joan C. Engelsman, *The Feminine Dimension of the Divine* (Philadelphia: Westminster Press, 1979), pp. 13ff. See also Antonio Morean, *Jung, Gods, and Modern Man* (Notre Dame, IN: University of Notre Dame Press, 1970).

28. Mircea Eliade, *A History of Religious Ideas, Vol. I From Stone Age to the Eleusinian Mysteries* (Chicago: University of Chicago Press, 1978), 20ff.

29. Marija Gimbutas, *The Language of the Goddess* (San Francisco: Harper & Row, 1989), xviiff. See also Elinor W. Gadon, *The Once and Future Goddess* (San Francisco: Harper & Row, 1989).

30. Pamela Berger, *The Goddess Obscured* (Boston: Beacon Press, 1985), pp. 49ff.

31. Engelsman, *The Feminine Dimension of the Divine*, p. 48.

32. Tikva Frymer-Kensky, *In the Wake of the Goddesses* (New York: The Free Press, 1992), p. 13.

33. Carroll Saussy, *God Images and Self-Esteem: Empowering Women in a Patriarchal Society* (Louisville: Westminster/John Knox Press, 1991), pp. 54ff.

34. See Moltmann-Wendel and Moltmann, *God—His and Hers*, p. 2.

35. Gerda Lerner, *The Creation of Patriarchy* (New York: Oxford University Press, 1986), p. 49.

36. See Charlene Spretnak, (ed.), *The Politics of Women's Spirituality* (New York: Doubleday, 1982), p. xii.

37. See Engelsman, *The Feminine Dimension of the Divine*, pp. 95ff. Philo seems to have transposed Wisdom into the Logos, and eventually this notion became applied to Jesus Christ and lost its feminine connotation.

38. Walter Gardini, "The Feminine Aspect of God in Christianity," in Ursula King (ed.), *Women in the World's Religions, Past and Present* (New York: Paragon House, 1986), pp. 58ff.

39. A seminal work here is Elisabeth Schüssler Fiorenza, *In Memory of Her*

(New York: Crossroad, 1984).
40. See Leonardo Boff, *The Maternal Face of God* (San Francisco: Harper & Row, 1987).

Chapter 3: God, Science, and Creation

1. A.R. Peacocke, *Creation and the World of Science* (Oxford: Clarendon Press, 1979), pp. 10ff.
2. John Durant, *Darwinism and Divinity* (London: Basil Blackwell, 1985), p. 10.
3. John Hedley Brooke, *Science and Religion* (New York: Cambridge University Press, 1991), p. 153.
4. Quoted in Durant, *Darwinism and Divinity*, p. 11.
5. Durant, *Darwinism and Divinity*, p. 1.
6. Holmes Rolston III, "Joining Science and Religion," in Robert Russell and others (eds.), *John Paul II on Science and Religion* (Vatican City: Vatican Observatory Publications, 1990), pp. 88-89.
7. See G.V. Coyne and others (eds.), *The Galileo Affair: A Meeting of Faith and Science* (Vatican: Specola Vaticana, 1985).
8. Quoted in Gerhard Staguhn, *God's Laughter: Man and His Cosmos* (San Francisco: HarperCollins, 1992), p. 79.
9. Staguhn, *God's Laughter*, p. 90.
10. Staguhn, *God's Laughter*, p. 84.
11. See Stephen Hawking, *A Short History of Time* (New York: Bantam, 1988), pp. 175ff.
12. A.R. Peacocke, "The New Biology and Nature, Man and God," in F. Kenneth Hare (ed.), *The Experiment of Life: Science and Religion* (Toronto: University of Toronto Press, 1983), pp. 27-88.
13. See Daniel Liderbach, *The Numinous Universe* (New York: Paulist Press, 1989).
14. See Fritjof Capra, *The Tao of Physics* (Boston: Shambhala, 1975); and R.J. Russell, W.R. Stoeger, and G.V. Coyne, *Physics, Philosophy and Theology: A Common Quest for Understanding* (Notre Dame, IN: University of Notre Dame Press, 1988).
15. Brian Swimme, *The Universe Is a Green Dragon* (Santa Fe: Bear and Co., 1985).
16. John H. Brooke, *Science and Religion* (Cambridge: Cambridge University Press, 1991), pp. 37ff.
17. Jaroslav Pelikan, *Issues in Evolution* (Chicago: University of Chicago Press, 1960), III, p. 29.
18. Russell, *John Paul II on Science and Religion*, pp. M4-M14.
19. Quoted in Peacocke, *Creation and the World of Science*, p. 64.
20. Ernan McMullin, "The Sciences and Theology," in A.R. Peacocke (ed.), *The Sciences and Theology in the Twentieth Century* (Notre Dame IN: University of Notre Dame Press, 1981), p. 49.
21. Pelikan, "Creation and Causality in the History of Christian Thought," III, 32.
22. John Haught, *The Cosmic Adventure* (New York: Paulist Press, 1991), pp. 23-24. This analogy was first used by Richard Overman.
23. Rolston, *Joining Science and Religion*, pp. 63-64.
24. See A.R. Peacocke, *God and the New Biology* (San Francisco: Harper & Row, 1986), p. 91.
25. Quoted in Rolston, "Joining Science and Religion," p. 69.
26. See Peacocke, *Creation and the World of Science*, p. 201.
27. See Sallie McFague, *Models of God* (Philadelphia: Fortress Press, 1988), pp.

69ff.; and *The Body of God: An Ecological Theology* (Minneapolis: Fortress Press, 1993).

28. Gibson Winter, *Liberating Creation: Foundations of Religious Social Ethics* (New York: Crossroad, 1981), pp. 40ff. See also Haught, *The Cosmic Adventure*, pp. 117ff.

29. Sean McDonagh, *The Greening of the Church* (Maryknoll, NY: Orbis Books, 1990), p. 110.

30. Rosemary Radford Ruether, *Gaia and God* (San Francisco: Harper-SanFrancisco, 1992), p. 195.

31. Ruether, *Gaia and God*, p. 197.

32. Dale and Sandy Larsen, *While Creation Waits* (Wheaton, IL: Harold Shaw Publishing, 1992), pp. 17ff.

33. Catarina J.M. Halkes, *New Creation* (Louisville: Westminister/John Knox Press, 1991), p. 80.

34. Thomas Berry, *The Dream of the Earth* (San Francisco: Sierra Club Books, 1988), p. 123. Berry points out that the Black Death killed off one-third of the population of Europe and deeply affected the religious attitudes of the people of the time.

35. See Matthew Fox, *Original Blessing* (Santa Fe: Bear and Co., 1983).

36. Lynn White, "The Historical Roots of Our Ecologic Crisis," *Science 155* (March 10, 1967), 1203-1207. For answers to White, see Bernhard Anderson, "Human Dominion over Nature," in Miriam Ward (ed.)., *Biblical Studies in Contemporary Thought* (Somerville, MA.: Greene, Hadden and Co., 1975), pp. 27-45; and James Barr, "Man and Nature; The Ecological Controversy and the Old Testament," in David and Eileen Spring (eds.), *Ecology and Religion in History* (New York: Harper & Row, 1974), pp. 48-75.

37. See John Cobb, *Is It Too Late? A Theology of Ecology* (Beverly Hills, CA: Bruce, 1972).

38. See Bernhard Anderson, "Creation and Ecology," in his edited volume, *Creation in the Old Testament* (Philadelphia: Fortress Press, 1984), pp. 155ff.

39. Sean McDonagh, *The Greening of the Church*, p. 119.

40. Anderson, "Creation and Ecology," p. 159.

41. Anderson, "Creation and Ecology," p. 169. See also Wesley Granberg-Michaelson, "Covenant and Creation," in C. Birch, W. Eakin, J. McDaniel (eds.), *Liberating Life: Contemporary Approaches to Ecological Theology* (Maryknoll, NY: Orbis Books, 1990), pp. 27ff.

42. McDonagh, *The Greening of the Church*, pp. 151ff.

43. See Gordon Zerbe, "The Kingdom of God and the Stewardship of Creation," in Calvin Dewitt (ed.), *The Environment and the Christian* (Grand Rapids: Baker Book Co.), pp. 73ff.

44. See Brennan R. Hill, *Jesus the Christ* (Mystic, CT: Twenty-Third Publications, 1991), p 135ff.

45. See McDonagh, *The Greening of the Church*, pp. 207-216.

46. Anne Lonergan and Caroline Richards, (eds.), *Thomas Berry and the New Cosmology* (Mystic, CT: Twenty-Third Publications, 1987), pp. 5ff.

47. Lonergan and Richards, *Thomas Berry and the New Cosmology*, p. 108.

48. Rosemary Radford Ruether, *New Women/New Earth: Sexist Ideologies and Human Liberation* (New York: Seabury Press, 1975), pp. 204ff. See also Carolyn Merchant, *The Death of Nature: Women, Ecology and the Scientific Revolution* (New York: Harper & Row, 1980).

49. Halkes, *New Creation*, p. 120. See also Catherine Keller, *From a Broken Web: Separation, Sexism and the Self* (Boston: Beacon Press, 1986).

50. Ruether, *Gaia and God*, pp. 252ff.

51. See Norman Myers, *Gaia: An Atlas of Planet Management* (New York: Doubleday, 1988).

52. See Charles Murphy, *At Home on Earth: Foundations for a Catholic Ethic of Environment* (New York: Crossroad, 1989); Charles Cummings, *Eco-Spirituality* (New York: Paulist Press, 1991); Jay B. McDaniels, *Earth, Sky, Gods and Mortals* (Mystic, CT: Twenty-Third Publications, 1990); Albert J. Fritsch, *Down to Earth Spirituality* (Kansas City: Sheed and Ward, 1992); Helder Camara, *Sister Earth: Ecology and the Spirit* (New Rochelle, NY: New City Press, 1990).

Chapter 4: Jesus of Nazareth

1 See John P. Meier, *A Marginal Jew: Rethinking the Historical Jesus* (New York: Doubleday, 1991), pp. 20ff.

2 Edward Schillebeeckx, *Jesus: An Experiment in Christology* (New York: Seabury Press, 1979), pp. 72ff.

3 Brennan Hill, *Jesus the Christ: Contemporary Perspectives* (Mystic, CT: Twenty-Third Publications, 1991), p. 40.

4. Michael L. Cook, *Guidelines for Contemporary Catholics: The Historical Jesus* (Chicago: Thomas More Press, 1986), pp. 16ff.

5. Gunther Bornkamm, *Jesus of Nazareth* (New York: Harper & Row, 1960); E.P. Sanders, *Jesus and Judaism* (Philadelphia: Fortress Press, 1985); James Mackey, *Jesus the Man and the Myth* (Mahwah, NJ: Paulist Press, 1979); Edward Schillebeeckx, *Jesus: An Experiment in Christology* (New York: Seabury Press, 1979); Walter Kasper, *Jesus the Christ* (Mahwah, NJ: Paulist Press, 1976); Gerald Sloyan, *Jesus in Focus* (Mystic, CT: Twenty-Third Publications, 1994); John Dominic Crossan, *The Historical Jesus* (San Francisco: HarperSanFrancisco, 1991). 6. See Richard A. Horsley and John Hanson, *Bandits, Prophets, and Messiahs: Popular Movements in the Times of Jesus* (Minneapolis: Winston Press, 1985); and Richard A. Horsley, *Jesus and the Spiral of Violence* (San Francisco: HarperSanFrancisco, 1987).

7. See Helmut Koe, *Ancient Christian Gospels: Their History and Development* (London, SCM Press,1990); and George W. MacRae, "Why the Church Rejected Gnosticism" in *Jewish and Christian Self-Definition* Vol. 1, *The Shaping of Christianity in the Second and Third Centuries,* E. P. Sanders (ed.) (Philadelphia: Fortress Press, 1980), pp. 126-133.

8. See Crossan, *The Historical Jesus.*

9. See Joseph Fitzmyer, *Responses to 101 Questions on the Dead Sea Scrolls* (New York: Paulist Press, 1993).

10. See M. McNamara, *Palestinian Judaism and the New Testament* (Wilmington, DE: Michael Glazier, 1983) and John Riches, *The World of Jesus: First-Century Judaism* (Cambridge: Cambridge University Press, 1990).

11. See S. Sandmel, *Herod, Profile of a Tyrant* (Philadelphia: Lippincott, 1967).

12. See Sean Freyne, *Galilee, Jesus and the Gospels* (Philadelphia: Fortress Press, 1988).

13. John P. Meier, *A Marginal Jew*, p. 277.

14. See James H. Charlesworth, *Jesus Within Judaism* (New York: Doubleday, 1988), pp. 101, 140ff.; Sherman E. Johnson, *Jesus and His Towns* (Wilmington: Michael Glazier, 1989); J. Wilkinson, *Jerusalem as Jesus Knew It: Archaeology as Evidence* (London, 1982).

15. For further background on the Essenes, see G. Vermes, *The Dead Sea Scrolls* (Minneapolis: Augsburg Fortress, 1981); Samuel Sandmel, *Judaism and Christian Beginnings* (New York: Oxford University Press, 1978); Helmer Ringgren, *The Faith of Qumran* (New York: Crossroad, 1995).

16. See Bernard J. Lee, *The Galilean Jewishness of Jesus* (Mahwah, NJ: Paulist

Press, 1988), pp. 73ff.

17. Irving M. Zeitlin, *Jesus and the Judaism of His Time* (New York: Polity Press, 1988), pp. 11ff.; and Anthony J. Saldarini, *Pharisees, Scribes, and Sadducees in Palestinian Society* (Wilmington, DE: Michael Glazier, 1988).

18. Wm. M. Thompson, *The Jesus Debate* (New York: Paulist Press, 1985), pp. 158ff.; see also John J. Carroll, "Luke's Portrayal of the Pharisees," *CBQ* 50 (Oct. 1988), 604-621.

19. Karl Rahner, *Foundations of Christian Faith* (New York: Crossroad, 1987), 264ff.

20. See E.P. Sanders, *Jesus and Judaism*, pp. 164ff.

21. See A.E. Harvey, *Jesus and the Constraints of History* (Philadelphia: Westminister Press, 1982), pp. 109ff. See also Howard Clark Kee, *Medicine, Miracle and Magic in the New Testament Times* (Cambridge, MA: Cambridge University Press, 1988).

22. Pheme Perkins, *Jesus as Teacher* (New York: Cambridge University Press. 1990), pp. 5-6. A strong case for Jesus assuming the role of cynic is built by John Dominic Crossan, *The Historical Jesus*, pp. 421ff.

23. Elizabeth Schüssler Fiorenza, *In Memory of Her: A Feminist Theological Reconstruction of Christian Origins* (New York: Crossroad, 1984), pp. 142ff.; see also Ben Witherington III, *Women in the Ministry of Jesus* (London: Cambridge University Press, 1988); Elizabeth M. Tetlow, *Women and Ministry in the New Testament* (New York: Paulist Press, 1989).

24. See Jane Kopas, "Jesus and Women: Luke's Gospel," *Theology Today* 43 (2) (July 1986), 195ff.

25. Anne Carr, *Transforming Grace* (San Francisco: Harper & Row, 1988), pp. 173ff.

26. Sandra M. Schneiders, "Women in the Fourth Gospel and the Role of Women in the Contemporary Church," *Biblical Theology Bulletin* 12 (2) (1982), 35-45. See also Elisabeth Schüssler Fiorenza, "Mary Magdalene: Apostle to the Apostles," *UTS Journal* (April 1975) 22ff.

27. A.E. Harvey, *Jesus and the Constraints of History*, p. 59. See also Schillebeeckx, *Jesus: an Experiment in Christology*, pp. 472ff.

Chapter 5: The Mysteries of Jesus Christ

1. Raymond E. Brown, *The Birth of the Messiah*, rev. ed. (New York: Doubleday, 1994), p. 8.

2. See H.C. Waetjen, "The Genealogy as the Key to the Gospel according to Matthew," *Journal of Biblical Literature* 95 (1979), 205-230.

3. See Raymond E. Brown, "The Meaning of the Magi; The Significance of the Star," *Worship* 49 (1975), 574-82.

4. Brown, *The Birth of the Messiah*, pp. 16ff.

5. Brown, *The Birth of the Messiah*, pp. 283ff.

6. See Richard Horsley, *The Liberation of Christmas* (New York: Crossroad, 1989), pp. 100ff.

7. See Janice Capel Anderson, "Mary's Difference: Gender and Patriarchy in the Birth Narratives," *Journal of Religion* 67 (2) (April 1987), 183-202.

8. Hill, *Jesus the Christ*, pp. 169ff.

9. See Donald Senior, *The Passion of Jesus in the Gospel of Mark* (Wilmington, DE: Michael Glazier, 1979).

10. See John T. Pawlikowski, "The Trial and Death of Jesus: Reflections in Light of a New Understanding of Judaism," *Chicago Studies* 25 (1) (1986), 78-84.

11. See Donald Senior, *The Passion of Jesus in the Gospel of Luke* (Wilmington, DE: Michael Glazier, 1986).

12. See Gerald O'Collins, *Interpreting Jesus* (New York: Paulist Press, 1983), pp. 82ff; Reginald H. Fuller and Pheme Perkins, *Who Is Christ?* (Philadelphia: Fortress Press, 1983), p. 109.

13. For an overview of these theories, see J.P.M. Sweet, "The Zealots and Jesus," in Ernst Bammel and C.F.D. Moule (eds.), *Jesus and the Politics of His Day* (Cambridge: Cambridge University Press, 1984), pp. 1-9.

14. E.P. Sanders, *Jesus and Judaism* (Philadelphia: Fortress Press, 1985), p. 301.

15. Donald Senior, *Jesus: A Gospel Portrait* (New York: Paulist Press, 1992), p. 122.

16. A.E. Harvey, *Jesus on Trial* (Atlanta: John Knox Press, 1976), p. 10.

17. James Mackey, *Jesus, the Man and the Myth*, p. 57.

18. Donald Senior, *The Passion of Jesus in the Gospel of Mark*.

19. See Sanders, *Jesus and Judaism*, pp. 295 ff.; Irving Zeitlin, *Jesus and the Judaism of His Time* (New York: Polity Press, 1988), p. 149.

20. Gerhard Lohfink, *The Last Days of Jesus* (Notre Dame, IN: Ave Maria Press, 1984), p. 13.

21. Zietlin, *Jesus and the Judaism of His Time*, pp. 152ff.

22. Raymond E. Brown, *The Death of the Messiah* (New York: Doubleday, 1994) Vol. 1. pp. 665ff.

23. Brown, *The Death of the Messiah*, Vol. 2, pp. 1088ff.

24. See Gerald O'Collins, *Jesus Risen* (Mahwah, NJ: Paulist Press, 1987), pp. 21ff.

25. Pheme Perkins, *Resurrection: New Testament Witness and Contemporary Reflection* (New York: Doubleday, 1984), pp. 38ff.

26. Walter Kasper, *Jesus the Christ* (New York: Paulist Press, 1976), p. 125.

27. See William. P. Loewe, "The Appearances of the Risen Lord: Faith, Fact, and Objectivity," *Horizons* 6 (1979), 178ff.

28. Perkins, *Resurrection*, p. 124.

29. James D.G. Dunn, *The Evidence for Jesus* (Philadelphia: Westminster Press, 1985), p. 59.

30. Reginald H. Fuller, *The Formation of the Resurrection Narratives* (Philadelphia: Fortress Press, 1980), p. 46.

31. William Thompson, *The Jesus Debate* (New York: Paulist Press, 1985), p. 423.

32. Kasper, *Jesus the Christ*, p. 39.

33. Schillebeeckx, *Jesus*, pp. 346ff, 643ff.

Chapter 6: Jesus the Christ

1. See Richard Norris, Jr. (ed.), *The Christological Controversy* (Philadelphia: Fortress Press, 1987), p. 3.

2. Jaroslav Pelikan, *The Christian Tradition*, Vol. 1: *The Emergence of the Catholic Tradition (100-600)* (Chicago: University of Chicago Press, 1971), pp. 173ff.

3. Leo Davis, *The First Seven Ecumenical Councils (325-787)* (Wilmington, DE: Michael Glazier, 1987), pp. 40ff.

4. See Justo Gonzalez, *The Story of Christianity*, vol. I: *The Early Church to the Dawn of the Reformation* (New York: Harper & Row, 1984), pp. 58ff.

5. Earl Richard, *Jesus, One and Many: The Christological Concept of the New Testament Authors* (Wilmington, DE: Michael Glazier, 1988), pp. 439ff.

6. See Charles Kannengieser, "Arius and the Arians," *Theological Studies* 44 (Sept. 1983), 456-475.

7. For more background on this council, see Frances M. Young, *From Nicea to Chalcedon: A Guide to Literature and Its Background* (Philadelphia: Fortress Press, 1983).

8. See Hubert Jedin, *Ecumenical Councils of the Catholic Church* (New York:

Herder and Herder, 1960), pp. 28ff.
9. See Hill, *Jesus the Christ*, p. 227.
10. See Franz J. vanBeeck, "Ten Questions on Christology and Soteriology," *Chicago Studies* 25 (3) (1986), 269-278.
11. Russell Aldwindle, *Jesus: A Savior or the Savior? Religious Pluralism in Christian Perspective* (Macon: Mercer University Press, 1982), pp. 99ff.
12. See Gerald Sloyan, *Jesus: Redeemer and Divine Word* (Wilmington, DE: Michael Glazier, 1989), pp. 43ff.
13. See Arland J. Hultgren, *Christ and His Benefits: Christology and Redemption in the New Testament* (Philadelphia: Fortress Press, 1987), pp. 5ff.
14. See Karl Rahner, *Foundations of Christian Faith* (New York: Crossroad, 1987), p. 288.
15. See Xavier Léon-Dufour, *Dictionary of Biblical Theology* (New York: Desclee Co., 1967), p. 134.
16. See Denis Edwards, *What Are They Saying About Salvation?* (New York: Paulist Press, 1986), pp. 8ff.
17. Martin Hengel, *The Atonement* (Philadelphia: Fortress Press, 1981), pp. 65 ff.
18. Sloyan, *Jesus: Redeemer and Divine Word*, pp. 49ff.
19. See Gabriel Daly, *Creation and Redemption* (Wilmington, DE: Michael Glazier, 1989) pp. 184ff.
20. See G.R. Evans, *Anselm and Talking About God* (Oxford: Clarendon Press, 1978).
21. See Edward Schillebeeckx, *Christ: The Experience of Jesus as the Lord* (New York: Seabury Press, 1980), pp. 64ff.
22. See Claus Bussman, *Who Do You Say? Jesus Christ in Latin American Theology* (Maryknoll, NY: Orbis Books, 1985), p. 11.
23. See "Justice in the World," in David J. O'Brien and Thomas A. Shannon, (eds.), *Renewing the Earth: Catholic Documents on Peace, Justice, and Liberation* (New York: Doubleday, 1977), p. 391.
24. Gustavo Gutiérrez, *A Theology of Liberation* (Maryknoll, NY: Orbis Books, 1973).
25. See Leonardo Boff, *Jesus Christ Liberator* (Maryknoll, NY: Orbis Books, 1978), pp. 279ff.
26. Ignacio Ellacuría, *Freedom Made Flesh* (Maryknoll, NY: Orbis Books, 1976), p. 46.
27. See Segundo Galilea, "Jesus' Attitude Toward Politics: Some Working Hypotheses," in J. Míquez-Bonino (ed.), *Faces of Jesus* (Maryknoll, NY: Orbis Books, 1984), p. 96.
28. See Gutiérrez, *A Theology of Liberation*, p. 170.
29. See Christopher Rowland and Mark Corner, *Liberation Exegesis* (Atlanta: John Knox Press, 1990), p. 47.
30. Gutiérrez, *A Theology of Liberation*, p. 176.
31. See Juan Luis Segundo, *The Historical Jesus of the Synoptics* (Maryknoll, NY: Orbis Books, 1985), p. 197.
32. Boff, *Jesus Christ Liberator*, p. 290.
33. See Alfred T. Hennelly (ed.), *Liberation Theology: A Documentary History* (Maryknoll, NY: Orbis Books, 1990), p. 304.

Chapter 7: The Church of Jesus Christ

1. See Francis Schüssler Fiorenza, *Foundational Theology: Jesus and Church* (New York: Crossroad, 1984), pp. 60ff.
2. Edward Schillebeeckx, *Church: The Human Story of God* (New York: Crossroad, 1990), p. 111.

3. Daniel J. Harrington, S.J., *God's People in Christ* (Philadelphia: Fortress Press, 1980), pp. 17ff.

4. See Schillebeeckx, *Church*, p. 139.

5. See Francis J. Cwiekowski, *The Beginnings of the Church* (New York: Paulist Press, 1988), pp. 40ff.

6. Ben F. Meyer, *The Early Christians* (Wilmington, DE: Michael Glazier, 1986), pp. 37ff.

7. See Cwiekowski, *The Beginnings of the Church*, pp. 66ff.

8. Robert Kress, *The Church* (New York: Paulist Press, 1985), pp. 39ff.

9. Eric Jay, *The Church: Its Changing Image Through Twenty Centuries* (Atlanta: John Knox Press, 1980) I, p. 8. See also Wayne Meeks, *The First Urban Christians* (New Haven: Yale University Press, 1983).

10. Jay, *The Church*, p. 9.

11. George H. Tavard, *The Church, Community of Salvation* (Collegeville, MN: Liturgical Press, 1992), pp. 35ff.

12. Vincent Donovan, *The Church in the Midst of Creation* (Maryknoll, NY: Orbis Books, 1989), pp. 8ff.

13. Martin Hengel, *Between Jesus and Paul* (London: Fortress Press, 1983), p. 58.

14. See Meyer, *The Early Christians*, pp. 57ff.

15. Cwiekowski, *The Beginnings of the Church*, pp. 73ff.

16. Raymond E. Brown, *The Churches the Apostles Left Behind* (New York: Paulist Press, 1984), pp. 124ff.

17. Raymond E. Brown and John P. Meier, *Antioch and Rome: New Testament Cradles of Catholic Christianity* (New York: Paulist Press, 1983), pp. 23ff.

18. Brown and Meyer, *Antioch and Rome*, pp. 48ff.

19. Cwiekowski, *The Beginnings of the Church*, pp. 98ff.

20. Brown and Meier, *Antioch and Rome*, pp. 92ff.

21. Brown and Meier, *Antioch and Rome*, pp. 124ff.

22. Brown and Meier, *Antioch and Rome*, pp. 98ff.

23. Brown and Meier, *Antioch and Rome*, pp. 100ff.

24. See Raymond E. Brown and others, *The New Jerome Biblical Commentary* (Englewood Cliffs, NJ: Prentice Hall, 1990) 43: 4ff. See Eugene LaVerdiere, *Luke* (Wilmington, DE: Michael Glazier, 1982).

25. See Brown, *The Churches the Apostles Left Behind*, p. 28.

26. Raymond E. Brown, *The Community of the Beloved Disciple* (New York: Paulist Press, 1979), pp. 33ff.

27. Cwiekowski, *The Beginnings of the Church*, p. 164.

28. See Helen Doohan, *Leadership in Paul* (Wilmington, DE: Michael Glazier, 1984); Wilfrid Harrington, *Jesus and Paul* (Wilmington, DE: Michael Glazier, 1987); Gerd Theissen, *The Social Setting of Pauline Christianity* (Philadelphia: Fortress Press, 1982); and Pheme Perkins, *Ministering in the Pauline Churches* (New York: Paulist Press, 1982).

29. Brown, *The Churches the Apostles Left Behind*, p. 48.

30. Brown and others, *The New Jerome Biblical Commentary*, 54: 6. See E. Schweizer, *The Letter to the Colossians* (Minneapolis: Fortress Press, 1982).

31. See Daniel J. Harrington, *Light of All Nations* (Wilmington, DE: Michael Glazier, 1982), pp. 16ff.

32. Cwiekowski, *The Beginnings of the Church*, pp. 159ff.

33. For a thorough background on these essentials, see Rudolf Schnackenburg, *The Church in the New Testament* (New York: Herder and Herder, 1965).

Chapter 8: Reform and Renewal

1. Derek Holmes, *A Short History of the Catholic Church* (New York: Paulist

Press, 1984), p. 78.

2. Adrian Hastings, "Catholic History from Vatican I to John Paul II," in Adrian Hastings (ed.), *Modern Catholicism: Vatican II and After* (New York: Oxford University Press, 1991), p. 1ff.

3. Peter Hebblethwaite, "John XXIII," in Hastings, *Modern Catholicism*, pp. 28ff.

4. Eugene C. Bianchi, "A Democratic Church: Task for the Twenty-First Century," in Eugene C. Bianchi and Rosemary Radford Ruether (eds.), *A Democratic Catholic Church* (New York: Crossroad, 1992), p. 49.

5. "The Church in the Modern World," #1 in Walter Abbott (ed.), *The Documents of Vatican II* (New York: Guild Press, 1966).

6. Hastings, *Modern Catholicism*, pp. 5ff.

7. Bianchi and Ruether, *A Democratic Catholic Church*, p. 9.

8. Jay P. Dolan, "The Desire for Democracy in the American Catholic Church," in Bianchi and Ruether, *A Democratic Catholic Church*, pp. 113ff.

9. Charles Curran, "What Catholic Ecclesiology Can Learn from Official Catholic Social Teaching," in Bianchi and Ruether, *A Democratic Catholic Church*, pp. 94ff.

10. See Francis Schüssler Fiorenza and John P. Galvin (eds.), *Systematic Theology* (Philadelphia: Fortress Press, 1991), p. 38. The notion of church as sacrament was developed by Karl Rahner and Otto Semmelroth previous to Vatican II. See Avery Dulles, *A Church to Believe In* (New York: Crossroad, 1984), pp. 46 ff. and Peter Fink, "The Church as Sacrament and the Sacramental Life of the Church," in Lucien Richard and others (eds.), *Vatican II: The Unfinished Agenda* (New York: Paulist Press, 1987), pp. 71-82.

11. Avery Dulles, S.J., *A Church to Believe In* (New York: Crossroad, 1984), pp. 45ff.

12. Quoted in Avery Dulles, *The Catholicity of the Church*, p. 128.

13. "Dogmatic Constitution on the Church," #1 in Walter Abbott (ed.), *The Documents of Vatican II*. See Francine Cardman, "One Treasure Only: Vatican II and the Ecumenical Nature of the Church," in Lucien Richard and others (eds.), *Vatican II: The Unfinished Agenda*, pp. 174-190.

14. See Thomas Ryan, *A Survival Guide for Ecumenically Minded Christians* (Collegeville, MN: Liturgical Press, 1989).

15. "Dogmatic Constitution on the Church," #16 in Abbott, *The Documents of Vatican II*.

16. Dulles, *The Catholicity of the Church*, p. 160. See also Karl Rahner, *Concern for the Church* (New York: Crossroad, 1981), p. 26.

17. Eugene Kennedy, *Tomorrow's Catholic, Yesterday's Church* (New York: Harper & Row, 1988), p. 41.

18. Vincent Donovan, *The Church in the Midst of Creation* (Maryknoll, NY: Orbis Books, 1989), pp. 105ff. See Heinrich Fries and Karl Rahner, *The Unity of the Churches* (Philadelphia: Fortress Press, 1985).

19. See Karl Rahner, "The Sinful Church in Decrees of Vatican II," in *Theological Investigations* (Baltimore: Helicon, 1969), VI, pp. 270-294.

20. Donovan, *The Church in the Midst of Creation*, pp. 106ff.

21. Francis A. Sullivan, *The Church We Believe In* (New York: Paulist Press, 1988), p. 85.

22. Dulles, *A Church to Believe In*, pp. 49ff. See also Eric G. Jay, *The Church: Its Changing Image Through Twenty Centuries* (Atlanta: John Knox Press, 1980), pp. 120ff.

23. Karl Rahner, "Basic Theological Interpretation of The Second Vatican Council," *Theological Investigations* (New York: Crossroad, 1981), XX, pp. 77-89.

24. See Donovan, *The Church in the Midst of Creation*, p. 106.

25. Dulles, *The Catholicity of the Church*, pp. 108ff. See Lucien Richard, "Mission and Inculturation: The Church in the World," in Richard, *Vatican II: The Unfinished Agenda*, pp. 93-113.

26. Donovan, *The Church in the Midst of Creation*, pp. 106ff.

27. Sullivan, *The Church We Believe In*, p. 155.

28. Francis Schüssler Fiorenza, *Foundational Theology*, pp. 85ff.

Chapter 9: Mission and Ministry

1. Avery Dulles, "The Church and the Kingdom," in Eugene LaVerdiere (ed.), *A Church for All Peoples* (Collegeville, MN: Liturgical Press, 1993), p. 14.

2. John Paul II, "Redemptoris Missio," (Washington, DC: USCC, 1990), p. 9.

3. See Anthony J. Gittins, *Bread for the Journey: The Mission of Transformation and Transformation of Mission* (Maryknoll, NY: Orbis Books, 1993), p. 7.

4. "The Church Today," #11 in Walter Abbott (ed.), *The Documents of Vatican II* (New York: Guild Press, 1966).

5. Francis Schüssler Fiorenza, *Fundamental Theology* (New York: Crossroad, 1984), pp. 197ff.

6. Schüssler Fiorenza, *Fundamental Theology*, pp. 197ff.

7. Schüssler Fiorenza, *Fundamental Theology*, pp. 204ff.

8. See David J. O'Brien and Thomas A. Shannon (eds.), *Renewing the Earth: Catholic Documents on Peace, Justice and Liberation* (New York: Doubleday, 1977), pp. 33ff.

9. O'Brien and Shannon, *Renewing the Earth*, pp. 36ff. For an overview of this and other periods see Charles Curran and Richard McCormick (eds.), *Official Catholic Social Teaching: Readings in Moral Theology, No. 5* (New York: Paulist Press, 1986).

10. See Joe Holland and Peter Henriot, *Social Analysis: Linking Faith and Justice* (Maryknoll, NY: Orbis Books, 1980), xvii ff. See Roland Foley, "Pope as Prophet: The New Social Encyclical," *America* (30 April, 1988), 447ff.

11. Michael Amaladoss, "The Church as Servant of the Coming of the Kingdom," in Gerald Anderson and others (eds.), *Mission in the 1990's* (Grand Rapids: Eerdmans, 1991), pp. 4ff.

12. Gustavo Gutiérrez, *Las Casas: In Search of the Poor of Jesus Christ* (Maryknoll, NY: Orbis Books, 1993), p. 29.

13. Gerald Arbuckle, *Earthing the Gospel: An Inculturation Handbook for the Pastoral Worker* (Maryknoll, NY: Orbis Books, 1990), p. 12.

14. See Anthony Bellagamba, *Mission and Ministry in the Global Church* (Maryknoll, NY: Orbis Books, 1992), pp. 1-9.

15. John Paul II, "Redemptoris Missio," pp. 89ff.

16. See Hans Küng and others (eds.), *Christianity and World Religions* (New York: Doubleday, 1986).

17. See Leonardo Boff, *Ecclesiogenesis: The Base Communities Reinvent the Church* (Maryknoll, NY: Orbis Books, 1986).

18. G. Anderson and others (eds.), *Mission in the 1990's*, p. 73.

19. See Lavinia Byrne, *Women Before God: Our Own Spirituality* (Mystic, CT: Twenty-Third Publications, 1988); and Teofilo Cabestrero, *Ministers of God, Ministers of the People* (Maryknoll, NY: Orbis Books, 1982).

20. Wahlbert Buhlmann, *With Eyes to See* (Maryknoll, NY: Orbis Books, 1990), pp. 6-7.

21. Edward Schillebeeckx, *The Church: The Human Face of God* (New York: Crossroad, 1990), pp. 19ff. See also Nathan Mitchell, *Mission and Ministry* (Wilmington, DE: Michael Glazier, 1982), pp. 72-136; and T. O'Meara, *Theology of Ministry* (New York: Paulist Press, 1983), pp. 76-94.

22. Schillebeeckx, *The Church,* p. 119.

23. Bernard Cooke, *Ministry to Word and Sacrament* (Philadelphia: Fortress Press, 1976), pp. 199ff. See Paul Bernier, *Ministry in the Church* (Mystic, CT: Twenty-Third Publications, 1992), pp. 31ff.; and Kenan Osborne, *Priesthood* (New York: Paulist Press, 1988), pp. 40-85.

24. Edward Schillebeeckx, *Ministry: Leadership in the Community of Jesus Christ* (New York: Crossroad, 1981), pp. 37ff.

25. Schillebeeckx, *The Church,* p. 59.

26. Bernier, *Ministry in the Church,* pp. 87ff. A collection of early articles on the diaconate by Karl Rahner can be found in *Foundations for the Renewal of the Diaconate* (Washington, DC: USCC, 1993). See also A. Lemaire, "From Service to Ministries: Diakonia in the First Two Centuries," *Concilium* 10, 8 (Dec. 1972), 35-49.

27. See Michael Kwatera, *The Liturgical Ministry of Deacons* (Collegeville, MN: Liturgical Press, 1985); and Patrick McCaslin and Michael Lawler, *The Sacrament of Service* (New York: Paulist Press, 1986).

28. U.S. Bishops Committee on the Liturgy, *The Deacon: Minister of Word and Sacrament* (Washington, DC: USCC, 1979), p. 22.

29. Bernier, *Ministry in the Church,* pp. 89ff.

30. Edward Schillebeeckx, *The Church With a Human Face: A New and Expanded Theology of Ministry* (New York: Crossroad, 1985), pp. 41ff.

31. See "The Dogmatic Constitution on the Church," #10, Abbott, *The Documents of Vatican II.*

32. Jay Dolan and others (eds.), *Transforming Parish Ministry: The Changing Roles of Catholic Clergy, Laity and Women Religious* (New York: Crossroad, 1989), pp. 5ff.

33. Dolan and others, *Transforming Parish Ministry,* pp. 594ff. See Kenan Osborne, *Priesthood.*

34. Kenan Osborne, *Ministry* (New York: Paulist Press, 1993), p. 571.

35. Osborne, *Ministry,* p. 572.

36. Schillebeeckx, *The Church with a Human Face,* p. 151.

37. Cooke, *Ministry to Word and Sacrament,* pp. 79ff.

38. J.M.R. Tillard, *The Bishop of Rome* (Wilmington, DE: Michael Glazier, 1982), pp. 36 ff., 46ff.

39. Cooke, *Ministry to Word and Sacrament,* p. 432.

40. Patrick Granfield, *Limits of the Papacy* (New York: Crossroad, 1987), p. 3. See Michael Miller, *What Are They Saying about Papal Primacy?* (New York: Paulist Press, 1983).

41. Osborne, *Ministry,* p. 594.

Chapter 10: The Sacrament of the Eucharist

1. Philippe Rouillard, "From Human Meal to Christian Eucharist," in *Living Bread, Saving Cup: Readings on the Eucharist,* R. Kevin Seasoltz (ed.) (Collegeville, MN: Liturgical Press, 1982), pp. 140-56.

2. Hill, *Jesus the Christ,* pp. 119ff.

3. David N. Power, *The Eucharistic Mystery* (New York: Crossroad, 1992), pp. 31ff.

4. Rouillard, "From Human Meal to Christian Eucharist," pp. 144ff.

5. Jerome Kodell, O.S.B., *The Eucharist in the New Testament* (Collegeville, MN: Liturgical Press/Michael Glazier Books, 1988), pp. 17ff.

6. Xavier Léon-Dufour, S.J., *Sharing the Eucharistic Bread* (Mahwah, NJ: Paulist Press, 1982), pp. 17ff.

7. Léon-Dufour, S.J., *Sharing the Eucharistic Bread,* p. 15.

8. Léon-Dufour, S.J., *Sharing the Eucharistic Bread*, pp. 50ff.
9. Léon-Dufour, S.J., *Sharing the Eucharistic Bread*, pp. 96ff.
10. Léon-Dufour, S.J., *Sharing the Eucharistic Bread*, p. 101.
11. Léon-Dufour, S.J., *Sharing the Eucharistic Bread*, pp. 82-95; Power, *The Eucharistic Mystery*, pp. 32ff.
12. Power, *The Eucharistic Mystery*, pp. 294ff.
13. Monika Hellwig, *The Eucharist and the Hunger of the World* (2nd ed.) (Kansas City: Sheed and Ward, 1994); see also Power, *The Eucharistic Mystery*, p. 295.
14. Roulliard,"From Human Meal to Christian Eucharist," pp. 126ff.
15. Kodell, *The Eucharist in the New Testament*.
16. Léon-Dufour, *Sharing the Eucharistic Bread*, pp. 41, 194.
17. Rouillard, "From Human Meal to Christian Eucharist," pp. 146ff.
18. Gary Macy, *The Banquet's Wisdom: A Short History of the Theologies of the Last Supper* (Mahwah, NJ: Paulist Press, 1992), p. 29.
19. Karl Rahner, *Foundations of Christian Faith*, trans. William Dych (New York: Crossroad, 1978), p. 426.
20. Max Thurian, *The Mystery of the Eucharist* (Grand Rapids: Eerdmans, 1981), pp. 19ff.
21. Power, *The Eucharistic Mystery*, p. 320.
22. Thomas Merton, *The Living Bread* (New York: Farrar, Straus and Cudahy, 1956), pp. 28ff.; see also Thurian, *The Mystery of the Eucharist*, pp. 19ff.
23. Power, *The Eucharistic Mystery*, p. 323.
24. David N. Power, "Eucharist" in *Systematic Theology*, Francis Schüssler Fiorenza and John P. Galvin (eds.) (Minneapolis: Augsburg Fortress, 1991), II, pp. 274.
25. Power, "Eucharist" in *Systematic Theology*, II, p. 269; see also Fritz Chenderlin, *"Do This as My Memorial": The Semantic and Conceptual Background and Value of Anamnesis in 1 Cor 11:24–25* (Rome: Biblical Institute Press, 1982).
26. Power, *The Eucharistic Mystery*, p. 44.
27. Power, *The Eucharistic Mystery*, p. 49.
28. Jerome Murphy-O'Connor, "The Eucharist and Community," in *Living Bread, Saving Cup*, p. 21.
29. Léon-Dufour, *Sharing the Eucharistic Bread*, p. 104.
30. Léon-Dufour, *Sharing the Eucharistic Bread*, p. 113.
31. Macy, *The Banquet's Wisdom*, pp. 18ff.
32. Macy, *The Banquet's Wisdom*, p. 23.
33. Thurian, *The Mystery of the Eucharist*, pp. 31-46.
34. Macy, *The Banquet's Wisdom*, p. 41.
35. Macy, *The Banquet's Wisdom*, pp. 71ff.
36. Power, "Eucharist" in *Systematic Theology*, II, pp. 278.
37. John H. P. Reumann, *The Supper of the Lord* (Philadephia: Fortress Press, 1985), p. 104.
38. See William R. Crockett, *Eucharist: Symbol of Transformation* (Collegeville, MN: Liturgical Press/Pueblo Books, 1989), pp. 128ff.
39. Quoted in Thurian, *The Mystery of the Eucharist*, p. 42.
40. Reumann, *The Supper of the Lord*.
41. Crockett, *Eucharist*, pp. 14ff.
42. Thurian, *The Mystery of the Eucharist*, p. 45.
43. Reumann, *The Supper of the Lord*, p. 104.
44. Crockett, *Eucharist*, pp. 231ff.
45. See Warren A. Quanbeck, *Search for Understanding: Lutheran Conversation with Reformed, Anglican and Roman Catholic Churches* (Minneapolis: Augsburg,

1972); and Paul Empie, *Lutherans and Catholics in Dialogue* (Philadelphia: Fortress Press, 1975).

46. Reumann, *The Supper of the Lord,* p. 109.

47. See Julian Charly, *The Anglican-Roman Catholic Agreement on the Eucharist* (Bramcote, Notts: Grove Books, 1971); and Leonard Swidler, (ed.), *The Eucharist in Ecumenical Dialogue* (Mahwah, NJ: Paulist Press, 1976).

48. See World Council of Churches, *Faith and Order Paper, No. 111* (Geneva, 1982).

Chapter 11: The Sacrament of Marriage

1. Walter Kasper, *Theology of Christian Marriage* (New York: Crossroad, 1983), p. 26.

2. Leonardo Boff, "The Sacrament of Marriage," in *The Sacraments: Readings in Contemporary Sacramental Theology,* Michael Taylor (ed.) (New York: Alba House, 1981), p. 197.

3. Theodore Mackin, *What Is Marriage?* (Mahwah, NJ: Paulist Press, 1982), pp. 22ff.

4. For further comments, see Theodore Mackin, *The Marital Sacrament* (Mahwah, NJ: Paulist Press, 1989), pp. 65ff.

5. The word here is *mysterion,* which later was translated as *sacramentum* in the Vulgate translation of the Bible. This led some to use this as proof that marriage was a sacrament. In fact the notion was not introduced theologically until the time of Saint Augustine, and only in the twelfth century was marriage presented as a sacrament and included in the seven sacraments of the church.

6. Mackin, *What Is Marriage?,* p. 131.

7. Michael G. Lawler, *Marriage and Sacrament: A Theology of Christian Marriage* (Collegeville, MN: Liturgical Press, 1993), p. 56.

8. Lawler, *Marriage and Sacrament,* pp. 58ff.

9. Mackin, *What Is Marriage?,* pp. 198ff.

10. Mackin, *What Is Marriage?,* p. 226.

11. Mackin, *What Is Marriage?,* pp. 267-68.

12. Mackin, *What Is Marriage?,* pp. 22ff., points out that in the first millennium not a single scholar attempted a painstaking analysis of Ephesians 5: 21–32.

13. Mackin, *What Is Marriage?,* p. 32.

14. Mackin, *The Marital Sacrament,* pp. 274-75.

15. Edward Schillebeeckx, *Marriage: Human Reality and Saving Mystery* (Kansas City: Sheed and Ward, 1965), pp. 332ff.

16. Schillebeeckx, *Marriage,* pp. 312ff.

17. Schillebeeckx, *Marriage,* pp. 325ff.

18. Mackin, *The Marital Sacrament,* p. 412.

19. Papal and conciliar documents on marriage are summarized in William Urbine and William Seifert, *On Life and Love: A Guide to Catholic Teaching on Marriage and Family* (Mystic, CT: Twenty-Third Publications, 1993).

20. Mackin, *What Is Marriage?,* pp. 543ff.

21. Harville Hendrix, *Getting the Love You Want* (New York: HarperCollins, 1988), pp. 47-55.

22. Evelyn Eaton Whitehead and James D. Whitehead, *Marrying Well: Stages on the Journey of Christian Marriage* (New York: Doubleday, 1983), p. 21.

23. Lawler, *Marriage and Sacrament,* pp. 1ff.

24. See Lawrence Wrenn, "Refining the Essence of Marriage," *The Jurist,* 46 (1986), 539ff.

25. Aaron T. Beck, *Love Is Never Enough* (New York: HarperCollins, 1989), pp. 169ff.

26. "The Pastoral Constitution on the Church in the Modern World," #48, in Walter Abbott (ed.), *The Documents of Vatican II* (New York: Guild Press, 1966).

27. William Roberts, "Theology of Christian Marriage," in *Alternative Futures for Worship, Vol 5: Christian Marriage,* Bernard Cooke (ed.) (Collegeville, MN: Liturgical Press, 1987), p. 48; see also Lawler, *Marriage and Sacrament,* pp. 4ff.

28. Karl Rahner, "Marriage as a Sacrament," in *Theological Investigations, Volume X* (New York: Crossroad, 1973), pp. 205ff.

29. Jared Wicks, "Marriage: An Historical and Theological Overview" in *The Sacraments,* ed. Michael Taylor (New York: Alba House, 1981), p. 190.

30. Rahner, *Foundations of Christian Faith,* p. 204.

31. Denis F. O'Callaghan, "Faith and the Sacrament of Marriage," *Irish Theological Quarterly,* 52 (1986), 175ff.; see also Brennan R. Hill, "Marriage as Sacrament: A Theology in Transition," *Melita Theologica,* Vol. XLII (1991), #1, 42-60; Ladislas Orsy, "Faith, Sacrament, Contract, and Christian Marriage: Disputed Questions," *Theological Studies,* 43 (1982), 390ff.; and Michael Lawler, *Secular Marriage, Christian Sacrament* (Mystic, CT: Twenty-Third Publications, 1985), pp. 60ff.

32. Kathleen Fischer Hart and Thomas Hart, *The First Two Years of Marriage* (Mahwah, NJ: Paulist Press, 1983), pp. 60ff.

33. Karl Rahner, *Foundations of Christian Faith* (New York: Crossroad, 1987), p. 419.

34. Eileen Zielget Silbermann, *The Savage Sacrament: A Theology of Marriage after American Feminism* (Mystic, CT: Twenty-Third Publications, 1983).

35. Juan Luis Segundo, *The Sacraments Today* (Maryknoll, NY: Orbis Books, 1986), pp. 15ff.

Chapter 12: Initiation, Forgiveness, and Healing

1. Aidan Kavanagh, *The Shape of Baptism: The Rite of Christian Initiation* (Collegeville, MN: Liturgical Press/Pueblo Books, 1974), p. 7.

2. Kenan B. Osborne, *The Christian Sacraments of Initiation* (Mahwah, NJ: Paulist Press, 1987), pp. 25ff.

3. Kavanagh, *The Shape of Baptism,* p. 14.

4. Thomas Marsh, *The Gift of Community: Baptism and Confirmation* (Collegeville, MN: Liturgical Press/Michael Glazier Books, 1984), pp. 49ff.

5. Kavanagh, *The Shape of Baptism,* p. 19.

6. Rudolph Schnackenburg, *Baptism in the Thought of St. Paul* (New York: Herder and Herder, 1964), pp. 55ff.

7. Johannes Quasten, *Patrology* (Westminster, MD: Newman Press, 1951), I, p. 214.

8. Kavanagh, *The Shape of Baptism,* p. 56. For a detailed account of how the present catechumenate is carried out, see Thomas H. Morris, *The RCIA: Transforming the Church* (Mahwah, NJ: Paulist Press, 1989).

9. *Catechism of the Catholic Church* (Washington DC: United States Catholic Conference, 1994), #1261.

10. Osborne,*The Christian Sacraments of Initiation,* pp. 83ff.

11. Osborne, *The Christian Sacraments of Initiation,* p. 121.

12. Gerard Austin, *Anointing with the Spirit* (Collegeville, MN: Liturgical Press/Pueblo Books, 1975), pp. 4 ff.

13. Aidan Kavanagh, *Confirmation: Origins and Reform* (Collegeville, MN: Liturgical Press/Pueblo Books, 1988), pp. 85ff.; and Paul Turner, *Confirmation: The Baby in Solomon's Court* (Mahwah, NJ: Paulist Press, 1993), pp. 106ff.

14. Kavanagh, *Confirmation: Origins and Reform,* pp. 3 ff., 69 ff; see also Aidan Kavanagh, "Confirmation: A Suggestion for Structure," *Worship,* 58 (1984), 386-

94; and Paul Turner, "The Origins of Confirmation: An Analysis of Aidan Kavanagh's Hypothesis," *Worship* 65 (1991), 320-38.

15. Turner, *Confirmation,* p. 2.

16. Osborne, *The Christian Sacrament of Initiation,* p. 134.

17. Monika K. Hellwig, *Sign of Reconciliation and Conversion: The Sacrament of Penance in Our Times* (Collegeville, MN: Liturgical Press/Michael Glazier Books, 1982), pp. 14ff.

18. Richard Gula, *To Walk Together Again: The Sacrament of Reconciliation* (Mahwah, NJ: Paulist Press, 1984), pp. 92ff.

19. Gula, *To Walk Together Again,* pp. 15ff.

20. Gula, *To Walk Together Again,* p. 189.

21. Hellwig, *Sign of Reconciliation and Conversion,* pp. 31 ff; see also J. M. Tillard, "The Bread and Cup of Reconciliation," in *Sacramental Reconciliation,* ed. Edward Schillebeeckx (New York: Herder, 1971).

22. Kenan B. Osborne, *Reconciliation and Justification* (Mahwah, NJ: Paulist Press, 1991), pp. 54ff.

23. Osborne, *Reconciliation and Justification,* pp. 84ff.

24. Osborne, *Reconciliation and Justification,* pp. 93ff.

25. G. Yule, "Luther's Understanding of Justification by Grace Alone in Terms of Catholic Theology," in *Luther, Theologian for Catholics and Protestants* (Edinburgh: T&T Clark, 1985), pp. 87ff.

26. Gula, *To Walk Together Again,* p. 217.

27. James Dallen, "Theological Foundations of Reconciliation," in *Reconciliation: The Continuing Agenda,* ed. Robert J. Kennedy (Collegeville, MN: Liturgical Press, 1987), pp. 14ff.; see also Lawrence E. Mick, *Penance: The Once and Future Sacrament* (Collegeville, MN: Liturgical Press, 1987), pp. 61ff.

28. Robert J. Kennedy, "The Rite of Reconciliation for Individual Penitents: Celebration of the Church," in *Reconciliation,* pp. 131ff.

29. Herman Hendrickx, *The Miracle Stories* (San Francisco: Harper & Row, 1987), p. 8.

30. Charles W. Gusmer, *And You Visited Me: Sacramental Ministry to the Sick & the Dying* (Collegeville, MN: Liturgical Press/Pueblo Books, 1984), pp. 7ff.

31. Gusmer, *And You Visited Me,* p. 6.

32. Morton T. Kelsey, *Healing and Christianity* (New York: Harper & Row, 1973), pp. 50ff., 134.

33. Gusmer, *And You Visited Me,* p. 85.

Index

Of Related Interest ...

Jesus the Christ
Contemporary Perspectives
Brennan Hill
Hill has managed to take a subject with countless disparate threads and weave them into a solid, scripturally reliable and often surprising portrait of Jesus of Nazareth and the Christ of Faith. This book is perfect for anyone anxious to learn more about Jesus as both a historical person and as a figure of belief.

ISBN: 0-89622-492-9, 308 pp, $14.95

The Catechism
Highlights & Commentary
Brennan Hill and William Madges
These two Xavier University theology professors explain the contents of the 700 plus pages of the new *Catechism of the Catholic Church*. Their interpretations are solidly supported by the best theological research available.

ISBN: 0-89622-589-5, 160 pp, $9.95

Faith, Religion and Theology
A Contemporary Introduction
Brennan R. Hill, Paul Knitter and William Madges
This book focuses on the nature of Christian faith, examines the reasons for the wealth of religious diversity and compares the fundamentalist approach to Scripture with the historical-critical approach. It serves as an introduction to the array of theologies, dealing with issues such as feminism, liberation, and nuclear and ecological issues.

ISBN: 0-89622-415-5, 388 pp, $14.95

Available at religious bookstores or from

XXIII TWENTY-THIRD PUBLICATIONS
P.O. Box 180 • Mystic, CT 06355 • 1-800-321-0411